The Social Psychology of
Inclusion and Exclusion

The Social Psychology of
Inclusion and Exclusion

Edited by

Dominic Abrams
University of Kent

Michael A. Hogg
University of Queensland

José M. Marques
University of Porto

Psychology Press
New York ▪ Hove

Published in 2005 by
Psychology Press
270 Madison Avenue
New York, NY 10016
www.psypress.com

Published in Great Britain by
Psychology Press
27 Church Road
Hove, East Sussex
BN3 2FA
www.psypress.co.uk

www.socialpsychologyarena.com

Copyright © 2005 by Taylor & Francis Books, Inc.

Psychology Press, is an imprint of the Taylor & Francis Group.
Printed in the United States of America on acid-free paper.

All rights reserved. No part of this book may be reprinted or reproduced or utilized in any form or by any electronic, mechanical, or other means, now known or hereafter invented, including photocopying and recording, or in any information storage or retrieval system, without permission in writing from the publishers.

10 9 8 7 6 5 4 3 2

Library of Congress Cataloging-in-Publication Data
   The Social psychology of inclusion and exclusion / edited by Dominic Abrams, Michael A. Hogg, José M. Marques.
      p. cm.
   Includes bibliographical references and index.
   ISBN 1-84169-073-2 (hardback : alk. paper)
   1. Marginality, Social. 2. Social groups. 3. Social psychology. I. Abrams, Dominic, 1958- II Hogg, Michael A., 1954- III. Marques, José M. (José Mendes)

HM1136.S64 2005
305—dc22
                                                                                             2004009908

To Ben, Zoë, and Alice

Contents

Acknowledgments ix
Contributors xi

1 A Social Psychological Framework for Understanding Social Inclusion and Exclusion 1
   Dominic Abrams, Michael A. Hogg, and José M. Marques

Section I: Individual Inclusion and Exclusion 25

2 Social Exclusion Increases Aggression and Self-Defeating Behavior while Reducing Intelligent Thought and Prosocial Behavior 27
   Jean M. Twenge and Roy F. Baumeister

3 Reacting to Ostracism: Retaliation or Reconciliation? 47
   Kipling D. Williams and Cassandra L. Govan

4 Stigma and Social Exclusion 63
   Brenda Major and Collette P. Eccleston

5 The Role of Exclusion in Maintaining Ingroup Inclusion 89
   Cynthia L. Pickett and Marilynn B. Brewer

6 Exclusion of the Self by Close Others and by Groups: Implications of the Self-Expansion Model 113
   Tracy McLaughlin-Volpe, Art Aron, Stephen C. Wright, and Gary W. Lewandowski Jr.

Section II: Group Dynamics of Inclusion and Exclusion 135

7 Managing Group Composition: Inclusive and Exclusive Role Transitions 137
   John M. Levine, Richard L. Moreland, and Leslie R. M. Hausmann

8 When Bad Becomes Good (and Vice Versa): Why Social   161
    Exclusion Is Not Based on Difference
    Dominic Abrams, Georgina Randsley de Moura,
    Paul Hutchison, and G. Tendayi Viki

9 Fringe Dwellers: Processes of Deviance and Marginalization
    in Groups   191
    Michael A. Hogg, Kelly S. Fielding, and John Darley

10 Delinquency: Cause or Consequence of Social Exclusion?   211
    Nicholas Emler and Stephen Reicher

Section III: Intergroup Inclusion and Exclusion   **243**

11 Social Inclusion and Exclusion: Recategorization and the   245
    Perception of Intergroup Boundaries
    John F. Dovidio, Samuel L. Gaertner, Gordon Hodson,
    Melissa A. Houlette, and Kelly M. Johnson

12 Intergroup Contact in a Divided Society: Challenging   265
    Segregation in Northern Ireland
    Miles Hewstone, Ed Cairns, Alberto Voci, Stefania Paolini,
    Frances McLernon, Richard J. Crisp, Ulrike Niens,
    and Jean Craig

13 Cognitive Representations and Exclusion of Immigrants: 293
    Why Red-Nosed Reindeer Don't Play Games
    Diana R. Rice and Brian Mullen

14 Attitudes toward Immigrants and Immigration: The Role of   317
    National and International Identity
    Victoria M. Esses, John F. Dovidio, Antoinette H. Semenya, and
    Lynne M. Jackson

Author Index   339

Subject Index   353

Acknowledgments

This book is the culmination of a combined effort that has involved an assorted array of our friends and coworkers. We are indebted to Alison Mudditt, Stacy Malyil, and Paul Dukes at Psychology Press for their advice, enthusiasm, and patience, to Graham Moffitt for his thorough preparation of the indexes and Veena Krishnan for her meticulous work at the production stage. We are grateful to Miles Hewstone, Diane Houston, Vicki Esses, Jack Dovidio, Julie Christian, Constantine Sedikides, and Alex Haslam for their support for the project. The ideas for this book were also supported through a seminar series sponsored by the Economic and Social Research Council (R451265070), the Academy of Social Sciences, the British Psychological Society, The European Association of Experimental Social Psychology, and the Society for the Psychological Study of Social Issues.

Notes on Contributors

Dominic Abrams is Professor of Social Psychology and Director of the Centre for the Study of Group Processes at the University of Kent. He received his BA from Manchester University (1979), an MSc from the London School of Economics (1980), and PhD from Kent (1984), after which he joined the faculty at Bristol and Dundee Universities before returning to Kent in 1989. He is currently Chair of the Research Board of the British Psychological Society, and coeditor of the journal, *Group Processes and Intergroup Relations* (Sage). He is an Academician of the Academy of Social Sciences and a Fellow of SPSSI. His research focuses on intergroup prejudice and discrimination and the personal and social regulation of behavior among group members.

Arthur Aron is Professor of Psychology at the State University of New York at Stony Brook. His research focuses on motivational, cognitive, and neural processes in close relationships, including their implications for intergroup contact and prejudice. Much of his research has been supported by the National Science Foundation; some of his current work is supported by the IRUL Foundation. He recently completed a 6-year-term as Associate Editor for the *Journal of Personality and Social Psychology*.

Roy F. Baumeister is the Eppes Professor of Psychology at Florida State University. He obtained his BA from Princeton University in 1974, his MA from Duke University in 1976, and his PhD from Princeton University in 1978. After a postdoctoral year at UC Berkeley, he joined the faculty at Case Western Reserve University, where he remained until 2003. Dr. Baumeister's research interests span the field of social psychology; he has done work on the self-personality, self-control, human sexuality, and social rejection. He is the author of over 200 scientific publications and 13 books.

Marilynn Brewer received her PhD in social psychology at Northwestern University in 1968 and is currently Professor of Psychology and Eminent Scholar in Social Psychology at the Ohio State University. Her primary area of research is the study of social identity and intergroup relations and she is the author of numerous research articles and books in this area. Dr. Brewer was recipient of the 1996 Lewin Award from SPSSI, the 1993 Donald T. Campbell award for Distinguished Contributions to Social Psychology from the Society for Personality and Social Psychology, and the 2003 Distinguished Scientist award from the Society of Experimental Social Psychology.

Ed Cairns is Professor of Psychology at the University of Ulster. He has spent thirty years studying the psychological aspects of political violence in relation to the conflict in Northern Ireland. He has been a visiting scholar at the Universities of Florida, Cape Town, and Melbourne. He is a Fellow of the British Psychological Society and past president of the Division of Peace Psychology of the APA.

Jean Craig (deceased) had been for many years a researcher with the Northern Ireland Civil Service employed on a wide variety of community-related research projects. In her spare time she had a passionate commitment to human rights, especially those concerning young people. At the time of her death (2000) she was seconded as a Research Officer to the Centre for the Study of Conflict at the University of Ulster.

Richard J. Crisp is a Reader in Social Psychology at the University of Birmingham. He obtained his BA from the University of Oxford and his PhD from Cardiff University. His research interests focus on cognitive and motivational models of group processes and intergroup relations. He received the British Psychological Society Award for Outstanding Doctoral Research Contributions to Psychology (2000) and the Society for the Psychological Study of Social Issues "Louise Kidder" Early Career Award (2003).

John Darley (PhD 1965, Harvard) is the Warren Professor of Psychology and a Professor of Psychology and Public Affairs at Princeton University. He is a past president of the American Psychological Society and a recipient of the Society of Experimental Social Psychology, Distinguished Scientific Award. His current research focuses on two topics: How incentive systems can induce corruption in groups striving to gain these incentives, and the principles citizens use to allocate punishments to moral transgressors.

John F. Dovidio (MA, PhD in Social Psychology from the University of Delaware) is Professor of Psychology at the University of Connecticut. Dr. Dovidio is currently Editor of the *Journal of Personality and Social Psychology—Interpersonal Relations and Group Processes*. He has been Editor of *Personality and Social Psychology Bulletin* and Associate Editor of *Group Processes and Intergroup Relations*. Dr. Dovidio's research interests are in stereotyping, prejudice, and discrimination; social power and nonverbal communication; and altruism and helping. He shared the 1985 and 1998 Gordon Allport Intergroup Relations Prize with Samuel Gaertner for their work on aversive racism and ways to reduce bias, and the 2000 Prize with Kerry Kawakami for their research on reducing spontaneous stereotyping.

Collette Eccleston is a PhD candidate in social psychology at the University of California, Santa Barbara. She is interested in the effects of stigmatization on self-esteem, group identification, and motivation. She is also interested in how individuals cope with membership in a stigmatized group. Her research addresses how belief in the legitimacy of the social system affects the use of coping strategies such as social comparison and selective devaluing. She is the recipient of a National Science Foundation Graduate Fellowship.

Nicholas Emler is Professor of Social Psychology at the University of Surrey, and has previously held appointments at the London School of Economics and at the Universities of Dundee, Oxford, and Rene Descartes (Paris). He has also been a visiting professor at Johns Hopkins University, the ecole des Hautes Etudes en Sciences Sociales Paris, and the Universities of Tulsa, Bologna, and Geneva. His interests are broadly in the area of moral psychology and this has included research on such topics as the development of socio-moral knowledge in childhood, delinquency, reputation management, political identity, and leadership.

Victoria Esses is Professor of Psychology at the University of Western Ontario, Canada. She is Associate Editor of *Group Processes and Intergroup Relations*, and has served as Associate Editor of *Personality and Social Psychology Bulletin*. Her research interests include intergroup relations, prejudice, and discrimination, with a particular interest in attitudes toward immigrants and immigration. Dr. Esses received the 1992 Otto Klineberg Intercultural and International Relations Award with Geoffrey Haddock and Mark Zanna for their work on intergroup attitudes. She is a consultant for Citizenship and Immigration Canada, and has designed government courses on public attitudes toward immigration and cultural diversity.

Kelly Fielding (PhD 2002, University of Queensland) is an Assistant Professor of Psychology at the University of Queensland. She has basic and applied research interests that span the areas of group processes and intergroup relations, and social and environmental sustainability. Her current research investigates responses to leadership, positive deviance, and the social-psychological determinants of pro-environmental behavior.

Samuel L. Gaertner is Professor of Psychology at the University of Delaware. He received his PhD from the City University of New York, Graduate Center in 1970. He shared the Gordon Allport Intergroup Relations Prize awarded by the Society for the Psychological Study of Social Issues in 1985 with John Dovidio for their work on aversive racism and also in 1998 for their work on the Common Ingroup Identity Model. In 2004, Professors Dovidio and Gaertner shared the SPSSI Kurt Lewin Memorial Award. Professor Gaertner is on the editorial boards of the *Journal of Personality and Social Psychology, Personality and Social Psychology Bulletin*, and *Group Processes and Intergroup Relations*.

Cassandra Govan completed her PhD in social psychology at Macquarie University in Sydney, Australia. She is currently a post-doctoral fellow in social and organizational behavior at Stanford Graduate School of Business.

Leslie Hausmann is currently pursuing a PhD in social psychology at the University of Pittsburgh. Her research interests encompass various aspects of stereotyping and prejudice. Her masters thesis investigated the relationships among different sources of motivation to control prejudice and the display of implicit prejudice. She is now completing her dissertation, which explores the role of communication in the development of stereotypes.

Miles Hewstone is Professor of Social Psychology and Fellow of New College, Oxford University. He has published widely on the topics of attribution theory, social cognition, stereotyping, social influence, and intergroup relations. His current research focuses on the reduction of intergroup conflict. He is cofounding editor of the *European Review of Social Psychology*, and a former editor of the *British Journal of Social Psychology*. He has twice been a Fellow at the Center for Advanced Study in the Behavioral Sciences, Stanford and is a Fellow of the British Academy and an Honorary Fellow of the British Psychological Society.

Gordon Hodson completed his PhD at the University of Western Ontario, and is an Assistant Professor at Brock University, Canada. His research interests involve stereotyping, prejudice, and discrimination, with a focus on individual differences, intergroup contact, and perceived threat.

Michael Hogg (PhD 1983, University of Bristol) is an Australian Professorial Fellow at the University of Queensland, with an honorary appointment as Visiting Professor of Psychology at the University of California, Santa Barbara. He is a Fellow of the Academy of the Social Sciences in Australia, and a fellow of the Society for the Psychological Study of Social Issues. Dr. Hogg's research is on group processes, intergroup relations, social identity, and self-conception. His current research focuses on leadership, differentiation within groups, and the motivational role of subjective uncertainty reduction in group and intergroup processes.

Melissa A. Houlette is currently an Assistant Professor at the College of Mount St. Joseph, holding a joint appointment in Behavioral Sciences and the Department of Business Administration. Her research interests include the causes and consequences of intergroup bias and the development of means to improve relations between groups, as well as decision-making processes and outcomes in groups. Her research seeks to combine the two areas of interest in an effort to integrate and extend the Common Ingroup Identity Model with work on information sharing and decision making in demographically diverse groups.

Paul Hutchison is a post-doctoral research fellow at the School of Psychology, University of Exeter. He graduated from the University of Abertay, Dundee, and received his MSc and PhD from the University of Kent. His primary research interests are in areas of intergroup relations, social perception and judgment, and group decision-making processes.

Lynne Jackson is an Assistant Professor at King's University College at the University of Western Ontario, in London, Canada. Her research deals with prejudice and group conflict, intergroup helping, the role of religion in social behaviour, and adult life transitions.

Kelly M. Johnson is a graduate student in social psychology at the University of Delaware. She received her MA in general/experimental psychology from California State University, Northridge. Her research interests are in the field of intergroup relations. She is particularly interested in the relationships among affect, status, and cognitive representations, and their effect on intergroup attitudes and behaviors.

John M. Levine is Professor of Psychology and Senior Scientist at the Learning Research and Development Center at the University of Pittsburgh. His research focuses on small group processes, including majority and minority influence, group socialization, shared reality, and group loyalty. He is a Fellow of APA and APS and has served as Editor of the *Journal of Experimental Social Psychology* and Executive Committee Chair of the Society of Experimental Social Psychology.

Tracy McLaughlin-Volpe is an Assistant Professor of Social Psychology at the University of Vermont. She earned her PhD at the State University of New York at Stony Brook and was a Postdoctoral Research Fellow for the Social Identity Consortium at the Graduate School and University Center of the City University of New York. Her primary research interests are in group processes, especially intergroup relations and prejudice.

Gary W. Lewandowski Jr. is an Assistant Professor of Social Psychology at Monmouth University in New Jersey. He received his BA from Millersville University of Pennsylvania, and then proceeded to receive his MA and PhD from the State University of New York at Stony Brook. His research focuses on how entering, maintaining, and losing romantic relationships influences the self.

Dr. Frances McLernon is a Lecturer in Social and Clinical Psychology at the University of Ulster in Northern Ireland. Her research interests include Northern Irish children's attitudes to war and peace before and after the paramilitary ceasefires, and the role of intergroup contact in the processes of forgiveness and reconciliation in Northern Ireland.

Brenda Major is a Professor of Psychology at the University of California, Santa Barbara. Her research addresses how people cope with prejudice, discrimination, devalued social identities, and stressful life events. She is particularly interested in psychological resilience—the personality characteristics and cognitive, emotional, and behavioral strategies that enable people to maintain their sense of self-esteem and well-being and strive despite negative life events and adversity. Her work has been funded by grants from the National Science Foundation and the National Institutes of Mental Health.

José M. Marques (PhD, Catholic University of Louvain at Louvain-la-Neuve) is Professor of Psychology and Head of the Social Psychology Graduate Training Program at the University of Porto. His areas of research include stereotyping and group perception with a special interest on group norms and reactions to group deviants in intergroup contexts.

Richard L. Moreland is Professor of Psychology and Management at the University of Pittsburgh. He is interested in many aspects of small groups, but especially changes in groups over time, including such phenomena as group formation and dissolution, group development, and group socialization. He is a Fellow of Divisions 8, 9, and 49 of APA and currently serves as Associate Editor for *Group Processes and Intergroup Relations* and *Organization Science*.

Brian Mullen is Professor of Psychology and Director of the Social Psychology Graduate Training Program at Syracuse University. His areas of research include the social cognition contributions to group and intergroup behavior, with a special interest in the cognitive representations of ethnic immigrant groups in ethnophaulisms. He also does research on the development, and application of, meta-analytic statistical techniques, and is currently working on a third-generation meta-analytic statistical software system.

Ulrike Niens received her PhD in Psychology from the University of Ulster in 2001. She is currently a research fellow with the UNESCO Centre, University of Ulster, where she is developing a research program focusing on education for citizenship and democracy in Northern Ireland. Her research interests include social identity, social change and political participation in divided societies.

Cynthia Pickett received her PhD in social psychology from Ohio State University in 1999. From 1999 to 2002, Dr. Pickett was Assistant Professor of Psychology at the University of Illinois at Urbana-Champaign and then joined the faculty at the University of Chicago in 2002. Dr. Pickett conducts research in the areas of social identity and intergroup relations, group perception and social cognition, and interpersonal rejection and has received funding for these projects from the National Science Foundation and the National Institutes of Mental Health.

Stefania Paolini is a Lecturer at the University of Newcastle, Australia. She obtained her *Laurea* degree from the University of Padua, Italy and her PhD from Cardiff University. Her research interests include stereotype change, intergroup contact, intergroup anxiety, and social cognition.

Georgina Randsley de Moura is a research associate in social psychology at the University of Kent, Canterbury, U.K. Her research interests are in the area of group processes, particularly related to political and organizational fields. She is currently investigating leadership and deviance, using Social Identity Theory and the Subjective Group Dynamics model as theoretical frameworks for her research.

Stephen D. Reicher is Professor of Psychology at the University of St. Andrews. His interest lies in processes of social identity and collective action and this has included work on such topics as crowd behavior, political rhetoric, nationalism and discrimination.

Diana R. Rice is Assistant Professor of Psychology at Tyndale University College. Her areas of research include social cognitive approaches to intergroup behavior, as well as the cognitive representations used when describing ethnic immigrant groups. She also conducts research on the cognitive representations used in categorizing and recognizing faces from ethnic in- and outgroups.

Antoinette H. Semenya received her master's degree in social psychology from the University of Western Ontario in 2001, and is completing her PhD in social psychology, under the guidance of Dr. Victoria M. Esses. Antoinette's research interests lie in the areas of intergroup relations, identity, and stigma. She is currently examining the ways in which perceptions of social power affect self and group processes among stigmatized group members. Upon completion of her PhD in 2005, Antoinette plans to pursue an academic career.

Jean M. Twenge is Assistant Professor of Psychology, San Diego State University. She obtained her BA/MA from the University of Chicago in 1993 and her PhD from the University of Michigan in 1998. She became interested in social rejection while working as a postdoctoral researcher at Case Western University from 1999 to 2001. Dr. Twenge also does meta-analyses of birth cohort changes in personality traits over time. She is the author of 40 publications, including 28 journal articles.

G. Tendayi Viki is a Lecturer in Forensic Psychology at the University of Kent. He received his PhD in forensic psychology from the University of Kent, Canterbury. His research interests include: intra- and intergroup dynamics, social-cognitive processes, contemporary sexism, rape myth acceptance, attitudes to crime and punishment, and behavioral variables in cancer prevention.

Alberto Voci is Associate Professor of Social Psychology at the University of Padova, Italy. His research interests are prejudice reduction, perceptions of group variability, the antecedents of ingroup bias and, more broadly, the motivational and cognitive processes related to the dynamics between personal and social identity.

Kipling Williams is Professor of Psychological Sciences at Purdue University in West Lafayette, Indiana. He worked on this chapter while Professor of Psychology at Macquarie University in Sydney Australia, with the assistance of an Australian Research Council Grant. He has authored or edited six books and has published over sixty articles and chapters on topics in group performance, social influence, psychology and law, and Internet research. He has co-convened the annual Sydney Symposium on Social Psychology (with the Joe Forgas and Bill von Hippel), and is currently President of the Society for Australasian Social Psychologists. His most recent books include *Ostracism: The Power of Silence* (2001), *The Social Outcast: Ostracism, Social Exclusion, Rejection, and Bullying* (expected 2005), *Social Motivation: Conscious and Unconscious Processes* (2004), *Social Judgments: Implicit and Explicit Processes* (2003), *The Social Self: Cognitive, Interpersonal and Intergroup Perspectives* (2002), *Social Influence: Direct and Indirect Processes* (2001), and *The Social Mind: Cognitive and Motivational Aspects of Interpersonal Behavior* (2001).

Stephen Wright is Associate Professor and Canada Research Chair in Social Psychology at Simon Fraser University. His research interests focus on intergroup relations, collective action, prejudice and prejudice reduction. He is currently an associate editor of *Personality and Social Psychology Bulletin*, has published numerous book chapters and articles in major social, educational, and cross-cultural psychology journals, and is the co-author of *Social Psychology in Cross-Cultural Perspective*.

1

A Social Psychological Framework for Understanding Social Inclusion and Exclusion

DOMINIC ABRAMS, MICHAEL A. HOGG, and JOSÉ M. MARQUES

This book draws together social psychological theory and research on social inclusion and exclusion. The rationale for the book is to understand inclusion and exclusion at different levels of explanation, and as involving different types of social psychological process. This chapter describes the central points made by each of the other chapters, and highlights key conclusions from each about evidence and its practical implications. This evidence is drawn together and provides the basis for an integrative conceptual framework that distinguishes features of social inclusion in terms of i) different levels of exclusionary relationship, ii) different modes of exclusion, and iii) different dynamics of exclusion within the relationship.

This book is about the social psychological phenomenology and dynamics of social inclusion and exclusion. We take as our starting point the assumption that social life is played out within a framework of relationships within which people seek inclusion and belongingness. Relationships necessarily include people, but they also have boundaries that by definition exclude other people. Frequently these boundaries are challenged or crossed. For example, families gain and lose new members through birth, death, marriage, and divorce; schools gain and lose students by virtue of time and age; adolescent peer groups hold the potential to enhance or to jeopardize the identities of their members; sports teams select and reject players as a function of ability and performance; judicial and political decisions are often intended to create the conditions for fairness, welfare, peace, but these decisions are influenced by the group's way of dealing with divergences and disagreement. At a macro-social level, countries may attract and repel individuals on the basis of race, ethnicity, occupation, or other statuses. Political or cultural alliances can provide a basis for the inclusion or exclusion of whole sections of the global community. In short, much of social life is about who we include, who we exclude, and how we all feel about it. The human passion for walls (e.g., Hadrian's Wall, the Berlin Wall, The Great Wall of China), fences (that between Mexico and the United States), dykes (e.g., Offa's Dyke), and ditches (around any number of British Castles) is no accident—it is a material manifestation of our need to manage inclusion and exclusion.

This book is intended both to reflect ongoing research and to contribute to a new research agenda that emphasizes the value of analyzing important aspects of social inclusion and exclusion from a social psychological perspective. The book brings together leading researchers in social psychology to explore different explanations and theories of how, when and why people become outsiders and insiders, and what the personal, social and cultural consequences may be. The book will be of central interest to social psychologists, and as it explores processes at the heart of human social existence it should have much to offer students of intercultural relations, sociology, political science, and social and public policy. It should also serve as a useful source for decision-makers and social policy makers, and provide an informative framework for practicing social scientists.

In this introductory chapter we have intentionally avoided extensive referencing (that is available throughout the book) and provided an overview and framework that maps out the central ideas developed in the book. There is a variety of different approaches to the theme of inclusion and exclusion. Within sociology these include classic sociological theory of alienation and anomie (e.g., Durkheim (1895), Merton (1938), the work of Simmel (1955), as well as ethnomethodological and symbolic interactionist accounts offered by Lemert (1967), Becker(1963), Scheff (1963), and Goffman (1961). However, until relatively recently there has not been a corresponding empirical analysis of mediating psychological processes. Societal diversity means that people may differ on various dimensions of comparison (e.g., ethnic, opinion, physiognomic). Sometimes people may consider diversity to be positive in the sense that it provides valued distinctiveness. At other times being separated from others may be highly aversive. The question is why particular differences are treated as so central a basis for social inclusion or exclusion at particular times.

SCOPE AND AIMS OF SOCIAL PSYCHOLOGICAL RESEARCH ON INCLUSION AND EXCLUSION

To address the question of what it is that transforms a person from being just "the same" or "different" to being an insider, an outsider or a "deviant" it is useful to think in terms of several different perspectives and levels of analysis.

We have organized the book to reflect differences in emphasis within the research literature. The chapters focus on different forms and types of actors and targets in the processes of inclusion and exclusion, ranging from the inclusion of others as part of the self-concept to societal level inclusion and exclusion of minority ethnic and immigrant groups. Social exclusion may cause harm but also bring psychological benefits, though not usually for both parties. Social inclusion and exclusion is a dialectic in which the parties may vary in their complicity or dispute. Some excluded parties may ultimately find ways to create a positive outcome for themselves; for instance, by redefining what is important or by exposing and challenging the legitimacy of the bases of exclusion.

Taken together the chapters provide a basis for a conceptual framework for analyzing and understanding social inclusion and exclusion. We draw this framework together at the end of this chapter. In general terms, we can characterize targets and sources of exclusion as either individuals or groups; the relationship context as ranging from transnational to intrapersonal; and the dynamics as involving degrees of interdependence, material or symbolic resources, a temporal dimension, and as invoking motives that center on opportunities or threats. Exclusion can arise in several forms or modes, ranging from the ideological to the physical, communicative, and purely cognitive.

Among the aims of this book is to help sustain the case for social psychology as a useful social science that is a worthwhile investment for public funds. Contributors to this volume were asked to describe their theoretical framework and research evidence, and also to explore some practical and policy implications of their work. Social psychologists tend to be cautious about forays into the policy arena, but increasingly it is the case that other social science disciplines are framing policy agendas, for example in economics, education, social welfare, health, and justice. Whereas some disciplines are guided by grand theory or statistical models, social psychologists are (necessarily) conservative and unwilling to generalize from evidence. However, there are undoubtedly clear and important regularities in the relationships between social contexts and behavior that are mediated by psychological processes, and we need to be able to make a case that we have something useful to say about these (see Brewer, 1995).

THE CHAPTERS

The book is organized into three sections, emphasizing individual, group and intergroup inclusion and exclusion, respectively.

Section A: Individual Inclusion and Exclusion

This section focuses on people's responses to being excluded in the context of interpersonal relationships (Jean Twenge & Roy Baumeister) and intragroup situations (Kipling Williams & Cassandra Govan), or because of stigmatizing features (Collette Ecclestone & Brenda Major). It also considers the cognitive processes and consequences of including others in the self-concept (Tracy McLaughlin-Volpe, Arthur Aron, & Stephen Wright), and the processes that narrow or broaden the range of others that include or exclude the self (Cynthia Pickett & Marilynn Brewer).

Jean Twenge and Roy Baumeister examine the nature of not belonging. Their premise is that the need to belong is fundamental to human life. How does an excluded person react to being left out of a relationship or isolated within society? Their thesis is that typically such rejected individuals react with anger and resentment, and retaliation. Social exclusion can set in train a dynamic that results in further exclusion, and ultimately conflict. Across a series of more than twenty vivid and powerful experiments they demonstrate the profoundly negative cycle that affects people who are excluded, either directly or prospectively (e.g., by the belief that they may spend their future alone and isolated). Excluded people become aggressive (even when unprovoked), defensive, uncooperative, unhelpful, self-defeating (e.g., they make less rational, healthy choices), and they shut off their emotional responses, perhaps engaging in defensive denial. They also perform worse on tasks such as intellectual tests.

The clear message is that being and feeling excluded is bad for people both psychologically and materially. Moreover, it is bad for the communities in which they exist, creating conditions that give rise to conflict, increased inequality, and mistrust. Surprisingly, reactions to rejection do not seem to depend on the rejected person's level of self-esteem. Instead, people who are more narcissistic are most likely to react hostilely following rejection—a finding that may be relevant to why particular individuals take extreme actions such as the Columbine High School shootings. However, the better news is that socially rejected people respond positively when offered acceptance; the cycle can be broken.

Kipling Williams and Cassandra Govan consider both the negative and more socially constructive reactions that result when people are ostracized within a group. They describe evidence from real interacting, as well as virtual, internet, groups in which individuals are ostracized. The evidence shows that ostracism from within a small group often prompts actions aimed at re-inclusion, such as conforming more to the group's norms.

An interesting difference between Williams and Govan and Twenge and Baumeister is that the latter do not find that self-esteem is implicated. However, Williams and Govan propose that whether positive or negative reactions follow ostracism depends on how a person can act to regain the four fundamental needs of belonging, self-esteem, control, and meaningful existence. Whereas threats to belonging and self-esteem should promote efforts to regain inclusion (generally pro-social action), threats to control and recognition provoke reactions to validate existence and regain control over others. Moreover, the public reactions of ostracized individuals may be conciliatory but implicitly or privately they may feel hurt and angry, and this may be conveyed implicitly in their behavior. Williams and Govan draw attention to the widely used method of "time out" to control children's behavior in classroom situations or in the home. They suggest that the particular method used for time outs could easily trigger more antisocial and negative reactions, rather than the compliance and desire for re-inclusion that teachers and parents aim for.

Brenda Major and Collette Eccleston move the focus from the particular to the general—to the experience of exclusion among people who are societally stigmatized. Stigmatization is dependent on specific societal contexts rather than inherent qualities of the stigmatized. Some stigmas are more pervasive (across situations) than others. However, exclusion based on stigma is distinguishable from other forms of exclusion because it depends on social consensus about the targets, tends to be shared among a set of people, and is often accompanied by a social justification or supportive ideology for moral exclusion.

Reasons for exclusion include the alleviation of discomfort, system justification, and status preservation for the members of majority groups. There may also be evolutionary reasons (Kurzban & Leary, 2001) that include avoiding poor partners for exchange, those who are diseased and outgroup members, or those who undermine group living. However, reactions to being stigmatized are not always negative. Different reactions are captured in a model of stress and coping that focuses on how stigmatized people regulate exposure to, cognitively appraise, and cope with stigma-based exclusion. For example, one reaction is to enhance one's desirability as a relationship partner for a non-stigmatized individual. Another reaction is to withdraw from situations that embody the threat of rejection. A third reaction is to find alternative bases of inclusion (e.g., within the stigmatized group), particularly when one's stigma is visible and associated with a group identity. A final response is to blame stigmatization on the prejudices of others. Indeed many stigmatized groups may provide a buffer against exclusion by providing their members with protected self-esteem and an ideological perspective that rejects the legitimacy of unfavorable evaluations.

Cynthia Pickett and Marilynn Brewer consider why group memberships are so important to people and how they respond to the threat of exclusion from their groups. Although marginalized individuals may attempt to become more prototypical (i.e., normative), another way that individuals can preserve an optimal identity is by clarifying the nature of intergroup distinctions and boundaries. Thus, it may be the marginal, rather than central, group members that display the most criticism, vigilance, and stringency over who is or is not included within the group. The, perhaps surprising, result is that those group members who are closest to outgroups are also those who resist similarities with the outgroups most energetically, and who perceive the groups in the most stereotypical way—perhaps a manifestation of the zealotry of new members whose membership credentials still need to be proven?

Couched in terms of the theory that people strive for an optimal balance between distinctiveness and assimilation in group memberships, the implications for pluralistic societies are interesting. Members of majority groups are likely to be able to enjoy both inclusiveness at a superordinate (e.g., national) level and distinctiveness at a subordinate (e.g., ethnic) level. However, minority group members face being peripheral in the superordinate context which may motivate either eschewing their subgroup identity or adopting it at the risk of becoming excluded from the mainstream.

Tracy McLaughlin-Volpe, Arthur Aron and Stephen Wright examine social inclusion and exclusion using their model of self-expansion. To the extent that the self can be expanded to encompass others, one's potential self-efficacy is increased (because of the associated access to resources those others imply), and this sense of self-efficacy is rewarding in itself. Much of the research described in the chapter concentrates on exclusion from close relationships (e.g., separation, divorce, loss of close friends), but the principles of the model apply also to groups. The model holds that people are selective in the relationships they incorporate into the self—only those that offer opportunities for self-expansion are likely to be attractive. As a result, the instability of a person's personal network, and potential losses from that network represent threats to the self-concept, and result in more negative self-descriptions and lowered self-efficacy.

McLaughlin-Volpe, Aron and Wright also propose people who are excluded do not merely feel miserable, they also feel frustrated that their capacity to act and achieve has been thwarted. An interesting implication of the self-expansion model is that responses to rejection may not always focus on the specific relationship that has been lost. If the bases of exclusion are unambiguous, the person may seek new relationships that allow self-expansion in other ways, or may re-emphasize existing relationships to bolster their importance. There may even be instances of exclusion that are experienced positively, such as when a relationship has broken down. If a relationship provides fewer benefits than expected, limits personal growth, or creates a barrier to forming relationships that bring better self-expansion prospects, people may actively provoke dissolution of the relationship.

There are policy implications for educational and organizational settings in which inclusion and exclusion are inevitable. Within such contexts more positive outcomes could be achieved if more attention was paid to the way exclusion may affect self-expansion, the social skills that are required to develop adequate self-expansion, the ways in which rejection is communicated, and the structural opportunities for members to find alternative routes for self-expansion (such as clubs, and small groups).

Section B: Group Dynamics of Inclusion and Exclusion

Section B focuses on mechanisms of inclusion and exclusion within groups, either as a natural part of the development and socialization processes of small groups (John Levine & Richard Moreland), as a function of the intergroup context in which people judge groups and individuals simultaneously (Dominic Abrams, Georgina Randsley de Moura, Paul Hutchison, & Tendayi Viki) or as a result of the motivational dynamics of self-categorization under uncertainty (Michael Hogg, Kelly Fielding, & John Darley). Nicholas Emler and Stephen Reicher concentrate on the specific group-based exclusion processes that surround delinquency.

A central problem for any group is to sustain its continuity and to thrive, while also being able to replace individual members or subgroups by including new members. The processes are necessarily dynamic and occur over time. To have a proper understanding of the mechanisms and processes that underpin inclusion and exclusion we need to understand how group composition is managed through social interaction and communication. John Levine and Richard Moreland analyze the way small groups manage the process of inclusion and exclusion of their members.

They propose that group socialization involves three psychological processes: evaluation, commitment, and role transition. Role transitions can be characterized as individuals' movement through the group in terms of inclusive (entry, acceptance) and exclusive (divergence and exit) phases. The interesting issue is how groups and individuals deal with discrepancies in readiness for such transitions. Levine and Moreland offer a typology of role transitions involving whether or not the group and individual share the same decision criteria for a role transition, have equivalent levels of commitment to one another, and are mutually unready, differentially ready or mutually ready for the transition.

For an inclusive transition, the group is likely to try to raise the individual's commitment and/or lower his or her decision criterion. Role transitions are also marked by particular events or ceremonies. However, as illustrated by numerous vivid examples, under different conditions these may be either positive or mild or negative, even punitive, reflecting the balance of the inclusion criteria and the commitment levels of the different parties. Most importantly, the intensity of the inclusion/exclusion process varies as individuals move towards and away from the group's core.

In the group socialization framework it is thought that individuals are more likely to seek inclusive than exclusive transitions. These transitions will reflect groups' capacities to satisfy motives such as a need to belong, a need for control and need for positive social identity. More generally, an important motivating principle in Levine and Moreland's group socialization model may be viewed as a group-level analog of the processes thought to guide self-expansion. In the self-expansion model, individuals are thought to be motivated by opportunities for increased potential efficacy. In the group socialization model, groups are thought to seek to include and exclude individuals in response to the potential contribution to the group. It is therefore interesting to consider whether some of the alternative routes to expansion described by McLaughlin-Volpe, Aron and Wright, might also have analogs at the group level.

Dominic Abrams, Georgina Randsley de Moura, Paul Hutchison, and Tendayi Viki consider the reasons why deviance and deviants within groups are rejected, tolerated, or even welcomed. They report a series of experimental and field studies testing predictions from the subjective group dynamics model, an extension of the social identity approach to groups. This proposes that part of the motivation for distinguishing deviant group members from others comes from the need to sustain the subjective validity of the group's core values, attitudes, and actions. When placed in the context of comparison with other groups, the issue is which group is accorded relatively greater validity. Consequently, people who identify with a group may wish not only to distance it from other groups but also to make stronger distinctions within their group between normative and deviant members.

The evidence shows that, even though people are well aware of differences within groups, they may only regard a member as atypical if that member is moving closer to an outgroup. Moreover, evaluations of deviant group members are more affected by the direction than the magnitude of deviation. Ingroup members who deviate towards an outgroup norm, and outgroup members who deviate toward an ingroup norm are especially likely to be accorded negative and positive evaluations, respectively, whereas members who deviate equally extremely in a direction away from opposing groups tend to be treated more like normative members. This pattern of evaluations increases as the intergroup comparisons become more salient. When ingroup deviants are criticized the aim is not necessarily to evict them from the group. Instead the priority may be to regain a sense of the validity of the ingroup's norms and standards. Thus, for example, positive stereotypes of the ingroup may be bolstered when a deviant member is evaluated negatively, and group members are more likely to derogate a deviant ex-leader than a deviant prospective leader, presumably because the latter has some legitimacy as a person who can redefine ingroup norms.

In a further extension of the model, Abrams and colleagues consider how manifestations of prejudice may change as children develop. Whereas younger children are likely to favor ingroup members over outgroup members purely on the basis of category membership, older children may favor specific individuals from both ingroups and outgroups using as a criterion the relative validation that the individuals provide for ingroup norms. Thus, problems such as bullying within schools may be viewed not only as part of a process of individual victimization, but of children's developing integration of intergroup and intragroup dynamics. Taken together, the research on the subjective group dynamics model helps to make sense of phenomena such as the way extreme group members may establish cults, when and why corruption and cheating are tolerated in institutions, business, and sport; different responses to whistleblowing or confessions; and why particular individuals are singled out to be targets of social pressure and bullying.

Michael Hogg, Kelly Fielding, and John Darley offer a slightly different analysis of marginalization within groups, also based on the social identity perspective. They augment this approach with both staffing theory and a perspective on attributional accounts and rationalizations. They consider that the direction of deviation (toward or away from the outgroup), the members' motivational orientation (for uncertainty reduction or for identity enhancement) and self-attribution of the deviant's actions will be especially influential. In line with Levine and Moreland's thinking, marginalization is seen as a last, rather than first, resort of groups. It only occurs if socialization attempts fail. Leaders, by being able to define the ingroup prototype, are in a particularly strong position to marginalize other members. However, groups may be more or less dependent on particular members (or numbers of members), and may also actively value dissenters as a way of ensuring they are flexible enough to tackle complex problems. Similarly, some members may actively seek deviant status (see also Pickett and Brewer's, and Emler and Reicher's chapters), or to set a new more extreme position to define the group norm.

Hogg, Fielding and Darley draw out different motivational possibilities from Abrams and colleague's analysis of pro-norm and anti-norm deviance. When solidarity and entitativity are particularly important to members they will emphasize uncertainty reduction, and will hence be intolerant towards both negative and positive deviants. However, when group status and valence are threatened, members will focus on negative deviants for marginalization. Moreover, if a positive deviant (e.g., outstanding performer) attributes their deviance to a property of the group, they are more likely to be accepted than if they take personal credit. Conversely, if a negative deviant attributes their actions to the group they are more likely to be a target for rejection. Several experimental studies are reported that are in line with this analysis. These dynamics of marginalization have clear implications for the way organizations manage diversity, particularly in a culture that stresses recognition of individual's contributions and sets them apart from the group.

Nicholas Emler and Stephen Reicher consider whether delinquency is best analyzed as a cause or as a consequence of social exclusion. Earlier chapters demonstrate very clearly that being excluded results in negative psychological and behavioral outcomes. Yet it would be wrong to depict people who are marginalized only as victims. They may play a very active role in their own marginalization. In keeping with the theme of the book as a whole, Emler and Reicher emphasize that exclusion from one social group or system may be complemented by inclusion (or self-inclusion) in another. They describe how adolescents become divided in their views of institutional authority, with a minority reaching the conclusion that such authority is unjust and illegitimate. Emler and Reicher's reputation management model of delinquency draws extensively from sociological theory, and holds that delinquency involves both opposition to institutional authority—a rejection of the values and norms of a dominant (and rejecting) group—and a positive orientation to maintaining a valued public identity within a subcultural context.

There are several important strands of evidence that demonstrate why delinquency is more appropriately characterized as a group process than as individual pathology. These include substantial attitude-based sex differences in delinquency, and the fact that delinquency is not closely associated with lack of success in school. Delinquent acts are primarily conducted as part of a group activity and a public activity. Delinquents are keenly aware of their audience and seek to manage their reputation, and part of that reputation involves establishing distance from a key outgroup—the system. Thus, delinquency is characterized not only by exclusion from the mainstream, but by inclusion in a group defined in terms of opposition to authority. However, delinquent young people are not entirely adrift. They sustain close relationships with parents and family, they aspire to normal futures (jobs, partners etc), they are keen to avoid prison or a criminal record. There is a "bulge" of delinquency that peaks at age 15 or so. The practical implications of this analysis for how society manages delinquency are quite far reaching. Emler and Reicher stress that the task is to avoid forms of action that perpetuate exclusion or impede reinclusion. Therefore the risks of excessively punitive reactions to delinquency, that then perpetuate it at this stage are very high. Instead, systems of restorative justice should offer much better prospects.

Section C: Intergroup Inclusion and Exclusion

The final section examines how intergroup relationships can be transformed by the inclusion of out-groups at different levels—either by redefining intergroup boundaries, forming cross-group relationships, or by maintaining subordinate and superordinate group identities (John Dovidio, Samuel Gaertner, Gordon Hodson, Melissa Houlette, and Kelly Johnson). The way in which intergroup boundaries are represented has important implications for intergroup relations and the success of intergroup contact, for example in Northern Ireland (Miles Hewstone, Ed Cairns, Alberto Voci, Stephania Paolini, Frances McLernon, Richard Crisp, Ulrike Niens, & Jean Craig). This section also considers the direct and indirect implications for social exclusion of the way images of immigrant and minority ethnic groups are represented in public literature and the media (Diana Rice and Brian Mullen), and concludes with the issue of how intergroup attitudes may relate to inclusion and exclusion of groups at the level of nationality (Victoria Esses, John Dovidio, Antoinette Semenya, & Lynne Jackson).

John Dovidio, Samuel Gaertner and their colleages analyze the nature of social inclusion and exclusion in terms of their Common Ingroup Identity Model (CIIM) of prejudice. Their work examines how the reframing of social category boundaries can transform outsiders into insiders and how this subsequently determines attitudes, relationships and behavior toward other group members. Inevitably, however, there are limits to recategorization.

There are many factors that can create a salient category division between groups. Therefore categorization itself can be viewed as an outcome, and subsequently a mediator, of the relationship between the social context and intergroup biases. Rather like the self-expansion model, the central idea in the CIIM is that once a set of people are defined as part of the ingroup they will be treated in a similar way to other ingroup members. Thus recategorization of former outgroups as part of a superordinate ingroup is a major tool for battling intergroup prejudice. Unlike self-categorization theory or the self-expansion model, Dovidio and colleages note that once people are part of a common ingroup they may begin to differentiate more as individuals, and that this too will help to reduce intergroup bias. There is now a large body of laboratory and field evidence to support the CIIM's proposition that a common ingroup identity reduces negative affective reactions, bias and behavior, and increases commitment (e.g., within organizations).

In keeping with several current models of identity, the CIIM also allows that people may seek simultaneous membership of a superordinate and subordinate groups—a dual identity in which people feel they belong to different groups that are "playing on the same team". However, dual identification may be of greater benefit only under certain conditions. In Dovidio and colleages' research dual identity is linked to less bias in high schools, but it is associated with more bias in the context of stepfamilies and corporate mergers. Whereas a "one-group" identity is most appealing and beneficial for members of majority groups (who sustain their status and do not lose distinctiveness) a dual identity is likely to be more comfortable and constructive for members of minority groups. This poses a practical problem of how to ameliorate intergroup biases when different groups are likely to respond differently to the prospect of a common identity. Current evidence suggests that, over time, a common superordinate level of identity is likely to bring most benefits for all groups.

Miles Hewstone, Ed Cairns, Alberto Voci, Stefania Paolini, Frances McLernon, Richard Crisp, Ulrike Niens, & Jean Craig provide a detailed "case study" of chronic mutual social exclusion-segregation between communities in Northern Ireland. The categorical basis of segregation in Northern Ireland is religion (though not religiousness), but segregation finds its expression in the political and education separation of the Catholic and Protestant communities. Although both communities are largely Caucasian, the differences are indicated by markers such as accent, name, facial structure, dress, area of residence, and school name. This illustrates how, when a social grouping is important to its members they will find cues that clarify category membership (rather than the other way around).

Hewstone and colleagues report evidence of the forms and degree of segregation that exists, and the historical and social mechanisms that work strongly against integration and positive contact. They focus on the role of affective processes in mediating between intergroup contact and positive intergroup relations. Intergroup friendship covaries with reduced anxiety during intergroup encounters, and both are associated with reduced intergroup bias. Equally important are factors that moderate the impact of contact. There is some evidence that it is beneficial to maintain the salience of intergroup boundaries during contact with individual outgroup members, so that positive experiences are generalized to the group as a whole. In contrast to Dovidio and colleagues' chapter, here it is argued that the ideal scenario is one in which group memberships are salient, but at the same time the contact is interpersonal.

Hewstone and colleagues present a variety of forms of evidence showing that those who have had more contact with outgroup members are more favorably inclined toward mixing with that group. In particular, intergroup friendship is associated with reduced anxiety, which in turn is associated with lowered prejudice, especially when people also report being highly aware of their group memberships during contact. Both direct and indirect contact (i.e., having an ingroup friend who has an outgroup friend) are associated with reduced anxiety and prejudice.

One of the key challenges in Northern Ireland is that schools are segregated. The evidence suggests that opportunities for contact predict the amount of contact, and that more recent (e.g., teenage) contact has a stronger influence on university students' outgroup attitudes than early (primary school) contact. The policy implications of this research include investigating the opportunities for indirect contact, working on ensuring that when contact does happen it is characterized by opportunities to form friendships, and working toward less segregated schooling.

Diana Rice and Brian Mullen consider the way that the social imagery of particular groups may generate or sustain their exclusion from wider society. Ethnophaulisms, or ethnic slurs, are used routinely in dominant cultures' depictions of minority groups. Ethnophaulisms have important implications for the cognitive representation of those groups as they encapsulate the group in simplified imagery that can be characterized in terms of physical traits, personal traits, personal names, food habits, group names, and other features. More simplified representations use fewer types of features. Using archival evidence of the complexity and valence of ethnophaulisms in society over different time periods, Rice and Mullen show that ethnic minorities that are represented in simpler terms are also often described in more negative terms. Moreover, there is a tendency for smaller, less familiar and more foreign groups to be represented more simply and negatively.

Cognitive representations are associated with important direct and indirect manifestations of discrimination. Across 19 different migrant groups from Europe to the United States, and over a 150-year period, Rice and Mullen find a strong relationship between the complexity and valence of ethnophaulisms and direct exclusion evidenced through immigration quotas and naturalization rates for each group. Indirect forms of exclusion are even more strongly related to the cognitive representations of minority groups. In children's literature, children from ethnic groups with ethnophaulisms of lower complexity were also represented with smaller heads and simpler speech.

Overall, an important finding to emerge from this work is that complexity rather than valence tends to be the most important predictor of negative outcomes. A simplified representation of a group reduces that group's scope to demonstrate its variability and avoid to stereotyping. As well as highlighting the need to investigate indirect exclusion more extensively, Rice and Mullen draw some interesting policy implications. One is that the simplification of the way groups are characterized can itself be exclusionary, even when the valence is positive. A further problem is that smaller or more distant groups may simply be left out of education about other ethnicities, which may be taken to imply that they have no complexity. Thus, it is not enough merely to present children with instances of members of other groups; those instances must also be complex and varied. Intriguingly, there is some evidence that people can be trained to think about objects in more multidimensional terms, and that this can transfer to the way they think about people. This evidence suggests some interesting ways that educators could develop teaching about ethnic and cultural diversity.

In the final chapter, Victoria Esses, John Dovidio, Antoinette Semenya, and Lynne Jackson consider the implications of inclusionary attitudes in the context of the global community. On the one hand we are encouraged to think in global terms (e.g., climate change or disaster management), but on the other to be committed and loyal to our own nations or regions (e.g., "fortress Europe" or Basque separatism). An important factor in how these perspectives meld is likely to be the degree of threat that is posed by the inclusion of external communities.

Based on social identity theory it is predicted that people who identify strongly with their nation will be inclined to derogate immigrant populations. However, national identity can take different forms, including patriotism (loyalty and positive affect) and nationalism (a cognitive orientation towards national superiority) and civic/cultural (voluntary) versus nativist (birthright) definitions. Evidence and research from around the world suggest that people with more nativist and nationalist orientations are more likely to adopt exclusionary attitudes towards immigrants, whereas patriotism is not implicated in the same way. Moreover, people with more internationalist attitudes tend to be favorably inclined toward immigrants. Based on the Common Ingroup Identity Model, Esses and her colleages offer a strategy for improving attitudes towards immigrants and immigration, particularly the attitudes of people most likely to be prejudiced. In one study they predict and find that persuasive messages that stress a common civic/cultural national identity significantly improves attitudes toward immigrants, but not toward immigration per se. In a second study persuasive messages were oriented toward a common international identity based on internationalism. This time, those prone to be prejudiced showed significant improvements in their attitudes to immigration but not toward immigrants.

The practical implications of this work are that there are effective ways in which openness to cultural and ethnic diversity can be fostered without undermining important social identities, such as those based on nationality. The particular forms taken by national and international identity are likely to have a direct bearing on how people respond to potential inclusion of new groups. If national identity is based on nationalism, and if that nationalism has a nativist basis, it is likely to provoke defensive and negative reactions to immigrants. On the other hand educational and social interventions that promote patriotic national identity based on civic definitions, together with an internationalist perspective, seem likely to promote more positive attitudes toward immigrant groups.

WHAT DO WE KNOW ABOUT THE SOCIAL PSYCHOLOGY OF INCLUSION AND EXCLUSION?

Table 1.1 lists some of the central conclusions and themes to emerge from the different chapters in this book. We have organized this summary in terms of four headings: the psychological effects of exclusion; the motives likely to be invoked by exclusion; the likely reactions or responses to being in an exclusionary relationship; and potential avenues for intervention to deal with negative consequences of exclusion.

The effects of exclusion are almost wholly negative, whether conceived in broad terms such as the loss of important parts of the self, or in more specific terms such as the particular negative emotions or defensive reactions that follow. Of course the exception is when someone is excluded from an undesirable relationship or group. But, although this might free someone from a stigmatizing association, it is likely that the positive aspect is the implicit or explicit inclusion in a more positive set of relationships; that is, subjectively it is removal of exclusion. Moreover, most people probably do not engage in counterfactual thinking about all the negative relationships they could have been excluded from.

We were struck by the diverse array of motives that have been proposed relating to exclusion and inclusion. These range from broad evolutionary needs to more specific goals such as the desire to maintain a particular reputation. Specific motivations may well be linked to specific forms of exclusion or specific types of relationship, but the overarching principle appears to be that exclusion provokes attempts to establish a legitimate place in the social world. That is, people want to be confident that they are part of a relationship or group that gives them meaning, security, and positive prospects.

TABLE 1.1 Effects, Motives, Responses and Intervention in Social Exclusion

Psychological effects of exclusion	Motives invoked by exclusion	Likely responses to exclusion	Examples of potential interventions
Contraction of self	Evolutionary	Attempt reinclusion (e.g., reassert loyalty)	Recategorization through common group membership and communication techniques (e.g., internationalism)
Self-concept threat	Need to belong	Find alternative bases of inclusion in same or different relationship	Recognize diversity but encourage dual identity (super-ordinate plus (superordinate levels of relationship)
Lowered self-esteem	Need for meaningfulness, validity, certainty	Find alternative source of validation	Encourage and use complex representations of members of excluded groups
Anger	Need for (optimal) distinctiveness	Reassert boundaries to clarify who included in which categories	Create opportunities to build relationships across the divide (e.g., intergroup friendships and indirect contact)
Frustration	Need for positive self-concept (via evaluation of self, group etc).	Express hostility toward source and others (e.g., prejudice, unhelpfulness)	Provide alternative opportunities for self-expansion for excluded people
Emotional denial	Potential self-efficacy	Find alternative basis for control and efficacy	Prevent marginalization by establishing transparent and trustworthy procedures for justice
Cognitive impairment	Reputation management	Reappraise situation or cause of exclusion (e.g., define it as illegitimate by attributing to prejudice)	Break the link between exclusion at the superordinate and subordinate levels of relationship
	Gains versus losses	System justification/rejection	Limit damage of necessary exclusion by better communication, e.g., offer less threatening attributions for exclusion
	Avoidance of threat or discomfort	Avoidance—withdraw, hide basis of exclusion or regulate exposure to source, engage in in self-defeating behavior	

The evidence about how people respond to exclusion appears to be quite consonant with Tajfel and Turner's (1979) analysis of intergroup status differences, which proposed reactions of objective and social competition, social change, social creativity, and social mobility, to which can be added disidentification (Hogg & Abrams, 1988; Ellemers, Spears, & Doosje, 2002). At a more abstract level these strategies can be considered as a general means of identity-maintenance. They seem to fall into five types of response. One response is to fight back. A second is to sustain reinclusion by various means, ranging from ingratiation to reinforcing boundaries that exclude others and reinstate one's own inclusion. A third response is to attempt to reestablish control over the relationship. If all of this fails, a fourth type of response is to question the legitimacy of the exclusion, or question the reasons for it. Finally, a fifth response is to withdraw from the relationship and attempt to move into other, more accepting relationships.

What are the practical implications of all this work? The chapters themselves refer to inclusion and exclusion in a very wide variety of forms and contexts, ranging from the experience of ostracism within an ad hoc group to the cognitive and motivational underpinnings of nationalism and prejudice against immigrants. Are there some common conclusions about the way negative effects of social exclusion can be mitigated?

A strong theme that emerges from the chapters is that the way different individuals and groups are represented should be a good candidate for intervention. Encouraging more inclusive ("one group") representations seems a promising avenue, but it is also clear that the desire for distinctiveness has to be addressed. This may be done by encouraging close individual relationships across group boundaries, and by focusing on complex features that work against simplified and stereotypic imagery. Moreover, the reframed more inclusive relationship has to offer both parties some gains. Even when exclusion in one relationship is unavoidable it seems likely that the more negative consequences can be reduced by finding alternative relationships within which inclusion can be established.

A Framework for Understanding the Psychology of Social Inclusion and Exclusion

Drawing together the ideas in this book we think it is possible to develop a more restricted and coherent conceptual framework for researching social inclusion and exclusion. We acknowledge the intellectual debt we owe to all the contributors to the book in helping us think about this framework, and we apologize for misinterpretations or omissions of crucial elements. The elements of this framework are listed in Table 1.2.

Sources and Targets of Exclusion and Inclusion
One way to characterize social exclusion is in terms of sources and targets. Social categories

TABLE 1.2 A Conceptual Framework for Social Inclusion and Exclusion

Relationship context of exclusion/inclusion	Modes/forms of exclusion	Dynamics of exclusion/inclusion relationship
Transnational	Ideological/Moral	Independent vs. interdependent relationship
Societal	Representational	Consensual vs. contested exclusion
Institutional	Categorical	Involves material vs. symbolic resources
Intergroup	Physical	Outcome vs. process focus
Intragroup	Communicative	Shorter vs. longer temporal perspective
Interpersonal		Opportunity vs. threat motivations
Intrapersonal		

and groups are clearly one type of target of exclusion, particularly if they are minorities, are unfamiliar, or pose any kind of threat. Social categories, and more often groups, are also powerful agents of exclusion. By their very nature, they have the capacity to include and exclude people, and must do so to exist as categories or as groups. Individuals are highly likely to be the targets of exclusion, particularly if they have a poor fit with a group. Moreover, individuals may be excluded from relationships either because they belong to an excluded group, or because of something unique about them as a person.

In contrast, it is unlikely that individuals are readily able to engineer exclusion, unless they have an unusual level of personal power, are supported psychologically by an ingroup, or can draw on a principle of exclusion that is defined at a more abstract level of relationship. Therefore, we believe there is likely to be an asymmetry in control over inclusion/exclusion processes. In general, the group has more power over the individual than individuals do over one another or over groups. This may be reflected even at the interpersonal level. It seems likely that interpersonal exclusion is more potent if it also removes access to an important social network, effectively reducing a person's social capital.

The Relationship Context of Exclusion and Inclusion
Exclusion and inclusion can happen at many different levels. We think it is useful to distinguish those that are associated with different forms of exclusion. At the most general and abstract level is exclusion based on large scale geographical, religious or ethnic differences—where the humanity or rights of entire sections of the global community are diminished or ignored. This transnational level encompasses exclusion based on nationality, and based on cultural and economic divides such as the more and less developed economic blocks, Islamic vs. Christian countries, geopolitical classifications (e.g., the "axis of evil") and so on.

The next level is societal; the consensual exclusion of particular sets of people within a particular society (e.g., stigmatization of people who are obese or have mental health problems). Next is the institutional level, where different institutions within society may select different groups or individuals, and define their own criteria for inclusion and exclusion, whether these be active (e.g., setting of quotas) or apparently passive (e.g., "neutral" selection criteria for admission). At the next level, is intergroup exclusion whereby particular groups sustain boundaries that establish their differences from other groups. Intergroup exclusion is likely to be more manifest and explicit than other forms because it often involves direct competition or conflict between groups. Then there is intragroup exclusion within which groups define the criteria by which members are allowed to define themselves and be treated as legitimate members.

The final two levels are the interpersonal and intra-personal. Interpersonal exclusion refers to denial of access to a relationship such that one person excludes another. Intrapersonal exclusion refers to a cognitive and emotional frame that enables or prevents a person from considering opportunities for inclusion in the first place (e.g., a white person could not easily conceive of becoming black). This is, in a sense, the relationship with oneself, which defines the scope or possibilities for one's inclusion in other relationships.

These relationship contexts should each have distinct manifestations of social exclusion and inclusion, but they are not mutually exclusive. For example, societal exclusion, which may be manifested in general attitudes toward various stigmatizing conditions, could well be expressed concretely in an instance of interpersonal exclusion of a stigmatized person from becoming a friend. Moreover, intergroup exclusion can, and is likely to, occur within the context of higher levels of abstraction. Generally, we think the more abstract levels of exclusion provide a context and pretext for the more specific and concrete levels, whereas the reverse is less likely to be true.

Forms and Modes of Exclusion and Inclusion

We expect there should be a degree of correspondence between the abstractness of the relationship and the mode of exclusion and inclusion that operates within the relationship. A relatively abstract form of exclusion is based on broad social ideology, moral conventions and principles. For example, execution of multiple murderers represents a consensus within society that such acts are outside its moral boundaries (cf. Reed & Aquino, 2003) and therefore it is legitimate to remove the perpetrator permanently. However, it is equally unacceptable for individuals to take personal revenge, and therefore such exclusion has to be mediated by complex legislative and institutional systems.

A second abstract, but less formal, type of exclusion happens in terms of social (and cognitive) representations. To the extent that groups and individuals can be characterized in simple, perhaps dehumanized or infrahumanized, terms, it is much easier to exclude the entire set. Different groups and individuals are accorded different degrees of entitativity and essence (Hamilton, Sherman, & Rodgers, 2004), which in turn implies different kinds of expectations and treatment. This form of exclusion does not require an ideological framework or set of rules. However, it is likely to be reflective of exclusion, as well as being highly implicated as a causal factor that perpetuates exclusion.

A third form of exclusion, which may range from relatively abstract to relatively specific, is the process of categorization. The simple act of partitioning people into different social categories necessarily involves over inclusion and exclusion of members in terms of the assumed sharedness of their characteristics with others of the same category. Notice, however, that as we move towards the more concrete forms, there is also potential for greater flexibility and likelihood of flux or change. Whereas ideology, law, and morality are hard to change, and whereas social imagery may be well established and pervasive, categories can be reassigned, or their meanings or relevance can change relatively quickly depending on the context.

As exclusion becomes more concrete it is also likely to be manifested in more specific ways. The most obvious manifestation is physical segregation, which may vary in the extent to which it is institutionalized and enforced. Physical segregation can range from societal, such as Apartheid or the Berlin Wall, to the interpersonal such as presence of a garden fence, or the distance apart that two people sit in a room (e.g., Macrae, Bodenhausen, Milne, & Jetten, 1994).

Exclusion and inclusion may also be achieved through particular communicative practices (e.g., speech accommodation or divergence, use of more abstract descriptions, non-verbal actions, ostracism), the most obvious being a simple instruction to "go away". Such instances of exclusion are likely to be easier to detect and prevent than the more abstract forms. However, we believe that often the concrete manifestations are likely to be the tip of an iceberg of exclusion at higher levels of abstraction, and although melting the tip might be sufficient to save the ship on one occasion, eventually the iceberg will resurface albeit with a slightly altered shape.

Dynamics of Exclusion and Inclusion

Interdependence

Processes of exclusion are highly dynamic, in the sense that they involve change in a relationship, in which at least two parties have potential for influence. These dynamics vary on several continua. One is whether the parties relate to one another as independent or interdependent entities. Targets of social exclusion may be unaware that they are excluded by a particular source, or they may not care, perhaps because they see opportunities for inclusion by other sources as sufficient. Sources of exclusion may use exclusion criteria that are general and thereby exclude others with whom there is no obvious form of interdependence.

There may be various system justification accounts that underpin independent exclusion, as may be the case in residential segregation such as "white flight", in which economically advantaged majority group members move to live in areas that "have the best schools". This leaves the "worst schools" in areas populated by economically disadvantaged minorities (cf. Bobo, 1988). Resistance and reaction to social exclusion is unlikely to be strong or coherent unless people are aware of the relevant interdependencies involved.

Even when relationships are interdependent exclusion may in some cases be consensual. For example, boys and girls in elementary school seem quite happy to self-segregate for purposes of play and social activities. Doctors and nurses, academic teachers and college cleaners may be quite happy to dine in different workplace canteens or common rooms. Men and women seem reasonably content with the idea that they should use different rest rooms in public buildings. Likewise, people may choose to exit relationships consensually (as members retire from groups, are relocated by organizations, as people develop different interests or as couples separate to move to different locations). Whether consensual or not, the outcomes may vary in terms of their desirability for building a more stable or progressive society, and should not be assumed to be unproblematic, either conceptually or practically.

The types of exclusion that are more likely to concern researchers and policy makers are those involving conflict or threat. In these situations exclusion is likely to be contested and the dynamics are likely to involve a struggle over who is excluded and on what basis.

Resources

When exclusion is contested it is likely that both the parties are attentive to their access to valued resources. In addition to material outcomes, the resources are social and psychological, including symbolic elements such as prestige, esteem and respect, independence, self-determination, and other qualities. Distributive or procedural issues, or both, are likely to be relevant to exclusion relationships. We assume that most individuals and groups generally seek to optimize or maximize their resources, and it is hardly surprising that they do so, in part, by denying resources to others (cf. Sherif, 1966). The problem for society is that early social disadvantage in terms of education, health, and housing are well established predictors of future exclusion (cf. the idea of social capital Portes, 1988; Putnam, 2000). Without some social management these resource inequalities can generate various forms of social decay or unrest (see also Klandermans, 1997).

Unequal access to power also makes it possible that people may be excluded when others rule their behavior to be "illegal". Justice-based exclusion is potentially explosive because it depends on consensus about the legitimacy of the system and rules that are imposed. When that consensus breaks down, the formerly excluded party is likely to react with anger, and the former excluders to become defensive and even more exclusive, as can be witnessed in the conflicts in Palestine, and more generally between Western and Islamic cultures.

It seems likely that the dynamics of exclusion at more abstract levels of relationship generally center on symbolic resources and processes, whereas the dynamics in less abstract levels of relationship are likely to have a relatively greater emphasis on the more tangible material outcomes. For example, governments are likely to justify tax breaks to the wealthy using procedural principles and system-justifying values such as equality of opportunity, whereas individuals in a work group are likely to apply a distributive rule that everyone pays the same amount into the pool for lottery tickets, regardless of their status or income (cf. Tyler & Blader, 2000).

Temporality

A third element in the dynamics of social inclusion and exclusion is time. Time can be conceived either as history (e.g., consider the sunk costs for each side in the conflict between communities in Northern Ireland), or as the time that it takes for inclusion and exclusion to happen. At more abstract levels of relationship, inclusion and exclusion seem likely to occur over a longer time course and changes in the form or mode will also take more time. Moreover, relationships that have been exclusive for longer periods of time seem likely to become represented at more abstract levels (e.g., enshrined in religious doctrine or in law). The exclusion is gradually more likely to become defined culturally in terms of the natural essence of the included and excluded parties (e.g., untouchables in Indian society), and to be seen as inevitable. Thus, over time there is likely to be a tendency for social exclusion to become consolidated.

Time also provides an important element in change, however, because of the individual and collective memories (see Pennebaker, Pàez & Rimé, 1997) and expectations that may surround social exclusion. Moreover, changing levels of inclusion at a more abstract level may provide the impetus for subsequent changes at a lower level. For example, as issues of equality and diversity become more strongly framed by an overarching human rights agenda, principles of freedom and equality that govern treatment of different ethnic or religious groups within society may also have an impact on the perceived legitimacy of differential treatment of men and women within those groups. Likewise, the success of one minority group in gaining rights may spur others on to act in similar ways. From the majority perspective, the threats or opportunities posed by one group or individual in the past may encourage a more exclusive or inclusive approach, respectively, to others in the present and future.

Motivational orientation

These dynamics of consensus and conflict can also be framed in terms of the motivational orientations involved. The contrasting elements of approach/avoidance, promotion/prevention, challenge/threat are well documented as individual action tendencies or motives in social psychology (Blascovich & Mendes, 2000; Mackie & Smith, 2002; Shah & Higgins, 2001). To apply these to social exclusion it is necessary to consider these assertive and aversive orientations from the perspective of more than one actor.

We think the most pertinent and general motives are the elements of opportunity and threat that inclusion and exclusion are likely to present to the parties involved. Depending on the balance of opportunities and threats/costs, each party will gravitate toward social exclusion or inclusion of the others. The dynamics are made more complex because these opportunities and threats may not correspond at different levels of relationship. For example, it may be highly effective to exclude a non-cooperative or lazy group member in order to improve the performance of one's group. However, there may be institutional or legislative reasons why it is not possible to evict that person. The opportunity that encourages exclusion at the local level is outweighed by the costs of doing so at the more abstract level. Conversely, even though a country may impose severe restrictions on immigration because of ideological and nationalistic sentiment, it may be that within a particular field (e.g., medicine) a chronic shortage of qualified candidates can only be met using immigrant workers. Thus a manager may have to actively recruit members from that group. The threat that encourages exclusion at the more abstract and distal level of relationship is outweighed by the opportunities that encourage inclusion at the more concrete level.

CONCLUSION

We hope that readers will find the chapters in this book thought provoking and that the book itself will be a stimulus for further research into the social psychology of exclusion and inclusion. Our offering of a conceptual framework is intended to provide a structure within which the specific ideas from each chapter can be located. However, we are well aware that there are plenty of other ways of cutting the cake, and our inclusive attempts may not have been optimal. We look forward to developing the framework and deriving additional testable hypotheses from it in the future.

REFERENCES

Becker, H. S. (1963). *Outsiders: Studies in sociology of deviance*. New York: Free Press.

Blascovich, J., & Mendes, W. B. (2000). Challenge and threat appraisals: The role of affective cues. In J. Forgas (Ed.), *Feeling and thinking: The role of affect in social cognition* (pp. 59–82). Cambridge UK: Cambridge University Press.

Bobo, L. (1988). Group conflict, prejudice and the paradox of contemporary racial attitudes. In P. Katz & D. A. Taylor (Eds.), *Eliminating racism: Profiles in controversy* (pp. 85–114). New York: Plenum.

Brewer, M. B. (1985). Experimental research and social policy: Must it be rigor versus relevance? *Journal of Social Issues, 41*(4) 159–176.

Durkehim, E. (1895/1938). *The rules of sociological method.* New York: Free Press.
Ellemers, N., Spears, R., & Doojse, B. (2002). Self and social identity. *Annual Review of Psychology, 53,* 161–186.
Goffman, E. (1961). *Asylums.* New York: Doubleday.
Hamilton, D. L., Sherman, S. J., & Rodgers, J. S. (2004). Perceiving the groupness of groups: Entitativity, homogeneity, essentialism and stereotypes (pp. 39–60). In Y. Yzerbyt, C. M. Judd, & O. Corneille (Eds.), *The psychology of group perception: Perceived variability, entitativity and essentialism.* New York: Psychology Press.
Hogg, M. A., & Abrams, D. (1988). *Social identifications: A social psychology of intergroup relations and group processes.* London: Routledge.
Kaplan, H. B. & Johnson, R. J. (2001). *Social deviance: Testing a general theory.* New York: Kluwer Academic/Plenum.
Klandermans, B. (1997). *The social psychology of protest.* Oxford: Blackwell.
Kurzban, R. & Leary, M. R. (2001). Evolutionary origins of stigmatization: The functions of social exclusion. *Psychological Bulletin, 12,* 187–208.
Lemert, E. M. (1967). *Human deviance, social problems and social control.* Englewood Cliffs, NJ: Prentice Hall.
Mackie, D. M. & Smith, E. R. (2002). Intergroup emotions and the social self: Prejudice reconceptualized as differentiated reactions to out-groups. In J. P. Forgas & K. D. Williams (Eds.), *The social self: Cognitive, interpersonal, and intergroup perspectives* (pp. 309–326). Philadelphia, PA:Psychology Press.
Macrae, C. N., Bodenhausen, G. V., Milne, A. B., & Jetten, J. (1994). Out of mind but back in sight: Stereotypes on the rebound. *Journal of Personality and Social Psychology, 67,* 808–817.
Merton, R. K. (1938). Social structure and anomie. *American Social Science Review, 3,* 672–682.
Pennebaker, J. W., Pàez, D., & Rimé, B. (Eds.) (1997). *Collective memory of political events: Social psychological perspectives.* Mahwah, NJ: Lawrence Erlbaum Associates.
Portes, A. (1988). Social capital: Its origins and applications in modern sociology. *Annual Review of Sociology, 24,* 1024–1047.
Putnam, R. D. (2000). *Bowling alone: The collapse and revival of American community.* New York: Simon & Schuster.
Reed, A., & Aquino, K. F. (2003). Moral identity and the expanding circle of moral regard toward outgroups. *Journal of Personality and Social Psychology, 84,* 1270–1286.
Scheff, T. J. (1963). The role of the mentally ill and the dynamics of mental disorder. *Sociometry, 26,* 436–453.
Shah, J., & Higgins, E. T. (2001). Regulatory concerns and appraisal efficiency: The general impact of promotion and prevention. *Journal of Personality and Social Psychology, 80,* 693–705.
Sherif, M. (1966). *In common predicament: Social psychology of intergroup conflict and cooperation.* Boston: Houghton-Mifflin.
Simmel, G. (1955). *Conflict and the web of group affiliations.* Glencoe, IL: Free Press.
Tajfel, H., & Turner, J. C. (1979). An integrative theory of intergroup conflict. In W. G. Austin, & S. Worchel (Eds.), *The social psychology of intergroup relations* (pp. 33–47). Monterey, CA: Brooks/Cole.
Tyler, T. R., & Blader, S. L. (2000). *Cooperation in groups: Procedural justice, social identity, and behavioral engagement.* Philadelphia, PA: Psychology Press.

Section I

Individual Inclusion and Exclusion

2

Social Exclusion Increases Aggression and Self-Defeating Behavior while Reducing Intelligent Thought and Prosocial Behavior

JEAN M. TWENGE and ROY F. BAUMEISTER

Across more than 20 experiments, we find that social exclusion leads to almost uniformly negative outcomes. Socially excluded people are more aggressive even toward innocent targets, are less willing to help or cooperate, engage in self-defeating behaviors like risk-taking and procrastination, and perform poorly on analytical reasoning tasks. Narcissists show a higher level of aggression after rejection, and self-esteem has no effect. Aggression after rejection can be prevented under some circumstances, usually when the target may provide some social acceptance (when further interaction is expected, or when the target is not too low- or high-status). Socially excluded people do not show mood deficits in self-report measures; in fact, excluded people report less emotion on implicit measures of mood. Rejected participants who denied the rejection and reported a more positive mood were more aggressive. Thus rejected people may be engaging in defensive denial of emotion, a cognitive state which might explain the negative consequences found across these studies.

Almost everyone has had the experience of feeling socially excluded: being alone on a Saturday night and feeling lonely; being rejected by peers, perhaps by means of cruel teasing; experiencing a divorce or the breakup of a romantic relationship; or having a friend cancel a social occasion because she found something more interesting to do. Because being with people is such a fundamental human need (Baumeister & Leary, 1995), these experiences can have a strong impact.

How do people react to social exclusion and rejection? We have begun to answer this question through a series of laboratory experiments. This research has concentrated on six main areas: aggression, prosocial behavior, self-defeating behavior, cognitive performance, individual differences, and emotion. We will discuss each of these areas in turn after outlining the general theory that provides a framework for the research.

THE NEED TO BELONG

Many things motivate human beings: the need for food, the need for shelter, the need to eat ice cream while watching late-night television (obviously some needs are more fundamental than others). After primary needs such as food and shelter are satisfied, the need to belong is among the strongest of human motivations (Baumeister & Leary, 1995). People go to extraordinary lengths to affiliate with others, be liked by others, and belong to groups. These needs might have arisen from evolutionary pressures; our ancestors who were excluded from social groups often died because they found it difficult to hunt, gather, and defend themselves against predators with only an army of one (e.g., Ainsworth, 1989; Axelrod & Hamilton, 1981; Barash, 1977; Bowlby, 1969; Buss, 1990, 1991; Hogan, Jones, & Cheek, 1985; Moreland, 1987). In addition, people excluded from groups were, almost by definition, unlikely to reproduce themselves. Thus the solitary hunters we described in the previous sentence were, most likely, no one's ancestors, even if they did manage to live out a normal lifespan.

Mark Leary and his colleagues have proposed that low self-esteem often results from feelings of rejection and loneliness (e.g., Leary & Baumeister, 2000; Leary, Tambor, Terdal, & Downs, 1995; Leary & Downs, 1995). Thus when people feel disliked by others, they often internalize these feelings and come to feel dislike for themselves. Leary suggests that self-esteem acts as a "sociometer" that measures a person's prospects for belongingness. High self-esteem means that one is the sort of person with whom others will want to affiliate, and low self-esteem means that one is the sort of person who may be neglected or even shunned by others. Because the need to belong is a powerful motivator, self-esteem acts as a "gas gauge" for our "fuel tank" of stored belongingness; people will make every effort to replenish it if it gets too low.

In our research, we sought to expand upon this previous research, addressing the behavioral consequences of social exclusion. When people are rejected by others, how do they react? When people hear they are likely to be alone later in life, what patterns can we find in their subsequent behavior?

Aggression: If You Can't Join Them, Beat Them

Over the past few years, Americans have been shocked and saddened by a series of shootings at our nation's high schools. In most of these cases, the perpetrators have been young men who felt rejected and bullied by their peers (Leary, Kowalski, Smith, & Phillips, 2003). The example of school violence is not an isolated one: social rejection or exclusion often leads to impulsive acts. Children who are rejected by their peers are more aggressive (Coie, 1990; Newcomb, Bukowski, & Pattee, 1993), and many perpetrators of violence are young men who feel cut off from close relationships with family members as well as with age mates (Garbarino, 1999; Walsh, Beyer, & Petee, 1987).

Adults are not immune to this effect. For example, single men commit more crimes than married men do, even when age is controlled (Sampson & Laub, 1993). They are more likely to be arrested for speeding or reckless driving (Harrington & McBride, 1970), and are more likely to be involved in car accidents (Harano, Peck, & McBride, 1975), especially those related to alcohol (Richman, 1985). In general, single people abuse alcohol and drugs at a higher rate than married people (Williams, Takeuchi, & Adair, 1992). These trends also appear in society at large. In the United States, social bonds between people have weakened in recent decades (Fukuyama, 1999; Putnam, 2000) at the same time that impulsive antisocial behaviors such as crime, drug abuse, and violence have increased.

All of these sources and trends suggest that social exclusion is correlated with increased aggressive and antisocial behavior. However, the opposite relation is actually more logical: when one is rejected, it makes sense to be less aggressive and more prosocial, in an attempt to win back friends and establish affiliation. In fact, Williams, Cheung, and Choi (2000) found that participants who were ostracized were later more likely to conform to other's judgments, which those researchers regarded as prosocial act designed to make the person more appealing to potential group members. Whether social exclusion is related to more aggressive or less aggressive behavior, the previous research gives little suggestion of the direction of causation. For example, social exclusion could cause aggression, but it is equally plausible that aggressive behavior could cause exclusion by others. Mediation by negative emotion might also occur. Given these unanswered questions, we undertook a series of experimental studies to address the question of social exclusion and aggression (see Table 2.1).

The most straightforward tests of the link between social exclusion and aggression occurred in Experiments 4 and 5 of Twenge, Baumeister, Tice, and Stucke (2001). In Experiment 4, participants spent the first 15 minutes of the study interacting with a group of their same-sex peers. They were then placed in separate rooms and asked to nominate the two group members they wanted to work with on a subsequent task. By random assignment, half of the participants then heard that none of the other participants had chosen them (this was the rejected condition). The other half heard that everyone had chosen them (accepted condition). All participants were then provoked: they received a very negative evaluation of an essay that they had written, supposedly issued by a

TABLE 2.1 Summary of Results of Laboratory Studies of Social Exclusion

Project/dependent variable	Effect of exclusion
Aggression (Twenge, Baumeister, Tice, & Stucke, 2001; Twenge & Cacho, 2003)	Blasting unpleasant noise, negative job evaluation. Only occurs in some situations.
Prosocial behavior (Twenge, Ciarocco, Cuervo, Bartels, & Baumeister, 2004)	Donating less money, volunteering less time, not helping experimenter, not cooperating in game
Self-defeating behavior (Twenge, Catanese, & Baumeister, 2002)	Risky lottery choice, choice of unhealthy behaviors, procrastination
Cognitive performance (Baumeister, Twenge, & Nuss, 2002)	Poor performance on: IQ test, GRE reading comprehension, GRE analytical reasoning
Individual differences: Narcissism and self-esteem (Twenge & Campbell, 2003)	Narcissism leads to aggression; self-esteem has no effect
Mood and emotion (Twenge, Catanese, & Baumeister, 2003; Twenge & MacDonald, 2004)	No effects or very weak effects on explicit measures; less emotion on implicit measures

new participant who had just arrived at the lab (and thus not one of the people who had accepted or rejected them). Participants then played a noise-blasting game with this new person; they were told that whoever lost a reaction time trial would hear a blast of noise, the intensity and duration of which was controlled by the other player. Thus participants had a weapon that they could use to hurt another human being. We wanted to know if rejected participants would be more or less aggressive than accepted participants.

The results clearly showed that rejected participants were more aggressive toward the person who insulted them. Rejected participants blasted louder noise at their opponents and were also more aggressive on a composite measure of aggression (consisting of noise loudness and duration). The two conditions did not differ on a self-report measure of emotion, and the results linking social exclusion and aggression did not change when controlled for negative or positive emotion.

In the next study, we sought to broaden the focus. The preceding study showed that rejected people became highly aggressive toward someone who insulted and provoked them. Would they also be aggressive toward someone who had not insulted and provoked them? We used the same procedure save one important change: in this study, the other person did not deliver any critical insulting evaluation to the participants. They did not receive any evaluation of their essay from the opponent; in fact, they had no interaction at all with the person with whom they played the noise-blasting game. The results showed that rejected participants were still significantly more aggressive than participants who had been accepted: they blasted louder noise and for a longer time. Thus social exclusion causes an increase in aggressive behavior even toward an innocent target.

We obtained converging evidence for these conclusions by using a different manipulation of social exclusion and a different measure of aggression. In this experiment, we manipulated social exclusion by giving participants false feedback on a personality test. In the crucial condition (future alone), participants heard that they were likely to be alone later in life. In contrast, participants in the future belonging condition heard that they would have good relationships throughout life. We also included a misfortune control group, who heard that they would likely be accident prone in the future (thus a negative outcome, but one unrelated to relationships). After receiving the future prediction, all participants were then provoked by a negative essay evaluation. They were told that the person who had evaluated their essay had applied for a research assistant position that was very competitive; the participant was asked to evaluate the applicant, rating him/her on a list of attributes. Thus, the participant could hurt or help someone who had insulted them. Written evaluations have been used to measure aggression in several other studies (e.g., Kulik & Brown, 1979; Ohbuchi, Kameda, & Agarie, 1989; O'Neal & Taylor, 1989; for a review, see Baron & Richardson, 1994, pp. 64–66).

Consistent with the results of the noise-blasting studies, participants who heard that they were likely to be alone later in life were more aggressive toward the person who had insulted them, issuing a sharply negative job evaluation. In contrast, the future belonging and misfortune control groups gave neutral evaluations of the applicant. The difference with the misfortune control group is informative; the forecast of a negative future is apparently not the cause of the heightened aggression. Only the forecast of a lonely future causes a notable increase in aggression.

Last, we sought to establish whether excluded individuals would also be aggressive toward someone who praised them. We used the same procedure as in the previous study, except participants received a positive evaluation of their essay. Under these circumstances, we found that all participants gave a positive evaluation of the applicant, with no differences between the future alone, future belonging, and misfortune control. Thus socially excluded participants are more aggressive than others when they are insulted and when they are neither insulted nor praised; however, they are not more aggressive toward someone who praises them.

Thus, this series of experiments shows that social exclusion can cause a marked increase in aggressive behavior. The average effect size for this set of studies is 1.33, meaning that rejected individuals scored 1.33 standard deviations higher on measures of aggression compared to the control groups. Anything over 0.80 standard deviations is conventionally regarded as a large effect, so the impact of social exclusion appears to be quite large. Several other researchers have replicated or partially replicated these results, also finding that social exclusion leads to increased aggression (Buckley, Winkel, & Leary, 2004; Kirkpatrick, Waugh, Valencia, & Webster, 2002; Warburton, Williams, & Cairns, 2003).

Why does social exclusion lead to increased aggression? Negative emotional states do not seem to be the culprit, as they did not mediate the effect in any of the studies. Although definitive evidence is not available, it seems plausible that socially excluded individuals become antisocial because they no longer see the point in being prosocial. When we are accepted, our social behavior is shaped by the demands of others; when we are rejected, we may indulge our more selfish and base impulses and act more aggressively.

We have begun to explore which situations cause aggression after rejection, and which can prevent it (Twenge & Cacho, 2003). In one experiment, half of the participants heard that they would interact with their game partner later, and the other half heard that they would not (the usual situation). When rejected participants heard that they would interact with their game partner, they were no longer aggressive. In the second study, rejected and accepted participants were told that their game partners were accepted by another group, rejected by another group, or simply members of another group (neutral). Rejected participants were not aggressive toward neutral group members, but were aggressive toward both accepted and rejected targets. Thus aggression after rejection is heightened when participants do not expect to interact further with the target of their aggression, and when they believe that the target is either different from them (accepted) or low status (rejected). On the other hand, aggression after rejection does not occur when participants expect to interact with their game partner, and when they believe that the target is from another group. This is consistent with the motivational theory of belongingness (Baumeister & Leary, 1995), which predicts that rejected people should seek acceptance in order to regain social ties. These results show that rejected people will act prosocially when they interact with those who may provide social acceptance (a future interaction partner, or another group member who is not too high or too low in status).

Prosocial behavior: Help! I Need Somebody

Although we find that social exclusion causes aggressive behavior, it could be that excluded individuals could act in prosocial ways when they are given the explicit opportunity to do so. Thus we undertook another series of experiments to explore a possible link between social exclusion and prosocial behavior. Previous evidence and theory suggests that social exclusion could cause either increased or decreased prosocial behavior.

If people are strongly motivated to form and maintain social bonds (Baumeister & Leary, 1995), then the loss of social connection frustrates this basic human need. This should motivate people to desire new connections. By helping others and cooperating with them, people could presumably prove their social value to others; in this way they could induce others to like and depend on them. It seems only rational that the socially excluded person would try harder to get along with others, and an increase in prosocial behavior seems a promising way to accomplish this. There is some empirical evidence to support this idea (e.g., Gardner, Pickett, & Brewer, 2000; Williams et al., 2000; Williams & Sommer, 1997).

The opposite prediction, that social exclusion could reduce prosocial behavior, is also plausible. Under this view, prosocial behavior depends on believing one is part of a community in which people mutually seek to aid, support, and love each other. When people are excluded, their motivation to perform such behaviors would be reduced or eliminated. Excluded people might feel that following social rules is no longer necessary, or that there is no point in continuing to make any such efforts or sacrifices. In many cases, doing what is prosocial and right for the group conflicts with self-interest. Most conceptions of virtue and socially desirable behavior promote prosocial actions that go against the individual's own wishes and desires (e.g., Hogan, 1973; Baumeister & Exline, 1999). For example, children must be socialized into helping others (Cialdini & Kenrick, 1976; Cialdini, Kendrick, & Baumann, 1981; Perry, Perry, & Weiss, 1986). Freud (1930) proposed that the superego (an internal system of restraint) is crucial for making civilized communal life possible: It emerges as a capacity to thwart instinctual or selfish interests in order to pursue actions that are valued by the group. Without the socializing context provided by social inclusion, the psychological restraints that support prosocial behavior may be diminished, and the prosocial impulse might be extinguished.

Prior research also provides correlational support for a connection between social rejection and decreased prosocial behavior, although it is unclear what causes what. Numerous correlational studies have found that children who are rejected by their peers act less prosocially than children who are accepted by their peers (Asher & Coie, 1990; Coie & Dodge, 1988; Gest, Graham-Berman, & Hartup, 2001; Mize & Ladd, 1988; Wentzel & Erdley, 1993; Wentzel & McNamara, 1999). Many studies have found that prosocial actions are more highly correlated with social acceptance than antisocial actions are (Asher & Renshaw, 1981; Bukowski & Newcomb, 1984; Hartup, Glazer & Charlesworth, 1967; Parkhurst & Asher, 1992; Schonert-Reichl, 1999). However, these findings are correlational, so it is unclear if social exclusion causes less prosocial behavior or vice versa.

We performed a series of experimental studies to determine if social exclusion causes more or less prosocial behavior (Twenge et al., 2004). In the first experiment, we used the future outcomes manipulation mentioned previously: future alone participants heard that they were likely to be alone later in life, compared to three control groups (future belonging, misfortune control, and a pure control group hearing no future prediction). After the manipulation, the experimenter gave each participant two dollars in quarters. She then mentioned that the laboratory was taking up a collection for the Student Emergency Fund, and pointed to a collection box on the table. The amount of money donated by each participant served as the measure of prosocial behavior. The results were striking: on average, future alone participants donated less than $0.40, while participants in the other three conditions donated an average of $1.50—that is, nearly three times as much. Only 37% of the Future Alone participants made any donation at all, whereas every single participant (100%) in the other three conditions gave at least something. These results were not mediated by either self-reported emotion or by state self-esteem.

In the second experiment, we manipulated social exclusion via acceptance or rejection by peers. The experimenter said that the participant could not complete the regular part of the experiment, so he or she could either leave or could help the experimenters by doing between one and three short studies for the remainder of the hour. The experimenter explained that the experimental credit would be the same either way. The results of this experiment again showed that excluded participants were markedly less helpful. Rejected participants volunteered for only 0.30 extra experiments, whereas accepted participants volunteered for 1.70 experiments on average. Only 20% of rejected people volunteered to help at all, whereas 90% of accepted people volunteered to help with at least one study.

The first two experiments both measured prosocial behavior that involved the sacrifice of self-interest: participants were asked to give up a scarce resource (either money or time). In the third experiment, we measured a prosocial behavior that did not involve a noticeable sacrifice. We manipulated social exclusion using the prediction of future outcomes. After the participant completed an emotion measure, the experimenter reached toward a shelf and knocked over a can of pencils. The measure of helping was the number of pencils the participant helped pick up from the floor. Even though this form of helping did not involve a sacrifice, socially excluded participants were still considerably less helpful compared to the people in the other groups. The future alone group barely helped at all; on average, they helped pick up less than one pencil. In contrast, the other groups helped pick up between eight and nine pencils on average. Only 15% of the Future Alone participants helped pick up any pencils at all, compared to the 64% who helped in the other three conditions. These effects were not mediated by mood, and trait self-esteem was not a significant moderator variable. Thus, again, socially excluded people were less helpful than others.

In the last three experiments, we measured prosocial behavior in a mixed-motive game. After receiving the prediction of different future outcomes, participants played the Prisoner's Dilemma game with a computer program (they believed they were playing with another participant). In this game, participants choose to either cooperate or compete on each turn; a point matrix rewards players when both cooperate, takes points off when both compete, and awards more points to the competitor when one player competes and the other cooperates. Overall, cooperating results in a higher point total at the end of the game. In two experiments, the computer was programmed to begin by competing and then play a tit-for-tat strategy; in the other, it was programmed to cooperate on the first turn before playing tit-for-tat. All three experiments produced the same result: future alone participants chose to cooperate significantly less often than the other groups. This occurred even though cooperating would have given the greatest return to the self in yielding a higher point total and thus more money. In the last experiment, the experimenter was blind to condition and the social exclusion feedback was delivered on paper, yet those who received the prediction of a life alone still cooperated on fewer turns.

We measured seven different possible mediating variables across these six experiments: mood, state self-esteem, ego shock, belongingness, trust, control, and state self-awareness. None mediated the effect. Thus the mediator remains elusive.

Nevertheless, the results of these studies are quite consistent and striking. Socially, exclusion causes people to become less helpful in general. They are less helpful toward a specific person who asks for help or toward a vaguely defined category of needy comrades. They are less helpful toward a peer and toward a high status person. They are less helpful regardless of whether helping others would cost them something, cost them nothing, or even plausibly benefit them.

Self-Defeating Behavior: If It Feels Good Right Now, Do It

Self-defeating behavior has long been a puzzle to psychology, leading some theorists to propose that people have innate self-destructive tendencies (Freud, 1965/1933; Menninger, 1966/1938; Piers & Singer, 1971/1953). However, there is very little evidence that people ever explicitly wish or try to bring suffering, harm, or failure upon themselves, and the hypothesis of self-destructive desires (whether innate or acquired) is not supported by research (see Baumeister, 1997; Baumeister & Scher, 1988). Instead, most self-defeating behavior results when people choose pleasurable short-term outcomes that carry long-term costs, rather than more beneficial long-term outcomes. Another route to self-defeating outcomes is poor self-regulation and the selection of counterproductive strategies based on a misunderstanding of self and the world.

Previous research has found a correlational link between social exclusion (that is, not having close, meaningful relationships) and self-defeating behavior. Suicide is the ultimate self-defeating act, and people with fewer social attachments are more likely than others to commit suicide (Baumeister, 1990; Durkheim, 1897/1951; Trout, 1980). Single people are more likely to abuse alcohol and drugs (Williams et al., 1992), which is sometimes regarded as a self-defeating pattern. In addition, married people are often mentally and physically healthier than single, divorced or widowed individuals (Bloom, White, & Asher, 1979; DeLongis, Folkman, & Lazarus, 1988; Goodwin, Hunt, Key, & Samet, 1987;

Lynch, 1979; Williams et al., 1992). These health problems may well be linked to self-defeating behaviors and poor self-regulation, because poor regulation of many behaviors (e.g., overeating, smoking, failing to exercise, alcohol, and drug addiction) causes harm to health. As with many of the previous studies on social exclusion, however, these studies are correlational and cannot establish causation.

We again used laboratory manipulations of social exclusion, this time measuring several self-defeating behaviors (Twenge et al., 2002). All of these experiments used the future alone manipulation, in which participants hear they are likely to be alone later in life (compared to the future belonging and misfortune control groups).

To study self-defeating behavior, we began by adapting a procedure that measured preference for a foolish, risky choice over an objectively superior play-it-safe option (Leith & Baumeister, 1996). Participants were given a choice between two lotteries. The risky choice offered a small chance of winning a moderate amount of money (2% and $25), whereas the safe choice offered a large chance of winning a small amount of money (70% and $2). In both cases, losing entailed the stressful experience of hearing a tape of very unpleasant noise. Worked out mathematically, the safe choice was by far the most beneficial, offering the greatest payout in the long run and a lesser chance of hearing the noise. Thus, choosing the risky lottery was a self-defeating choice. Sure enough, 85% of the participants in the two control conditions favored the play-it-safe option. But socially excluded people were much more likely to choose the risky lottery choice (about 66% of the time). The effect was not mediated by mood.

Next, we measured self-defeating behavior by asking participants to make three choices related to health. They could either receive a candy bar or a granola bar, either read a magazine or fill out a health questionnaire, and either sit idly or run in place before measuring a pulse. In each case, the second choice was explicitly presented as healthier. Thus the first item in each pair, although being more pleasurable, was also less healthy and thus self-defeating in the long run. Consistent with the previous results, socially excluded participants made fewer healthy choices (0.78), compared to 1.94 in the other conditions.

In yet another study, we measured procrastination, which is a classic self-defeating behavior. After hearing the future prediction, participants were told that they would take a predictive and important math test later in the experiment. They were given 15 minutes in which they could practice for the test (using a series of very boring math problems), do nothing, or actively procrastinate by reading magazines or playing video games. The experimenter watched from behind a one-way mirror, recording how the participants spent their time. The results showed that the future alone participants spent nearly half of their time procrastinating (7.12 minutes), compared to only three minutes on average for the participants in the other two conditions. Thus the future alone participants were much more likely to procrastinate by doing pleasurable things rather than concentrating on boring math problems that nevertheless might help them do better on an upcoming test.

Overall these results show that excluded participants are more likely to engage in self-defeating behaviors. Somewhat to our surprise, none of the effects were mediated by mood. Across all of our studies, we have found very few significant differences in mood, and these studies used three different self-report mood measures. Apparently social exclusion bypasses negative mood and goes straight to causing self-defeating behavior. Another possibility for a mediator is cognitive disorientation, possibly including a loss of future orientation and a failure of rational, meaningful thought (e.g., Baumeister, 1990; Pennebaker, 1989; Pennebaker, Czajka, Cropanzano, & Richards, 1990; Wyer & Srull, 1986). This disorientation may be what impairs people's ability to self-regulate their behavior effectively and do things that will be good for them in the long run. This is one reason why we proceeded to study cognitive performance in our next series of studies.

Cognitive Performance: Social Exclusion Reduces Intelligent Thought

Like many of the topics we have addressed, competing predictions can be made about the effect of social exclusion on intelligent thought. Social exclusion could lead to increased intelligent thought. If one is going to survive alone, considerable cognitive skills are necessary, and so it would be adaptive to become more mentally focused after being excluded from a social group. After all, survival often requires that many tasks (such as obtaining and preparing food) must be carried out successfully, and the lone individual cannot count on others to assist him or her. Hence one might expect social exclusion to stimulate intelligent thinking.

On the other hand, intelligent thought may have arisen in the first place as a tool for facilitating social groups and their interaction. Reasoning about social relationships is one of the most complex tasks many people perform on a daily basis. Given this, the socially isolated individual may have less need for intelligent thought.

These competing predictions motivated us to examine how social exclusion might affect measures of cognitive performance. We used the future alone manipulation in a series of experiments described here (Baumeister et al., 2002). In the first experiment, participants took the General Mental Abilities Test (Janda, Fulk, Janda, & Wallace, 1995; reprinted in Janda, 1996), which is a paper-and-pencil intelligence test. Participants were given six minutes to answer as many questions as they could. Future alone participants answered significantly fewer questions correctly, as compared to those in the future belonging and misfortune control groups. Future alone participants also attempted significantly fewer problems on the IQ test. These results were not mediated by mood.

The second experiment used a more complex design. We measured cognitive *encoding* for half of the participants, who received the exclusion manipulation, read two reading passages, and were then informed that the exclusion manipulation was not true. They then answered a series of questions about the reading passages. Thus they read the passages under the influence of exclusion but answered the questions after the manipulation had been nullified by the debriefing. In the *recall* condition, the other half of the participants read the two passages, received the exclusion manipulation, and then answered the questions. Thus these participants read the passages under normal conditions but answered the questions under the influence of social exclusion. This way we could ascertain whether social exclusion impaired encoding (reading) or recall, or both. In addition, the reading passages included one difficult passage and one easy passage.

The results showed that social exclusion affected only one type of cognitive performance: recall of the difficult passage. There were no differences on either passage in the encoding conditions, and no differences in performance on either recall or encoding of the easy passage. Thus encoding of information seems unaffected, while recall of complicated information is affected by social exclusion.

However, these results may have been caused by the reasoning required in the questions about the difficult passage. Socially excluded participants had no trouble recalling information about the easy passage, and those questions were straightforward. The questions on the difficult passage, however, required a higher level of thought and reasoning. Thus in the third experiment we assigned some participants to a simple recall task (remembering nonsense syllables they had learned), whereas other participants were given questions from a GRE analytical test that included difficult logic and reasoning problems. The results showed that social exclusion affected only performance on the analytical problems. Recall of nonsense syllables was not affected. Thus the cognitive impairment engendered by social exclusion focuses on higher-order reasoning, and not the simple recall of items.

Overall, these results suggest that social exclusion reduces intelligent thought but not information encoding or simple recall. Socially excluded participants answered fewer IQ test questions correctly, had more trouble recalling information about a difficult reading passage, and performed poorly in analytical reasoning. In contrast, socially excluded participants were able to encode information, recall information about an easy reading passage, and recall nonsense syllables effectively.

Individual Differences: Narcissism and Self-esteem

The previous studies have shown that social exclusion has strong and consistent effects on people, causing increased aggression, decreased prosocial behavior, more self-defeating behavior, and diminished cognitive performance. However, it seems plausible that there are individual differences in responses to exclusion. In particular, some people may be more aggressive than others after experiencing rejection by peers. We hypothesized that individuals high in narcissism might react to rejection with higher levels of anger and aggression (Twenge & Campbell, 2003). In a first study, we asked participants to recall a time when they had felt rejected, and to respond to a series of emotion words describing how they felt during this real-life experience. After controlling for passive negative emotions such as sadness, there was a significant correlation between trait narcissism and feelings of anger after rejection. Trait self-esteem was not correlated with anger. In the second study, we manipulated social rejection as we did in several studies mentioned above; participants met in the laboratory, chose people for further interaction, and then learned that either no one or everyone had chosen them. Narcissism was significantly correlated with feelings of anger after rejection, but not feelings of anger after acceptance.

We then moved on to examining behavioral aggression. We used the same noise-blasting game employed in the aggression studies presented earlier in the chapter: participants believe they are playing a computer game against another person, and they can choose the level and duration of noise they blast against their opponent. In this study, participants experienced a rejection by their peers and were then told they would play the game with someone from their group (thus someone who rejected them). Individuals high in narcissism were significantly more aggressive toward someone who had rejected them, compared to those low in narcissism. Self-esteem was unrelated to aggressive responding. These results are consistent with other findings indicating that high narcissism predisposes people toward aggression and hostility, whereas standard self-esteem measures show no effect (Bushman & Baumeister, 1998). Social exclusion apparently brings out the hostile tendencies of narcissists.

Would rejected narcissists also be aggressive toward a new person after experiencing a social rejection? In the last study, we found that narcissism was again correlated with aggression even when participants believed they were blasting noise against a new person—someone who had arrived late at the laboratory and thus not a member of the group who had issued the rejection. We also included a control group of accepted individuals in this study; there was no correlation between narcissism and aggression after participants were socially accepted.

These results provide an interesting application to the school shootings that have occurred across the United States in the past several years. Almost all of the school shooters experienced rejection and cruel teasing at the hands of their peers (Leary et al., 2003). In addition, the shooters at Columbine High School displayed narcissistic tendencies, stating that they could make people believe anything and debating which Hollywood director would film their story. Many pundits have suggested that boys who perpetrate school violence are low in self-esteem. Our results, however, suggest that self-esteem has no relation to aggressive behavior after social rejection. Instead, high narcissism (which could be mistaken for high self-esteem) is a significant predictor of whether someone will turn aggressive after experiencing a social rejection.

Emotion and Mood

Across all of our experiments, we rarely find any mood effects. Socially rejected people do not report more negative moods than those who have been accepted (the few differences we find are small and suggest that rejected people are in a neutral mood rather than a negative one). This has held true across a one-item mood measure, two standardized measures, a three-item measure used by Williams et al. (2000), and a long list of negative and positive mood words (Twenge et al., 2003). In addition, mood does not mediate any of the behavioral effects (even researchers who usually find mood effects after exclusion find that it does not mediate the effects on behavior: e.g., Buckley et al. in press).

We have begun to measure mood using more subtle and implicit measures. In two experiments, participants were seated in front of a computer that ostensibly flashed a word on the screen at subliminal speed. Across 18 trials, participants were asked to circle the word they thought they saw among four choices (one choice was an emotion word, and the others were neutral words). Rejected participants circled fewer emotion words than control and accepted participants (Twenge et al., 2003; Twenge & MacDonald, 2004). In another study, participants completed word stems that could form either negative mood words or neutral words (e.g., FE __ __ can be finished as either fear or feet). Excluded participants completed fewer stems with emotion words than control participants. This was especially striking because the effect was for negative emotion words: one would expect excluded participants to be in a more negative mood and thus think of negative emotion words, but the opposite was true (Twenge & MacDonald, 2004).

It seems plausible that rejected people are in denial about the negative experience of rejection. In one of the word flashing studies, participants also played the noise-blasting aggression game with a new partner. These results provided evidence for defensive denial among rejected participants: there was a positive correlation between aggression and positive emotion words circled, and a negative correlation between aggression and negative words circled (Twenge & MacDonald, 2004). Thus rejected participants who reported being in the best mood (more positive, less negative) were the most aggressive toward an innocent target. Rejected participants, who heard that no one chose them after a group interaction, were also asked how many people they believed actually chose them. There was a positive correlation between aggression and believed acceptance; rejected participants who maintained that more people actually chose them were more aggressive toward a new person. Thus rejected people who are in denial (who circle positive words, do not circle negative words, and believe more people chose them) subsequently lash out with aggression.

CONCLUSIONS

The results of these studies suggest that social exclusion has broad and powerful effects on behavior. Moreover, most of these effects appear to be undesirable. Our hypotheses about how being rejected or excluded might cause people to turn over a new leaf, seek new ways of making friends, become helpful or altruistic toward new potential partners, and even become more thoughtful were repeatedly contradicted.

Instead, the effects of social exclusion were uniformly, even disturbingly undesirable. We found that rejected people became more aggressive, not just toward people who had rejected them, but toward new people who had provoked them—and ominously, toward new "innocent bystanders" who had not done anything to them. Rejected people spared some people, however: those who had been friendly; those who they expected to interact with in the future; and those they believed came from another social group but were not too high- or low-status.

Further, socially excluded people showed broad declines in prosocial behavior. They were less generous toward needy fellow students, toward an experimenter who asked for a favor, and toward someone who simply needed a little help after a mishap. They were less cooperative toward a peer in a mixed-motive game. They were unhelpful regardless of whether helping would cost them money and effort, would cost them essentially nothing, or might even benefit them.

Just as social exclusion made people less desirable partners to others, it also made people less prone to take care of themselves. Social exclusion apparently causes self-defeating behavior. Rejected people took more foolish risks, made more unhealthy choices, and procrastinated more than people who had been accepted.

Intelligent thought is apparently another casualty of social exclusion. We found that socially excluded people performed more poorly on an intelligence test and on tests of complex reasoning. On simple, straightforward cognitive tasks they seemed to do as well as others. Thus, the higher cognitive functions appear to suffer in the wake of rejection.

Last, we found that people with inflated views of self and a strong motivation to garner the admiration of others—namely narcissists—exhibited the strongest negative reactions to social exclusion. These were particularly prone to exhibit aggression in the wake of being rejected. Such individuals are known to have hostile tendencies, and social rejection appears to bring these out.

Perhaps ironically, the only sphere in which we failed to find substantial negative effects in the wake of social exclusion is emotion. In fact, implicit measures show that excluded people avoid emotion. This may, in fact, be the cause for many of the behavioral effects we find: in defensively controlling their emotion, rejected people have fewer resources with which to control aggressive impulses, help others, focus on longer-term outcomes so as not to self-defeat, and think analytically.

In any case, these findings confirm the view of human beings as highly social creatures with a strong need to belong. Multiple forms of desirable, adaptive behavior appear to break down when individuals are excluded by social groups. To find a fully functioning human being, it may be generally necessary to look in the middle of a rich, supportive social network.

REFERENCES

Ainsworth, M. D. (1989). Attachments beyond infancy. *American Psychologist, 44*, 709–716.

Asher, S. R., & Coie, J. D. (1990). *Peer rejection in childhood*. New York: Cambridge University Press.

Asher, S. R., & Renshaw, P. D. (1981). Children without friends: Social knowledge and social skill training. In S. R. Asher & J. M. Gottman (Eds.), *The development of children's friendships* (pp. 273–296). New York: Cambridge University Press.

Axelrod, R., & Hamilton, W. D. (1981). The evolution of cooperation. *Science, 211*, 1390–1396.

Barash, D. P. (1977). *Sociobiology and behavior*. New York: Elsevier.

Baron, R. A., & Richardson, D. R. (1994). *Human Aggression* (2nd ed.). New York: Plenum.

Baumeister, R. F. (1990). Suicide as escape from self. *Psychological Review, 97*, 90–113.

Baumeister, R. F. (1997). Esteem threat, self-regulatory breakdown, and emotional distress as factors in self-defeating behavior. *Review of General Psychology, 1*, 145–174.

Baumeister, R. F., & Exline, J. J. (1999). Virtue, personality, and social relations: Self-control as the moral muscle. *Journal of Personality, 67*, 1165–1194.

Baumeister, R. F., & Leary, M. R. (1995). The need to belong: Desire for interpersonal attachments as a fundamental human motivation. *Psychological Bulletin, 117*, 497–529.

Baumeister, R. F., & Scher, S. J. (1988). Self-defeating behavior patterns among normal individuals: Review and analysis of common self-destructive tendencies. *Psychological Bulletin, 104*, 3–22.

Baumeister, R. F., & Tice, D. M. (1990). Anxiety and social exclusion. *Journal of Social and Clinical Psychology, 9*, 165–195.

Baumeister, R. F., Twenge, J. M., & Nuss, C. K. (2002). Effects of social exclusion on cognitive processes: Anticipated aloneness reduces intelligent thought. *Journal of Personality and Social Psychology, 83*, 817–827.

Bloom, B. L., White, S. W., & Asher, S. J. (1979). Marital disruption as a stressor: A review and analysis. *Psychological Bulletin, 85*, 867–894.

Bowlby, J. (1969). *Attachment and loss: Vol. 1. Attachment*. New York: Basic Books.

Buckley, K., Winkel, R., & Leary, M. (2004). Reactions to acceptance and rejection: Effects of level and sequence of relational evaluation. *Journal of Experimental Social Psychology, 40*, 14–28.

Bukowski, W. M., & Newcomb, A. F. (1984). Stability and determinants of sociometric status and friendship choice: A longitudinal perspective. *Developmental Psychology, 20*, 941–952.

Bushman, B. J., & Baumeister, R. F. (1998). Threatened egotism, narcissism, self-esteem, and direct and displaced aggression: Does self-love or self-hate lead to violence? *Journal of Personality and Social Psychology, 75*, 219–229.

Buss, D. M. (1990). The evolution of anxiety and social exclusion. *Journal of Social and Clinical Psychology, 9*, 196–210.

Buss, D. M. (1991). Evolutionary personality psychology. *Annual Review of Psychology, 42*, 459–491.

Cialdini, R. B., & Kendrick, D. T. (1976). Altruism as hedonism: A social development perspective on the relationship of negative mood state and helping. *Journal of Personality and Social Psychology, 34*, 907–914.

Cialdini, R. B., Kendrick, D. T., & Baumann, D. J. (1981). Effects of mood on prosocial behavior in children and adults. In N. Eisenberg-Berg (Ed.), *The development of prosocial behavior*. New York: Academic Press.

Coie, J. D. (1990). Toward a theory of peer rejection. In S. R. Asher & J. D. Coie (Eds.), *Peer rejection in childhood* (pp. 365–401). New York: Cambridge University Press.

Coie, J. D., & Dodge, K. A. (1988). Multiple sources of data on social behavior and social status in the school: A cross-age comparison. *Child Development, 59*, 815–829.

DeLongis, A., Folkman, S., & Lazarus, R. S. (1988). The impact of daily stress on health and mood: Psychological and social resources as mediators. *Journal of Personality and Social Psychology, 54*, 486–495.

Durkheim, E. (1951). *Suicide* (J. A. Spaulding & G. Simpson, Trans.). New York: Free Press. (Original work published 1897)

Freud, S. (1930). *Civilization and its discontents* (J. Riviere, Trans.). London: Hogarth Press.

Freud, S. (1965). *New introductory lectures on psychoanalysis* (J. Strachey, Trans.). New York: Norton. (Original work published 1933)

Fukuyama, F. (1999). *The great disruption: Human nature and the reconstitution of social order*. New York: Free Press.

Garbarino, J. (1999). *Lost boys: Why our sons turn violent and how we can save them*. San Francisco: Jossey-Bass.

Gardner, W. L., Gabriel, S., & Diekman, A. (2000). The psychophysiology of interpersonal processes. In J. T. Cacioppo, L. G. Tassinary, & G. G. Bertson (Eds.), *The Handbook of Psychophysiology* (2nd ed., pp. 643–664). Cambridge, MA: Cambridge University Press.

Gardner, W. L., Pickett, C. L., & Brewer, M. B. (2000). Social exclusion and selective memory: How the need to belong influences memory for social events. *Personality and Social Psychology Bulletin, 26*, 486–496.

Gest, S. D., Graham-Bermann, S. A., & Hartup, W. W. (2001). Peer experience: Common and unique features of number of friendships, social network centrality, and sociometric status. *Social Development, 10*, 23–40.

Goodwin, J. S., Hunt, W. C., Key, C. R., & Samet, J. M. (1987). The effect of marital status on stage, treatment, and survival of cancer patients. *Journal of the American Medical Association, 258*, 3125–3130.

Gottlieb, J., & Carver, C. (1980). Anticipation of future interaction and the bystander effect. *Journal of Experimental Social Psychology, 16*, 253–260.

Harano, R. M., Peck, R. L., & McBride, R. S. (1975). The prediction of accident liability through biographical data and psychometric tests. *Journal of Safety Research, 7*, 16–52.

Harrington, D. M., & McBride, R. S. (1970). Traffic violations by type, age, sex, and marital status. *Accident Analysis and Prevention, 2*, 67–79.

Hartup, W. W., Glazer, J. A., & Charlesworth, R. (1967). Peer reinforcement and sociometric status. *Child Development, 38*, 1017–1024.

Hedge, A., & Yousif, Y. H. (1992). Effects of urban size, urgency, and cost on helpfulness: A cross-cultural comparison between the United Kingdom and the Sudan. *Journal of Cross-Cultural Psychology, 23*, 107–115.

Hogan, R. (1973). Moral conduct and moral character: A psychological perspective. *Psychological Bulletin, 79*, 217–232.

Hogan, R., Jones, W. H., & Cheek, J. M. (1985). Socioanalytic theory: An alternative to armadillo psychology. In B. R. Schlenker (Ed.), *The self and social life* (pp. 175–198). Newberry Park, CA: Sage.

Janda, L. (1996). *The psychologists' book of self-tests.* New York: Berkley.

Janda, L. H., Fulk, J., Janda, M., & Wallace, J. (1995). The development of a test of General Mental Abilities. Unpublished manuscript, Old Dominion University.

Kirkpatrick, L. A., Waugh, C. E., Valencia, A., & Webster, G. D. (2002). The functional domain specificity of self-esteem and the differential prediction of aggression. *Journal of Personality and Social Psychology, 82*, 756–767.

Kulik, J. A., & Brown, R. (1979). Frustration, attribution of blame, and aggression. *Journal of Experimental Social Psychology, 15*, 183–194.

Leary, M. R. (1990). Responses to social exclusion: Social anxiety, jealousy, loneliness, depression, and low self-esteem. *Journal of Social and Clinical Psychology, 9*, 221–229.

Leary, M. R., & Baumeister, R. F. (2000). The nature and function of self-esteem: Sociometer theory. In M. Zanna (Ed.), *Advances in experimental social psychology* (Vol. 32, pp. 1–62). San Diego, CA: Academic Press.

Leary, M. R., & Downs, D. L. (1995). Interpersonal functions of the self-esteem motive: The self-esteem system as a sociometer. In Kernis, M. (Ed.), *Efficacy, agency, and self-esteem* (pp. 123–144). New York: Plenum.

Leary, M. R., Kowalski, R. M., Smith, L., & Phillips, S. (2003). Teasing, rejection, and violence: Case studies of the school shootings. *Aggressive Behavior, 29*, 202–214.

Leary, M. R., Tambor, E. S., Terdal, S. K., & Downs, D. L. (1995). Self-esteem as an interpersonal monitor: The sociometer hypothesis. *Journal of Personality and Social Psychology, 68*, 518–530.

Leith, K. P., & Baumeister, R. F. (1996). Why do bad moods increase self-defeating behavior? Emotion, risk taking, and self-regulation. *Journal of Personality and Social Psychology, 71*, 1250–1267.

Lynch, J. J. (1979). *The broken heart: The medical consequences of loneliness.* New York: Basic Books.

Menninger, K. (1966). *Man against himself.* New York: Harcourt, Brace & World. (Original work published 1938)

Mize, J., & Ladd, G. W. (1988). Predicting preschoolers' peer behavior and status from their interpersonal strategies: A comparison of verbal and enactive responses to hypothetical social dilemmas. *Developmental Psychology, 24*, 782–788.

Moreland, R. L. (1987). The formation of small groups. In C. Hendrick (Ed.), *Group processes: Review of personality and social psychology* (Vol. 8, pp. 80–110). Newberry Park, CA: Sage.

Newcomb, A. F., Bukowski, W. M., & Pattee, L. (1993). Children's peer relations: A meta-analytic review of popular, rejected, neglected, controversial, and average sociometric status. *Psychological Bulletin, 113*, 99–128.

Ohbuchi, K., Kameda, M., & Agarie, N. (1989). Apology as aggression control: Its role in mediating appraisal of and response to harm. *Journal of Personality and Social Psychology, 56*, 219–227.

O'Neal, E. C., & Taylor, S. L. (1989). Status of the provoker, opportunity to retaliate, and interest in video violence. *Aggressive Behavior, 15*, 171–180.

Parkhurst, J. T., & Asher, S. R. (1992). Peer rejection in middle school: Subgroup differences in behavior, loneliness, and interpersonal concerns. *Developmental Psychology, 28*, 231–241.

Pennebaker, J. W. (1989). Stream of consciousness and stress: Levels of thinking. In J. S. Uleman, & J. A. Bargh (Eds.), *Unintended thought*. New York: The Guilford Press.

Pennebaker, J. W., Czajka, J. A., Cropanzano, R., & Richards, B. C. (1990). Levels of thinking. *Personality and Social Psychology Bulletin, 16*, 743–757.

Perry, L. C., Perry, D. G., & Weiss, R. J. (1986). Age differences in children's beliefs about whether altruism makes the actor feel good. *Social Cognition, 4*, 263–269.

Piers, G., & Singer, M. (1971). *Shame and guilt: A psychoanalytic and cultural study*. New York: Norton. (Original work published 1953)

Putnam, R. D. (2000). *Bowling alone: The collapse and revival of American community*. New York: Simon & Schuster.

Richman, A. (1985). Human risk factors in alcohol-related crashes. *Journal of Studies on Alcohol, 10*, 21–31.

Sampson, R. J., & Laub, J. H. (1993). *Crime in the making: Pathways and turning points through life*. Cambridge, MA: Harvard University Press.

Schonert-Reichl, K. A. (1999). Relations of peer acceptance, friendship adjustment, and social behavior to moral reasoning during early adolescence. *Journal of Early Adolescence, 19*, 249–279.

Trout, D. L. (1980). The role of social isolation in suicide. *Suicide and Life-Threatening Behavior, 10*, 10–23.

Twenge, J. M., Baumeister, R. F., Tice, D. M., & Stucke, T. S. (2001). If you can't join them, beat them: Effects of social exclusion on aggressive behavior. *Journal of Personality and Social Psychology, 81*, 1058–1069.

Twenge, J. M., & Cacho, J. (2003). When does social rejection lead to aggression? Exploring situational and target effects. *Personality and Social Psychology Bulletin* (Unpublished manuscript).

Twenge, J. M., & Campbell, W. K. (2003). "Isn't it fun to get the respect that we're going to deserve?" Narcissism, social rejection, and aggression. *Personality and Social Psychology Bulletin, 29*, 261–272.

Twenge, J. M., Catanese, K. R., & Baumeister, R. F. (2002). Social exclusion causes self-defeating behavior. *Journal of Personality and Social Psychology, 83*, 606–615.

Twenge, J. M., Catanese, K. R., & Baumeister, R. F. (2003). Social exclusion and the deconstructed state: Time perception, meaninglessness, lethargy, lack of emotion, and self-awareness. *Journal of Personality and Social Psychology, 85*, 409–423.

Twenge, J. M., Ciarocco, N. J., Cuervo, D., Bartels, J. M., & Baumeister, R. F. (2004). Social exclusion reduces prosocial behavior. *Journal of Personality and Social Psychology* (Unpublished manuscript).

Twenge, J. M., & MacDonald, D. (2004). Evidence for defensive denial after social rejection. Manuscript in preparation.

Walsh, A., Beyer, J. A., & Petee, T. A. (1987). Violent delinquency: An examination of psychopathic typologies. *Journal of Genetic Psychology, 148*, 385–392.

Warburton, W., Williams, K. D., & Cairns, D. (2003, April). *Effects of Ostracism and Loss of Control on Aggression*. Paper presented at the 32nd Annual Meeting of the Society of Australasian Social Psychology, Bondi Beach, Australia.

Wentzel, K. R., & Erdley, C. A. (1993). Strategies for making friends: Relations to social behavior and peer acceptance in early adolescence. *Developmental Psychology, 29*, 819–826.

Wentzel, K. R., & McNamara, C. C. (1999). Interpersonal relationships, emotional distress, and prosocial behavior in middle school. *Journal of Early Adolescence, 19*, 114–125.

Williams, D. R., Takeuchi, D. T., & Adair, R. K. (1992). Martial status and psychiatric disorders among blacks and whites. *Journal of Health and Social Behavior, 33*, 140–157.

Williams, K. D., Cheung, C. K. T., & Choi, W. (2000). CyberOstracism: Effects of being ignored over the Internet. *Journal of Personality and Social Psychology, 79*, 748–762.

Williams, K. D., & Sommer, K. L. (1997). Social ostracism by one's coworkers: Does rejection lead to loafing or compensation? *Personality and Social Psychology Bulletin, 23*, 693–706.

Wyer, R. S., & Srull, T. K. (1986). Human cognition in its social context. *Psychological Review, 93*, 322–359.

3

Reacting to Ostracism: Retaliation or Reconciliation?

KIPLING D. WILLIAMS and CASSANDRA L. GOVAN

Considerable attention has recently been given to reactions to ostracism (Williams, 1997; Williams & Zadro, 2001), rejection (Nezlek, Kowalski, Leary, Blevins, & Holgate, 1999), and exclusion (Baumeister & Tice, 1990). Without exception, the consequences of exclusion on the targeted individual are negative. These reactions include negative moods, hurt feelings, feelings of isolation, loss of belonging, self-esteem, and meaningful existence. What has differed, however, has been the behavioral reactions to the exclusion. Several studies show evidence of behavioral supplication, and several studies show evidence of what appears to be the direct opposite pattern of behavioral reactions to exclusion. Clearly, we have an interesting conundrum: does being excluded by others cause people to try to regain their inclusionary status or does it cause antisocial behavior? In this chapter, we examine the current literature and derive hypotheses that suggest which of these behavioral reactions will occur. Three recent studies will be summarized that support these predictions.

INTRODUCTION AND OVERVIEW

After nearly a century of neglect, social psychologists have recently devoted considerable attention to ostracism (Williams, 1997, 2001; Williams & Zadro, 2001), rejection (Leary, 2001; Nezlek et al., 1997), and social exclusion (Baumeister & Tice, 1990). Although each of these phenomena may have distinctive features, all involve the implied exclusion of an individual by another individual or group. Uniformly, the self-reported reactions by targets of exclusion are negative. These often include negative mood, hurt feelings, feelings of isolation, loss of belonging, control, self-esteem, and meaningful existence. What appear to be wildly divergent however, are the behavioral reactions to the exclusion.

Whereas some studies show evidence of ingratiation and desires for inclusion, other studies demonstrate antisocial reactions and desires for retaliation. In one study, ostracized individuals worked harder on a group task (Williams & Sommer, 1997) and in another, they were more likely to conform to a new group's incorrect perceptual judgments (Williams, Cheung, & Choi, 2000). Alternatively, socially excluded individuals were more likely to retaliate, and show anger (Twenge, Baumeister, Tice, & Stucke, 2001), leading some to speculate that the rejection felt by those few students at Columbine High School may have led to their subsequent violence (Leary, Kowalski, Smith, & Phillips, 2003; Williams, 2001).

Social ostracism is a strong force and leads to negative self-reported feelings and meaningful behavioral consequences. But why do individuals sometimes react in ways that will likely improve their inclusionary status, whereas in other instances, in ways that almost assure future exclusion and rejection? This is the focus of the present chapter. One question that often arises when one is presented with these opposing results is: which findings are correct? Do socially excluded people react prosocially or antisocially? We think this line of inquiry is unproductive and quite possibly obfuscates an intriguing, yet complex, phenomenon. The better question, we argue, is: under what conditions does ostracism lead to behaviors that will reinstate the individual in the group (or another group), and under what conditions will social exclusion lead to behaviors that are antisocial?

First, we will examine in detail the studies that have found prosocial, or inclusionary, reactions. Then we will do the same for those studies showing antisocial, or retaliatory, reactions. We will then discuss two possible explanations for these apparently contradictory reactions, and will finally present three studies that will test these explanations. We will conclude with a conceptualization of the ostracized individual who is torn between two powerful, primal forces.

The Power of Silence

Over a hundred years ago, William James's observation on social exclusion and being ignored foreshadowed the competing forces acting on individuals that could lead to either response:

A man's social self is the recognition which he gets from his mates. We are not only gregarious animals, liking to be in sight of our fellows, but we have an innate propensity to get ourselves noticed, *and noticed favorably*, by our kind. No more fiendish punishment could be devised, were such a thing physically possible, than that one should be turned loose in society and remain absolutely unnoticed by all the members thereof. If no one turned around when we entered, answered when we spoke, or minded what we did, but if every person we met 'cut us dead,' and acted as if we were non-existing things, *a kind of rage and impotent despair* would ere long well up in us, from which the cruelest bodily tortures would be a relief; for these would make us feel that however bad might be our plight, we had not sunk to such a depth as to be unworthy of attention at all. (James, 1890, pp 293–294, emphasis added)

James predicted a need to be *noticed favorably*, which is consistent with reacting to ostracism in ways that makes one more appealing to others. He also predicted feelings of *rage* that would surface if one felt nonexistent and cut dead by others. Are these alternative responses contradictory, or can they coexist within the same individual?

STUDIES FINDING PROSOCIAL REACTIONS TO OSTRACISM

Several studies have shown support for the idea that individuals who are ostracized, excluded, or rejected behave in ways that will increase their inclusionary status. These behaviors range from working harder in group settings, to conforming to group perceptions, to being more sensitive to information about others. These sorts of reactions make intuitive sense: if individuals have been rejected, they want to be reincluded. In order to be reincluded (by the rejecting person/group or a new person/group), they make themselves appear more attractive by acting in prosocial or conciliatory ways. Indeed, it makes theoretical sense as well: Baumeister and Leary (1995) state "The general argument is that deprivation of belongingness should lead to a variety of affiliative behaviors . . ." (p. 508).

For example, Snoek (1962) manipulated whether or not confederates rejected participants (by not talking to them) for personal or impersonal reasons. When rejected for personal reasons—they were deemed unworthy of membership—Snoek found that participants desired social reassurance and chose to continue their membership in the group.

Predmore and Williams (1983) used a ball-tossing task to ostracize or include male students. Afterwards, the students were expecting to take part in a task that required good hand-eye co-ordination, but were told they could work alone, with the same group (who had ostracized or included them) or with a new group. Ostracized individuals were more likely to request working with another group than to work with the same group or to work alone. Included participants were most likely to want to work with the same group. These results suggest a desire to be with others, perhaps with the hope of being included and accepted by new people. A truly antisocial response would have been to request working alone.

Williams and Sommer (1997) used a ball-tossing paradigm and found that compared to included females, ostracized females worked harder for their group on a subsequent collective task (i.e., the individual contributions were combined to form a group total) than on a coactive task (i.e., the individual contributions were not combined). The authors interpreted the extra effort exerted by the ostracized females in the collective task as a tactic to increase their inclusionary status, as if the ostracized individual was thinking, "If I work hard for the group, they might appreciate me." In this study, the apparent ingratiating behavior was directed toward the sources of the ostracism. However, there is also evidence to suggest that ostracized individuals will act in an ingratiating way towards a new neutral group (i.e., a group that had nothing to do with the ostracism).

Gardner, Pickett, and Brewer (2000) found that after participants took part in a 3-way conversation, participants who were excluded from the conversation (compared to those who were included) were more likely to remember information presented that pertained to people, rather than other categories. We agree with the authors' interpretation that, like hunger, when people are deprived of the social need of belonging, they will engage in cognitive activity that helps them satisfy their need. By remembering and paying close attention to information about people, individuals would more likely be successful in future social interactions.

Zadro and Williams (1998) used the train ride paradigm (Williams & Zadro, 2001) in which three participants engaged in a role-play activity based upon a brief script that they read prior to embarking on the 5-minute trip. All participants were informed that one of the three individuals on the train row told on the other two classmates for talking during a lecture. The two classmates were told to initially argue with the tattle-tail, then to ignore and exclude him or her for the rest of the trip. As usual, targets of ostracism reported lower levels of belonging, self-esteem, control, and meaningful existence, whereas the ostracizers reported feeling a stronger bond with their co-ostracizer and feelings of power and control. Of interest to this chapter, however, was the finding that compared to the other participants, ostracized individuals who held an unpopular stance on the issue of the Monarchy in Australia were more likely to overestimate how likely other students held the same opinions. The authors interpreted this finding as evidence that when one's feelings of belonging and meaningful existence are threatened, individuals will engage in any means available to be similar to others. By believing in their similarity, they are not retaliating or being hostile, but rather, they are trying to fit in.

Williams et al. (2000) created an Internet game called Cyberball in which participants were either included or ostracized in a game of virtual ball toss. The participant played the game with two other players, who were supposedly simultaneously logged on to the game web site, but in fact were preprogrammed icons that either included or ostracized the participant in the game. In Study 1, they found that the more the individual was ostracized (which varied from overinclusion to inclusion to partial ostracism to complete ostracism), the more they reported the game to be aversive and unpleasant. Indeed, they reported lower levels of belonging and self-esteem that was shown to mediate their unpleasant feelings. In Study 2, following the game of Cyberball, participants were reassigned to a new group of five other individuals and were given a perception task where they were to make judgments. The participant was always the last person in the group of six people to make their judgments (of course, the other five people were not real, but preprogrammed responses from the computer). Ostracized participants were more likely to conform to the unanimous (incorrect) judgments of the others in their group than were included participants. Thus, it appears that ostracized participants bolstered their inclusionary status with this new group to avoid future rejection.

Finally, taking a functional or socio-evolutionary perspective, it is clear from anthropological, sociological, and the animal literatures that ostracism is ubiquitous across time, cultures, and even species (Gruter & Masters, 1986; Williams, 2001). Ostracism is used as a form of discipline and for correcting the unwanted behavior of individuals or small groups. In many instances, the result of ostracism (sometimes called time-out, excommunication, silencing, sending someone off to Coventry) is that the ostracized individual corrects his or her behavior so as to be acceptable to the group in order that they can be reincluded. If ostracism was not generally effective in bringing the undesirable behavior of individuals back to acceptability, then it seems unlikely that ostracism would be practiced universally.

STUDIES FINDING ANTISOCIAL REACTIONS TO OSTRACISM

The first author recently visited a prison in which the wife of a famous football player was talking with female inmates about her highly publicized spouse-abuse case. When her husband returned home from a road-trip, he confronted her about the large credit card bill. She started yelling at him about how she hated him being away for so long, and he responded by saying that he would not talk to her if she was going to carry on in such an abusive manner. After several minutes of silence, the wife started hurling insults at her husband to get a response, but the husband acted as though he had not heard her. Finally, enraged, she threw a marble ashtray at his head, taking a chunk out of his skull, which then led to the much-publicized physical fight. Clearly, in this case, the wife reacted aggressively to the source of the ostracism.

A variety of studies suggest a link between ostracism, ignoring, and/or rejection and antisocial responses. For example, Gottman's (1979, 1980) research with married couples suggests that silence can trigger violence. Geller, Goodstein, Silver, and Sternberg (1974) found that ignored females were less likely to reward the ignoring confederates. Craighead, Kimball, and Rehak

(1979) found that individuals who imagined being ignored indicated that they would be more likely to feel frustration and anger, passivity and disengagement.

Thompson and Richardson (1983) used a paradigm in which a dyad would reject an individual. They found that rejected individuals retaliated against the rejectors, especially against dyads composed of a male who initiated the rejection and a female who followed suit. Several studies found that ignored or rejected individuals were less likely to want to work with the rejecting group, although in most cases this preference was qualified by either individual differences (i.e., those low in self-esteem, Dittes, 1959; those high in public self-consciousness, Fenigstein, 1979) or situational factors (i.e., those who were ignored for impersonal reasons, Snoek, 1962). Insko and Wilson (1977) instructed groups of three participants to engage in a series of two-person conversations, that is, during each of these conversations, the third member of the group was left out. The experimenter imposed an ostensible time constraint, such that one member conversed once with the other two, but the other two had not conversed with each other. Even though the exclusion was clearly not the "fault" of the participants, participants rated the group member they had not conversed with as less likeable and less interpersonally attractive on a variety of dimensions.

In research pertinent to organizations, Faulkner (1998) found that individuals who were ostracized for whistle blowing were more likely to retaliate against the ostracizers, and Cheung (1999) found that customers who did not receive a reply from the company to their email enquiries were less likely to patronize the company. All of these studies involved self-reported or behavioral responses that were not prosocial, but were also not necessarily aggressive.

More recently, in a series of clever laboratory studies, Twenge et al. (2001) found that participants who were given "forecasts" of a life without meaningful friendships were more likely to be aggressive. Participants completed a personality test and were given bogus feedback. Some were told that their personality profile suggested that their future would be full of meaningful relationships (Future Belonging). Others were told that their profile suggested that they would be accident-prone (Misfortune). The Misfortune group's forecast served as a control group for an unpleasant, but nonexclusionary future. A final group were told that they would be alone, that their life would lack any meaningful relationships after they were past their mid-twenties (Future Alone).

In this series of five studies, Twenge et al. found consistent support for the antisocial responses to exclusion. This response was even found towards a neutral participant—someone who had not excluded or insulted the participant. Whether the exclusion was due to a forecast of a lonely life, or being told that no one wanted to work with them, excluded participants seemed to respond in antisocial, possibly aggressive ways. Apart from being antisocial, such responses would also be unlikely to be attractive to other individuals or groups. Thus, these responses would appear to be inconsistent with Baumeister and Leary's (1995) premise that sensing rejection and exclusion will direct individuals to behave in ways that improves their inclusionary status. (For a more detailed description of the studies, see Twenge & Baumeister, this volume).

In a series of Internet studies, Williams et al. (2002) also found some support for an antisocial response to ostracism. In one study (Study 2) participants were either included or ostracized in a chat-room discussion about thoughts and experiences of their first year at university. Confederates played the parts of the two other members of the chat room. All participants were included for the first 4 minutes of the conversation. Following this introductory period participants were either ignored for the remaining 5 minutes of conversation (ostracism condition), or they continued to be included (inclusion condition). The postexperimental questionnaire included evaluative ratings of the two other participants in the chat room and a rating of how much the participant would like to be friends with the other two participants. Ostracized participants rated the confederates less positively than included participants, and also reported less desire to be friends with them.

In Study 3, again, participants were either included or ostracized in a chat-room discussion, but they were also either agreed with or disagreed with, regarding their opinion of the Sydney Olympics. In this study, the introductory period (where all participants were included) lasted for 2 min, and inclusion/ostracism period of the chat-room lasted for 10 minutes. Regardless of whether participants were agreed with or not, ostracized participants reported that they liked the two confederates less than included participants.

What was interesting about both Studies 2 and 3 was that some ostracized participants were showing evidence of what we termed "virtual bravado." That is, they were confronting the other two participants in the chat-room and demanding an explanation, or were behaving provocatively by intruding in the two-way conversation with a monologue. This kind of reaction has never happened in the face-to-face conversation paradigm. Face-to-face ostracized participants typically withdraw without seeking clarification, without trying to interrupt, and without getting visibly angry. However, we noticed our chat-room ostracized participants seeking clarification (e.g., "Hey, are you there?" "Why aren't you answering my questions?" "Are you ignoring me?"), leaning forward toward their screen, interrupting (e.g., "so, as I was saying"), or getting angry (e.g., "Jeez, you guys are rude!"), or even starting a conversation with themselves. Take this participant's response as an example:

u 2 can keep talking btw yourselves and ignore me I don't mind!!! . . . maybe I should start a conversation with myself . . . hi, how are yah . . . I'm fine how are you . . . I'm fine too . . . come on talk to me! I feel like a nigel . . . oh okay now you gonna answer her I bet . . . I asked that question only 2000 years ago.

Clearly, the passive despondency observed in the face-to-face ostracism sessions does not generalize to chat rooms. Perhaps hostile responses are more likely to occur in chat rooms because individuals feel more anonymous, or because they do not have to endure the painful nonverbal signs of rejection that they are forced to observe when face-to-face.

There has been speculation that the perpetrators of 15 school shootings in American high schools were victims of ostracism, rejection, and malicious teasing in their schools (Leary et al., 2003; Williams, 2001), and the perpetrator of the recent school shooting in Germany, although not an outcast, was upset about being expelled from his school (Andrews, 2002; Biehl, 2002; Lemonick, 2002). Their reaction to this treatment was obviously extremely antisocial and aggressive, but whether their behavior was due to, or partially instigated by ostracism, is difficult to determine. After all, it is not surprising that after shooting one's peers one attempts to provide a plausible explanation and justification. Also, there are probably thousands of students who are bullied and ostracized; yet violent outbreaks are thankfully rare. Additionally, other, perhaps more potent factors may contribute to such extreme violence, including feelings of depersonalization and deindividuation that might increase adherence to violent role models or in-group members (see Reicher, Spears, & Postmes, 1995).

EXPLANATIONS FOR THE DIVERGENT FINDINGS

Studies that show evidence of conciliatory, prosocial, or ingratiating responses following ostracism are based primarily on the tenet that individuals will attempt to behave in affiliative ways if they fear their inclusionary status is threatened. Studies that find aggression following ostracism, exclusion, or rejection either lack any explanation for the effect (Twenge et al., 2001) or point to frustration, anger, hurt feelings, and other forms of negative affect that might lead individuals to lash out, either in retaliation, or in the form of displaced aggression toward neutral others (Leary et al., 2003).

We suggest two plausible explanations for the apparent contradictions. One, guided by the framework of Williams's model of ostracism, suggests that two sets of needs that are threatened by ostracism can result in oppositional reactions. The second is that individuals' primal, automatic responses are retaliatory, but their strategic and controlled reactions are to be seen as good and attractive, so that they can be reincluded.

Competing Needs Explanation

Williams's (1997, 2001) model of ostracism may help us understand the opposing reactions to ostracism. The core of this model is that ostracism is suggested to uniquely threaten four fundamental human needs: belonging, self-esteem, control, and meaningful existence. After experiencing an incident of ostracism, the target will react in ways to regain the lost needs.

Apart from being intuitively appealing, reacting in an ingratiating way to ostracism is also consistent with Williams's model of ostracism (1997, 2001). These effects were predicted by Williams's model, which was partially based on reasoning put forth by Baumeister and Leary (1995). Most pertinent to the ingratiating response are the needs of belonging and self-esteem. After an ostracism incident, the individual may act in ingratiating ways to (a) regain inclusion by the source of the rejection, or (b) prevent ostracism from another individual or group. These behaviors should bolster the individual's feelings of belongingness and self-esteem.

The ingratiating response is consistent with Baumeister and Leary's predictions regarding social exclusion and the need to belong. Baumeister and Leary (1995) suggest that the need to belong is a fundamental motivation, and that to keep this need satisfied, individuals avoid rejection. One could avoid rejection by steering clear of situations in which rejection is likely, or, by repairing one's behavior in order to get reaccepted by the excluding group, or to be accepted by new groups. Threats to self-esteem ought to follow the same course. According to Leary, Tambor, Terdal, and Downs (1995), self-esteem is nothing more than a "sociometer" that provides feedback to the individual about his or her inclusionary status. Thus, self-esteem, like belonging, should direct the individual to behave in a prosocial manner to increase the chances of reinclusion.

There are, according to Williams's model, two other needs that ostracism threatens: control and meaningful existence. When ignored and excluded, individuals are unable to control the social situation. No matter what is said or done, the sources of ostracism appear to be unaffected. Ostracism also communicates to individuals a lack of recognition of their existence. Indeed, it is a poignant metaphor for one's nonexistence or death. Unlike the needs of self-esteem and belongingness, regaining the needs of control and recognition might *not* direct ostracized individuals to behave in an ingratiating manner. Instead, they may be more motivated to provoke reactions in order to validate their existence and to exert control over others.

At present, most studies in our laboratory have found that ostracism reduces participants' self-reported levels of all four needs (belonging, control, self-esteem, and meaningful existence), thus it is difficult to tease apart the possibility that the belonging/self-esteem needs are competing with the control/meaningful existence needs. Future research should try to determine methods by which the two sets of needs are differentially affected by ostracism, to see if they lead to either pro- or anti-social responses. We now turn our attention to another possible explanation, and present three studies that shed some light on its viability.

Implicit/Explicit Reactions Explanation

In a recent article by Wilson, Lindsey, and Schooler (2000), the authors propose a model of dual attitudes. The authors suggest that it is possible to have disparate implicit and explicit attitudes towards the same attitude object. The authors further suggest that the implicit attitude is the default, whereas the explicit attitude only overrides the implicit attitude if the individual has the cognitive capacity available to do so. Similarly, we suggest that individuals have dual responses to events. That is, individuals may represent their responses one way when measured explicitly, but another way when measured implicitly. Thus, after an ostracism incident, individuals may have implicit responses to retaliate, but explicit responses to ingratiate.

Think of it this way: Ostracized individuals are angry that they have been ignored. If there were no consequences, they would love to vent their anger. But, they realize that an angry response would leave them in a position where further exclusion would be almost guaranteed—after all, who wants to associate with someone who is angry or violent? So, the ostracized individual acts in a way that will hopefully get them reincluded in the group that ignored them (or a new group). Wilson et al. (2000) describe research that suggests that the implicit attitude comes to the surface when (a) participants are responding under time pressure, (b) participants are cognitively busy when responding, or (c) the measure is an implicit measure (e.g., Implicit Association Test [IAT], Thematic Apperception Test [TAT], etc.). Perhaps, then, studies that show prosocial reactions (e.g., working harder: Williams & Sommer, 1997; conformity: Williams et al., 2000) are examining behaviors or self-reports under conditions that promote explicit reactions, whereas those that find antisocial responses (e.g., Twenge et al., 2001 studies; Virtual Bravado: Williams et al., 2002) are examining behaviors that are perceived to be less diagnostic of one's motives, and are therefore, implicit. We present three experiments that begin to shed some light on this possibility.

Three Experiments

Experiment 1: Attraction to Group Leaders
In her honors thesis, Amy Wheaton manipulated ostracism and inclusion through the use of the ball-toss paradigm, and then had participants rate their attraction and interest in a videotaped presentation by a leader of an ostensible campus organization. Individuals were randomly assigned to watch one of two videotaped presentations in which the reputability of the attire of the spokesperson for the group, and the reputability of the group that he represented were co-manipulated.

In the socially reputable group condition, the actor wore smart casual clothes and described the group's main purpose as helping students to grow and reach their full potential by giving members the skills that could help them empower and improve both their personal and future business life. He went on to describe group discussions and group activities, which focused on improving studying habits and helping members to choose the best career path. In the socially deviant group condition, the actor wore a tie-dyed gown, beads, and an African hat woven out of bright multicolored thread. The aim was to make him up to appear like a stereotypical new-age guru, or cult leader. In this condition, the purpose of the group was described as to help students to move into a higher state of consciousness and cosmic awareness, by giving members the skills needed to access their psychic powers and engage in out of body experiences. He went on to describe discussions and group activities, which focused on learning how to harness members' energies in order to experience such things as soul travel, time travel, levitation, and psycho kinesis.

The results of this experiment demonstrated that regardless of how reputable the group's leader and group was, ostracized individuals were more attracted to the leader than included individuals. We interpret this result as another indication that ostracized individuals have an increased desire to be included, so much so that other groups, no matter how strange, seem attractive and desirable to them.

So, rather than feeling negative, disparaged, and resentful of other groups, this research indicates that ostracized individuals may be more tolerant and open to (even susceptible or vulnerable to) overtures by new groups. Because the measures taken were self-reports that would be viewed by the experimenter, perhaps participants, were engaging in impression management. If, however, participants feelings or inclinations were assessed in such a way that allowed for enough attributional ambiguity so that antisocial responses could be successfully disguised, we may have shown opposite results.

Experiment 2: Train ride We (Williams, Case, Govan, & Zadro, 2002) recently conducted a large role-playing experiment that tested further the possible inclinations ostracized individuals had toward either prosocial or antisocial behavior. In this study, we examined the impact of being the sole target of ostracism compared with having a cotarget. Participants were instructed to act as if they were sitting in a train carriage. We manipulated whether participants were sitting in groups of three or in groups of four. In the 3-person groups, two participants were instructed to ignore the other participant. In the 4-person groups, two participants were instructed to ignore the other two participants. We found that although targets felt lower on all four needs than sources, targets in 3-person groups felt lower on all four needs than targets in 4-person groups. Thus, having a cotarget buffered all of the deleterious effects of being ignored. More interestingly, although targets felt more anger than sources overall, targets in 3-person groups felt more anger than targets in 4-person groups. So, not only did having a cotarget seem to prevent threats to the needs, it also made targets less angry about the ostracism. A caveat for these results is in order: all results were based on self-reports. It may well be that ostracized groups, if given the chance, would be more inclined and able to retaliate than ostracized individuals (see e.g., research on the discontinuity effect by Insko and his colleagues, 1987, 1998).

Experiment 3: Ostracism and prejudice: Explicit and implicit

To examine the possibility of disparate implicit and explicit responses to ostracism, we (Williams, Case, & Govan, 2002) examined included and ostracized participants' implicit and explicit attitudes towards Aboriginal and White Australians. Participants were either included or ostracized from a game of Cyberball. Following the game, participants completed an Implicit Association Test (IAT; Greenwald, McGhee, & Schwartz, 1998) that examined their implicit attitudes towards Aboriginal and White Australians, and modern and old fashioned forms of Aboriginal prejudice (Pedersen & Walker, 1997). Thus, indications of prejudice were assessed from a very implicit measure to a very explicit measure. Additional measures of needs and mood were also taken. Compared to included participants, ostracised individuals were equally prosocial in their responses to the explicit measures (old fashioned and modern prejudice), yet there was a significant difference in the IAT results, suggesting that ostracised participants were showing more implicit prejudice towards Aboriginals than included participants.

These results provide evidence consistent with the *dual responses* explanation suggested earlier. At an explicit level, ostracized participants want to appear inclusive, tolerant, and socially acceptable, thus they portray themselves as egalitarian and nonprejudiced. However, at the implicit level, they are hurt and angry and will vent their anger on the most accessible targets; in this case, Aboriginals. Therefore, both prosocial and antisocial responses reside within the same person. Which set of responses emerge depends on the method of assessment: implicit measures elicit implicit responses; explicit measures elicit explicit responses.

CONCLUSIONS

Ostracism, rejection, exclusion—no matter what label we give it, is extremely unpleasant to receive. There seems to be little contention in the literature that ostracized individuals feel sad *and* angry, and that they report lower levels of belonging, self-esteem, control, and meaningful existence. The debate that has arisen in the literature concerns how a target of ostracism responds. They can become ingratiating, apparently to increase their inclusionary status, or they can become aggressive, which would seem to ensure their future exclusion.

We reviewed this literature and offered a few plausible explanations for this apparent conundrum. One possibility is that the need for belonging and self-esteem may pull toward inclusionary reactions and the need for control and meaningful existence may pull toward antisocial reactions. Which ever set of needs is most threatened will dictate the direction of response. Another possibility is that both reactions are triggered in the individual: anger and retaliation at an implicit level, and hopes for reinclusion at the explicit level. Depending upon whether the response is likely to be noted and evaluated by others (an explicit response) or disguised and attributionally ambiguous (an implicit response), one response may trump the other.

Our current research provides evidence for both explanations. We are currently designing experiments to test both of these explanations more directly to determine whether one or both explanations are capable of explaining these opposing reactions. We are also examining the possibility that for ostracism to result in aggression, a substantial loss of control must accompany or follow the ostracism. The "life alone" paradigm by Twenge and Baumeister, for example, if believed fully, would lead participants to believe that there was nothing that could be done to change the prognosis. In support of this contention, Wayne Warburton (2002) found that aggressive responses (in the form of delivering a larger amount of hot sauce to a neutral third party who was known to dislike hot sauce) only occurred in response to ostracism when there was also a subsequent loss of control. The results of such studies will further our theoretical understanding of the processes involved in ostracism, exclusion, and rejection, and may provide mechanisms for society to direct the behaviors of ostracized individuals to prosocial, rather than antisocial, responses.

Intervention and Policy Implications

One of the most prevalent uses of culturally sanctioned ostracism is the employment of "time-out" disciplinary procedures in homes and schools. When children misbehave, parents and teachers are strongly discouraged (even outlawed) from using corporal punishment, even spanking. Contrarily, it is widely viewed as enlightened to use time-out as a means to correct unwanted behavior. Although time-out seems to enjoy worldwide endorsement, the procedures used in its name are highly variable. In school, some children are sent to another room, usually alone, for undetermined amounts of time. Other times, the child is somehow branded (by wearing a hat or arm band, or sitting in a corner) while remaining in the same room, with the understanding that everyone in the room ignores him or her until the teacher says otherwise. In essence, children are ostracized, socially or physically, as a means to correct their behavior.

We suspect that all methods of time-out are not the same, and that some might be less effective and more harmful than others. By stripping a child of any sense of belonging, control, self-esteem, or meaningful existence, teachers may unwittingly be triggering a sequence of attention-seeking, maladaptive, and aggressive behaviors, rather than socially desirable and constructive behaviors. Although this issue requires scrutiny and research attention, it is our belief that policy makers who encourage the use of time-out become mindful of how the procedure is to be used. From our research findings, it would seem prudent to provide children with some sense of control over when they can rejoin the class. For example, children could be told that when they feel they can behave co-operatively, they can return to their seat. This way, the temporary loss of belonging occurs without a total loss of control, allowing the child to feel the aversiveness of social exclusion, without an insatiable desire to reclaim attention.

REFERENCES

Andrews, D. L. (2002, April 26). Shooting rampage at German school. *The New York Times*, p. A1.

Baumeister, R. F., & Leary, M. R. (1995). The need to belong: Desire for interpersonal attachments as a fundamental human motivation. *Psychological Bulletin, 117*, 497–529.

Baumeister, R. F., & Tice, D. M. (1990). Anxiety and social exclusion. *Journal of Social and Clinical Psychology, 9*, 165–195.

Biehl, J. K. (2002, April 27). 18 die in German high school shooting: Ex-student targets teachers, kills self. *Boston Globe*, p. A1.

Cheung, C. K. T. (1999). *Ostracizing clients on the Internet: The effects of not responding to electronic mail enquiries*. Unpublished master's thesis, University of New South Wales, Sydney, Australia.

Craighead, W. E., Kimball, W. H., & Rehak, P. J. (1979). Mood changes, physiological responses, and self-statements during social rejection imagery. *Journal of Consulting and Clinical Psychology, 47*, 385–396.

Dittes, J. E. (1959). Attractiveness of group as function of self-esteem and acceptance by group. *Journal of Abnormal and Social Psychology, 59*, 77–82.

Faulkner, S. J. (1998). *After the whistle is blown: The aversive impact of ostracism*. Unpublished doctoral dissertation, University of Toledo, Ohio.

Fenigstein, A. (1979). Self-consciousness, self-attention, and social interaction. *Journal of Personality and Social Psychology, 37*, 75–86.

Gardner, W., Pickett, C. L., & Brewer, M. B. (2000). Social exclusion and selective memory: How the need to belong influences memory for social events. *Personality and Social Psychology Bulletin, 26*, 486–496.

Geller, D. M., Goodstein, L., Silver, M., & Sternberg, W. C. (1974). On being ignored: The effects of violation of implicit rules of social interaction. *Sociometry, 37*, 541–556.

Gottman, J. (1980). Consistency of nonverbal affect and affect reciprocity in marital interaction. *Journal of Consulting and Clinical Psychology, 48*, 711–717.

Gottman, J. M. (1979). *Marital interaction: Experimental investigations*. New York: Academic Press.

Greenwald, A. G., McGhee, D. E., & Schwartz, J. K. L. (1998). Measuring individual differences in implicit cognition: The implicit association test. *Journal of Personality and Social Psychology, 74*, 1464–1480.

Gruter, M., & Masters, R. D. (1986). Ostracism as a social and biological phenomenon: An introduction. *Ethology and Sociobiology, 7*, 149–158.

Insko, C. A., Pinkley, R. L., Hoyle, R. H., Dalton, B., Hong, G., Slim, R., et al. (1987). Individual-group discontinuity: The role of intergroup contact. *Journal of Experimental Social Psychology, 23*, 250–267.

Insko, C. A., Schopler, J., Pemberton, M. B., Wieselquist, J., McIlraith, S. A., Currey, D. P., et al. (1998). Long-term outcome maximization and the reduction of interindividual–intergroup discontinuity. *Journal of Personality and Social Psychology, 75,* 695–710.

Insko, C. A., & Wilson, M. (1977). Interpersonal attraction as a function of social interaction. *Journal of Personality and Social Psychology, 35,* 903–911.

James, W. (1890). *Principles of Psychology, Vol. 1.* New York: Dover.

Leary, M. R. (Ed.). (2001). *Interpersonal Rejection.* New York: Oxford University Press.

Leary, M. R., Kowalski, R. M., Smith, L., & Phillips, S. (2003). Teasing, rejection, and violence: Case studies of the school shootings. *Aggressive Behavior, 29,* 202–214.

Leary, M. R., Tambor, E. S., Terdal, S. K., & Downs, D. L. (1995). Self-esteem as an interpersonal monitor: The sociometer hypothesis. *Journal of Personality and Social Psychology, 68,* 518–530.

Lemonick, M. D. (2002, May 6). Germany's Columbine. *Time Magazine (New York), 159 (18),* 36–39.

Nezlek, J. B., Kowalski, R. M., Leary, M. R., Blevins, T., & Holgate, S. (1997). Personality moderators of reactions to interpersonal rejection: Depression and trait self-esteem. *Personality and Social Psychology Bulletin, 23,* 1235–1244.

Pedersen, A., & Walker, I. (1997). Prejudice against Australian aborigines: Old fashioned and modern forms. *European Journal of Social Psychology, 27,* 561–587.

Predmore, S. J., & Williams, K. D. (1983, May). *The Effects of Social Ostracism on Affiliation.* Paper presented at the meeting of the Midwestern Psychological Association, Chicago.

Reicher, S. D., Spears, R., & Postmes, T. (1995). A social identity model of deindividuation phenomena. *European Review of Social Psychology, 6,* 161–198.

Snoek, J. D. (1962). Some effects of rejection upon attraction to a group. *Journal of Abnormal and Social Psychology, 64,* 175–182.

Thompson, H. L., & Richardson, D. R. (1983). The Rooster Effect: Same-sex rivalry and inequity as factors in retaliative aggression. *Personality and Social Psychology Bulletin, 9,* 415–425.

Twenge, J. M., Baumeister, R. F., Tice, D. M., & Stucke, T. S. (2001). If you can't join them, beat them: Effects of social exclusion on aggressive behavior. *Journal of Personality and Social Psychology, 81,* 1058–1069.

Warburton, W. (2002). *Aggressive responses to ostracism: The role of loss of control and narcissism.* Unpublished honours thesis, Macquarie University, Sydney.

Williams, K. D. (1997). Social ostracism. In R. Kowalski (Ed.), *Aversive interpersonal behaviors* (pp. 133–170). New York: Plenum.

Williams, K. D. (2001). *Ostracism: The power of silence.* New York: Guilford.

Williams, K. D., Case, T. I., & Govan, C. L. (2002, March). Impact of Ostracism on Social Judgments: Explicit and Implicit Responses. Conference presentation at the Sydney Symposium of Social Psychology, Sydney.

Williams, K. D., Case, T. I., Govan, C. L., & Zadro, L. (2002, May). *Effects of social ostracism on sources and targets.* Conference presentation at the Midwestern Psychological Association, Chicago, IL.

Williams, K. D., Cheung, C. K. T., & Choi, W. (2000). Cyberostracism: Effects of being ignored over the Internet. *Journal of Personality and Social Psychology, 79,* 748–762.

Williams, K. D., Govan, C. L., Croker, V., Tynan, D., Cruikshank, M., & Lam, A. (2002). Investigations into differences between social and cyber ostracism. *Group Dynamics: Theory, Research, and Practice*.

Williams, K. D., & Sommer, K. L. (1997). Social ostracism by coworkers: Does rejection lead to social loafing or compensation. *Personality and Social Psychology Bulletin, 23*, 693–706.

Williams, K. D., & Zadro, L. (2001). Ostracism: On being ignored, excluded, and rejected. In M. Leary (Ed.), *Interpersonal rejection* (pp. 21–53). New York: Oxford Press.

Wilson, T. D., Lindsey, S., & Schooler, T. Y. (2000). A model of dual attitudes. *Psychological Review, 107*, 101–126.

Zadro, L., & Williams, K. D. (1998, April). Riding the 'O' train: A role-play exercise to examine social ostracism. *Proceedings of the Society for Australasian Social Psychology*, Christchurch, NZ.

4

Stigma and Social Exclusion

BRENDA MAJOR and COLLETTE P. ECCLESTON

Exclusion is an essential aspect of stigmatization. Excluding the stigmatized serves several functions for those who exclude, including self-esteem enhancement, anxiety reduction, system justification, and reduction of the costs associated with group living. Exposure to stigma-based exclusion is a stressor, however, for those who are excluded. We propose that how individuals respond to this stressor is a function of (a) how they regulate exposure to the stressor of stigma-based exclusion, (b) how they cognitively appraise stigma-based exclusion, and (c) the coping strategies they use to deal with exclusion that is appraised as stressful. Individuals who are potential targets of stigma-based exclusion will not necessarily suffer from lower self-esteem or reduced well-being if they avoid stigma-based exclusion, do not appraise stigma-based exclusion as stressful, or if they use coping strategies that are effective at managing the internal or external demands posed by stigma-based exclusion that is appraised as threatening. Coping strategies discussed include enhancing one's relational desirability, seeking alternative bases of inclusion, withdrawing from domains in which one is likely to be excluded, and attributing exclusion to prejudice rather than personal characteristics.

> I have a twenty-seven year old son who will not speak to me because I am mentally ill. . . . I found a missing persons service for him, wrote him letters, and he refuses to contact me. And the feedback I got from the missing persons service was he doesn't want to be associated with a mentally ill mother
>
> (Wahl, 1999, p. 52).

The need to form and maintain lasting, positive, and significant relationships with others is a fundamental human motive (Baumeister & Leary, 1995). People strongly desire social attachments, exert considerable energy to develop and sustain them, and are adversely affected by their dissolution or absence (Baumeister & Leary, 1995; Williams, 2001). The need to belong may be evolutionarily adaptive. Infants who desire and are successful at maintaining secure attachments with their caregivers are more likely to survive (Bowlby, 1969). Human beings who lived in groups and sought and sustained supportive relationships with others may have been more likely to survive and reproduce than those who lived alone (Leary, 2001). Whereas the experience of inclusion is frequently accompanied by positive emotions, the experience of being excluded typically leads to negative emotions, including sadness, loneliness, jealousy, anger, shame, and anxiety (Baumeister & Tice, 1990; Leary, 1990). Individuals who chronically expect rejection from others are more likely to have low self-esteem, be depressed, and experience high levels of negative affect than those who typically expect to be accepted by others (Mendoza-Denton, Purdie, Downey, Davis, & Pietrzak, 2002).

Rejection and exclusion, however, are an inevitable part of social life. Everyone is rejected or left out by others at one time or another. People have only a limited amount of time and energy to devote to social relationships. Hence, each individual must carefully choose with whom they want to spend time and develop a relationship (Leary, 2001). A choice to spend time with one individual necessarily inhibits opportunities to spend time with another. Failure to put boundaries and limits on inclusion of others can lead to a "saturated self" in which the individual is overwhelmed by excessive relationships (Gergen, 1991). Consequently, the experience of being a target of exclusion and rejection is unavoidable. This experience, however, is not distributed equally across society. In every society there are some categories of individuals who are systematically devalued and excluded from a broad array of social relationships and social domains. These individuals are stigmatized.

In its most basic terms, stigma refers to a mark or sign of disgrace or discredit. In ancient Greece, the mark was a literal one, burnt or cut into the body to advertise that the bearer was a contemptible person. Goffman defined stigma as an attribute that extensively discredits the individual, reducing him or her "from a whole and usual person to a tainted, discounted one" (1963, p. 3). Jones et al. (1984) proposed that a person is stigmatized when a "mark" (a deviation from the norm) is linked to dispositions that discredit the bearer of the mark. Crocker, Major, and Steele (1998) argued that stigmatization occurs when a person possesses (or is believed to possess) "some attribute, or characteristic, that conveys a social identity that is devalued in a particular social context" (p. 505). Goffman (1963) distinguished among three general categories of stigmatizing conditions: "blemishes of individual character," "abominations of the body," and "tribal stigmas." Blemishes of individual character are stigmas that reflect or are assumed to reflect immoral or deviant behavior. In contemporary American society, the mentally ill, homosexuals, and criminals are examples of this type of stigma. Abominations of the body refer to stigmas that arise from physical disfigurement or physical deviations from what is considered "normal." Paraplegics, the overweight, and the facially disfigured are examples of this type. Tribal stigmas are based on membership (typically inherited) in despised racial, ethnic, or religious groups. African Americans, Native Americans, and Jews fit into this category of stigma.

Stigma can be distinguished from deviance. Deviance refers to a divergence from the normal, a statistically infrequent occurrence. Some deviant characteristics may be viewed positively (Frable, Blackstone, & Scherbaum, 1990). In contrast, stigma is always negative. The qualities that members of stigmatized groups are believed to possess makes them somehow spoiled. As Goffman puts it, "we believe the person with a stigma is not quite human" (p. 5). Indeed, Leyens (Leyens et al., 2000, 2001) demonstrated that members of stigmatized groups are often regarded as "infrahumans," in that they are viewed as lacking in the possession of distinctly human characteristics such as secondary emotions. In addition, because deviance is a matter of numerical representation, if enough people come to possess a certain quality or belong to a certain group, it is no longer considered deviant. For example, Archer (1985) discusses the fact that premarital sexual relationships, which were considered deviant in the seventeenth century, ceased to be so in the eighteenth century following an increase in the rate of out of wedlock pregnancies. However, with stigmatization, numerical representation does not solve the problem. Obesity is widespread in the United States; yet overweight people are severely stigmatized. Women comprise approximately half the population and yet they experience many of the trials of a stigmatized group. In many cultures throughout the world, women are devalued and denied the right to political participation, employment, mobility, and education, among other things.

Stigma can also be distinguished from low status, although stigmatized individuals tend to often occupy positions of low status and have less social power. Again, the stigmatized bear a mark that deems them less than a whole person, not deserving of the rights given to most members of the society in which they reside. For example, in the United States slaves were counted as three fifths of a person and thus not benefiting from rights accorded Americans such as representation in Congress and voting. Similarly, women in the United States were not allowed to vote until 1920, because they were not believed to have the reasoning ability to vote responsibly. Certainly, the inability to secure the basic rights accorded to other citizens results in the stigmatized having low social power.

Some scholars stress the extent to which stigmatization exists in the eye of the beholder, rather in a particular attribute. Crocker et al. (1998) argue that stigma is contextual—it is experienced within specific social contexts, and with respect to specific others. As the context (and audience) changes, so too does the experience of stigma. Characteristics that are stigmatizing in some contexts (dark skin color among a group with white skin) are not stigmatizing in other contexts (dark skin color among a group of others with similarly dark skin). Thus, according to this perspective, all individuals are potentially vulnerable to experiencing stigma. The pervasiveness and severity of stigmatization varies profoundly, however, depending on whether one is a member of a chronically high or low status group. For example, even though a male among a group of female rape victims might feel stigmatized in that particular context, he is unlikely to feel similarly stigmatized in most contexts. Highly obese individuals in America, in contrast, are likely to feel stigmatized in their interactions with most people, and in most contexts. In contrast to this contextual view of stigma, other scholars (e.g., Kurzban & Leary, 2001) propose that some characteristics are universally stigmatized, and point to cross-cultural similarity in what groups are targeted for stigmatization.

Exclusion is an essential aspect of stigmatization. Indeed, Miller and Kaiser (2001) observe that stigma is so intimately related to rejection and exclusion that prejudiced attitudes towards members of stigmatized groups frequently are measured by asking people to indicate the social distance they want to keep between themselves and members of the stigmatized group. Leary and Schreindorfer (1998) explicitly incorporated this association between stigma and exclusion in their definition of stigma. They proposed that stigmatization occurs "when a shared characteristic of a category of people becomes consensually regarded as a basis for dissociating from (that is, avoiding, excluding, ostracizing, or otherwise minimizing interaction with) individuals who are perceived to be members of that category" (p. 15).

Several aspects of stigma-based exclusion set it apart from most other types of exclusion. First, in contrast to exclusion based on idiosyncratic attitudes or preferences, stigma-based exclusion is *consensual*. There is general agreement within a culture that certain types of people should be excluded. Consequently, those who are stigmatized are likely to experience exclusion and rejection more pervasively than those who are not stigmatized. They are likely to be excluded by a wider array of individuals, excluded more frequently, and from more domains of social life than are those who are excluded purely for idiosyncratic reasons. Second, exclusion based on stigma, particularly tribal stigmas such as race or religion, is typically *shared* with others who share the same attribute, who belong to the same category. Thus, exclusion is based on a social identity, not simply a personal identity. This shared aspect of stigma-based exclusion allows for the use of several coping strategies not available to those excluded for purely personal reasons. Third, stigma-based exclusion is often considered *justified*. That is, there is often agreement within a culture that exclusion of the stigmatized is legitimate (Crandall, 1994). Opotow (1990) referred to this as "moral exclusion," observing that groups are morally excluded when they are perceived as "outside the boundary in which moral values, rules, and considerations of fairness apply" (p. 173). In the United States, for example, almost every state has a law preventing homosexuals from legally marrying. Homosexuals are also denied access to certain forms of government security clearance (Herek, 1990), and the bylaws of many churches prevent homosexuals from occupying positions of leadership within the church. Likewise, many

Americans consider it justifiable to exclude the overweight from positions in the public eye, such as being TV spokespersons, actors, receptionists, or airline attendants. This presumed justifiability of excluding the stigmatized can lead to more severe negative treatment than is meted out to those excluded for more idiosyncratic reasons. Because those who are morally excluded are seen as nonentities or undeserving, harming them appears acceptable, appropriate, or just (Opotow, 1990). For example, after the September 11th terrorist attacks, many Americans felt morally justified in expressing negative views about Muslims, supporting racial profiling of Muslims, imposing stricter immigration laws against Muslims, and committing violence against Muslim Americans.

WHY ARE THE STIGMATIZED EXCLUDED?

Stigmatization and accompanying exclusion are so ubiquitous that some scholars suggest that these processes must serve important psychological functions for the stigmatizer (see Crocker et al., 1998; Kurzban & Leary, 2001 for a review). One function that excluding the stigmatized may serve is to enhance personal or group self-esteem. Individuals are motivated to maintain a positive view of the self (Tesser, 1988) and the groups to which they belong (Tajfel & Turner, 1986). Through processes of downward comparison and derogation, excluding those who are stigmatized may help those who are not stigmatized to feel better about themselves and their group (Tajfel & Turner, 1986; Wills, 1981). Although one could presumably exclude and discriminate against any number of outgroups in order to satisfy this need, social norms dictate who should and who should not be excluded and discriminated against (Abrams & Hogg, 1988). Exclusion and discrimination are most likely to occur when such behavior is perceived as justifiable or legitimate (Jetten, Spears, Hogg, & Manstead, 2000).

The stigmatized also may be excluded to alleviate discomfort and anxiety on the part of the non-stigmatized. For example, people tend to feel uncomfortable around people who are mentally ill, in part because they are perceived as unpredictable and dangerous (Farina, 1998; Farina & Ring, 1965). The mentally ill are especially likely to be excluded from situations that would involve intimate contact, such as working relationships, friendships and romantic relationships. Indeed, individuals often prefer to work alone rather than with a person they believe to be mentally ill (Farina & Ring, 1965). Sixty-eight percent of mentally ill persons reported feeling excluded or shunned by others at least sometimes (Wahl, 1999).

Another reason that some types of stigmatized individuals may be excluded is because they remind the nonstigmatized of their own vulnerability and mortality. This may apply in particular to people who are diseased, disfigured or disabled. According to terror management theory, human beings have considerable anxiety about our own mortality (Solomon, Greenberg, & Pyszczynski, 1991). One way of managing the terror of our impending death is simply to avoid people or situations that remind us of death. A more sophisticated way of managing terror is to create a cultural worldview, that is, a shared understanding of reality that imposes order on the random events of the world. The cultural worldview allows the individual to believe that bad things don't happen to good people and that literal or figurative immortality is possible if one upholds the values of the culture. Because the worldview buffers us from existential terror, individuals who challenge the cultural worldview by thinking or behaving differently are susceptible to stigmatization and exclusion. The self-esteem enhancement and anxiety reduction perspectives provide insights into why some groups and not others are stigmatized within a given culture. These perspectives have difficulty, however, explaining why the stigmatized themselves often show evidence of outgroup favoritism and ingroup derogation (see Crocker et al., 1998).

System justification perspectives can explain this phenomenon. According to these perspectives, stigmatization serves to justify existing social inequalities (Jost & Banaji, 1994; Sidanius & Pratto, 1993). People are motivated to justify the social, economic, and political systems in which they live. To do this, members of a society make attributions about the positive and negative characteristics and deservingness of members of different social groups on the basis of the current social structure. These attributions justify, and make seem reasonable, the different roles and rewards that different people experience in society. For example, stereotyping African Americans as submissive and childlike, but at the same time uncivilized and nonhuman, justified their enslavement (Jahoda, 1999). Excluding African Americans from virtually all aspects of society reinforced the idea that they were not human, and justified their being treated as simply property. In addition, excluding members of low-status groups from gaining access to positions of high status in society helps to maintain status differences. At least until 1964, when the Civil Rights Act was passed, African Americans were systematically denied access to areas of social life that were literally or symbolically related to improving their status, including institutions of higher education, the political system, and particular neighborhoods. Even today, more than 35 years after the Civil Rights act was passed in the United States, African Americans are still being denied access to symbols of high status in America. The system justification perspective not only accounts for within culture agreement on who is stigmatized, but also explains why members of stigmatized groups sometimes show favoritism toward the nonstigmatized. Of course, power differences between the stigmatized and the nonstigmatized also contribute to this tendency. The system justification perspective does not, however, explain why some groups appear to be stigmatized and excluded across a number of different cultures, and across historical time periods.

Recent evolutionary perspectives on the function of stigmatization attempt to fill this gap (Kurzban & Leary, 2001; Neuberg, Smith, & Asher, 2000). According to evolutionary perspectives, the purpose of society is to increase individuals' chances of surviving and passing on their genes. Living in a social group is likely to increase reproductive fitness both directly (e.g., individuals with whom one can mate are available) and indirectly (individuals with whom one can co-operate to achieve mutual goals such as building shelters are available). Sociality also has its limits, however. Certain aspects of group living, such as competition and conflict, are threats to reproductive fitness. Thus, individuals are social to the extent that it is beneficial to reproductive fitness, and not social if it is disadvantageous to fitness. The crucial problem for social creatures is deciding who is likely to be associated with the benefits of being social versus who is likely to be associated with its costs.

According to Kurzban and Leary (2001), stigmatization is a result of mechanisms evolved for deciding who is unlikely to increase one's reproductive fitness, and hence should be excluded from social interaction. In particular, they suggest that the phenomenon of stigma derives from cognitive adaptations designed to solve three problems. First, adaptations evolved to exclude people who are poor partners for social exchange. This is likely to lead to avoidance and exclusion of those who are perceived as unpredictable (e.g., the mentally ill) (because of unpredictability), those who do not follow social norms (e.g., homosexuals), those who "cheat" (e.g., criminals), as well as people who are perceived to have nothing to give (e.g., the homeless, the elderly). Second, adaptations evolved to exclude other individuals from reaping the benefits of membership in one's ingroup, and to exploit excluded individuals. The purpose of groups is to provide the individual with an opportunity to accomplish things that he or she would not have been able to do as an individual. Therefore, individuals are motivated to join powerful groups from whom they can benefit, in part by exploiting outgroup members. Outgroups should be stigmatized and excluded from economic and societal benefits in order to protect the ingroup from exploitation by them. Examples are exclusion of members of other racial, ethnic, and religious groups. Third, adaptations evolved to prevent contact with people likely to carry communicable pathogens. Because people are motivated to survive and pass on their genes, they want to avoid individuals who may infect them with a parasite or a contagious disease. This should lead to stigmatization and physical exclusion of people known or believed to have a disease (e.g., cancer, AIDS, leprosy), or whose physical appearance is suggestive of illness or disease (e.g., the disfigured, the disabled). These three bases of exclusion—of poor partners for exchange, of those suspected of carrying disease, and of outgroups—are reminiscent of Goffman's (1963) typology of stigmas—blemishes of character, abominations of the body, and tribal stigmas.

Neuberg et al. (2000) also argue that people who decrease the likelihood that living in a group will be beneficial will be stigmatized. They suggest that group living is highly adaptive for survival and passing on one's genes. Therefore, individuals who in some way appear to threaten the effective functioning of groups will be stigmatized. The fundamental benefit of group living is sharing. Sharing is only a benefit, however, if everyone shares. Consequently, individuals who are seen as nonreciprocating, such as thieves or physically disabled individuals who are unable to reciprocate will be stigmatized. Individuals who intentionally exploit the co-operative tendencies of others, such as cheaters and traitors, should also be stigmatized. Third, living in a social group involves creating norms and socialization practices. Therefore, individuals who threaten the socialization process of the group, such as homosexuals or individuals with different religious beliefs will be stigmatized. Finally, outgroups will be stigmatized, especially when they are perceived as threatening the ingroup's ability to gain resources.

In sum, exclusion of the stigmatized may serve a variety of psychological functions. Evolutionary accounts of the functions of stigmatization and exclusion help to explain the commonalties across cultures in targets of stigmatization. These accounts are less successful, however, in explaining the considerable variation that occurs both within and across cultures, and across time, in stigmatization. Furthermore, they have some difficulty explaining the contextual nature of the predicament of stigma. Nonetheless, they provide an interesting and provocative account for the pervasiveness of stigmatization across cultures and time.

Psychological Consequences of Stigma-Based Exclusion

Because psychological well-being is at least partly dependent on inclusion (Leary, 1990) and the perception that one is valued by others (Pyszczynski, Greenberg, & Solomon, 1997), it is often assumed that frequent rejection and exclusion inevitably will result in profoundly negative psychological consequences for its targets (Baumeister & Leary, 1995; Leary, 2001; Williams, 2001). Leary (2001), for example, asserts that the perception that others do not value their relationships with us as much as we desire is "virtually always accompanied by emotional distress" (p. 9). With respect to stigmatization, a number of scholars have argued that repeated exposure to prejudice and discrimination inevitably will leave a "mark of oppression" on the personalities and self-esteem of its victims (e.g., Allport, 1954/1979; Cartwright, 1950; Erikson, 1956). For example, Dorwin Cartwright argued, "To a considerable extent, personal feelings of worth depend on the social evaluation of the group with which a person is identified. Self-hatred and feelings of worthlessness tend to arise from membership in underprivileged or outcast groups" (1950, p. 440).

There is little doubt but that the stigmatized are harmed in multiple ways by the blatant and subtle forms of exclusion that they endure (see Major, Quinton, & McCoy, 2002). The stigmatized are systematically excluded from education, employment, occupational advancement, housing, education, and quality medical care. This compromises their physical and emotional well-being, especially if structural discrimination is repeated, pervasive, and severe (Allison, 1998; Clark, Anderson, Clark, & Williams, 1999). The stigmatized are also often targets of violence, resulting in physical as well as psychological harm (Herek, 2000). Perceiving that oneself or one's group is a victim of pervasive discrimination typically is associated with lower self-esteem and poorer well-being (Major, Quinton, & McCoy, 2002). Contrary to the "inevitable mark of oppression" hypothesis, however, members of chronically stigmatized groups frequently do not exhibit signs of poor mental health and/or low self-esteem (Crocker & Major, 1989; Diener & Diener, 1996; Rosenberg & Simmons, 1972). Indeed, on the basis of their review of more than 20 years of empirical research, Crocker and Major (1989) concluded that members of stigmatized groups often have levels of global self-esteem as high or higher than members of nonstigmatized groups. Findings such as these led scholars to focus on mechanisms of resilience rather than vulnerability among members of stigmatized groups (e.g., Crocker & Major, 1989; Crocker et al., 1998).

Contemporary research illustrates that there is not a one-to-one relationship between exposure to stigma-based rejection and exclusion and outcomes such as self-esteem and emotional well-being. Some stigmatized individuals and groups demonstrate high self-esteem, despite consistent exclusion from many types of social relationships, whereas others do not. For example, on average, African Americans, have higher self-esteem than European-Americans (Twenge & Crocker, 2002), but overweight women have lower self-esteem than nonoverweight women (Miller & Downey, 1999). Among those who are overweight, some individuals have high self-esteem, whereas others do not (Friedman & Brownell, 1995). In addition, the same individual may show different responses to prejudice as the context changes, as research on stereotype threat demonstrates (Steele & Aronson, 1995).

We believe that this variability can be understood by conceptualizing responses to stigma-based rejection within a stress and coping model (e.g., Major & Schmader, 1998; Major et al., 2002; Major, Quinton, McCoy, & Schmader, 2000; Miller & Major, 2000). According to our perspective, exposure to stigma-based exclusion is a stressor. How individuals respond to this stressor is a function of (a) how they *regulate exposure* to the stressor of stigma-based exclusion, (b) how they *cognitively appraise* stigma-based exclusion, and (c) the *coping strategies* they use to deal with exclusion that is appraised as stressful. Individuals who are potential targets of stigma-based exclusion will not necessarily suffer from lower self-esteem or reduced well-being if they avoid stigma-based exclusion, do not appraise stigma-based exclusion as stressful, or if they use coping strategies that are effective at managing the internal or external demands posed by stigma-based exclusion that are appraised as threatening. In the following sections we consider various ways in which the stigmatized may na-based exclusion and the implications of these responses for ...d emotional well-being.

RESPONSES TO THE THREAT OF STIGMA-BASED EXCLUSION

Members of stigmatized groups respond to rejection and exclusion in various ways (Allport, 1954/1979; Goffman, 1963; Jones et al., 1984). Allport distinguished between extropunitive and intropunitive "ego defenses" used by victims of prejudice. Extropunitive defenses attack the source of the difficulty; victims who adopt these strategies blame the rejecter or excluder rather than themselves. By contrast, victims employing intropunitive strategies take the responsibility for rejection and exclusion upon themselves. Other distinctions include individual versus group-level reactions to exclusion and devaluation (Ellemers & Van Rijswijk, 1997), social mobility, social creativity, or social change responses to a devalued social identity (Tajfel & Turner, 1986), and problem-focused versus emotion-focused coping responses to stigmatization (Miller & Major, 2000).

According to Leary (2001), people react to the specific threat of interpersonal rejection and exclusion in one of three primary ways: by enhancing their relational value to other people, by seeking alternative relationships in which they will be more highly valued, and/or by withdrawing. Crocker and Major (1989) identified three cognitive processes that the stigmatized may employ to buffer their self-esteem from threat (a) selectively comparing outcomes with members of their own group, rather than with members of nonstigmatized groups, (b) selectively devaluing those attributes on which their group fares poorly and valuing those attributes on which their group excels, and (c) attributing negative feedback to the prejudiced attitudes of others toward their group rather than to their own deservingness. In the following section, we consider how the stigmatized may respond to the threat of stigma-based rejection and/or exclusion using Leary's and Crocker and Major's frameworks.

Enhance One's Desirability as a Relational Partner

One way in which the stigmatized may react to stigma-based exclusion is by seeking to enhance their desirability to the nonstigmatized as relationship partners. One approach to this is by attempting to eliminate one's stigmatizing condition. Dieting to achieve weight loss, undergoing cosmetic surgery to alter the signs of aging or body parts considered less than perfect, going to therapy to overcome mental illness and addictions, obtaining an education to overcome poverty, and attending elocution courses to conquer a stammer are all examples of behavioral attempts by the stigmatized to eliminate a stigma. Of course, this strategy is only available to individuals whose stigmas are indeed under their control. The repeated failure experienced by most dieters suggests that such attempts may often not be successful.

A second way in which members of stigmatized groups may attempt to enhance their attractiveness is by distancing themselves from their own stigmatized group. They may, for example, attempt to set themselves apart from the group through their behavior, so as to communicate, "I am not like them." Steele and Aronson (1995) found that when African American college students felt threatened by negative stereotypes about their group, they disavowed having interests and preferences consistent with stereotypes of their group (e.g., liking rap music). Kaiser and Miller (2001) found that women who thought they were going to be evaluated by a sexist judge described themselves in less feminine terms than did women who did not anticipate a sexist evaluator.

Perhaps the ultimate form of attempting to distance oneself from one's stigmatized group is to conceal or disguise one's stigma, and thereby "pass" as nonstigmatized. People attempt to conceal a wide variety of stigmatizing conditions, including homosexuality, mental disorders, physical illnesses, and a host of behaviors that might be considered "blemishes of character" (e.g., an addiction, a prior criminal conviction). Concealment is an option primarily for those whose stigmas are invisible, or at least not readily apparent. Even highly visible identities, however, may be temporarily concealable. For example, interacting via the telephone or the Internet is one way in which the stigmatized may participate in social interactions without their stigma being known. Furthermore, some features, such as light skin, may blur the boundaries that distinguish members of stigmatized groups from members of nonstigmatized groups. This may allow members of stigmatized racial, ethnic, or religious groups to "pass" as members of nonstigmatized groups, and hence be included by those groups.

Fear of social disapproval and rejection are the most common reasons reported for keeping aspects of identity secret (Pennebaker, 1993). Bisexuals' and homosexuals' level of openness about their sexuality is influenced more by their beliefs about how others will judge them than by how much they accept their own sexuality (Franke & Leary, 1991). Three quarters of individuals who have had a mental illness avoid disclosing it to individuals outside of their family (Wahl, 1999). In several studies of psychological responses to abortion, Major and colleagues asked women, just prior to having an abortion and again subsequent to their abortion, who they had told of their pregnancy and abortion. Prior to their abortion, less than twenty-five percent of the women said they had told a parent of their pregnancy, and only two-thirds said they had told a friend (Major et al., 1990; Major, Zubek, Cooper, Cozzarelli & Richards, 1997). In another study, Major and Gramzow (1999) found that two years postabortion, 57% of women said that they had felt a need to keep the abortion secret from family and 45% said that they needed to keep it a secret from friends. Forty-seven percent also said they thought others would look down upon them if they knew about the abortion. These measures were strongly positively correlated, suggesting that fear of social disapproval prompted many women to conceal their abortion.

Concealing a stigma may not only allow a person to avoid social disapproval, but may also preserve important social relationships that could be threatened if the stigma was known. People often conceal their stigma from some, but disclose their stigmatized status to other individuals who they feel confident will not exclude them as a result (Major, Richards, Cooper, Cozzarelli, & Zubek, 1998). Revealing a stigma to close others who are not supportive is particularly painful. For example, Major et al. (1998) asked women who said they had revealed their abortion to a close other as to how supportive this person had been. Women who said that a partner, friend, or family member to whom they had revealed their abortion was not extremely supportive were more depressed one month after their abortion than women who said they had concealed their abortion from that person. Some researchers conclude that the negative effects of revealing a stigma on social interactions are so consequential that individuals who can conceal their stigma are better off psychologically than those who cannot (Jones et al., 1984).

Concealment, however, also can be psychologically costly. Goffman (1963) termed individuals whose stigmas are visible as "discredited," but those whose stigmas are invisible as "discreditable." Individuals who conceal or disguise a stigma may not only suffer from fear that their stigma will be discovered, but may also fear social disapproval for having tried to conceal it. This may lead to anxiety in social interactions with the nonstigmatized. Avoiding discovery may also require vigilance to avoid giving the secret away (Smart & Wegner, 1999). Most people feel a compelling need to disclose important aspects of their identity. Failure to do so is associated with poorer physical health and emotional well-being (Pennebaker, 1997). HIV infection, for example progresses more rapidly among HIV-seropositive gay men who conceal their homosexual identity than it does among those who are "out," unless they are high in rejection sensitivity (Cole, Kemeny, & Taylor, 1997; Cole, Kemeny, Taylor, & Visscher, 1996). Major and Gramzow (1999), described earlier, found that feeling a need for secrecy about the abortion was related to higher levels of thought suppression and intrusive thoughts of the abortion, and to decreases in emotional well-being from preabortion to two years postabortion. Concealment also deprives the stigmatized individual of the benefits of ingroup social comparisons, self-validation, and ingroup social support.

A final way in which stigmatized individuals may seek to enhance their relationship desirability is by overcompensating—exerting more effort in the relationship, or developing and refining their interaction skills so that they are particularly socially skillful (Miller & Myers, 1998). They often try harder and are more persistent than the nonstigmatized in social situations (Dion & Stein,

1978). The stigmatized often express the belief that they have to work harder to receive the same evaluations as the nonstigmatized. All of these attempts to improve desirability as relationship partners to the nonstigmatized can be considered various ways of seeking to avoid or reduce exposure to stigma-based exclusion.

Withdraw

A second response to stigma-based exclusion is to withdraw from relationships, domains, and situations in which exclusion is anticipated. Those who are overweight, for example, may avoid striking up friendships with others who are highly attractive, or going to places where they feel they will be rejected because of their weight, such as singles bars, the beach, or the gym (Myers, 1998). Students who are members of groups that are stereotyped as being intellectually inferior may drop out of school (Steele, 1997). Homosexuals may avoid attending churches where they anticipate that they will not be welcome. Ethnic minorities may avoid communities that exclude members of their ethnicity. Women may avoid interactions with men who are reputed to be sexist (Fitzgerald, Swan, & Fisher, 1995).

Often, however, physical withdrawal is not an option for the stigmatized. They must go to school or to work, even though they face rejection and exclusion by their teachers, supervisors, classmates, or coworkers. In such cases, members of stigmatized groups may psychologically withdraw by disengaging their self-esteem from domains in which negative outcomes are anticipated or experienced (Crocker et al., 1998; Major & Schmader, 1998). They also may disengage their self-esteem from the evaluations of individuals who reject or exclude them. To the extent that self-esteem is not contingent upon inclusion in certain domains or acceptance by particular individuals, rejection or exclusion is less likely to be threatening to self-esteem. Several scholars propose that this is a strategy used by African Americans to cope with the negative outcomes they often face in the academic domain (Ogbu, 1991; Steele, 1997). Ogbu (1991) suggests that African American students define academic success as antiblack, thereby ascribing doing well in school as undesirable. Steele and his colleagues (Steele, 1997; Steele & Aronson, 1995) suggest that African Americans may disidentify from school to protect their self-esteem from negative stereotypes about their group's intellectual ability. From a coping perspective, strategies of psychological withdrawal reduce the extent to which stigma-based exclusion is appraised as a self-relevant threat.

One negative consequence of psychological withdrawal from domains where one fears exclusion is that it reduces motivation to persist in those domains. This can be costly if the domain is important for future success, such as performance in school or work. Another consequence is that others may also use physical or psychological withdrawal as a rationale to justify further exclusion of the stigmatized from the domain in question. They may conclude that the stigmatized are just not interested in or capable of performing well in the domain.

Seek Alternative Bases of Inclusion

A third response to stigma-based exclusion is to seek alternative relationships in which to feel valued and included. Individuals need to belong (Baumeister & Leary, 1995), but they do not need to belong to all groups. Indeed, an individual's position within their ingroup, that is, the respect he or she receives from other ingroup members, is more strongly related to personal self-esteem than is the group's position in society as a whole (Tyler, Degoey, & Smith, 1996). Consequently, identifying and affiliating with other individuals who are similarly stigmatized may be an important coping response to stigma-based exclusion. There is some evidence that exclusion by an outgroup causes increased identification with the ingroup. Jetten, Branscombe, Schmitt, and Spears (2001) found that customers at a body piercing shop who read that individuals with body piercings could expect negative discriminatory treatment from the public subsequently felt closer to other body piercers than customers who read they could expect positive reactions from the public. In addition, the more customers identified with body piercers, the higher was their collective self-esteem (i.e., the more positively they viewed body piercers). Collective self-esteem was not directly affected by the discrimination manipulation.

Seeking inclusion by others who are similarly stigmatized is likely to have a number of psychological benefits. Affiliation with similarly stigmatized others provides opportunities for self-validation, sharing of experiences, and social support, all of which may help buffer the stigmatized from stigma-based exclusion (Frable, Platt, & Hoey, 1998). Affiliating with others who are similarly stigmatized may also facilitate redefining the value of the very characteristics for which one's group is excluded (e.g., "Black is beautiful," Tajfel & Turner, 1986). Thus the ingroup offers an alternative to the general negative perception of the group that is held by society. Affiliating with and being included by others similarly stigmatized also facilitates ingroup social comparisons (Major, 1994). Comparing with others who are similarly stigmatized, rather than with the nonstigmatized, may help to protect the self-esteem of the stigmatized from painful upward comparisons (Crocker & Major, 1989). Among members of stigmatized groups, group identification typically is positively associated with self-esteem and mental health (Branscombe, Schmitt, & Harvey, 1999).

The availability of alternative relationships in which the stigmatized can feel valued and included is likely to be greater for people who are visibly than invisibly stigmatized. It is difficult to seek out similar others if one cannot identify who they are. Frable, Platt, & Hoey (1998) found that people with invisible stigmas were less likely to interact with others who shared their stigma or be aware that they were interacting with a stigmatized other than were people with visible stigmas. People with invisible stigmas also had lower self-esteem and were more anxious and depressed than people with visible stigmas or nonstigmatized individuals. Frable et al. (1998) suggest that because people with invisible stigmas have fewer opportunities to interact with others who visibly share the same identity, they are more susceptible to the culture's negative views of the group. Although face-to-face interaction may be less likely for those with invisible stigmas, the internet has provided a way for these individuals to affiliate with similarly stigmatized others. Individuals with invisible stigmas who actively participate in an internet community and for whom this community is important experience greater self-acceptance than individuals who do not participate in such groups (McKenna & Bargh, 1998).

Alternative inclusive relationships also may be more available for those whose stigma is associated with a recognizable group identity. Individuals whose stigmas are based on recognizable tribal stigmas, such as race, sex, or ethnicity, are more likely to identify themselves as group members than are individuals whose stigma results from a "blemish of character" or an "abomination of the body." Separatist movements, in which groups segregate themselves from society at large and focus on developing their own culture, as is the case with some members of the deaf community, are an extreme form of seeking alternative bases of inclusion.

Despite the many apparent benefits of identifying with similarly stigmatized others, there may be some costs. Ironically, strong identification with a stigmatized group may increase one's vulnerability to rejection and exclusion of the group. When the group is an important part of the self, distinctions between the personal and the collective self may be blurred. Consequently, stigma-based exclusion may be just as painful as exclusion based on unique personal characteristics. Individuals who are not highly identified with their stigmatized group, in contrast, may be less negatively affected by group-based exclusion because they view the exclusion as not really being about them personally. McCoy and Major (2003), for example, found that among low gender-identified women who were negatively evaluated by a male, self-esteem was higher if the women thought the male was sexist than if they thought he was not sexist. Among highly gender-identified women who received a similar negative evaluation, in contrast, being able to attribute the negative evaluation to sexism did not buffer self-esteem.

Selective affiliation with others who are similarly stigmatized may also prompt further exclusion by the outgroup. When members of a stigmatized group affiliate primarily or exclusively with each other, members of nonstigmatized outgroups may interpret those actions as exclusionary. Anecdotal evidence suggests that on college campuses, some students complain that organizations based on racial minority group membership are just as exclusionary as if such groups existed for white students. Nonstigmatized group members are likely to view these groups as evidence of reverse discrimination, leading to increased hostility toward, and exclusion of the stigmatized.

Attribute Exclusion to Discrimination

Another coping response to stigma-based exclusion is to deflect the exclusion away from the personal identity by attributing it to the prejudice of others toward one's social identity—one's stigmatized group (Crocker & Major, 1989; Major & Crocker, 1993). Attributing negative outcomes to prejudice against one's group should protect affect and self-esteem relative to making attributions to "internal, stable, and global causes such as a lack of ability" (Crocker & Major, 1989, p. 613). This hypothesis is based on theoretical models of emotion that posit that attributing negative events to causes external to the self (such as another's bigotry) protects self-esteem relative to attributing them to one's own lack of deservingness. Consistent with this hypothesis, women who can attribute a negative evaluation to the sexism of a male are less depressed than those who cannot make this attribution (Crocker, Voelkl, Testa, & Major, 1991; Experiment 1); African Americans who can attribute an interpersonal rejection to the racism of a white evaluator tend to have higher self-esteem than those who cannot (Crocker et al., 1991; Experiment 2), and men and women who imagine that they are excluded from a course by a sexist professor have significantly higher self-esteem than men and women who imagine that they are excluded by a professor who thinks they are stupid (Major, Kaiser, & McCoy, 2003).

There are some caveats to this pattern, however. First, as noted above, attributions to discrimination are more likely to protect self-esteem if the target is not highly identified with his or her stigmatized group (McCoy & Major, 2003). In addition, attributions to prejudice are more likely to protect self-esteem if prejudice is blatant rather than ambiguous. For example, in one study (Major, Quinton, & Schmader, 2003), women overheard a confederate make one of three comments while they were waiting to receive feedback on a test. In one condition, the confederate stated that she had heard the evaluator was sexist (blatant), in a second she stated that she had heard the evaluator graded men and women differently (ambiguous) and in a third condition she made a neutral comment. Women subsequently received negative feedback on their test and completed measures of self-esteem. Self-esteem was higher in the blatant condition than either the ambiguous or neutral conditions, which did not differ from one another.

Because attributing rejection or exclusionary treatment to discrimination involves the judgment that the treatment was based on one's social identity or group membership (Major et al., 2002), such attributions should be more prevalent among those who are highly identified with their group, and hence for those to whom the group is likely to be a salient aspect of identity.

Consistent with this latter prediction, in the study by Major et al. (2003) described above, women high in gender identification were more likely to attribute their feedback to discrimination in the ambiguous condition than were women low in gender identification. One might also expect that attributions to discrimination would be more prevalent among those individuals whose stigma more readily allows them to make group-level attributions than individual-level attributions for rejection. Some stigmas have more of a group identity than do other stigmas. Tribal stigmas, for example, are based on membership in a particular outgroup, often one that is easily recognizable (e.g., race, ethnicity, gender), and that has its own unique norms and values. People who are stigmatized because of "blemishes of individual character" (e.g., criminals, addicts, cheaters), or "abominations of the body" (e.g., the obese, the disfigured), in contrast, have a less clearly defined collective identity. The absence of a collective identity means that exclusion and rejection are experienced and interpreted as *personal* rejections, rather than as rejections that are *shared* with similar others. Exclusion of the personal self is more threatening than is exclusion of the collective self (Gaertner, Sedikides, & Graetz, 1999). Although we know of no direct evidence, we suspect that stigmatized individuals who lack an identity as being members of a group are more vulnerable to stigma-based exclusion than those who have a sense that they belong to a stigmatized group. This may be one reason why support groups for people with cancer, AIDS, and other stigmas promote well-being; they provide not only opportunities for social support, but also a mechanism for forming a collective identity and group-level attributions.

Attributions to discrimination also require the judgment that stigma-based exclusion or rejection is unjust, or illegitimate (Major et al., 2002). It is possible for individuals to recognize that their social identity was responsible for their exclusion, but not see this as unfair (e.g., "I did not get the job because people like me are not as qualified, capable, etc., as others"). Some stigmas are perceived (by both self and others) to reflect a "moral failing" of the individual, thus justifying exclusion (Crocker & Major, 1994). People with stigmas that are perceived to be controllable, for example, are often seen as morally suspect. It is assumed that they must have a "blemish of character;" otherwise the stigma would not have occurred, or would be eliminated. Rejection and exclusion of those with controllable stigmas is seen as justified, even by the stigmatized themselves (Crandall, 1994; Rodin, Price, Sanchez, & McElligot, 1989). People whose stigmas are perceived as controllable are judged as more responsible and blameworthy, are more likely to be targets of anger, and are less likely to be helped than those whose stigmas are seen as uncontrollable (Weiner, Perry, & Magnusson, 1988). Examples of stigmas that are perceived to be controllable include obesity, homosexuality, AIDS, criminality, addictions, and many forms of mental illness. Even if the onset of the stigma itself is not perceived as controllable, beliefs about control encourage judgments of responsibility for overcoming problems created by the stigma (Brickman et al., 1982). "Abominations of the body," even though not perceived as controllable, are also often seen as reflecting some moral imperfection of the person.

People who have stigmas that are perceived to be controllable are more vulnerable to stigma-based rejection than those whose stigmas are not perceived as controllable. For example, overweight women rejected by a man who knew their weight were more likely to blame the rejection on their weight than were nonoverweight women, but they were not more likely to blame the rejection on the man's prejudice (Crocker, Cornwell, & Major, 1993). Furthermore, attributing rejection to weight was not self-protective for these overweight women. Quinn and Crocker (1999) found that perceptions of control and Protestant Ethic beliefs (a legitimizing ideology) were negatively associated with psychological well-being among women who perceived themselves as very overweight, but were positively associated with well-being among nonoverweight women or women who perceived themselves as moderately overweight. Although we know of no direct evidence of this, we suspect that individuals who perceive their stigma as controllable are also less likely to self-identify as members of a "group" than those who perceive their stigmas as uncontrollable. Consequently, the former experience rejection and exclusion more personally, and less collectively, than the latter.

CONCLUSIONS

In this chapter we considered the nature of stigma-based exclusion, the reasons why it may occur, and the psychological responses of those who are excluded because of their stigma (See Table 4.1). Several aspects of stigma-based exclusion distinguish it from exclusion based on idiosyncratic preferences. First, there is typically consensual agreement within a culture that the stigmatized should be excluded; second, the experience of stigma-based exclusion is shared with others who belong to the same category, and third, stigma-based exclusion is often considered justified. Exclusion of the stigmatized may serve a variety of functions for those who exclude, including enhancing personal or group self-esteem, reducing anxiety, and justifying existing social inequalities. According to evolutionary perspectives, exclusion of the stigmatized enhances reproductive fitness by excluding those who are potential threats to group living.

Although frequent rejection and exclusion are assumed to result inevitably in lower self-esteem, there is not a one-to-one relationship between membership in a stigmatized group and low self-esteem. We propose that variability in self-esteem between stigmatized groups, within stigmatized groups, and within the same individual across contexts can be understood by considering how the stigmatized regulate exposure to, cognitively appraise, and cope with

TABLE 4.1 Types of Responses to Stigma-Based Exclusion

Enhance relational desirability	Seek alternative bases of inclusion	Avoid situations where exclusion is anticipated	Deflect exclusion from personal self
Eliminate stigma	Increase identification with stigmatized group	Physical withdrawal	Attribute exclusion to group-based discrimination
Distance self from stigmatized group	Selectively affiliate with ingroup members	Psychological disengagement	
Conceal or pass as nonstigmatized			
Overcompensate for stigma			

stigma-based exclusion. We considered four general responses the stigmatized might make to stigma-based exclusion. First, they may seek to enhance their desirability to the nonstigmatized as relationship partners. Examples include attempting to eliminate the stigmatizing condition, distancing from the stigmatized group, concealing the stigma, and overcompensating in relationships. Each of these can be considered ways to avoid or reduce exposure to stigma-based exclusion.

Second, the stigmatized may withdraw physically from relationships or situations in which they fear rejection or exclusion. When physical withdrawal is not possible, the stigmatized may withdraw psychologically by disengaging their self-esteem from domains or relationships. Physical withdrawal avoids exposure to stigma-based exclusion, whereas psychological withdrawal reduces the extent to which exclusion is cognitively appraised as threatening.

A third response to stigma-based exclusion is to seek alternative bases of inclusion, such as by affiliating and/or identifying with others who are similarly stigmatized. Affiliation with others who share one's stigma provides opportunities for self-validation, sharing of experiences, social support, ingroup social comparisons, and developing a collective identity. This important coping response is likely to be more readily available to individuals whose stigma is visible and/or is associated with a recognized group identity, such as those with tribal stigmas.

A fourth response to stigma-based exclusion is to blame it on others' prejudice against one's stigmatized group, rather than on oneself. Attributions to prejudice and/or discrimination involve the judgments that the rejection is group-based, rather than individually based, and is unjust. The ability to blame exclusion on discrimination protects self-esteem for two reasons. First, it makes exclusion a shared experience, rather than an individual experience; it is collective rather than personal. Second, exclusion is unjust and undeserved; it is not a reflection of one's personal deficiencies or moral failings. Two implications follow from this analysis. First to the extent that the stigmatized adopt a collective identity, that is, see themselves and others who share their stigma as members of the same *group*, their self-esteem is more likely to be buffered from exclusion. Second, to the extent that the stigmatized see their exclusion as *unjust and undeserved*, self-esteem is also more likely to be protected from exclusion. By capitalizing on these principles, activist groups such as the Gray Panthers, Gay and Lesbian Alliance Against Defamation, National Association to Advance Fat Acceptance, and The National Alliance of The Disabled make strides not only toward fostering a positive identity among the stigmatized, but also toward seeking social change.

REFERENCES

Abrams, D., & Hogg, M. A. (1988). Comments on the motivational status of self-esteem in social identity and intergroup discrimination. *European Journal of Social Psychology, 18*, 317–334.

Allison, K. W. (1998). Stress and oppressed category membership. In J. K. Swim and C. Stangor (Eds.), *Prejudice: The target's perspective* (pp. 145–170). San Diego, CA: Academic Press.

Allport, G. (1954/1979). *The nature of prejudice*. New York: Doubleday Anchor.

Archer, D. (1985). Social deviance. In G. Lindzey and E. Aaronson (Eds.), *Handbook of social psychology* (3rd ed., pp. 743–803). New York: Random House.

Baumeister, R. F., & Leary, M. R. (1995). The need to belong: Desire for interpersonal attachments as a fundamental human motivation. *Psychological Bulletin, 117*, 497–529.

Baumeister, R. F., & Tice, D. M. (1990). Anxiety and social exclusion. *Journal of Social and Clinical Psychology, 9*, 165–195.

Bowlby, J. (1969). *Attachment and loss, Vol 1: Attachment*. New York: Basic Books.

Branscombe, N. R., Schmitt, M. T., & Harvey, R. D. (1999). Perceiving pervasive discrimination among African Americans: Implications for group identification and well-being. *Journal of Personality and Social Psychology, 77*, 135–149.

Brickman, P., Rabinowitz, V. C., Karuza, J., Jr., Coates, D., Cohn, E., & Kidder, L. (1982). Models of helping and coping. *American Psychologist, 37*, 368–384.

Cartwright, D. (1950). Emotional dimensions of group life. In M. L. Raymert (Ed.), *Feelings and emotions* (pp. 439–447). New York: McGraw Hill.

Clark, R., Anderson, N. B., Clark, V. R., & Williams, D. R. (1999). Racism as a stressor for African Americans: A biopsychosocial model. *American Psychologist, 54*, 805–816.

Cole, S. W., Kemeny, M. E., & Taylor, S. E. (1997). Social identity and physical health: Accelerated HIV progression in rejection-sensitive gay men. *Journal of Personality and Social Psychology, 72*, 320–335.

Cole, S. W., Kemeny, M. E., Taylor, S. E., Visscher, B. R., & Fahey, J. L. (1996). Accelerated course of human immunodeficiency virus infection in gay men who conceal their homosexual identity. *Psychosomatic Medicine, 58*, 219–231.

Crandall, C. S. (1994). Prejudice against fat people: Ideology and self-interest. *Journal of Personality and Social Psychology, 66*, 882–894.

Crocker, J., Cornwell, B., & Major, B. (1993). The stigma of overweight: Affective consequences of attributional ambiguity. *Journal of Personality and Social Psychology, 64,* 60–70.

Crocker, J., & Major, B. (1989). Social stigma and self-esteem: The self-protective properties of stigma. *Psychological Review, 96,* 608–630.

Crocker, J., & Major, B. (1994). Reactions to stigma: The moderating role of justifications. In M. P. Zanna & J. M. Olson (Eds.), *The psychology of prejudice: The Ontario symposium* (Vol. 7, pp. 289–314). Hillsdale, NJ: Erlbaum.

Crocker, J., Major, B., & Steele, C. (1998). Social stigma. In D. Gilbert, S. T. Fiske, & G. Lindzey (Eds.), *Handbook of social psychology* (4th ed., pp. 504–553). Boston: McGraw Hill.

Crocker, J., Voelkl, K., Testa, M., & Major, B. (1991). Social stigma: The affective consequences of attributional ambiguity. *Journal of Personality and Social Psychology, 60,* 218–228.

Diener, E., & Diener, M. (1996). Most people are happy. *Psychological Science, 7,* 181–185.

Dion, K. K., & Stein, S. (1978). Physical attractiveness and interpersonal influence. *Journal of Experimental Social Psychology, 14,* 97–108.

Ellemers, N., & Van Rijswijk, W. (1997). Identity needs versus social opportunities: The use of group-level and individual-level identity management strategies. *Social Psychology Quarterly, 60,* 52–65.

Erikson, E. H. (1956). The problem of ego identity. *Journal of the American Psychoanalytic Association, 4,* 56–121.

Farina, A. (1998). Stigma. In Kim Tornvall & Ed Mueser (Eds.), *Handbook of social functioning in schizophrenia* (pp. 247–279). Boston: Allyn & Bacon.

Farina, A. & Ring, K. (1965). The influence of perceived mental illness on interpersonal relations. *Journal of Abnormal Psychology, 70,* 47–51.

Fitzgerald, L. F., Swan, S., & Fischer, K. (1995). Why didn't she just report him? The psychological and legal implications of women's responses to sexual harassment. *Journal of Social Issues, 51,* 117–138.

Frable, D. E., Blackstone, T., & Scherbaum, C. (1990). Marginal and mindful: Deviants in social interactions. *Journal of Personality and Social Psychology, 59,* 140–149.

Frable, D. E., Platt, L., & Hoey, S. (1998). Concealable stigmas and positive self-perceptions: Feeling better around similar others. *Journal of Personality and Social Psychology, 74,* 908–922.

Franke, R., & Leary, M. R. (1991). Disclosure of sexual orientation by lesbians and gay men: A comparison of private and public processes. *Journal of Social and Clinical Psychology, 10,* 262–269.

Friedman, M. A., & Brownell, K. D. (1995). Psychological correlates of obesity: Moving to the next research generation. *Psychological Bulletin, 117,* 3–20.

Gaertner, L., Sedikides, C., & Graetz, K. (1999). In search of self-definition: Motivational primacy of the individual self, motivational primacy of the collective self, or contextual primacy? *Journal of Personality and Social Psychology, 76,* 5–18.

Gergen, K. J. (1991). *The saturated self: Dilemmas of identity in contemporary life.* New York: Basic Books.

Goffman, E. (1963). *Stigma: Notes on the management of spoiled identity.* Englewood Cliffs, NJ: Prentice-Hall.

Herek, G. M. (1990). Gay people and government security clearances: A social science perspective. *American Psychologist, 45*, 1035–1042.

Herek, G. M. (2000). The psychology of sexual prejudice. *Current Directions in Psychological Science, 9*, 19–22.

Jahoda, G. (1999). Images of savages: Ancient roots of modern prejudice in Western culture. New York: Routledge.

Jetten, J., Branscombe, N. R., Schmitt, M. T., & Spears, R. (2001). Rebels with a cause: Group identification as a response to perceived discrimination from the mainstream. *Personality and Social Psychology Bulletin, 27*, 1204–1213.

Jetten, J., Spears, R., Hogg, M. A., & Manstead, A. S. R. (2000). Discrimination constrained and justified: Variable effects of group variability and in-group identification. *Journal of Experimental Social Psychology, 36*, 329–356.

Jones, E. E., Farina, A., Hastorf, A. H., Markus, H., Miller, D. T., & Scott, R. A. (1984). *Social stigma: The psychology of marked relationships*. New York: Freeman.

Jost, J. T., & Banaji, M. R. (1994). The role of stereotyping in system-justification and the production of false consciousness. *British Journal of Social Psychology, 33*, 1–27.

Kaiser, C. R., & Miller, C. T. (2001). Reacting to impending discrimination: Compensation for prejudice and attributions to discrimination. *Personality and Social Psychology Bulletin, 27*, 1357–1367.

Kurzban, R. & Leary, M. R. (2001). Evolutionary origins of stigmatization: The functions of social exclusion. *Psychological Bulletin, 12*, 187–208.

Leary, M. R. (1990). Responses to social exclusion: Social anxiety, jealousy, loneliness, depression, and low self-esteem. *Journal of Social and Clinical Psychology, 9*, 221–229.

Leary, M. R. (2001) Toward a conceptualization of interpersonal rejection. In Mark R. Leary (Ed.), *Interpersonal rejection* (pp. 3–20). New York: Oxford University Press.

Leary, M. R., & Schreindorfer, L. S. (1998). The stigmatization of HIV and AIDS: Rubbing salt in the wound. In V. J. Derlega & A.P. Barbee (Eds.), *HIV and social interaction* (pp. 12–29). Thousand Oaks, CA: Sage.

Leyens, J., Paladino, P. M. Rodriguez-Torres, R., Vaes, J., Demoulin, S., Rodriguez-Perez, A., et al. (2000). The emotional side of prejudice: The attribution of secondary emotions to ingroups and outgroups. *Personality and Social Psychology Review, 4*, 186–197.

Leyens, J., Rodriguez-Perez, A, Rodriguez-Torres, R., Gaunt, R, Paladino, P. M., Vaes, J., et al. (2001). Psychological essentialism and the differential attribution of uniquely human emotions to ingroups and outgroups. *European Journal of Social Psychology, 31*, 395–411.

Major, B. (1994). From social inequality to personal entitlement: The role of social comparisons, legitimacy appraisals, and group membership. In M. P. Zanna (Ed.), *Advances in Experimental Social Psychology* (Vol. 26, pp. 293–348). San Diego: Academic Press.

Major, B., Cozzarelli, C., Sciacchitano, A. M., Cooper, M. L., Testa, M., & Mueller, P. M. (1990). Perceived social support, self-efficacy, and adjustment to abortion. *Journal of Personality and Social Psychology, 59*, 452–463.

Major, B., & Crocker, J. (1993). Social stigma: The affective consequences of attributional ambiguity. In D. M. Mackie & D. L. Hamilton (Eds.), *Affect, cognition, and stereotyping: Interactive processes in intergroup perception* (pp. 345–370). New York: Academic Press.

Major, B., & Gramzow, R. H. (1999). Abortion as stigma: Cognitive and emotional implications of concealment. *Journal of Personality and Social Psychology, 77*, 735–745.

Major, B., Kaiser, C., & McCoy, S. K. (2003). It's not my fault: When and why attributions to prejudice protect self-esteem. *Personality and Social Psychology Bulletin, 29*, 772–781.

Major, B., Quinton, W. J., & McCoy, S. K. (2002). Antecedents and consequences of perceiving the self as a target of discrimination: Theoretical and Empirical Advances. In M. P. Zanna (Ed.), *Advances in Experimental Social Psychology, 34* (pp. 251–330). New York: Academic Press.

Major, B., Quinton, W. J., McCoy, S. K., & Schmader, T. (2000). Reducing prejudice: The target's perspective? In S. Oskamp (Ed.), *Reducing prejudice* (pp. 211–237). New York: Sage.

Major, B., Quinton, W. J., & Schmader, T. (2003). Attributions to discrimination and self-esteem: Impact of group identification and situational ambiguity. *Journal of Experimental Social Psychology, 39*, 220–231.

Major, B., Richards, C., Cooper, M. L., Cozzarelli, C., & Zubek, J. (1998). Personal resilience, cognitive appraisals, and coping: An integrative model of adjustment to abortion. *Journal of Personality and Social Psychology, 74*, 735–752.

Major, B., & Schmader, T. (1998). Coping with stigma through psychological disengagement. In J. K. Swim & C. Stangor (Eds.), *Prejudice: The target's perspective*. San Diego, CA: Academic Press, Inc.

Major, B., Zubek, J. M., Cooper, M. L., Cozzarelli, C., & Richards, C. (1997). Mixed messages: Implications of social conflict and social support within close relationships for adjustment to a stressful life event. *Journal of Personality and Social Psychology, 72*(6), 1349–1363.

McCoy, S. K., & Major, B. (2003). Group identification moderates emotional responses to perceived prejudice. *Personality and Social Psychology Bulletin, 29*, 1005–1017.

McKenna, K. Y. A., & Bargh, J. A. (1998). Coming out in the age of the Internet: Identity "demarginalization" through virtual group participation. *Journal of Personality and Social Psychology, 75*, 681–694.

Mendoza-Denton, R., Purdie, V. J., Downey, G., Davis, A., & Pietrzak, J. (2002). Sensitivity to race-based rejection: Implications for African-American students' transition to college. *Journal of Personality and Social Psychology, 83*, 896–918.

Miller, C. T., & Downey, K. T. (1999). A meta-analysis of heavyweight and self-esteem. *Personality and Social Psychology Review, 3*, 68–84.

Miller, C. T., & Kaiser, C. R. (2001). Implications of mental models of self and others for the targets of stigmatization. In: Mark R. Leary (Ed.), *Interpersonal rejection* (pp. 189–212). New York: Oxford University Press.

Miller, C. T., & Major, B. (2000). Coping with stigma and prejudice. In T. F. Heatherton, R. E. Kleck, M. R. Hebl, & J. G. Hull (Eds.), *The social psychology of stigma* (pp. 243–272). New York: Guilford.

Miller, C. T., & Myers, A. M. (1998). Compensating for prejudice: How heavyweight people (and others) control outcomes despite prejudice. In J. K. Swim &

C. Stangor (Eds.), *Prejudice: The target's perspective* (pp. 191–218). San Diego, CA: Academic Press, Inc.

Myers, A. M. (1998). *Fat, stigma and coping: Relation to mental health symptoms, body image and self-esteem.* Unpublished doctoral dissertation, University of Vermont.

Neuberg, S. L., Smith, D.M., & Asher, T. (2000). Why people stigmatize: Toward a biocultural framework. In T. F. Heatherton, R. E. Kleck, M. R. Hebl, & J. G. Hull (Eds.), *The social psychology of stigma* (pp. 31–61). New York: Guilford Press.

Ogbu, J. U. (1991). Minority coping responses and school experience. *Journal of Psychohistory, 18,* 433–456.

Opotow, S. (1990). Moral exclusion and injustice: An introduction. *Journal of Social Issues, 46,* 173–182.

Pennebaker, J. W. (1993). Social mechanisms of constraint. In D. M. Wegner & J. W. Pennebaker (Eds.), *Handbook of mental control* (pp. 200–219), Englewood Cliffs, NJ: Prentice Hall.

Pennebaker, J. W. (1997). *Opening up: the healing power of expressing emotions* (Rev. ed.). New York: Guilford Press.

Pyszczynski, T., Greenberg, J., & Solomon, S. (1997). Why do we need what we need? A terror management perspective on the roots of human social motivation. *Psychological Inquiry, 8,* 1–20.

Quinn, D. M., & Crocker, J. (1999). When ideology hurts: Effects of belief in the Protestant ethic and feeling overweight on the psychological well-being of women. *Journal of Personality and Social Psychology, 77,* 402–414.

Rodin, M., Price, J., Sanchez, F., & McElligot, S. (1989). Derogation, exclusion, and unfair treatment of persons with social flaws: Controllability of stigma and the attribution of prejudice. *Personality and Social Psychology Bulletin, 15,* 439–451.

Rosenberg, M., & Simmons, R. G. (1972). *Black and white self-esteem: The urban school child.* Washington, DC: American Sociological Association.

Sidanius, J., & Pratto, F. (1993). The dynamics of social dominance and the inevitability of oppression. In P. Sniderman & P. E. Tetlock (Eds.), *Prejudice, politics, and race in America today.* Stanford, CA: Stanford University Press.

Smart, L., & Wegner, D. M. (1999). Covering up what can't be seen: Concealable stigma and mental control. *Journal of Personality and Social Psychology, 77,* 474–486.

Solomon, S., Greenberg, J., & Pyszczynski, T. (1991). A terror management theory of social behavior: The psychological functions of self-esteem and cultural worldviews. In M. P. Zanna (Ed.), *Advances in experimental social psychology* (Vol. 24, pp. 93–159). San Diego, CA: Academic Press.

Steele, C. M. (1997). A threat in the air: How stereotypes shape intellectual identity and performance. *American Psychologist, 52,* 613–629.

Steele, C. M., & Aronson, J. (1995). Stereotype threat and intellectual performance of African Americans. *Journal of Personality and Social Psychology, 69,* 797–811.

Tajfel, H., & Turner, J. C. (1986). The social identity theory of intergroup behavior. In S. Worchel & W. G. Austin (Eds.), *The psychology of intergroup relations* (pp. 7–24). Chicago, IL: Nelson-Hall.

Tesser, A. (1988). Toward a self-evaluation maintenance model of social behavior. In L. Berkowitz (Ed.), *Advances in experimental social psychology: Vol. 21. Social psychological studies of the self: Perspectives and programs* (pp. 181–227). San Diego: Academic Press.

Twenge, J., & Crocker, J. (2002). Race, ethnicity, and self-esteem: Meta-analyses comparing Whites, Blacks, Hispanics, Asians, and Native Americans, including a commentary on Gray-Little and Hafdahl. *Psychological Bulletin, 128*, 371–408.

Tyler, T., Degoey, P., & Smith, H. (1996). Understanding why the justice of group procedures matters: A test of the psychological dynamics of the group-value model. *Journal of Personality and Social Psychology, 70*, 913–930.

Wahl, O. (1999). *Telling is risky business: mental health consumers confront stigma*. New Brunswick: Rutgers University Press.

Weiner, B., Perry, R. P., & Magnusson, J. (1988). An attributional analysis of reactions to stigmas. *Journal of Personality and Social Psychology, 55*, 738–748.

Williams, K. (2001). *Ostracism: The power of silence*. New York: Guilford Press.

Wills, T. A. (1981). Downward comparison principles in social psychology. *Psychological Bulletin, 90*, 245–271.

5

The Role of Exclusion in Maintaining Ingroup Inclusion

CYNTHIA L. PICKETT and MARILYNN B. BREWER

In this chapter, we address the idea that being restrictive and excluding others from the ingroup may serve an important function for group members. Ingroup exclusion may be one way by which individuals are able to enhance their own feelings of ingroup inclusion. A second goal of this chapter is to explore some of the consequences of this greater exclusiveness for perceptions of the ingroup and the outgroup. We argue that due to their different concerns, peripheral group members and core members may hold very different perceptions of the ingroup and outgroup. In addition, a person's relative standing within the group may affect their perceptions of the intergroup context itself—that is, the extent to which they notice and defend against the proximity of a relevant outgroup. We conclude the chapter by considering some of the implications of this work for intergroup relations in pluralistic societies.

A curious phenomenon, which seems to occur across a variety of social groups, is that the staunchest supporters and defenders of a group's standards, values, and norms are often not the most typical or central members of the group. In fact, those who are the *least* secure in their membership status (e.g., new members of a group or marginalized members) are sometimes the most likely to adhere to the group's standards (e.g., Schmitt & Branscombe, 2001) and show bias toward other members (e.g., Moreland, 1985). For example, new pledges to a sorority house are often more likely, than the more senior sorority members, to wear clothing with sorority letters and to attend functions held by the sorority. Ironically, these noncentral group members may be even more likely than those who truly embody the group attributes to notice and punish others for violating the norms and standards of the group. When given the power, marginal group members may also be more discriminating in determining who should belong in the group and who should be excluded—for example, when it is time to decide on the next group of new pledges. Thus, individuals' status within a group, that is, established member versus newcomer, can have important implications for how these individuals behave and for the dynamics within the group (see Levine & Moreland, 1994; Moreland, Levine, & Cini, 1993).

Why does this phenomenon occur and what purpose does it serve for the individual? And perhaps more interestingly, how is it that someone who knows that their position within a group is threatened or marginal feels that they have the authority to judge whether others meet the standards for ingroup membership? The goal of this chapter is to address these issues and review research that indicates that being restrictive and excluding others from the ingroup may serve an important function for group members. Ingroup exclusion may be one way that individuals are able to enhance their own feelings of ingroup inclusion. To be able to say that another person does not belong in the group is perhaps the ultimate symbol of ingroup belonging. A second goal of this chapter is to explore some of the consequences of this greater exclusiveness for perceptions of the ingroup and the outgroup. We argue that due to their different concerns, peripheral group members (who are concerned about their ingroup status) and core members may hold very different perceptions of the ingroup and outgroup. In addition, a person's relative standing within the group may affect their perceptions of the intergroup context itself—that is, the extent to which they notice and defend against the proximity of a relevant outgroup. We conclude the chapter by considering some of the tradeoffs that group members may make in order to achieve feelings of secure ingroup inclusion.

THE DESIRE FOR INGROUP BELONGING

Before beginning a discussion of how individuals cope with marginal ingroup status, it is important to first consider why feeling marginal would be considered to be unpleasant and aversive for group members. Research on the need to belong (e.g., Baumeister & Leary, 1995; Gardner, Pickett, & Brewer, 2000; Nezlek, Kowalski, Leary, Blevins, & Holgate, 1997) suggests that individuals require connectedness and belonging with others in order to function optimally. Rejection and exclusion from social relationships takes a toll on its targets and can lead to anxiety (Baumeister & Tice, 1990), negative affect (Marcus & Askari, 1999; Williams, Cheung, & Choi, 2000) and depressed self-esteem (Leary, 1990; Leary, Tambor, Terdal, & Downs, 1995). When this rejection occurs over long periods of time loneliness (Jones, 1990; Jones, & Carver, 1991; Peplau & Perlman, 1982) and depression (Leary, 1990) may result. The clear message from these various lines of research is that without belonging and connectedness with others, humans experience adverse consequences in terms of their health, adjustment, and well-being (Baumeister & Leary, 1995). Thus, marginal ingroup status may be distressing because it signals that a source of belongingness is threatened and may be stripped from the individual.

Attachment theorists such as Bowlby (1969) argued that individuals have a strong need to form interpersonal attachments and require intimate contact with others in order to feel a sense of security. Although focusing on the mother-child pair specifically, Bowlby (1969) argued that a "dynamic equilibrium" (p. 236) exists between the mother and child such that distance between the two is allowed to develop, but whenever the distance becomes too great, either the mother or the child is likely to become upset and act in ways to reduce that distance. A similar type of dynamic exists within groups. Membership in a group typically engenders a sense of similarity with the other members of the group and the knowledge (at least implicitly) that some tie or connection exists between the members of the group. These ties often imply an obligation to the group (i.e., that as a member you are expected to work in ways to promote and help the group). But these ties also imply that as a group member, one can rely on the other members of the group for support, security, and safety. For this reason, too much distance (psychologically or physically) between the self and the group can lead to distress, as it implies a lack of self-ingroup attachment and the potential loss of the ingroup as a source of support.

Following this logic, Smith, Murphy, and Coats (1999) recently applied an attachment-theory perspective to social groups. Smith et al. proposed that two dimensions underlie attachment to groups—*attachment anxiety* and *avoidance*. Secure ingroup attachment involves being low in attachment anxiety (i.e., feeling like a worthy group member and expecting groups to be accepting) and being low in avoidance (i.e., accepting of dependency and intimacy within groups). In other words, security within groups involves both the willingness to rely on the group and the belief that the group will be supportive of the self in times of need. What is important to note about Smith et al.'s analysis is that they argued that individuals differ in how they relate to their ingroups and that issues of attachment (the extent to which one is accepted within the group and the extent to which one feels worthy of that group membership) can be more or less problematic for group members. For a variety of reasons (which may or may not be based in reality) group members may feel that they are not truly accepted or valued in the group. These feelings and insecurities should lead to actions that would enhance belonging, for example, finding ways to please the group and conforming to group norms. Interestingly, Smith et al. note that a person who scores low on their scale of avoidance (meaning that the person desires closeness with the group) and who is high in group identification, that is, considers the group to be an important part of the self, might also be high in attachment anxiety. In other words, this person's experience with the group might be characterized by worries of acceptance and fears of rejection by the group, and this person should be quite vigilant for anything that signals the potential loss of the security that the group provides. It is this worry and fear that is predicted to lead to behaviors that would increase belonging in order to reduce this anxiety.

The attachment theory model offered by Smith et al. (1999) presumes that the various attachment styles represent relatively stable individual differences and that group members may differ from each other in their scores on the attachment anxiety and avoidance scales, and thus differ in their attachment styles. However, it is also possible to consider differences in the desire for ingroup inclusion and belonging in terms of intraindividual variation. In different situations and at different points in time, the same individual may require more or less ingroup inclusion. This is the perspective taken by optimal distinctiveness theory (ODT; Brewer, 1991, 1993; Brewer & Pickett, 1999). According to ODT, the need for assimilation is a fundamental human motive. But unlike theories that suggest that individuals achieve a sense of belonging through interpersonal relationships and similarity to other individuals (e.g., Baumeister & Leary, 1995; Codol, 1984; Snyder & Fromkin, 1980), ODT stresses the importance of social identities as a basis for assimilation need satisfaction. Identification with social groups involves the depersonalization of the self (Turner, Hogg, Oakes, Reicher, & Wetherell, 1987) such that the self becomes defined by the group's attributes, and the most salient features of the self-concept are those that the person has in common with the other members of the group (Brewer, 1991). Because of this depersonalization, group identification can be thought of as the expansion of the self to include others, which results in feelings of similarity and closeness to the other members of the group. Because of the role that group identities serve in meeting individuals' need for assimilation, marginal group status should be distinctly threatening because it implies that the group member may not really be that similar or close to the other members of the group, which would then lead to less need satisfaction. Thus, as an individual's status in the group changes, his or her need for assimilation should also vary accordingly.

Taken together, this body of research suggests that group memberships are quite important because they meet individuals' needs for belongingness, security, and assimilation. When a member of a group is led to believe that he or she is not a typical group member or is not fully accepted as part of the group, the person should experience distress to the extent that the person relies on that particular group for the satisfaction of belongingness, security, or assimilation needs. The question that we now turn to is what can group members do to attempt to reestablish secure ingroup standing. We will focus first on some fairly routine methods for achieving greater inclusion, and then examine how the exclusion of others may also be used to achieve this end.

ESTABLISHING INGROUP INCLUSION

Altering the Self as a Means of Attaining Ingroup Inclusion

Although individuals may be acknowledged as being members of a particular social group, these individuals can vary greatly in their prototypicality.

According to self-categorization theory, "the more a group member differs from outgroup members and the less he or she differs from other ingroup members (i.e., the more this person exemplifies what ingroup members share and what they do not share with the outgroup), the more that individual will be perceived as prototypical of the group" (Oakes, Haslam, & Turner, 1998, p. 80). Thus, if a person feels threatened by the fact that he or she is a marginal or peripheral group member, then one way of fixing the problem is to alter the self to become more prototypical.

In our own laboratory, we have demonstrated that threatening an individual's standing in the group, that is, giving the person feedback that indicates that he or she is on the margins of the ingroup, resulted in increased levels of self-stereotyping. Adopting the traits that are considered to be stereotypical of the ingroup and considering them to be more self-descriptive aligns the self more closely with the ingroup and makes a person appear more prototypical of the group. In these studies (Pickett, Bonner, & Coleman, 2002), we experimentally aroused participants' need for assimilation by telling them that their score on a personality test was very discrepant from the typical or average score of other ingroup members. (Control or no-need-arousal participants were told that their score was quite close to the ingroup mean.) Importantly, across these studies, some participants were told that their score was discrepant and far below the ingroup mean, whereas other participants were told that their score was discrepant and far *above* the ingroup mean. Participants were then provided with a list of traits and embedded in this list were traits that had been pretested as being stereotypical of the ingroup in addition to several stereotype-irrelevant traits.

We predicted that compared to controls, participants who felt marginal would rate the stereotype-relevant traits as being more descriptive of themselves, that is, engage in greater self-stereotyping. We also predicted that this self-stereotyping response would occur regardless of the direction of the self-ingroup discrepancy, that is, being either above or below the ingroup mean. In both cases, an individual should feel as if his or her position within the ingroup is threatened. This is not to say, however, that directional differences do not impact perceptions of prototypicality (see Abrams, Marques, Bown, & Dougill, 2002; Abrams, Marques, Bown, & Henson, 2000). A near-peripheral position (a placement within the ingroup that is close to the distribution or mean of an outgroup) is usually experienced as more threatening than a far-peripheral position (a placement within the ingroup that is farther away from the distribution or mean of an outgroup). And deviance in an antinorm direction is typically perceived as more deviant than deviance in a pronorm direction (e.g., Abrams et al., 2000). But in both situations, individuals should be motivated to achieve greater ingroup inclusion and therefore should exhibit increased self-stereotyping in response to feedback regarding their position within the ingroup.

Strong support was found for the predicted self-stereotyping response across the three studies (see Figure 5.1 for the data from Study 1 of

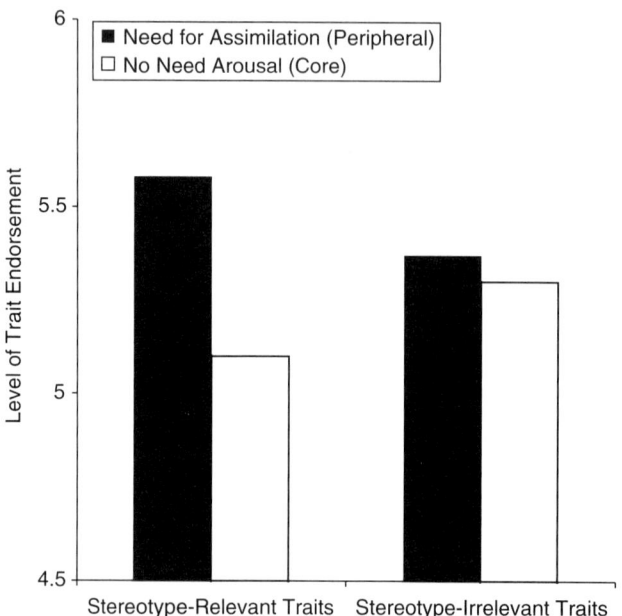

FIGURE 5.1 Self-stereotyping among university honors students. Adapted from C. L. Pickett, B. L. Bonner, & J. M. Coleman (2002). Motivated self-stereotyping: Heightened assimilation and differentiation needs result in increased levels of positive and negative self-stereotyping. *Journal of Personality and Social Psychology, 82,* 543–562.

Pickett et al., 2002). As shown in Figure 5.1, when participants were told that their personality score indicated that they are quite different from other members of the group (in this case university honors students), these participants compensated by perceiving stereotypical ingroup traits (but not the stereotype-irrelevant traits) as being more descriptive of the self. Study 2 of Pickett et al. (2002) indicated that this effect occurs regardless of the direction of the discrepancy (above or below the ingroup mean, although in both cases participants were in a near-peripheral position) and that identification level may moderate this effect when the stereotype of the ingroup is not overwhelmingly positive. In addition, the third study of this paper indicated that these self-stereotyping effects may have both private and public components. Participants in Study 3 were asked to describe themselves verbally to a hypothetical ingroup member (the ingroup in Study 3 was sorority members) and these descriptions were videotaped and coded for stereotypicality, that is, the extent to which the sorority member appeared to be *social, outgoing, snobby,* and *superficial.* These videos were also coded on a set of stereotype irrelevant traits—*mature, funny,* and *hostile.* As shown in Figure 5.2 (which are the results from the high identifiers in the study), marginal ingroup status led these sorority members to

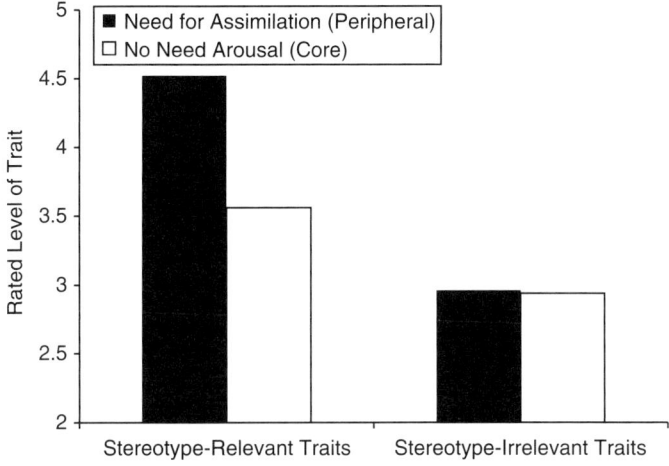

FIGURE 5.2 Stereotypical self-presentation among sorority members. Adapted from C. L. Pickett, B. L. Bonner, & J. M. Coleman (2002). Motivated self-stereotyping: Heightened assimilation and differentiation needs result in increased levels of positive and negative self-stereotyping. *Journal of Personality and Social Psychology, 82*, 543–562

present themselves in a more stereotypical fashion compared to control participants. These data suggest then that one response to marginal ingroup status (particularly among high identifiers) is to change how one perceives oneself and how one presents oneself to others.

Other researchers have found similar effects of marginal ingroup status on individuals' self-perceptions. Burris and Jackson (2000) gave participants who were either high or low on a measure of intrinsic religious orientation—the extent to which a person is devoutly committed to religion as an end in itself—false feedback that either threatened or bolstered their self-perceptions on a dimension that was important to religious group membership (helpfulness). Participants in the threat condition were specifically told that compared to other group members, they ranked lower in helpfulness than they actually perceived themselves to rank (as indicated by their pretest scores). Participants who were high in intrinsic religious orientation responded to threat by showing a significant increase in how identified they were with the group and how good and worthy they felt as group members, as evidenced by their scores on specific collective self-esteem items (Luhtanen & Crocker, 1992). From our standpoint, what is particularly notable about Burris and Jackson's (2000) study is that when the group membership was important, threats to the participants' standing in the group led to the compensatory response of seeing the self as *more* aligned with the ingroup.

One conclusion that may be drawn from these studies is that changing oneself to be more prototypical (to the extent that this is possible) is one potentially effective means of dealing with threatened standing within a group. However, changing the self is not the only option available for achieving greater ingroup inclusion. Although not immediately obvious as a strategy for gaining greater inclusion, in the next section of this chapter, we argue that excluding others may also be a way that marginal group members can bolster feelings of inclusion and ingroup belonging.

Exclusion as Means of Attaining Ingroup Inclusion

A principal task for groups is regulating group membership. Groups do not exist in isolation. To the contrary, a group is usually defined in relation to some other group, and the differences between the groups can be critically important to the existence of both groups. As noted by Turner, Oakes, Haslam, and McGarty (1994), social identities are "self-categories that define the individual in terms of his or her shared similarities with members of certain social categories in contrast to other social categories" (p. 454). What defines women and men are the differences between the groups, for example, the ability to nurse babies. Because the very definition of the group may rest on such differences, maintaining the integrity of the group requires that the group be comprised of individuals who possess the shared attributes of the group and who conform to the expected differences between the ingroup and the outgroup. Thus, if one were to consider a person who could not nurse children as a member of the category women, this would blur the boundaries between the ingroup and the outgroup and may be perceived as a threat to the group's existence.

For this reason, group members need to be fairly careful when judging whether others belong to the ingroup. Research on the ingroup overexclusion effect (Capozza, Dazzi, & Minto, 1996; Leyens & Yzerbyt, 1992; Yzerbyt, Leyens, & Bellour, 1995) demonstrates that when deciding the group membership of another individual, people are more careful when the individual is a potential ingroup member. The cost of making an error is more serious when judging a person as ingroup member versus an outgroup member, and thus group members tend to take more time (Yzerbyt et al., 1995) and employ more stringent criteria (e.g., Castano, Yzerbyt, Bourguigon, & Seron, 2002) when judging whether someone is a potential ingroup member compared to when the judgment is whether the person is a potential outgroup member.

This research suggests that ingroup overexclusion is a fairly general phenomenon. However, as noted by Castano et al. (2002), people may exhibit more or less ingroup overexclusion as a function of their levels of group identification and also perhaps as a function of their status within the group, that is, being a newcomer or peripheral member as opposed to a core member of the group. Displaying stronger overexclusion can be seen as a self-presentational method of demonstrating to the other ingroup members that one is truly committed and loyal to the ingroup (e.g., Noel, Wann, & Branscombe, 1995). However, in addition to these self-presentational reasons for exhibiting greater exclusion, marginal group members may be especially exclusionary because they are more concerned than core members with maintaining the integrity of group boundaries and the clarity of intergroup distinctions. As noted earlier, prototypicality is determined both by intragroup similarities and intergroup differences (Turner et al., 1987; Turner et al., 1994). A highly prototypical group member is someone who is not only very similar to other ingroup members but is also very different from members of the outgroup. Thus, prototypicality depends on the intergroup context and intergroup comparisons (Abrams & Hogg, 1990; Hogg & Abrams, 1988; Oakes et al., 1998).

What this means for the peripheral group members is that they not only need to be concerned with being similar to other ingroup members, but also concerned that they are not confused with the outgroup. Going back to the example of men and women again, if a defining intergroup distinction is that men have short hair and women have long hair, then a woman who feels that her status in the group women is marginal (perhaps because she has medium-length hair) should want to change herself to be more prototypical—that is, grow her hair longer. But at the same time, this woman should also be concerned that it is indeed the case that all members of the outgroup have short hair and that all members of the ingroup have long hair. If this distinction were blurred, then it would then call into question the validity of the dimension on which the woman was attempting to assert her prototypicality. The ideal situation would be for the woman to have long hair and know that the only other longhaired people in the ingroup are women and all short-haired people are men. Then she can be assured that her long hair stands up as a badge of secure ingroup inclusion.

This line of reasoning may seem paradoxical because it is possible to imagine that another response to marginal ingroup status would be to simply relax the group boundaries and define the ingroup more flexibly. This indeed may be the typical response of people who are not identified with the group and who do not use the group as a basis for need satisfaction. However, the strategy of relaxing group boundaries would likely result in the marginal group member feeling that he or she belongs to neither ingroup nor the outgroup. If women can have short or long hair, then certainly having short hair would not call into question the woman's membership in the ingroup. However, given that men also have short hair, the lack of clear boundaries should act as a barrier to developing feelings of prototypicality. Without clear intergroup boundaries, it is difficult to feel like a prototypical group member, because what it means to be prototypical is in part defined by difference from the outgroup. Blurring the boundaries of the ingroup should result in feeling less inclusion and belonging because the marginal group member may feel lumped in with the outgroup or like a member of neither the ingroup or outgroup.

One piece of evidence that supports this notion is data that comes from our own laboratory (Pickett et al., 2002; Study 3) where we manipulated ingroup

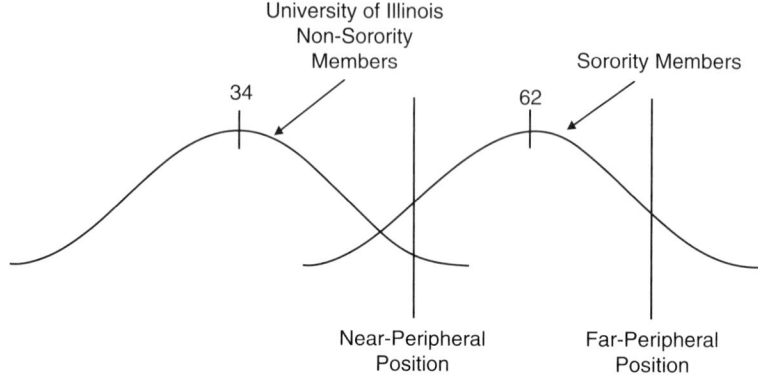

FIGURE 5.3 Feedback provided to participants to manipulate ingroup status and comparative context

status and the relevant comparative context (see Figure 5.3). More specifically, some participants were given bogus feedback on a personality test and were told that their score places them near the ingroup mean (only 1 point away). This was the control condition. Another group of participants was told that their score places them far above the ingroup mean (by 14 points) and also far away from the outgroup mean (by 42 points). In other words, these participants were in a far-peripheral position (see Jetten, Spears, & Manstead, 1997). Another group of participants were placed in a near-peripheral position, which meant that they were 14 points below the ingroup mean and only 14 points away from the outgroup mean.

In both cases, the near- and far-peripheral ingroup members were 14 points from the ingroup mean, but in one case (the near-peripheral condition) participants were also close to the outgroup mean which should have called into question how different the participant really is from members of the outgroup. What one would expect then is that the near-peripheral group member would feel less prototypic than the far-peripheral group member. This is indeed what was found. Participants in this study were asked how their personality feedback made them feel about themselves and were asked to provide a response using a 7-point scale anchored by 1 (*very different from other sorority members*) and 7 (*very similar to other sorority members*). Thus, higher numbers reflect greater perceived prototypicality. Although both the far- ($M = 4.58$) and near- ($M = 2.91$) peripheral group members felt significantly less prototypic than controls ($M = 5.79$), it was quite clear that the near-peripheral group members felt especially non-prototypic. The difference between the far- and near-peripheral group members was significant.

This supports self-categorization theory's notion that prototypicality is not simply a function of closeness or nearness to the ingroup, but that feelings of prototypicality are also derived from the intergroup context (Turner et al., 1987). When participants did not need to worry about being confused with outgroup members (the far-peripheral condition) they felt relatively less nonprototypic. Interestingly, even when outsiders are judging the prototypicality of a group member, they also take into account the intergroup context. Abrams et al. (2000) found that pronorm deviants (group members who deviate from the group norm by holding an extreme ingroup position) were seen as more prototypic than antinorm deviants (group members who reject their group's norms or favor the normative attitudes of an outgroup) even though both types of deviants were, of course, seen as less prototypic than normative group members. In addition, this effect was exacerbated when the intergroup context was made explicit as opposed to when participants were focused only on the ingroup (Abrams et al., 2000, 2002). These data suggest that perceived nearness to the outgroup is an important factor in determining a group member's prototypicality and that restoring feelings of prototypicality and inclusion will in some cases require marginal group members to engage in actions that would clarify intergroup boundaries.

So far, we have discussed the importance of intergroup distinctions for perceptions of prototypicality, but is it actually the case that marginal group members are more focused on maintaining intergroup distinctions than are core members of the ingroup? Our own research (Pickett & Brewer, 2001) and that of others (e.g., Schmitt & Branscombe, 2001) indicate that this is indeed the case. In one study (Pickett & Brewer, 2001), participants (who were all Arts and Humanities majors) were given bogus personality feedback, and some were told that their score was quite similar to other members of the ingroup (control condition), while others were told that their score was very different from other ingroup members and was, in fact, equidistant from the ingroup and outgroup (Natural Sciences students) means (a near-peripheral position). Participants then completed, as part of the study, an ingroup exclusion task adapted from Yzerbyt, Castano, and Seron (1998). In this task participants were presented with a list of 22 stereotypical traits of Arts and Humanities students and were asked to indicate which of the traits they felt were needed in order for someone to be considered an Arts and Humanities student at Ohio State University (OSU). The specific instructions were as follows:

On this page is a list of personality characteristics. What we would like for you to do is review these traits and then indicate which traits you believe are necessary in order for a person to be considered an Arts and Humanities student at OSU. In other words, if you were to meet an unknown person and wanted to be confident that that person is an Arts and Humanities student, which of the following traits must that person possess? It is important that you answer efficiently—in other words, please select the minimum number of traits that you believe are necessary in order to make an accurate judgment of whether the person is an Arts and Humanities student. Please indicate which trait(s) you have selected by writing them in on the blank lines at the bottom of the page.

The questionnaire was set up so that participants had to actively select traits that they felt were necessary in order for a person to be considered an Arts and Humanities student.

The ingroup exclusion task presumes that the more traits a person selects, the more restrictive he or she is being in judging who can be deemed to be an ingroup member. Furthermore, to the extent that membership in the group requires possessing more stereotypical traits, the group itself should become more distinct from the outgroup (Natural Sciences students). For this reason, we predicted that peripheral group status, which is assumed to arouse feelings of assimilation need, would lead participants to select a greater number of stereotypical traits compared to control participants. As predicted, peripheral group members selected on average 5.40 stereotypical traits as being necessary for ingroup membership, whereas control participants selected only 4.17 traits on average, and these two means differed significantly from each other.

Even though the peripheral group members had just received feedback indicating that they themselves are not typical group members, these peripheral members were the most discerning in judging whether another individual possesses the requisite credentials to be included in the ingroup. Again, this may seem paradoxical, and the adage that "people in glass houses should not throw stones" would seem to indicate that the most threatened individuals should be the least likely to cast judgment on others. However, because increased prototypicality is contingent on clear intergroup boundaries, marginal group members should be particularly sensitive to the intergroup context and, for their own sake, reject those who fall less clearly within the confines of the ingroup.

One implication of peripheral group members' desire to maintain clear intergroup distinctions is that they should evaluate more negatively those ingroup members who fail to maintain the distinctiveness of the ingroup. In other words, they should like other non-prototypical group members less than other prototypical group members. In a study involving men as the ingroup, Schmitt and Branscombe (2001) manipulated prototypicality by telling some men that they scored low on a masculinity scale and were well below the average range for men. This was the low prototypicality condition. In the high prototypicality condition, participants were given a masculinity score that placed them well within the average range for the ingroup. Participants then read about a prototypical male and a non-prototypical male and were asked to provide a rating for how much they liked each of the males. The results of this study indicated that among highly identified men, feeling peripheral led them to like the non-prototypical male less. Together with our own work (Pickett & Brewer, 2001), Schmitt and Branscombe's (2001) study suggests that feeling marginal can lead individuals to both dislike and actively reject non-prototypical ingroup members.

Much of the traditional work on social identity theory (e.g., Tajfel, Billig, Bundy, & Flament, 1971), focused on intergroup bias as a means through which groups achieve positive distinctiveness. Allocating more points to the ingroup versus the outgroup and evaluating the ingroup more positively than the outgroup can be seen as ways of asserting the difference between the ingroup and outgroup (and the ingroup's superiority). One would expect then that marginal ingroup status should affect levels of intergroup bias. Research by Branscombe and her colleagues (Branscombe, Ellemers, Spears, & Doosje, 1999; Noel et al., 1995) helps illustrate this idea. When an individual faces acceptance threat—feelings of insecurity regarding one's good standing within a group—that individual is expected to "experience an intrapsychic need to clarify what group he or she belongs to" (Branscombe et al., 1999, p. 51). Empirically, individuals have been shown to respond to marginal group membership by derogating outgroup members (Noel et al., 1995), adopting extreme attitudes (Wetherell, 1987), and by exhibiting ingroup favoritism (Jetten, Branscombe, & Spears, 2002). In general, each of these methods has the effect of distancing the ingroup from the outgroup. In addition, when made public, these actions can also be used to convey to other ingroup members that one is a good and loyal member of the ingroup (see Branscombe et al., 1999).

In summary, we have proposed that marginal ingroup members must take on the dual task of establishing greater similarity to other ingroup members and reifying intergroup distinctions in order to achieve greater ingroup prototypicality. Although only a handful of studies have directly examined the relationship between peripheral ingroup status and sensitivity to the intergroup context, the studies do converge on the same finding—that is, that peripheral group members seem to care more about ingroup–outgroup differences. Compared to core members, peripheral group members tend to dislike and exclude non-prototypical ingroup members more, engage in more derogation or 'sliming' (Branscombe et al., 1999) of outgroup members, and tend to evaluate the outgroup less favorably, especially when they anticipate becoming more prototypical in the future (Jetten et al., 2002).

Tradeoffs in Service of Attaining Ingroup Inclusion: Individual Versus Collective Self

A running assumption throughout this chapter is that individuals are generally quite concerned about their standing within their various ingroups because social groups meet certain basic level individual needs—that is, security and belonging. However, attaining secure ingroup inclusion may come at a cost—in particular, a cost to the individual's personal identity or individual self. It is often assumed that one of the primary goals of human existence is the attainment of positive self-regard and self-enhancement. Hence people may engage in a variety of strategies to promote the perception that they are good, worthy, likeable individuals—for example, strategic self-presentation (Jones & Pittman, 1982) and flattering social comparisons (e.g., Tesser, 1988). The issue that our present analysis raises is what potential costs to the personal self are entailed when striving to assimilate more fully into a social group, and, in particular, what happens when self-enhancement motives and assimilation motives are at odds?

First of all, it is important to note that when social identities are freely chosen, it is likely that individuals will choose to identify with social groups that are relatively positively valued in society (although positivity is not the sole concern in determining group identification; see Brewer, 1991; Hogg & Mullin, 1999). But to the extent that one's social groups are positively valued and possess positive stereotypes, then processes such as self-stereotyping should be fairly nonproblematic. When the traits that comprise the group stereotype are positive then perceiving these traits as being more descriptive of the self can enhance both personal and collective self-esteem (Luhtanen & Crocker, 1992). However, many social groups are not positively valued and are negatively stereotyped, for example, stigmatized groups such as racial and ethnic minorities. In these cases, being more prototypical may entail perceiving oneself in terms of the negative group stereotype and acting in a negative stereotypical manner (see Shih, Pittinsky, & Ambady, 1999). In our own research (Pickett et al., 2002) we found that when highly identified sorority members were given feedback indicating that they were peripheral, they engaged in greater negative self-stereotyping and more negative stereotypical self-presentation. More specifically, these women acted more snobbish and superficial than core members and believed that traits such as *materialistic*, *stuck-up*, and *spoiled* were more self-descriptive. Although measures of personal self-esteem were not included in this study, a question that these data often raise is whether the sorority members felt worse about themselves personally after describing themselves in such a negative manner. One can also imagine that behaviors such as outgroup derogation and purposefully excluding others from the ingroup may be at variance with individuals' personal standards and values. When this is the case, how do group members resolve this potential conflict?

In general, we believe that this situation is not as problematic as it may seem. As noted by Brewer and Gardner (1996), the individual and collective selves represent distinct levels of self-representation and are associated with different basic social motives. When the individual self (the individuated self-concept) is salient, self-interest is the predominant motivation. However, when the collective self is salient, then the basic social motivation is the collective welfare of the group. This suggests then that when group members are engaging in ingroup assimilation processes, they are most likely focused on the collective self and motives associated with the individual self are relatively less important. Feelings of self-worth and self-esteem are derived from the knowledge that one is a good and worthy *group member*, and not that one is a good and worthy *individual* per se (see Hogg & Abrams, 1988). In short, when collective identities are salient, the basis for self-worth shifts, and actions that might normally make a person feel badly about themselves when their individual self is salient may be a nonissue when the collective self predominates.

CONSEQUENCES OF MARGINAL INGROUP STATUS FOR INGROUP AND OUTGROUP PERCEPTIONS

An interesting implication of the greater focus on intergroup differentiation by marginal group members is that their perception of the ingroup may differ dramatically from those who are core members. Put differently, the view from the edge of a group may be quite different than the view from the center. This should be particularly the case to the extent that the dimensions on which the group is being judged are subjective and potentially malleable by the perceiver. In the previous section, we emphasized the importance of clear intergroup boundaries for the prototypicality of individual group members. Being stringent about who may belong to the ingroup and evaluating nonprototypical ingroup members less favorably are two means of maintaining intergroup distinctions. For example, Marques, Abrams, and Serodio (2001) found that group members judged a deviant group member more negatively when the ingroup was perceived as heterogeneous (i.e., lacking clear boundaries) than when the ingroup was relatively homogeneous. In other words, when the ingroup norm was insecure, group members were more motivated to derogate a deviant ingroup member in order to revalidate the norm.

However, another (and perhaps subtler) means of maintaining group boundaries is to alter mentally how one perceives the ingroup and the outgroup. More specifically, enhancement of both ingroup and outgroup homogeneity increases intergroup contrast, which reinforces assimilation within the ingroup. If a woman wants to see males and females as very distinct from each other, she may simply come to believe that, as a group, women are very similar to each other and men are very similar to each other. The woman may also call on the stereotypes that exist of men and women and perceive members of each of the groups as conforming more closely to their respective group stereotypes.

In the study by Pickett and Brewer (2001), these predictions were tested by asking peripheral and core group members (of the group of Arts and Humanities students) to rate how homogenous they perceived members of the ingroup and outgroup to be. As a measure of perceived ingroup and outgroup homogeneity, we used what Park and Judd (1990) term a "similarity task." In this task, participants were asked to rate how similar they believed Arts and Humanities students were along four different dimensions—personality, academic ability, social life, and in general. Participants made these ratings on a 10-point scale that ranged from (1) *large differences* to (10) *all alike*. Participants repeated the similarity task a second time for Natural Sciences

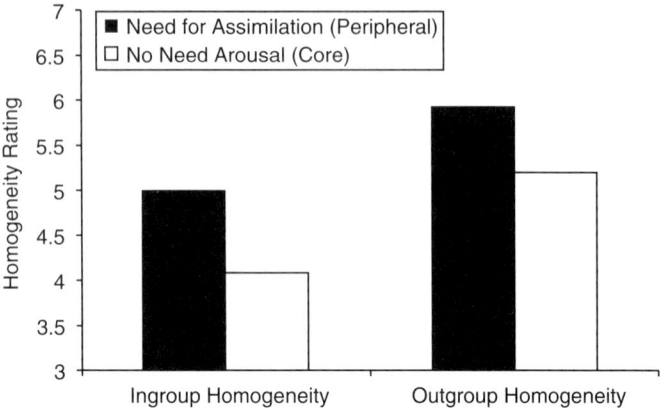

FIGURE 5.4 Perceived ingroup and outgroup homogeneity as a function of peripheral versus core ingroup status. Adapted from C. L. Pickett & M. B. Brewer (2001). Assimilation and differentiation needs as motivational determinants of perceived in-group and out-group homogeneity. *Journal of Experimental Social Psychology, 37*, 341–348

students, rating how similar they believed Natural Sciences students were in terms of the same four dimensions. Averaging across the four dimensions, a clear effect of ingroup status emerged (see Figure 5.4). Those participants who were given feedback that indicated that they were peripheral perceived both the ingroup and the outgroup to be more homogeneous than did control participants. This study was conducted within the framework of optimal distinctiveness theory (Brewer, 1991), which predicts that marginal ingroup status should arouse the need for assimilation. One method of satisfying this need (i.e., achieving greater ingroup inclusion) is to perceive the ingroup and outgroup as distinct from each other, which can be achieved via enhanced perceptions of ingroup and outgroup homogeneity.

In addition to measures of homogeneity, we also included measures of the perceived stereotypicality of the ingroup and outgroup. We used a version of Park and Judd's (1990) percentage estimates task. In this task, participants received a list of stereotypic traits of Arts and Humanities students followed by a list of stereotypic traits of Natural Sciences students and were asked to estimate the percentage (from 0% to 100%) of students within each of these groups that they believe possess each trait. Similar to the results from the homogeneity measures, peripheral members tended to see the ingroup ($M = 78.38$) and outgroup ($M = 75.45$) more stereotypically than did core members ($Ms = 70.41$ and 71.12, for the ingroup and outgroup respectively).

These results suggest that because peripheral ingroup status may motivate individuals (particularly those who are highly identified with the group) to establish clearer intergroup boundaries, peripheral and core members may end up perceiving the same group quite differently. Peripheral members may believe that the members of the group are fairly similar to one another, whereas core members may perceive much more heterogeneity in the group. Another implication is that core group members should not be as affected or bothered by the nearness of the outgroup as near-peripheral group members. In other words, being near the edge of the ingroup (and closer to the outgroup) should be especially threatening and may result in contrasting the outgroup away perceptually, that is, perceiving the outgroup as being more dissimilar to the ingroup than it really is.

Although we did not set out to test this hypothesis specifically, we do have some data that lend support to this idea. In Study 3 of Pickett et al. (2002), near-peripheral, far-peripheral, and core group members were asked to judge the perceived similarity of the ingroup (sorority members) to the outgroup (nonsorority members). Participants were specifically asked, "How did the feedback that about the SAQ make you feel about sorority members compared to other University of Illinois students?" Participants were given a 7-point rating scale that ranged from 1 (*very different from other U of I students*) to 7 (*very similar to other U of I students*) on which to provide their ratings. Although far-peripheral group members ($M = 2.79$) and core members ($M = 2.29$) did not differ significantly in their ratings of the perceived similarity of the outgroup to the ingroup, near-peripheral group members perceived more intergroup distance ($M = 1.78$) than did participants in the other two conditions. (The difference between the near-peripheral and far-peripheral conditions was marginally significant, $p = .09$.) These data suggest that where one stands within the group may play an important part in how one views both the ingroup and the outgroup, especially when the particular perception is malleable (e.g., judgments of similarity and difference).

Ironically, these differences in perception may allow core members to behave more freely within the group because their perception of what is "allowable" ingroup behavior is likely to be wider and more inclusive. In addition, core group members should generally be less threatened by and hostile to members of the outgroup because intergroup distinction is not as critical an issue for core members as it is for peripheral members. Thus, behaviors such as the formation of cross-group friendships and time spent with members of the outgroup may be influenced to a great extent by a person's position within the ingroup. Peripheral group members (who want to become less peripheral) may feel more limited in the activities that they can engage in and in the people that they can associate with because intragroup assimilation and intergroup differentiation are likely to be chronic concerns that may be compromised by certain actions on their part. Future research in this area should focus not only on the cognitive and affective consequences of peripheral versus core ingroup standing, but on potential behavioral outcomes as well.

IMPLICATIONS FOR PLURALISTIC SOCIETIES

In an earlier section we referred to possible trade-offs between personal self-enhancement and collective self needs in the pursuit of ingroup inclusion and differentiation. Similar trade-offs may be operative in the relationships between social identities at different levels of inclusiveness. Pluralistic or multicultural societies, for instance, are characterized as a system of nested identities with the nation-state as a superordinate identity encompassing ethnic or cultural group identities at the subgroup level. Pluralist policies are designed to promote strong and positive dual identifications at both levels of inclusion. However, it is often the case that cultural subgroups vary in status and representation at the superordinate level. A dominant majority group is perceived as prototypical of the national cultural identity, with minority subgroups relegated to marginal or peripheral inclusion. Under these circumstances, it is relatively easy for members of the majority subculture to identify at both their subgroup and the superordinate levels simultaneously. For them, subgroup distinctiveness and inclusion at the superordinate level are fully compatible since subgroup characteristics are central or prototypic of the nation as a whole (Mummendey & Wenzel, 1999).

For members of minority subgroups, however, there is less compatibility between meeting needs for differentiation at the subgroup level and inclusion at the superordinate level. As peripheral members of the superordinate, achieving inclusion involves eschewing aspects of their subgroup identity in order to assimilate to the national prototype and perhaps adopting a highly nationalistic form of national identity in order to secure their own inclusion by distancing from outgroup nations. Alternatively, they can choose to meet their primary identity needs at the subgroup level in which case any movement toward assimilation to the national prototype becomes a threat to ingroup distinctiveness and differentiation.

Consistent with this reasoning, a number of studies have found that among members of majority cultural groups, ethnic identification and national identification tend to be positively correlated. Among ethnic minorities, by contrast, this correlation is low or even negative, suggesting that national identity is perceived to be incompatible or in conflict with strong ethnic identity and loyalty (Sidanius, Feshbach, Levin, & Pratto, 1997; Sidanius & Petrocik, 2001; Sinclair, Sidanius, & Levin, 1998). At the same time, strongly identified minority group members may come to view the superordinate national group as homogeneous and overly inclusive. Assimilation to the national prototype then arouses the need for differentiation, protection of subgroup distinctiveness, and the risk of increased peripherality or exclusion.

This potential cycle of differentiation and exclusion presents a challenge to pluralistic ideology that seeks to promote both multiculturalism and national identification. Recognition and respect for subgroup differences are not of themselves sufficient to achieve both values. Rights and entitlements alone do not necessarily eliminate the trade-off between distinctiveness and inclusion. It may require a change in the nature of collective identity at the national level to eliminate the correlation between variation and deviance.

CONCLUSION

We began this chapter by considering why group memberships seem to matter so much to individuals and why being a marginalized member of a social group is often accompanied by a host of negative effects, for example, negative affect, anxiety, lower self-esteem (Leary, 1990). Because social groups satisfy very basic human needs (belonging, security, and assimilation), the potential loss of that group membership (as signaled by marginal ingroup status) can be extremely threatening. In response to this threat, individuals may attempt to change the self to become more prototypical, that is, engage in processes such as self-stereotyping (Pickett et al., 2002). However, because prototypicality is determined by both intragroup similarity *and* intergroup differences, marginal group members should also be very concerned (perhaps hyper-concerned) with maintaining clear intergroup distinctions and the integrity of ingroup and outgroup boundaries. Work from a variety of researchers demonstrates that marginal group members are more derogatory toward the outgroup (Branscombe et al., 1999; Jetten et al., 2002; Noel et al., 1995) and are more critical of nonprototypic ingroup members (Schmitt & Branscombe, 2001). When given the opportunity, marginal group members may also be more stringent in judging who should or should not be allowed to be a member of the ingroup (Pickett & Brewer, 2001).

In this chapter, we also considered some of the implications of marginal ingroup status for perceptions of the ingroup and outgroup. It is possible to make the ingroup and outgroup appear more distinct from each other by altering one's perceptions of how homogeneous the two groups are and of how stereotypical the group members are. Thus, peripheral group members should perceive the ingroup and outgroup as being more homogeneous than core members and should believe that the members of the group are more stereotypical. Our research (Pickett & Brewer, 2001) provided support for this hypothesis. Another implication is that marginal group members should be more sensitive to the relative distance of the outgroup (in terms of ingroup–outgroup similarity) than core members, and that this should be especially true for near-peripheral group members who are closest to (and thus more threatened by) the outgroup. Finally, we touched briefly on some issues of the potential costs and tradeoffs that are involved in attempting to achieve optimal ingroup inclusion. For individuals, positive self-enhancement and self-regard at the personal level may need to be sacrificed when engaging inclusion processes such as self-stereotyping and homogenization of the ingroup. For societies, national identity and tolerance for differentiation may come into conflict unless inclusion and distinctiveness are made fully compatible. Thus, the dynamic tension postulated by optimal distinctiveness theory underlies much of the politics of exclusion and inclusion.

REFERENCES

Abrams, D. & Hogg, M. A. (1990). Social identification, self-categorization and social influence. *European Review of Social Psychology, 1*, 195–228.

Abrams, D., Marques, J. Bown, N., & Dougill, M. (2002). Antinorm and pronorm deviance in the bank and on the campus: Two experiments on subjective group dynamics. *Group Processes and Intergroup Relations, 5*, 163–182.

Abrams, D., Marques, J. M., Bown, N., & Henson, M. (2000). Pronorm and antinorm deviance within and between groups. *Journal of Personality and Social Psychology, 78*, 906–912.

Baumeister, R. F., & Leary, M. R. (1995). The need to belong: Desire for interpersonal attachments as a fundamental human motivation. *Psychological Bulletin, 117*, 497–529.

Baumeister, R. F., & Tice, D. M. (1990). Anxiety and social exclusion. *Journal of Social and Clinical Psychology, 9*, 165–195.

Bowlby, J. (1969). *Attachment and loss: Vol. 1. Attachment.* New York: Basic Books.

Branscombe, N. R., Ellemers, N., Spears, R., & Doosje, B. (1999). The context and content of social identity threat. In N. Ellemers, R. Spears, and B. Doosje (Eds.), *Social identity: Context, commitment, content* (pp. 35–58). Oxford, England: Blackwell.

Brewer, M. B. (1991). The social self: On being the same and different at the same time. *Personality and Social Psychology Bulletin, 17*, 475–482.

Brewer, M. B. (1993). The role of distinctiveness in social identity and group behavior. In M. Hogg & D. Abrams (Eds.), *Group motivation: Social psychological perspectives.* London: Harvester Wheatsheaf.

Brewer, M. B., & Gardner, W. L. (1996). Who is this "we"? Levels of collective identity and self representations. *Journal of Personality and Social Psychology, 71*, 83–93.

Brewer, M. B., & Pickett, C. L. (1999). Distinctiveness motives as a source of the social self. In T. Tyler, R. Kramer, & O. John (Eds.), *The psychology of the social self* (pp. 71–87). Hillsdale, NJ: Lawrence Erlbaum.

Burris, C.T., & Jackson, L. M. (2000). Social identity and the true believer: Responses to threatened self-stereotypes among the intrinsically religious. *British Journal of Social Psychology, 39*, 257–278.

Capozza, D., Dazzi, C., & Minto, B. (1996). Ingroup overexclusion: A confirmation of the effect. *International Review of Social Psychology, 9*, 7–18.

Castano, E., Yzerbyt, V. Y., Bourguignon, D., & Seron, E. (2002). Who may enter? The impact of in-group identification on in-group/out-group categorization. *Journal of Experimental Social Psychology, 38*, 315–322.

Codol, J-P. (1984). Social differentiation and nondifferentiation. In H. Tajfel (Ed.), *The social dimension.* Cambridge: Cambridge University Press.

Gardner, W. L., Pickett, C. L., & Brewer, M. B. (2000). Social exclusion and selective memory: How the "need to belong" influences memory for social events. *Personality and Social Psychology Bulletin, 26*, 486–496.

Hogg, M. A., & Abrams, D. (1988). *Social identifications: A social psychology of intergroup relations and group processes*. London: Routledge.

Hogg, M. A., & Mullin, B-A. (1999). Joining groups to reduce uncertainty: Subjective uncertainty reduction and group identification. In D. Abrams & M. A. Hogg (Eds.), *Social Identity and Social Cognition*. Oxford: Blackwell.

Jetten, J., Branscombe, N. R., & Spears, R. (2002). On being peripheral: Effects of identity insecurity on personal and collective self-esteem. *European Journal of Social Psychology, 32*, 105–123.

Jetten, J., Spears, R., & Manstead, A.S.R. (1997). Distinctiveness threat and prototypicality: Combined effects on intergroup discrimination and collective self-esteem. *European Journal of Social Psychology, 27*, 635–657.

Jones, E. E., & Pittman, T. S. (1982). Toward a general theory of strategic self-presentation. In J. Suls (Ed.), *Psychological perspectives on the self* (Vol. 1, pp. 231–262). Hillsdale, NJ: Erlbaum.

Jones, W. H. (1990). Loneliness and social exclusion. *Journal of Social and Clinical Psychology, 9*, 214–220.

Jones, W. H., & Carver, M.D. (1991). The experience of loneliness: Adjustment and coping implications. In C. R. Snyder & D. R. Forsyth (Eds.), *Handbook of social and clinical psychology: The health perspective*. New York: Pergamon.

Leary, M. R. (1990). Responses to social exclusion: Social anxiety, jealousy, loneliness, depression, and low self-esteem. *Journal of Social and Clinical Psychology, 9*, 221–229.

Leary, M. R., Tambor, E. S., Terdal, S. K., & Downs, D. L. (1995). Self-esteem as an interpersonal social monitor: The sociometer hypothesis. *Journal of Personality and Social Psychology, 68*, 518–530.

Levine, J. M., & Moreland, R. L. (1994). Group socialization: Theory and research. In W. Stroebe & M. Hewstone (Eds.), *European review of social psychology* (Vol. 5, pp. 305-336). Chichester: John Wiley & Sons.

Leyens, J-P., & Yzerbyt, V. (1992). The ingroup overexclusion effect: Impact of valence and confirmation on stereotypical information search. *European Journal of Social Psychology, 22*, 549–569.

Luhtanen, R., & Crocker, J. (1992). A collective self-esteem scale: Self-evaluation of one's social identity. *Personality and Social Psychology Bulletin, 18*, 302–318.

Marcus, D. K., & Askari, N. H. (1999). Dysphoria and interpersonal rejection: A social relations analysis. *Journal of Social and Clinical Psychology, 18*, 370–384.

Marques, J. M., Abrams, D., & Serodio, R. G. (2001). Being better by being right: Subjective group dynamics and derogation of ingroup deviants when generic norms are undermined. *Journal of Personality and Social Psychology, 81*, 436–447.

Moreland, R. L. (1985). Social categorization and the assimilation of "new" group members. *Journal of Personality and Social Psychology, 48*, 1173–1190.

Moreland, R. L., Levine, J. M., & Cini, M. A. (1993). Group socialization: The role of commitment. In M. Hogg & D. Abrams (Eds.), *Group motivation: Social psychological perspectives* (pp. 105–129). London: Harvester-Wheatsheaf.

Mummendey, A., & Wenzel, M. (1999). Social discrimination and tolerance in intergroup relations: Reactions to intergroup difference. *Personality and Social Psychology Review, 3*, 158–174.

Nezlek, J. B., Kowalski, R. M., Leary, M. R., Blevins, T., & Holgate, S. (1997). Personality moderators of reactions to interpersonal rejection: Depression and trait self-esteem. *Personality and Social Psychology Bulletin, 23*, 1235–1244.

Noel, J. G., Wann, D. L., & Branscombe, N. R. (1995). Peripheral ingroup membership status and public negativity toward outgroups. *Journal of Personality and Social Psychology, 68*, 127–137.

Oakes, P., Haslam, S. A., & Turner, J. C. (1998). The role of prototypicality in group influence and cohesion: Contextual variation in the graded structure of social categories. In S. Worchel, J. F., Morales, D. Paez, & J-C. Deschamps (Eds.), *Social identity: International perspectives* (pp. 75–92). Thousand Oaks, CA: Sage.

Park, B., & Judd, C. M. (1990). Measures and models of perceived group variability. *Journal of Personality and Social Psychology, 59*, 173–191.

Peplau, L. A., & Perlman, D. (1982). *Loneliness: A sourcebook of current theory, research, and therapy*. New York: Wiley-Interscience.

Pickett, C. L., Bonner B. L., & Coleman J. M. (2002). Motivated self-stereotyping: Heightened assimilation and differentiation needs result in increased levels of positive and negative self-stereotyping. *Journal of Personality and Social Psychology, 82*, 543–562.

Pickett, C. L., & Brewer, M. B. (2001). Assimilation and differentiation needs as motivational determinants of perceived in-group and out-group homogeneity. *Journal of Experimental Social Psychology, 37*, 341–348.

Schmitt, M. T., & Branscombe, N. R. (2001). The good, the bad, and the manly: Threats to one's prototypicality and evaluations of fellow in-group members. *Journal of Experimental Social Psychology, 37*, 510–517.

Shih, M., Pittinsky, T. L., & Ambady, N. (1999). Stereotype susceptibility: Identity salience and shifts in quantitative performance. *Psychological Science, 10*, 80–83.

Sidanius, J., Feshbach, S., Levin, S., & Pratto, F. (1997). The interface between ethnic and national attachment: Ethnic pluralism or ethnic dominance? *Public Opinion Quarterly, 61*, 102–133.

Sidanius, J., & Petrocik, J. R. (2001). Communal and national identity in a multiethnic state: A comparison of three perspectives. In R. Ashmore, L. Jussim, & D. Wilder (Eds.), *Social identity, intergroup conflict, and conflict reduction* (pp. 101–129). New York: Oxford University Press.

Sinclair, S., Sidanius, J., & Levin, S. (1998). The interface between ethnic and social system attachment: The differential effects of hierarchy-enhancing and hierarchy-attenuating environments. *Journal of Social Issues, 54*, 741–757.

Smith, E. R., Murphy, J., & Coats, S. (1999). Attachment to groups: Theory and measurement. *Journal of Personality and Social Psychology, 77*, 94–110.

Snyder, C. R., & Fromkin, H. L. (1980). *Uniqueness: The human pursuit of difference*. New York: Plenum.

Tajfel., H., Billig, M. G., Bundy, R. P., & Flament, C. (1971). Social categorization and intergroup behavior. *European Journal of Social Psychology, 1*, 149–178.

Tesser, A. (1988). Toward a self-evaluation maintenance model of social behavior. In L. Berkowitz (Ed.), *Advances in experimental social psychology* (Vol. 21, pp. 181–227). New York: Academic Press.

Turner, J. C., Hogg, M. A., Oakes, P. J., & Reicher, S. D., & Wetherell, M. S. (1987). *Rediscovering the social group: A self-categorization theory.* Oxford: Blackwell.

Turner, J. C., Oakes, P. J., Haslam, S. A., & McGarty, C. (1994). Self and collective: Cognition and social context. *Personality and Social Psychology Bulletin, 20*, 454–463.

Wetherell, M. (1987). Social identity and group polarization. In J. C. Turner, M. A. Hogg, P. J. Oakes, S. D. Reicher, & M. S. Wetherell (Eds.), *Rediscovering the social group: A self-categorization theory.* Oxford: Blackwell.

Williams, K. D., Cheung, C. K. T., & Choi, W. (2000). Cyberostracism: Effects of being ignored over the Internet. *Journal of Personality and Social Psychology, 79*, 748–762.

Yzerbyt, V. Y., Castano, E., & Seron, E. (1998). *The ingroup overexclusion effect: The role of social identification and ingroup homogeneity.* Unpublished manuscript. Catholic University of Louvain.

Yzerbyt, V. Y., Leyens, J-P., & Bellour, F. (1995). The ingroup overexclusion effect: Identity concerns in decisions about group membership. *European Journal of Social Psychology, 25*, 1–16.

6

Exclusion of the Self by Close Others and by Groups: Implications of the Self-Expansion Model

TRACY McLAUGHLIN-VOLPE, ART ARON,
STEPHEN C. WRIGHT, and GARY W. LEWANDOWSKI JR.

This chapter examines the cognitive, affective, and motivational implications of the perceived exclusion of the self by close others and groups. Our examination builds on the self-expansion model and associated research, an approach which until now has focused mainly on the self's inclusion by close others and groups. Specifically, we extrapolate from existing findings and theory to consider why people seek to be included and avoid exclusion by others and groups, including a discussion of how social exclusion affects the way people perceive themselves. We then outline several strategies people use to avoid social exclusion, discuss the possibility that social exclusion is sometimes a welcome experience and conclude with suggestions for intervention and policy development.

THE SELF-EXPANSION MODEL

According to the self-expansion model (Aron & Aron, 1986; Aron, Aron, & Norman, 2001), the desire to expand the self is a basic human motive. Self-expansion is the desire to enhance one's potential self-efficacy by gaining or increasing one's access to material and social resources, perspectives, and identities (Aron & McLaughlin-Volpe, 2001). The model is similar to several theories of competence motivation, self-efficacy, intrinsic motivation, and self-actualization (e.g., Bandura, 1977; Deci & Ryan, 1987; Gecas, 1989; Higgins & Sorrentino, 1990; Maslow, 1970; Taylor, Neter, & Wayment, 1995; White, 1959). According to these theories, human beings are motivated to learn to control their environment, to experience themselves as capable and effective, and to bring themselves closer to their important life goals. The self-expansion model, however, differs from these other views of self-efficacy because it sees the desire to expand the self as primarily the desire to enhance *potential* efficacy—to gain access to the resources that make the achievement of goals possible. The actual achievement of goals is of only secondary importance. (For a recent elaboration of the motivational aspect of the model, see Aron, Norman, & Aron, 1998).

Further, according to the self-expansion model, one way that people gain access to desired resources, perspectives, and identities (especially when they may not be able to access these on their own) is by forming and maintaining close relationships with individual partners and with groups. In a close relationship, partners include each other into their self-conceptions, a process that affects how the partner is perceived and treated. Compared to strangers, for example, close relationship partners generally treat their partner to some extent as if they were self: They share important benefits with their close partners, see the world through their partner's eyes, and even—to a degree—take on their partners identities (Aron, Aron, Tudor, & Nelson, 1991; Aron & Fraley, 1999). In sum, the formation and maintenance of relationships with others appears to be a particularly satisfying and efficient way of achieving self-expansion because to the extent that in a close relationship one includes one's partner in the self, one can gain access to the partner's resources, perspectives, and identities (see Aron, Paris, & Aron, 1995).

Recently, the self-expansion model has been extended to consider the motivations for joining and identifying with groups (see Aron & McLaughlin-Volpe, 2001; Smith, 2002; Tropp & Wright, 2001). Wright, Aron, and Tropp (2002) propose that people are motivated to join groups, at least in part, because membership expands the self by offering access to the group's resources, perspectives, and identities. A person who, for example, joins a sorority can now access the material and social benefits this organization offers. In addition, the group becomes an important source of identity and the group's collective perspective (e.g., its worldviews, values, norms, etc.) can provide a framework for understanding and negotiating one's world.

To the extent that the inclusion of others and groups in the self allows for a rapid increase in desired potential self-efficacy, the experience is thought to be extremely pleasurable. Aron and colleagues (Aron & Aron, 1986; Aron et al., 1998) suggest that the experience of positive affect that accompanies self-expansion eventually functions as a secondary reinforcer and thus a motivator for self-expanding activities. Thus, initially, a desire to possess high levels of potential efficacy is the motivation for forming new relationships and joining new groups. However, over time the desire to experience the intensely positive feelings associated with the process of expanding becomes the primary motivation (cf. Pyszczynski, Greenberg, & Solomon, 1997). In addition, positive affect may function as a kind of measurement device for monitoring progress toward self-expansion, a notion similar to Carver and Scheier's (1990) self-regulatory process. Indeed, they argue that accelerations in the rate of progress in one's goals cause feelings of exhilaration.

Expansion of Self in Dyadic Relationships

The self-expansion model predicts that people will choose their friends carefully. Because we have only limited time and energy to invest in new relationships, we should be motivated to select friends who maximize our potential for self-expansion. In order to ensure optimal conditions for self-expansion, however, it is not enough to simply select those relationship partners who offer the most benefits. Self-expansion through self-other inclusion is much more likely when the relationship is stable and thus provides continued access to the partner. One way to ensure that a relationship will have a long life is to choose friends in whose eyes one is special and irreplaceable (Tooby & Cosmides, 1996). Consistent with this idea, people are attracted to high status others and report wanting desirable qualities in their partners, yet at the same time prefer partners who like and value them (Aron, Dutton, Aron, & Iverson, 1989; Baumeister & Wotman, 1992; Walster, Aronson, Abrahams, & Rottman, 1966). We also avoid relationship partners that limit self-expansion (Shaver & Buhrmester, 1983), who take advantage of us (Hatfield, Walster, & Traupmann, 1978; Leary, 2001), and who do not seem to value us (Kenny & Nasby, 1980). In sum, our desire to have partners and friends that offer maximal benefits appears to be balanced by the realization that only close and stable relationships with trustworthy and loyal others provide the ideal conditions for the achievement of self-expansion.

Expansion of Self through Group Membership

Group membership can provide multiple potential pathways to the achievement of self-expansion. Group membership gives the individual access to the resources (e.g., professional networks, protection), perspectives (e.g., a sense of history, a set of values), and identities (e.g., Lawyer, Canadian, Muslim) commensurate with that group identity. In addition, if membership is associated with interpersonal interactions between group members, it can provide the possibility of new interpersonal relationships and thus the inclusion of these individual others in the self.

Just as is the case for relationship partners, a group's attractiveness depends on the degree to which membership offers the potential for self-expansion. When group membership offers substantial benefits (in terms of the acquisition of resources, identities, and perspectives), people should be highly motivated to join and remain a part of the group. In support of this argument, people tend to be more attracted to higher status groups that hold access to a larger share of potential resources (Ellemers, 1993; Sachdev & Bourhis, 1991). However, because any opportunities for self-expansion provided by group membership depend on a person's standing within the group, the attractiveness of a given group should hinge importantly on whether or not the individual feels valued as a group member. People who know that they are highly desirable group members can not only trust that the group will be a stable and long-term source of self-expansion, but also that they will have priority access to the group's resources. Conversely, people whose status as group members is threatened cannot be sure that they will have continued access to the group's resources. Not surprisingly, threats to a person's status as a group member have been linked to efforts to strengthen one's position within the group (see Noel, Wann, & Branscombe, 1995) or when this is not possible to efforts to devalue the group (Dittes & Kelly, 1956; Snoek, 1962).

To summarize, people form close relationships with attractive partners and join desirable groups because access to the partner's and group's resources, perspectives, and identities increases their confidence that they can meet the demands of their world and achieve their goals. People who are successful in their attempts to expand the self-experience positive affect and increased self-esteem and these positive outcomes also serve as a secondary motivation for efforts to include others and groups in the self.

IMPLICATIONS OF THE SELF-EXPANSION MODEL FOR SOCIAL EXCLUSION

We propose that the self-expansion model offers a unique perspective on what it means to be excluded from dyadic relationships and social groups—why exclusion is generally an aversive experience—and offers specific predictions regarding the consequences of exclusion.

To the extent that the formation of successful bonds with others and groups is indeed an important avenue for self-expansion, exclusion from an interpersonal relationship or a group involves a direct loss to the present self as well as the loss of opportunities for future self-expansion. When we lose a valued relationship, for example, we not only lose the person's affection, but all the benefits that are and could potentially be provided by the partner. In addition, being rejected may make us feel less confident about our attractiveness to potential future relationship partners. Finally, along with the former partner people can also lose the social network associated with this partnership (Albrecht, 1980). According to one study, approximately 40% of the social network men and women had during marriage was lost upon separation (Rands, 1980), and the shrinking of one's social network in turn results in fewer new chances for social participation (Milardo, 1987). This is significant because the stability of a person's personal network ultimately impacts the individual's sense of self (McCall, 1982). Each person within the network provides a potential source of self-expansion. Therefore, the loss of each person in the network carries consequences for the self-concept similar in kind (if not in magnitude) to the loss of the partner.

The same logic applies to situations in which a person is excluded or rejected by a group. Being expelled from a group will result in a loss of all the psychological and material benefits that group offers. The predicted loss in potential self-efficacy would be exacerbated if this group is also a source of close interpersonal relationships. Thus, the self-expansion model predicts that social exclusion, whether by a relationship partner or a group, represents an attack on one's sense of self, and it is this assault on the self and the associated blow to one's sense of efficacy that, in part, account for the negative feelings associated with exclusion.

Cognitive Consequences of Social Exclusion

The self-expansion model suggests that targets of social exclusion lose access to important benefits provided by a relationship partner or group. To the extent that a relationship partner or group is included in one's conception of self, rejection is expected to result in reduced self-expansion, a stagnation of perceived self-expansion, or even negative self-expansion (a contraction of self). Usually focused on seeking out new opportunities for growth, excluded individuals must deal with a reduction in expansion potential or even a net loss in their sense of self. We propose that targets of social exclusion will be acutely aware of these changes in the self. They will feel less prepared to face present and future challenges and achieve future goals, and will experience decreases in perceived self-efficacy.

Research on relationship dissolution provides a vivid example of how people experience the predicted contraction of self. Recent divorcees commonly report feeling that they have "lost a part of themselves," "don't know who they are anymore," or feel "incomplete as people" because they no longer have access to the partner (Haber, 1990). Kohen (1981), for example, found that 60% of divorced women who were interviewed less than a year after relationship dissolution, used descriptors such as "nonperson," "not a part of life," or "depersonalized." Thus, relationship dissolution is painful because the loss of our partner quite literally deprives us of some of the resources, perspectives, and identities we use to construct our sense of self and thereby threatens our personal identity (Weigart & Hastings, 1977).

In a direct test of the self-expansion model in the context of social exclusion by a desired group, McLaughlin-Volpe (2002) hypothesized that students who had just found out that they had not been accepted into the sorority or fraternity of their choice would experience a contraction of self. Compared to students who had been accepted, they were expected to describe themselves with fewer self-attributes and report lower levels of self-efficacy. Indeed, taking into account each person's possibly self-expanding (experiences of acceptance) and contracting (experiences of rejection) events during the previous month, it was found that students with a negative balance (experiences of rejection outweighed experiences of acceptance) spontaneously listed significantly fewer unique self-descriptions, a smaller proportion of positive to negative self-descriptions, and reported significantly lower levels of self-efficacy. Thus, experiencing social exclusion had long-term consequences on a person's self-concept, and was associated with a much less diverse and expanded sense of self, more negative perceptions of self, and reduced levels of potential self-efficacy. In addition to changes in self-concept, rejected students also reported significantly more negative mood overall, as well as lower levels of self-esteem and life satisfaction. Affective consequences of social exclusion will be discussed in the next section.

Affective Consequences of Social Exclusion

The self-expansion model predicts that all forms of social exclusion are affectively unpleasant because they threaten the fulfillment of a basic drive. Deprived of their vehicle for self-expansion, targets of exclusion are unable to experience the pleasurable emotions that typically accompany self-expanding activities. To the extent that a relationship partner or group is seen as providing psychological and physical resources important for the achievement of goals (and/or as having the potential to provide these resources in the future), exclusion can seriously diminish present and potential self-efficacy. This loss of self-efficacy in turn can serve to undermine one's sense of control, a state that has been shown to be associated with a variety of negative outcomes, including feeling helpless, anxious, frustrated, and angry (e.g., Abramson, Seligman, & Teasdale, 1978; Deci & Ryan, 1991; Dweck & Leggett, 1988; Skinner, 1992).

Additionally, negative feelings such as sadness, anger, and possibly shame could result when the loss of acceptance spawns self-doubt as to whether one will be attractive to other desirable partners or groups. Finally, any negative effects resulting from social exclusion will likely be multiplied when a person is excluded from a group that also serves as a source of interpersonal relationships.

A large body of research has documented that people are generally very sensitive to social exclusion and respond to it with a range of negative emotions, including diminished self-esteem (Parkes, 1972; Spanier & Casto, 1979), depression (Hetherington, Cox, & Cox, 1978; Spanier & Casto, 1979; Sprecher, 1994), anger (Hetherington et al., 1978), anxiety, frustration, and despair (e.g., Leary, 1990). When anger is experienced it is often directed at the source of the exclusion (Pepitone & Wilpizeski, 1960). In a powerful illustration of the effects of even brief instances of social exclusion by two strangers, Geller, Goodstein, Silver, and Sternberg (1974) found that participants who were ignored by two confederates subsequently described themselves as alone, withdrawn, shy, anxious, and frustrated.

Other evidence for the affective consequences of social exclusion is provided by studies on the effects of perceived discrimination. Discrimination can be considered a form of social exclusion because experiences of discrimination communicate to their targets that they are not part of the ingroup and not valued as potential group members (Crocker, Major, & Steele, 1998). Affective responses to discrimination are strikingly similar to the responses documented in studies on the effects of rejection and ostracism. For example, Swim, Hyers, Cohen, and Ferguson (2001) reported that daily experiences with sexism were associated with feeling angry, anxious, and depressed as well as with lower social state self-esteem. Similarly, experiences of racism are generally associated with anger, anxiety, hopelessness, resentment, and fear (e.g., Armstead, Lawler, Gorden, Cross, & Gibbons, 1989; Branscombe, Schmitt, & Harvey, 1999).

In sum, experiences of any kind of rejection and social exclusion are generally painful and associated with a variety of negative emotions. Self-expansion theory proposes that these emotions are in part the result of the realization that one is denied access to the resources, perspectives, and identities of another or a group, which would have been available to the self had one not been excluded. Thus, exclusion represents the frustration of one's desire to expand the self, enhance potential self-efficacy, and experience the positive affect that accompanies this process.

Behavioral Consequences of Social Exclusion

The self-expansion model proposes that people are motivated to engage in relationships and join groups that function as stable and reliable vehicles for self-expansion. When faced with the possibility of social exclusion, people may therefore try to safeguard access to the benefits associated with relationships or groups and to self-expansion opportunities more generally by engaging in a number of relationship maintaining behaviors. We propose that people will respond to potential exclusion (a) by attempting to maintain or improve the threatened relationship or group membership as these represent existing opportunities for self-expansion, (b) by seeking out new relationships with individuals or groups that can replace the expansion opportunities threatened by the possible exclusion, (c) by reemphasizing other existing relationships or group memberships and thereby maximizing access to the expansion opportunities these provide, or (d) by any combination of these strategies. Any of these can be employed as preventive strategies before exclusion actually occurs (Vaughan, 1983) or as coping strategies during and after exclusion. While it is possible that some people will try to regain a sense of self-expansion in more individualistic ways by, for example, focusing on the development of personal resources (e.g., career, education), the present discussion will focus on social ways of responding to exclusion.

Maintenance and Improvement of the Threatened Relationship/Group Membership

Considering that people often have substantial investment in existing relationships and group memberships, we would expect to see a bias in favor of behaviors directed at relationship repair and the associated maintenance of access to existing expansion opportunities. This strategy to deal with the threat of exclusion makes sense for a variety of reasons. First, we often value and get attached to the benefits we are used to, and may see them as especially important in the face of potential loss. Second, when confronted with possible loss, we may become risk-averse, preferring to focus on relationships we know rather than risk the uncertainty of new relationships. Third, if the other or group is highly included in the self, it may be difficult to find an equivalent substitute. And, finally, in the face of potential exclusion we may not feel confident that we will be able to attract a new relationship partner or group.

The self-expansion model thus predicts that people respond to threats of exclusion with attempts to prevent or reverse the exclusion in order to be able to hold on to the resources, perspectives, and identities provided by the partner or group. A strategy that may be useful in preventing exclusion is to emphasize one's loyalty to the relationship partner or group. In a close relationship, for example, one may be especially attentive or accommodating. Group members may demonstrate their group-worthiness by behaving like prototypical group members or by working especially hard on behalf of the group.

These predictions are supported by the finding that targets of social exclusion typically respond with creative attempts to ingratiate themselves to the partner or group. For example, people have been shown to respond to social exclusion by increasing their conformity to group norms, avoiding conflict, working especially hard on collective tasks that benefit the group, and generally trying to present themselves in the best possible light (Baumeister & Leary, 1995; Brewer & Pickett, 1999; Ezrakhovich et al., 1998; Geller et al., 1974; Snoek, 1962; Williams & Somner, 1997). Compared to people with high social status in a particular group, peripheral group members are more likely to engage in strategic self-presentation to gain or regain acceptance by the group. They have been shown, for example, to engage in outgroup derogation (Noel et al., 1995) and to increase their liking for prototypical group members (Schmitt & Branscombe, 2001). Targets of social exclusion also sometimes find ways to attach themselves to the group symbolically. For example, Ko (1994) found that compared to included high school students, socially excluded students were more likely to use the pronoun "we" when asked to recall football games of their high school team.

However, other research has found that targets of social exclusion, when given the opportunity to do so, sometimes retaliate against the source of exclusion (Geller et al., 1974; Twenge, Baumeister, Tice, & Stucke, 2001). Because our model predicts that in most situations targets of social exclusion will prefer to accommodate to the group and save the threatened relationship, it is important to consider the circumstances that would favor retaliation. In general, people are surprisingly reluctant to give up on relationships (see Baumeister & Leary, 1995), preferring not to burn bridges and even maintaining relationships that are currently not central in our lives. This makes sense because future changes in life circumstances may lead one to desire or need benefits that are not provided by current relationships, but could potentially be provided by one's less central relationships or group memberships. Furthermore, a person's sense of potential self-efficacy is likely to be linked, in part, to the number of potential friends and potential ingroups that he or she can call upon. Thus, we predict that expressions of aggression against relationship partners and groups should be limited to situations in which social exclusion is experienced as definite, irreversible, and possibly illegitimate. In situations where one feels powerless to prevent exclusion, retaliation may serve to at least reestablish a sense of personal control. For example, in studies where participants are directly rejected, given an explicit reason for the social exclusion, and realize that they can do nothing to change the situation, they tend to express hostility toward and show little motivation to interact with the sources of rejection or to remain in the group (Pepitone & Wilpizeski, 1960; Snoek, 1962).

Many, if not most, instances of social exclusion, however, are rather ambiguous. Judging from informal conversations with U.S. college students, social exclusion is frequently experienced as a sense that friends or group members seem to have withdrawn slightly, are not calling as much as they used to, or seem less loyal. However, these subtle cues never quite add up to a feeling of explicit rejection. Ambiguity of this kind may allow the target of social exclusion to maintain the belief that not all is lost, that one's relationship or group status could improve. As long as targets perceive some hope for renewed inclusion, they should be motivated to appease the partner or group. In support of this idea, Ezrakhovich et al. (1998) found that ostracized participants worked harder on a subsequent group task when the reason for the ostracism was unclear, but not when it was clear. Similarly, Somner, Williams, Ciarocco, and Baumeister (2001) examined how much control participants felt they had over a situation depending on whether or not they knew why they were ostracized, and found that compared to participants who knew the reason for the ostracism, those who did not know it reported a greater sense of control. In sum, ambiguity in situations of social exclusion (e.g., the partner did not explicitly break off the relationship), while certainly stressful, may leave the target hope that the other(s) may be receptive to efforts to repair the relationship.

Seeking Out New Social Relationships with Individuals and Groups   A person, however, whose relationship has completely dissolved or

who has been explicitly expelled from a group would be expected to direct any attempts to restore a sense of potential self-efficacy at alternative sources of self-expansion. In cases where social exclusion is not ambiguous, we would therefore expect people to seek out new social relationships with individuals or groups, in an effort to maintain potential self-efficacy by acquiring new sources of self-expansion. There is some evidence that this is a fairly common strategy in the face of relationship dissolution: People often recover from heartbreak by engaging in a new romantic relationship (Baumeister & Dhavale, 2001). Hetherington et al. (1978) report that the year following divorce is often filled with a flurry of social activity during which men emphasize new social relationships, and that the most important factor for postdivorce adjustment is the establishment of new intimate relationships.

An experiment by Williams, Cheung, and Choi (2001) showed that people who are excluded by groups may use similar strategies. Participants playing a computer game in which they believed to be tossing a virtual flying disk with two other participants, were systematically excluded by the other players. In a subsequent perceptual judgment task with a different group, those people who had been excluded were more likely to conform to the new group, presumably in an effort to ingratiate themselves to this group. In other experiments, participants openly expressed that they would rather join a different group than engage in a group task with the ostracizing group (Predmore & Williams, 1983; Snoek, 1962). Also relevant are studies that suggest that targets of social exclusion appear to actively scan their environment for social opportunities. For example, Zadro & Williams (1998) found that participants who had been ostracized during a role-playing paradigm were more likely to overestimate the extent to which they thought that other people would agree with their attitudes and behaviors. While this finding has been interpreted as an attempt to regain a sense of belonging and control by assuming similarity, it could also simply be a way of signaling that one is available for a new relationship. Similarly, Gardner, Pickett, and Brewer (2000) demonstrated that regardless of whether participants were excluded from a dyad or a group in a simulated computer chat-room, they developed a memory bias for social events (both interpersonal and collective social events) when asked to recall events from a diary of an unknown person. That is, only those participants who had been excluded (and not those who had been accepted) selectively remembered explicitly social events, suggesting that when expansion of self is prevented, people seem motivated to redirect energies toward the fulfillment of this need (cf. Williams & Sommer, 1997).

Reemphasizing Already Existing Relationships/Group Memberships
A third strategy for maintaining expansion opportunities in the face of exclusion may be to emphasize already existing relationships with individuals and groups. To explain how existing relationships can serve to maintain

self-expansion, we have to first reiterate that the potential for self-expansion in relationships hinges on two variables: the attractiveness of the other or group in terms of the benefits they can provide and the willingness of the other or group to facilitate or at least permit perceived access to these benefits. (Some of the benefits provided by others and groups only require the partner or group to not actively interfere with the experience of the benefit, such as the benefit of identity or belonging or having the status of a best friend.) Thus, a good strategy for maximizing one's self-expansion potential is to seek out willing partners and groups that offer important benefits and invest in these relationships so that they become close and stable. Due to time-constraints, most people selectively invest in only a few relationships at a time. To the extent that a person also maintains some relationships and group memberships at a superficial level, these can become important sources of self-expansion when more central relationships begin to disintegrate. For example, Albrecht (1980) reports that following divorce, men *increased* participation in social clubs and organizations and women formed stronger bonds with family members.

Evidence for this hypothesis also comes from studies that examine peoples' responses to prejudice and discrimination. A number of studies have found that perceived prejudice and discrimination (i.e., exclusion), leads members of devalued groups to intensify their identification with their ingroup (e.g., Branscombe et al., 1999; Chavira & Phinney, 1991; Dion, 1975). Identification with one's own group in turn is related to well-being, lower depression (Arroyo & Zigler, 1995; Munford, 1994), higher self-esteem (e.g., Bat-Chava, 1994; Phinney, 1989; Rowley, Sellers, Chavous, & Smith, 1998), and more general psychological adjustment (Arroyo & Zigler, 1995). Thus, while it is possible that focusing on existing relationships also serves to reassure us of our worth (self-affirmation), many studies that examine peoples' responses to prejudice and discrimination suggest that reemphasizing existing relationships or group memberships can provide benefits that are consistent with self-expansion (e.g., Wong, Eccles, & Sameroff, 2003): Targets of discrimination often creatively adapt their "social interaction strategies in an attempt to achieve goals despite the existence of prejudice" (Miller & Kaiser, 2001, p. 83).

Imaginary Relationships with Individuals or Groups: Posing and Passing as a Group Member

There may be other, creative ways of dealing with exclusion while maintaining at least partial access to the benefits a person or group has to offer. As discussed earlier, when a group or person is perceived to represent a very large opportunity for self-expansion (i.e., one with extremely high status) rejection may be difficult to accept. It may seem impossible to find an alternative that could replace this partner or group, resulting in a strong desire to hold on at all costs. But what can a person do, who has been completely rejected and whose attempts to repair the relationship have failed? One strategy would be to pretend that the rejection has never occurred and continue to act as if one still was the spouse of a powerful person or the member of a prestigious group. Thus by living with an "assumed identity," a person may continue to access the group's perspectives (e.g., a particular worldview), and possibly even some of the group's resources (e.g., status). This type of strategy can make sense in situations where the individual can easily pass as a member of the desired group. For example, residents of what used to be East Germany are still frequently discriminated against when competing for jobs with former West Germans. To the extent that a person can successfully pass off as a West German (i.e., hide his or her East-German background and accent), he or she can gain access to desired resources (e.g., jobs). Obviously, this strategy comes with many costs to potential self-expansion, such as the stress of maintaining the pretense and the risk of discovery.

In sum, the self-expansion model predicts that the threat of social exclusion and the accompanying loss of potential self-efficacy will be associated with a diminished self-concept and negative affect. Thus, people have developed a range of strategies that can all be understood as means to help them maintain desired levels of potential self-efficacy in the face of social exclusion. These include efforts to improve or restore the threatened relationship, seeking out new sources of potential self-expansion including the reemphasis of a person's already existing relationships, and even maintaining an imaginary relationship with the desired person or group.

Variables that Influence the Choice of Responses to Social Exclusion

The self-expansion model suggests several variables that should moderate which of the several available strategies to maintain self-expansion a person would choose. In addition to the degree of exclusion discussed earlier, we propose that the desirability or attractiveness of the partner or group, the degree to which the person/group is included in the self, and a person's confidence in his or her ability to attract new partners or groups, should influence whether targets of exclusion choose to focus their energies on the existing relationship or whether they choose to look for alternative avenues for self-expansion.

Degree of Inclusion/Exclusion
When social exclusion is mild (as when group members express little interest in a person but do not explicitly reject him or her), a person may reasonably expect to be able to improve his or her standing in the group. However, when the rejection is explicit (as when a person is expelled from a group), efforts to repair the relationship are unlikely to improve matters. Snoek (1962) manipulated the severity of the rejection and found that strong rejection (whether attributed to personal or situational reasons) leads to a decrease in desire to rejoin the group and a parallel increase in

willingness to join another group. (See also Dittes & Kelly, 1956 for a study on the effect of perceived inclusion/exclusion on conformity.)

Desirability of the partner/group According to the self-expansion model, a person's motivation to reconnect to the rejecting partner or group depends in part on their desirability in terms of the number and kinds of benefits provided. Consistent with this prediction, Jackson and Saltzstein (1957) found that when a group is seen as highly attractive, even explicit social exclusion does little to reduce a person's attraction to the group. In fact, excluded group members rated the highly desirable group as even more attractive than accepted group members and conformed just as much to group norms in a subsequent perceptual judgment task. Thus, when a group is seen as highly desirable (i.e., when it is perceived to be a significant potential source of self-expansion), people appear motivated to remain in the group even in the face of explicit rejection.

The Degree of Inclusion of the Other/Group in the Self The motivation to hold on to existing relationships and resources should also depend in part on how close a person is to the partner or group (i.e., the degree to which the other/group has become included in the self.) People who feel especially close to another person and group members highly identified with a group are also likely to rely heavily on the benefits provided by the relationship or group membership. Findings from the divorce literature, for example, show that the more people were invested in their relationship and the more they relied on the partner for practical things and companionship, the more distress they experienced when the relationship dissolved (Chiriboga & Thurnher, 1980). Data from a diary study similarly shows that the effects of ostracism are stronger the closer the relationship is with the source of ostracism, and especially strong in the context of romantic relationships (Williams, Wheeler, & Harvey, 2001). Being ostracized by a friend or stranger had very little effect, but rejection from a romantic partner or family member was associated with high levels of concern and a strong need to apologize (and thus repair the relationship). Finally, Schmitt and Branscombe (2001) found that only group members highly identified with the group responded with attempts to ingratiate themselves to the group in response to information that their group-status was threatened.

High inclusion of the other/group in the self also means that "extraction" of that other/group from the self will likely be difficult and, even if successful, this extraction will likely result in a significant reduction in the size of the self (see page 117 for quotes from Kohen [1981] regarding divorcees' loss of self).

Confidence in One's Ability to Attract New Partners or Groups
A final moderator for how people will respond to ostracism or exclusion is the confidence they have in their ability to form successful new relationships with

individuals and groups. According to the sociometer theory (e.g., Leary, Haupt, Strausser, & Chokel, 1998), "... the self-esteem system ... is a subjective monitor or gauge of the degree to which the individual is being included and accepted versus excluded and rejected by other people" (p.1290). People low in self-esteem will thus have little confidence that they can easily replace their current relationship and would be expected to direct all their effort at repairing and regaining control of their threatened relationship/group membership (Somner et al., 2001). People high in self-esteem, on the other hand, are more likely to leave a relationship upon receiving ostracism than people low in self-esteem, presumably because they are more confident that they can form a new relationship (Somner et al., 2001). Finally, how confident we are in our ability to form new relationships may also depend on the size of our personal social network. Research on adjustment to marital separation finds that those individuals who engaged in more social activity during marriage and had maintained greater independence from their partner with regard to social and leisure activities were happier and less likely to be depressed after divorce (Chiriboga & Thurner, 1980; Thabes, 1997).

In sum, responses to social exclusion while generally directed at regaining a sense of self-expansion, are importantly influenced by several variables. These include the perceived degree of exclusion, the desirability of the person/group as a source of self-expansion, the degree of inclusion of the other/group in the self, and a person's confidence in their ability to attract new sources of self-expansion.

Positive Outcomes of Rejection/Exclusion

Social exclusion is widely held to be extremely aversive and, as we have seen, individuals devise many creative strategies to reverse or avoid its negative consequences. However, we propose that social exclusion can sometimes be a positive experience. Our discussion is inspired by findings that a substantial proportion of respondents in studies on relationship dissolution do *not* report experiencing distress (e.g., Stephen, 1987). Informal observations confirm that people sometimes provoke the breakup of a relationship and/or respond to experiences of social exclusion in unexpected ways by, for example, greeting the breakup with relief. Similarly, group members sometimes behave in a manner that they know will result in expulsion and former group members are sometimes quite happy to be free of the demands of membership. It seemed to us that these observations while puzzling at first sight can be understood within the framework of the self-expansion model. Specifically, we hypothesized that people provoke the breakup of a relationship or expulsion from a group or respond to such exclusion with relief when (a) the relationship partner or group is providing fewer benefits than expected and desired; (b) the relationship partner or group is limiting personal growth; or (c) the individual perceives access to other more desirable opportunities for self-expansion that are unavailable as long as the present relationship exists.

Relationships or Groups Provide Fewer Benefits than Expected and Desired When we enter relationships or join groups it is difficult to predict at the outset the extent to which these new experiences will allow us to gain new resources, identities, and perspectives. One reason for this difficulty is that people who are courting a potential partner and groups who recruit new members tend to present themselves in the best possible light. Over time and once the thrill and newness of the initial acquaintance process have passed, we may come to realize that a relationship or group has less to offer than we anticipated: Relationships grow boring, jobs fail to challenge, and groups are found to have little to offer. In such instances, people may welcome the termination of the relationship so that they can be free to pursue alternative avenues for self-expansion. In support of this notion, Sprecher (1994) found that boredom was one of the most commonly cited reasons for relationship breakups in college students.

Relationships or Groups Limit Personal Growth People may provoke or welcome social exclusion also when they feel that their ability to expand within or outside of the relationship or group is constrained. For example, people who desire more closeness than their partner, may feel that their partner is denying them full access to the benefits the relationship was expected to provide. Similarly, a marginal group member may resent receiving fewer benefits from group membership than central members of the group. In addition, people may welcome the dissolution of relationships that interfere with opportunities to expand in domains that are not directly related to the relationship (such as when a husband refuses to allow his wife to continue her education). In support of this idea, we find that the need for self-realization and personal growth has been linked to rising divorce rates (Thurner, Fenn, Melichar, & Chiriboga, 1983). Groups may also prevent their members from pursuing personal goals when these are seen as conflicting with the needs of the group. Street gangs, for example, have been reported to limit their members' ability to go to college.

Other More Desirable Oppportunities for Self-Expansion are Available A third possibility is that people provoke or welcome exclusion because they have opportunities for self-expansion that conflict with existing relationships or group memberships. We know, for example, that commitment in close relationships depends to a considerable degree on whether a person believes that he or she may be able to attract other more attractive relationship partners (Rusbult, 1983; Rusbult & Buunk, 1993). Because some partnerships—such as marriage—and some groups—such as certain fraternities—are exclusive and dictate that a person cannot belong to other potentially more desirable ones at the same time, they limit self-expansion. In addition, a person's ability to maintain a relationship or a group membership may be limited by constraints of time and energy because most relationships and group memberships require active maintenance behaviors (e.g., spending time with one's partner or group, going to meetings, paying membership fees, etc.). Thus, people may find themselves forced with a choice between two desirable and mutually exclusive partners or groups. Because it is impractical (and in most cultures frowned upon) to engage in more than one romantic relationship at a time, people will sometimes provoke a breakup in order to be free to pursue other potentially more expanding relationships.

While it is often possible to belong to several groups simultaneously, some groups demand exclusive loyalty and in other cases, time constraints, or value conflicts can force a person to give up one group in order to be maximally involved in another. In order to be able to join the more attractive group, the person may provoke exclusion from the original group by, for example, starting to miss important meetings or by violating group norms.

In sum, whenever peoples' needs to expand the self cannot be met (or at least are not optimally met) in existing relationships or groups, they may respond to social exclusion with relief because it allows them to pursue more suitable avenues for self-expansion or simply because they are now free from a relationship that restricted self-expansion through personal growth. We argue that just as people are motivated to protect relationships when they are self-expanding, they can also be motivated to abandon those same relationships when they find that these relationships cease to satisfy their expansion needs or when they have access to more desirable relationships.

IMPLICATIONS FOR INTERVENTION AND POLICY

The analysis of social exclusion from the perspective of the self-expansion model presented in this chapter was primarily designed to illuminate the reasons for why social exclusion is painful and how targets of social exclusion can be expected to respond to it. In the following section we suggest that the self-expansion model offers important insights for the analysis of social exclusion in applied settings. In particular, we believe that with the help of this framework it may be possible to identify those situations that are most likely to cause the strongest responses by victims of social exclusion as well as identify those individuals that may be most vulnerable in the face of social exclusion. At a recent symposium on social exclusion, audience members asked how the literature on social exclusion and ostracism can explain the actions of some of the perpetrators in the recent wave of high-school shootings, considering that some of the shooters, unexpectedly, were neither socially isolated nor lonely. Instead, they apparently had successful and stable social relationships. While there are undoubtedly a number of reasons for why these adolescents became determined to kill, it is interesting that in many cases they directed their anger primarily at the highly popular students (e.g., the "jocks") or the teachers—the groups that hold access to a large share of desired resources (e.g., status, power) and thus offer the highest potential for self-expansion (or the most power to deny desired self-expansion). Thus, individuals with strong self-expansion needs who feel that they have unjustly been denied access to desired self-expansion may be most likely to respond with anger and aggressive behavior.

Our analysis also points to the importance of social skills for people who are trying to overcome negative social experiences. As discussed, people engage in a wide variety of strategies to compensate for the experience of social exclusion and maintain their potential for self-expansion. However, in order for people to use any of these strategies, they must first acquire the requisite social skills. A lack of the social skills needed to form new relationships or join groups may identify those individuals most likely to suffer as a result of social exclusion and least likely to respond in socially desirable ways.

The self-expansion model also offers some suggestions as to how experiences of social exclusion and rejection can be buffered by the source of rejection. A graduate director who has to reject the majority of applicants to a popular graduate program or a coach who wants to exclude disruptive or ineffective team members can communicate his or her decision in a way that will help the excluded person understand that he or she can achieve self-expansion more optimally in other ways. One could, for example, make alternative sources of expansion available, minimize the perceived value of the program/team, and point out some of the person's strengths. These types of approaches may help people maintain adequate levels of self-esteem and self-efficacy in the face of rejection and give them the courage to approach other potential sources of self-expansion.

Finally, at the level of the institution, one may want to make sure that there are a wide variety of clubs, organizations, and teams available that provide opportunities for acceptance and self-expansion. Institutions in which a few select groups hold access to most of the resources are also most likely to create environments in which competition for membership in these groups is most severe and rejection is experienced as most devastating. However, a large and diverse offering of group memberships (that are all valued by the institution) may provide most students with the desired opportunities for belonging and self-expansion and create an atmosphere where the majority of students can achieve desired levels of self-efficacy.

CONCLUSION

In this chapter, we proposed that the self-expansion model can provide an integrative conceptual framework for understanding why human beings crave social inclusion in dyadic relationships and groups and attempt to avoid social exclusion. Self-expansion motives provide a novel motivational account of why people seek out close relationships and group acceptance and what determines their choice of relationship partners and groups, one that may prove a valuable complement to and could serve to integrate other existing perspectives. The self-expansion model further offers precise predictions regarding how people will respond cognitively, affectively, and behaviorally to perceived social exclusion and regarding the conditions that will moderate these responses. Finally, the self-expansion model provides a unique perspective on the conditions under which social exclusion may not be a universally negative experience.

REFERENCES

Abramson, L., Seligman, M., & Teasdale, J. (1978). Learned helplessness in humans: Critique and reformulation. *Journal of Abnormal Psychology, 87*, 49–74.

Albrecht, S. (1980). Reactions and adjustments to divorce: Differences in the experiences of males and females. *Family Relations, 29*, 59–68.

Armstead, C. A., Lawler, K. A., Gorden, C., Cross, J., & Gibbons, J. (1989). Relationship of racial stressors to blood pressure responses and anger expression in Black college students. *Health Psychology, 8*, 541–556.

Aron, A., & Aron, E. N. (1986). *Love as the expansion of self: Understanding attraction and satisfaction*. New York: Hemisphere.

Aron, A., Aron, E. N., & Norman, C. (2001). Self-expansion model of motivation and cognition in close relationships and beyond. In M. Clark & G. Fletcher (Eds.), *Blackwell's handbook of social psychology, Vol. 2: Interpersonal processes*. Oxford: Blackwell.

Aron, A., Aron, E. N., Tudor, M., & Nelson, G. (1991). Close relationships as including other in the self. *Journal of Personality and Social Psychology, 60*, 241–253.

Aron, A., Dutton, D. G., Aron, E., & Iverson, A. (1989). Experiences of falling in love. *Journal of Social and Personal Relationships, 6*, 243–257.

Aron, A., & Fraley, B. (1999). Relationship closeness as including other in the self: Cognitive underpinnings and measures. *Social Cognition, 17*, 140–160.

Aron, A., & McLaughlin-Volpe, T. (2001). Including others in the self: Extensions to own and partner's group memberships. In M. Brewer & C. Sedikides (Eds.), *Individual self, relational self, and collective self: Partners, opponents, or strangers*. Mahwah, NJ: Erlbaum.

Aron, A., Norman, C. C., & Aron, E. N. (1998). The self-expansion model and motivation. *Representative Research in Social Psychology, 22*, 1–13.

Aron, A., Paris, M., & Aron, E. N. (1995). Falling in love: Prospective studies of self-concept change. *Journal of Personality and Social Psychology, 69*, 1102–1112.

Arroyo, C. G., & Zigler, E. (1995). Racial identity, academic achievement, and the psychological well-being of economically disadvantaged adolescents. *Journal of Personality and Social Psychology, 69*, 903–914.

Bandura, A. (1977). Self-efficacy: Toward a unifying theory of behavioral change. *Psychological Review, 84*, 191–215.

Bat-Chava, Y. (1994). Group identification and self-esteem of deaf adults. *Personality and Social Psychology Bulletin, 20,* 494–502.

Baumeister, R. F., & Dhavale, D. (2001). Two sides of romantic rejection. In M. R. Leary (Ed.), *Interpersonal rejection* (pp. 55–71). New York: Oxford University Press.

Baumeister, R. F., & Leary, M. R. (1995). The need to belong: Desire for interpersonal attachments as a fundamental human motivation. *Psychological Bulletin, 117,* 497–529.

Baumeister, R. F., & Wotman, S. R. (1992). *Breaking hearts: The two sides of unrequited love.* New York: Guilford Press.

Branscombe, N. R., Schmitt, M. T., & Harvey, R. D. (1999). Perceiving pervasive discrimination among African Americans: Implications for group identification and well-being. *Journal of Personality and Social Psychology, 77,* 135–149.

Brewer, M. B., & Pickett, C. L. (1999). Distinctiveness motives as a source of the social self. In T. Tyler, R. Kramer, & O. John (Eds.), *The psychology of the social self* (pp. 71–87). Mahwah, NJ: Erlbaum.

Carver, C., & Scheier, M. (1990). Principles of self-regulation, action, and emotion. In E. T. Higgins & R. M. Sorrentino (Eds.), *Handbook of motivation and cognition: Foundations of social behavior* (Vol. 2). New York: Guilford.

Chavira, V., & Phinney, J. S. (1991). Adolescents' ethnic identity, self-esteem, and strategies for dealing with ethnicity and minority status. *Hispanic Journal of Behavioral Sciences, 13,* 226–227.

Chiriboga, D. A., & Thurnher, M. (1980). Marital lifestyles and adjustment to separation. *Journal of Divorce, 3,* 379–390.

Crocker, J., Major, B., & Steele, C. (1998). Social stigma. In D. M. Gilbert, S. T. Fiske, & G. Lindzey (Eds.), *The handbook of social psychology.* New York: McGraw Hill.

Deci, E. L., & Ryan, R. (1987). The support of autonomy and the control of behavior. *Journal of Personality and Social Psychology, 53,* 1024–1037.

Deci, E. L., & Ryan, R. M. (1991). A motivational approach to self: Integration in personality. In R. Dienstbier (Ed.), *Nebraska Symposium on Motivation: Volume 38. Perspectives on motivation.* Lincoln: University of Nebraska Press.

Dion, K. L. (1975). Womens' reactions to discrimination from members of the opposite sex. *Journal of Research in Personality, 9,* 294–306.

Dittes, J. E., & Kelley, H. H. (1956). Effects of different conditions of acceptance upon conformity to group norms. *Journal of Abnormal and Social Psychology, 53,* 100–107.

Dweck C. S., & Leggett, E. L. (1988). A social-cognitive approach to motivation and personality. *Psychological Review, 95,* 256–273.

Ellemers, N. (1993). The influence of socio-structural variables on identity management strategies. *European Review of Social Psychology, 4,* 27–57.

Ezrakhovich, A., Kerr, A., Cheung, S., Elliot, K., Jerrems, A., & Williams, K. D. (1998). *Effects of norm violation and ostracism on working with the group.* Presented at the Society of Australasian Social Psychologists, Christchurch, NZ.

Gardner, W. L., Pickett, C. L., & Brewer, M. B. (2000). Social exclusion and selective memory: How the need to belong influences memory for social events. *Personality and Social Psychology Bulletin, 26,* 486–496.

Gecas, V. (1989). Social psychology of self-efficacy. *American Sociological Review, 15*, 291–316.

Geller, D. M., Goodstein, L., Silver, M., & Sternberg, W. C. (1974). On being ignored: The effects of the violation of implicit rules of social interaction. *Sociometry, 37*, 541–556.

Haber, J. (1990). A family systems model for divorce and the loss of self. *Archives of Psychiatric Nursing, 4*, 228–234.

Hatfield, E., Walster, G. W., & Traupmann, J. (1978). Equity and premarital sex. *Journal of Personality and Social Psychology, 37*, 82–92.

Hetherington, E. M., Cox, M., & Cox, R. (1978). The aftermath of divorce. In J. Stevens & M. Matthews (Eds.), *Mother/child, father/child relationships*. Washington: National Association for the Education of Young Children.

Higgins, E. T., & Sorrentino, R. M. (1990). *Handbook of motivation and cognition: Foundations of social behavior*. New York: Guilford.

Jackson, J. M., & Saltzstein, H. D. (1957). The effect of person-group relationships on conformity processes. *Journal of Abnormal and Social Psychology, 57*, 17–24.

Kenny, D. A., & Nasby, W. (1980). Splitting the reciprocity correlation. *Journal of Personality and Social Psychology, 38*, 249–256.

Ko, T. (1994). *Social ostracism and social identity*. Unpublished master's thesis, University of Toledo.

Kohen, J. A. (1981). From wife to family head: Transitions in self-identity. *Psychiatry, 44*, 230–240.

Leary, M. R. (1990). Responses to social exclusion: Social anxiety, jealousy, loneliness, depression, and low self-esteem. *Journal of Social and Clinical Psychology, 9*, 221–229.

Leary, M. R. (2001). Toward a conceptualization of interpersonal rejection. In M. R. Leary (Ed.), *Interpersonal rejection* (pp. 3–20). New York: Oxford University Press.

Leary, M. R., Haupt, A. L., Strausser, K. S., & Chokel, J. T. (1998). Calibrating the sociometer: The relationship between interpersonal appraisals and state self-esteem. *Journal of Personality and Social Psychology, 74*, 1290–1299.

Maslow, A. H. (1970). *Motivation and personality*. New York: Harper & Row.

McCall, G. J. (1982). Becoming unrelated: The management of bond dissolution. In S. Duck (Ed.), *Personal relationships 4: Dissolving personal relationships* (pp. 211–231). New York: Academic Press.

McLaughlin-Volpe (2002). *Contraction of Self in Response to Social Exclusion*. Unpublished data.

Milardo, R. M. (1987). Changes in social networks of women and men following divorce: A review. *Journal of Family Issues, 8*, 78–96.

Miller, C. T., & Kaiser, C. R. (2001). A theoretical perspective on coping with stigma. *Journal of Social Issues, 57*, 73–92.

Munford, M. B. (1994). Relationship of gender, self-esteem, social class, and racial identity to depression in Blacks. *Journal of Black Psychology, 20*, 157–174.

Noel, J. G., Wann, D. L., & Branscombe, N. R. (1995). Peripheral ingroup membership status and public negativity towards outgroups. *Journal of Personality and Social Psychology, 68*, 127–137.

Parkes, C. M. (1972). *Bereavement: Studies of grief in adult life*. New York: International Universities Press.

Pepitone, A., & Wilpizeski, C. (1960). Some consequences of experimental rejection. *Journal of Abnormal and Social Psychology, 60*, 359–364.

Phinney, J. S. (1989). Stages of ethnic identity development in minority group adolescents. *Journal of Early Adolescence, 9*, 34–49.

Predmore, S., & Williams, K. D. (1983, May). *The Effects of Social Ostracism on Affiliation.* Paper presented at the meeting of the Midwestern Psychological Association, Chicago.

Pyszczynski, T. A., Greenberg, J., & Solomon, S. (1997). Why do we need what we need? A terror management perspective on the roots of human social motivation. *Psychological Inquiry, 8*, 1–20.

Rands, M. (1980). Changes in social networks following marital separation and divorce. In R. M. Milardo (Ed.), *Families and social networks*. Newbury Park, CA: Sage.

Rowley, S. J., Sellers, R. M., Chavous, T. M., & Smith, M. A. (1998). The relationship between racial identity and self-esteem in African-American college and high school students. *Journal of Personality and Social Psychology, 74*, 715–724.

Rusbult, C.E. (1983). A longitudinal test of the investment model: The development (and deterioration) of satisfaction and commitment in heterosexual involvement. *Journal of Personality and Social Psychology, 45*, 101–107.

Rusbult, C. E., & Buunk, B. P. (1993). Commitment processes in close relationships: An interdependence analysis. *Journal of Social and Personal Relationships, 10*, 175–204.

Sachdev, I., & Bourhis, R.Y. (1991). Power and status differentials in minority and majority group relations. *European Journal of Social Psychology, 21*, 1–24.

Schmitt, M. T., & Branscombe, N. R. (2001). The good, the bad, and the manly: Threats to one's prototypicality and evaluations of fellow in-group members. *Journal of Experimental Social Psychology, 37*, 510–517.

Shaver, P., & Buhrmester, D. (1983). Loneliness, sex-role orientation, and group life: A social needs perspective. In P. B. Paulus (Ed.), *Basic group processes* (pp. 259–288). New York: Springer-Verlag.

Skinner, E. A. (1992). Perceived control: Motivation, coping, and development. In R. Schwarzer (Ed.), *Self-efficacy: Thought control of action* (pp. 91–106). Washington, DC: Hemisphere.

Smith, E. R. (2002). Overlapping mental representations of self and group: Evidence and implications. In J. P. Forgas & K. D. Williams (Eds.), *The social self: Cognitive, interpersonal and intergroup perspectives* (pp. 21–35). New York: Psychology Press.

Snoek, J. D. (1962). Some effects or rejection upon attraction to a group. *Journal of Abnormal and Social Psychology, 64*, 175–182.

Somner, K. L., Williams, K. D., Ciarocco, N. J., & Baumeister, R. F. (2001). When silence speaks louder than words: Explorations into the intrapsychic and interpersonal consequences of social ostracism. *Basic and Applied Social Psychology, 23*, 225–243.

Spanier, G., & Casto, R. (1979). Adjustment to separation and divorce: An analysis of 50 case studies. *Journal of Divorce, 2*, 241–253.

Sprecher, S. (1994). Two sides to the breakup of a dating relationship. *Personal Relationships, 1*, 199–222.

Stephen, T. (1987). Attribution adjustment to relationship termination. *Journal of Social and Personal Relationships, 4*, 47–61.

Swim, J. K., Hyers, L. L., Cohen, L. L., & Ferguson, M. J. (2001). Everyday sexism: Evidence for its incidence, nature, and psychological impact from three daily diary studies. *Journal of Social Issues, 57*, 31–53.

Taylor, S. E., Neter, E., & Wayment, H. A. (1995). Self-evaluative processes. *Personality and Social Psychology Bulletin, 21*, 1278–1287.

Thabes, V. (1997). Survey analysis of women's long-term, postdivorce adjustment. *Journal of Divorce and Remarriage, 27*, 163–175.

Thurner, M., Fenn, C. B., Melichar, J., & Chiriboga, D. A. (1983). Sociodemographic perspectives on reasons for divorce. *Journal of Divorce, 6*(4), 25–35.

Tooby, J., & Cosmides, L. (1996). Friendship and the banker's paradox: Other pathways to the evolution of adaptations for altruism. *Proceedings of the British Academy, 88*, 119–143.

Tropp, L. R., & Wright, S. C. (2001). Ingroup identification as inclusion of ingroup in the self. *Personality and Social Psychology Bulletin, 27*, 585–600.

Twenge, J. M., Baumeister, R. F., Tice, D. M., & Stucke, T. S. (2001). If you can't join them, beat them: Effects of social exclusion on aggressive behavior. *Journal of Personality and Social Psychology, 81*, 1058–1069.

Vaughan, D. (1983). Uncoupling: The social construction of divorce. In H. Robboy & C. Clark (Eds.), *Social interaction* (pp. 405–422). New York: St. Martin's Press.

Walster, E., Aronson, V., Abrahams, D., & Rottman, L. (1966). Importance of physical attractiveness in dating behavior. *Journal of Personality and Social Psychology, 4*, 508–516.

Weigart, A. J., & Hastings, R. (1977). Identity loss, family, and social change. *American Journal of Sociology, 82*, 1171–1185.

White, R. W. (1959). Motivation reconsidered: The concept of confidence. *Psychological Review, 66*, 297–333.

Williams, K. D., Cheung, C. K. T., & Choi, W. (2000). Cyberostracism: Effects of being ignored over the internet. *Journal of Personality and Social Psychology, 79*, 748–762.

Williams, K. D., & Sommer, K. L. (1997). Social ostracism by one's coworkers: Does rejection lead to loafing or compensation? *Personality and Social Psychology Bulletin, 23*, 693–706.

Williams, K. D., Wheeler, L., & Harvey, J. (2001). Inside the social mind of the ostracizer. In J. Forgas, K. Williams, & L. Wheeler (Eds.), *The social mind: Cognitive and motivational aspects of interpersonal behavior*. New York: Cambridge Press.

Wong, C. A., Eccles, J. S., & Sameroff, A. (2003). The influence of ethnic discrimination and ethnic identification on African-American adolescents' school and socio-emotional adjustment. *Journal of Personality, 71*, 1197–1232.

Wright, S. C., Aron, A., & Tropp, L. R. (2002). Including others (and groups) in the self: Self-expansion and intergroup relations. In J. P. Forgas & K. D. Williams (Eds.), *The social self: cognitive, interpersonal, and intergroup perspectives* (pp. 343–363). New York: Psychology Press.

Zadro, L., & Williams, K. D. (1998, April). *Take the 'O' Train: Oblivious Versus Punitive Ostracism*. Presented at the Society of Australasian Social Psychologists, Christchurch, NZ.

Section II

Group Dynamics of Inclusion and Exclusion

7

Managing Group Composition: Inclusive and Exclusive Role Transitions

JOHN M. LEVINE, RICHARD L. MORELAND, and LESLIE R. M. HAUSMANN

*The management of group composition necessarily involves the inclusion and exclusion of members, which occurs via role transitions signaling changes in individuals' relationship to the group. Inclusive transitions (*entry, *when prospective members become new members, and* acceptance, *when new members become full members) signal movement toward the core of the group and increased status. Exclusive transitions (*divergence, *when full members become marginal members, and* exit, *when marginal members become ex-members) signal movement away from the core of the group and decreased status. Using a typology of role transitions that distinguishes cases in which groups and individuals are either mutually unready, differentially ready, or mutually ready for a transition, we discuss group expression and individual perception of inclusion/exclusion, as well as group pressure for transitions and individual resistance to such pressure. Finally, we discuss differences between and within inclusive and exclusive role transitions.*

A group's ability to achieve its goals, and sometimes its very survival, can depend on its composition, defined as the number and characteristics of its members (Moreland & Levine, 2003; Moreland, Levine, & Wingert, 1996). It is therefore not surprising that groups often devote substantial time and energy to trying to manage their composition.

One obvious management strategy is boundary control, which involves (a) bringing into the group people who are likely to help it and (b) ejecting from the group people who are likely to harm it (cf. Schneider, 1987; Wanous & Colella, 1989). Though boundary control is effective in many cases, it has some important drawbacks. One such drawback involves the difficulties associated with implementing this strategy. For example, groups that recruit new members often have problems identifying and attracting promising candidates, whereas groups that expel current members often have problems convincing these people to leave and adjusting to their departure.

Another drawback of boundary control derives from two related assumptions underlying the strategy, namely that people can relate to groups in only one of two ways (as nonmembers or members) and that a group's only task is to decide in which category particular people belong. A moment's reflection raises doubts about these assumptions. Rather than simply being members or nonmembers of groups, people can relate to groups in more differentiated ways. For example, they might be prospective members, newcomers, oldtimers, or ex-members. Group membership is thus not an all-or-none affair, but rather varies along an ingroup–outgroup continuum (Levine & Moreland, 1994; Moreland & Levine, 1982). This has important implications for the management of group composition. It suggests that a group must not only try to manage transitions across the boundary separating it from the social environment, but must also manage transitions across intragroup boundaries demarcating different roles that members can play.

Finally, it can be argued that the boundary-control strategy puts too much emphasis on member "selection" and too little emphasis on member "socialization." Although group composition can certainly be influenced by recruiting new members and expelling old members, it can also be affected by socializing people before and after they enter the group (Levine & Moreland, 1994; Moreland & Levine, 1982).

This line of reasoning suggests an intrinsic connection between managing group composition, on the one hand, and including/excluding group members, on the other hand. In this chapter, we offer an analysis of inclusion and exclusion based on the following assumptions. First, we assume that both inclusion and exclusion occur in the context of an ongoing relationship between the individual and the group, during which the individual moves through several phases of group membership. Second, we assume that inclusion occurs when the individual's perceived contributions to group goal attainment are positive, whereas exclusion occurs when the individual's perceived contributions are negative. Finally, we assume that the valence and intensity of inclusion and exclusion are signaled by the individual's role transitions between different phases of group membership. Our analysis of inclusion and exclusion is based on a model of group socialization that has proven useful for analyzing many small group phenomena, including commitment (Moreland, Levine, & Cini, 1993), role transitions (Moreland & Levine, 1984), treatment of newcomers (Levine & Moreland, 1991, 1999; Moreland & Levine, 1989, 2001), innovation (Levine & Moreland, 1985; Levine, Moreland, & Choi, 2001; Levine, Choi, & Moreland, 2003), group development (Moreland & Levine, 1988), trust (Moreland & Levine, 2002), and intergroup relations (Levine, Moreland, & Ryan, 1998).

GROUP SOCIALIZATION: A BRIEF OVERVIEW

Our model of group socialization is based on three psychological processes: evaluation, commitment, and role transition. Evaluation involves efforts by the group and the individual to assess the past, present, and probable future rewardingness of their own and alternative relationships. A group's evaluation of an individual is high insofar as his or her past, present, and anticipated future contributions to group goal attainment are greater than those of other people who were, are, or might be associated with the group. Similarly, an individual's evaluation of a group is high insofar as its past, present, and anticipated future contributions to personal need satisfaction are greater than those of other groups with which the individual was, is, or might be involved. Evaluation produces feelings of commitment between the group and the individual, which can rise and fall over time depending on each party's assessment of the rewardingness of their relationship.

Commitment has important consequences for both the group and the individual. For example, when a group is strongly committed to an individual, it will feel positive affect toward the person, attempt to fulfill his or her expectations, and work to gain or retain the person as a group member. Parallel responses will occur when an individual is strongly committed to a group. Role transitions are an especially important consequence of commitment. Both the group and the individual develop decision criteria (specific levels of commitment) that indicate when the individual should move from one phase of group membership to another. When either party's commitment rises or falls to its decision criterion, it will try to initiate a role transition. Such a transition will only occur, however, when both parties reach their respective decision criteria. Role transitions are major events, because they signal changes in the group's expectations for the individual and the individual's expectations for the group. The altered expectations that accompany role transitions lead to new evaluations by both parties, which in turn may produce changes in commitment and (when decision criteria are reached) additional role transitions. In this way, an individual's passage through a group can be conceptualized as a series of role transitions between different phases of group membership. Figure 7.1 illustrates a typical passage involving four role transitions (entry, acceptance, divergence, and exit) and five membership phases (investigation, socialization, maintenance, resocialization, and remembrance).

During the *investigation* phase, when the individual is a prospective member, the group engages in recruitment, looking for people who can contribute to the attainment of its goals. In a similar fashion, the individual engages in reconnaissance, looking for groups that can contribute to the satisfaction of personal needs. If the evaluation process causes the commitment of both parties to rise to their respective entry criteria (EC), then the role transition of *entry* occurs, and the person becomes a new member of the group.

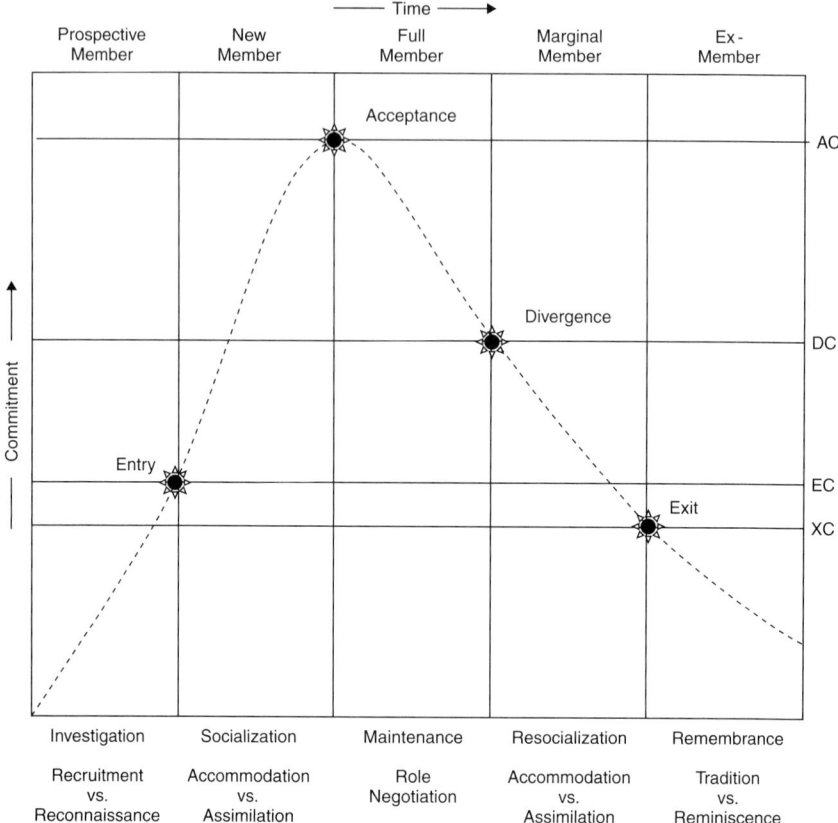

FIGURE 7.1   A model of group socialization

During the *socialization* phase, the group attempts to change the individual so that he or she contributes more to the attainment of its goals. Similarly, the individual attempts to change the group so that it contributes more to the satisfaction of personal needs. To the extent these efforts succeed, the individual experiences assimilation, and the group experiences accommodation. If the evaluation process causes the commitment of both parties to rise to their respective acceptance criteria (AC), then the role transition of *acceptance* occurs, and the person becomes a full member of the group.

During the *maintenance* phase, the group and the individual engage in role negotiation, with the goal of finding a specialized role for the individual (e.g., leader) that maximizes the group's ability to achieve its goals and the individual's ability to satisfy personal needs. If this negotiation succeeds, then the commitment levels of both parties remain high, and the person continues in the role of full member. But if this negotiation fails, then the commitment levels of both parties decline, perhaps falling to their respective divergence criteria (DC). If that happens, then the role transition of *divergence* occurs, and the person becomes a marginal member of the group.

During the *resocialization* phase, the group tries to change the individual to restore his or her contributions to the attainment of its goals. Similarly, the individual tries to change the group to restore its contributions to the satisfaction of personal needs. If sufficient assimilation and accommodation occur, then the commitment levels of both parties rise to their respective divergence criteria, producing a special role transition (*convergence*) that restores the individual to full membership. Often, however, commitment levels continue to fall, eventually reaching the group's and the individual's exit criteria (XC). At that point, the role transition of *exit* occurs, and the person becomes an ex-member of the group.

During the *remembrance* phase, both parties engage in a retrospective evaluation of their relationship. The group recalls its experiences with the individual, and the individual recalls his or her experiences with the group. These memories are often incorporated into the group's traditions and the individual's reminiscences. If the two parties continue to influence one another's outcomes, then they will also evaluate their current relationship. As time passes, the commitment levels of the two parties eventually stabilize, often at a low level.

Some constraints and limitations of this model should be acknowledged. First, although the model has a wide range of application, it is not meant to describe all kinds of groups. It applies primarily to small, autonomous, voluntary groups whose members interact on a regular basis, have affective ties to one another, share a common frame of reference, and are behaviorally interdependent. Second, Figure 7.1 presents an idealized representation of an individual's passage through a group and hence masks several complexities (Moreland & Levine, 1982). For example, group and individual commitment levels may change abruptly, rather than slowly. Moreover, group and individual decision criteria may shift over time, thereby influencing how long people spend in particular membership phases, and some decision criteria may vary in their relative positions (e.g., the entry criterion might be higher or lower than the exit criterion). In some cases, individuals may not pass through all five membership phases (e.g., a person might exit during the socialization phase if his or her commitment falls far enough, or a person might remain in the maintenance phase until his or her death). Finally, individual and group commitment levels and decision criteria may not be identical, which can produce conflict between the parties.

ROLE TRANSITIONS AND INCLUSION/EXCLUSION

Role transitions, which are the focus of our analysis of inclusion/exclusion, have received a good deal of attention. Both general discussions of the transition process (e.g., Ashforth, 2001; Ruble & Seidman, 1996; Trice & Morand, 1989; Van Gennep 1908/1960) and specific models of role entry and exit (e.g., Ashford & Taylor, 1990; Ebaugh, 1988; Louis, 1980; Nicholson, 1984; Van Maanen & Schein, 1979) have been offered. Because these transitions reflect profound changes in the individual's relationship to the group, they have information value for multiple audiences. Perhaps the most critical audience is the person (or persons) making the transition. Because different roles in a group carry different rights and responsibilities, new role occupants need to know when it is time to alter their behaviors toward and expectations for other members. In addition, these other members, who must adjust their own behaviors and expectations following a role transition, need to know when to make such adjustments. Role transitions also provide other members with information about the group's values and standards, which can affect their beliefs about their own chances of making these transitions. Finally, knowledge of role transitions is often beneficial to people outside the group, because it facilitates their interactions with the group (e.g., by clarifying which members should be contacted to solve particular problems) and helps them to understand the group's norms (e.g., by revealing what sorts of people the group promotes and demotes). Thus, a group's inclusion and exclusion activities can have ripple effects extending far beyond the targeted role occupants.

As the idealized commitment curve in Figure 7.1 indicates, the role transitions of entry and acceptance signal that the individual has moved *toward* the core of the group (full membership). In the case of entry, the individual has been promoted from prospective member to new member. In the case of acceptance, the individual has been promoted from new member to full member. Both of these role transitions thus reflect the group's increasing *inclusion* of the individual (cf. Schein, 1971). In contrast, the role transitions of divergence and exit signal that the individual has moved *away from* the core of the group. In the case of divergence, the individual has been demoted from full member to marginal member. In the case of exit, the individual has been demoted from marginal member to ex-member. Both of these role transitions thus reflect the group's increasing *exclusion* of the individual.

Our analysis will view the group as the source of inclusion/exclusion and the individual as the target. This focus derives from our interest, noted earlier, in the strategies that groups use to manage their composition. But this does not mean we believe that groups are all powerful when it comes to including and excluding individuals. Quite the contrary. According to the group socialization model, role transitions cannot occur unless both the group's and the individual's commitment levels reach their respective decision criteria. Thus, in order to produce a role transition, the group must gain the individual's co-operation (or at least acquiescence), which is often easier said than done. It is worth noting that groups do not communicate inclusion solely by encouraging inclusive transitions and exclusion solely by encouraging exclusive transitions. Inclusion can also be communicated by discouraging exclusive transitions, and exclusion can also be communicated by discouraging inclusive transitions. Moreover, groups can communicate inclusion and exclusion before and after role transitions occur, as well as during them.

A Typology of Role Transitions

Our group socialization model identifies six factors that can influence whether or not a role transition will occur—the group's and the individual's decision criteria, commitment levels, and readiness for the role transition (defined as whether or not their commitment levels have reached their respective decision criteria). Figure 7.1 depicts the simplest case, in which the group and the individual have the same decision criteria for each role transition, are equally committed to one another throughout their relationship, and thus are always mutually ready or mutually unready for a given transition. However, the reality of group life is often much more complex. Groups and individuals can have different decision criteria, feel different levels of commitment, and be differentially ready for a role transition (because only one party's commitment has reached its decision criterion).

Figure 7.2 contains a 2 (decision criteria) × 2 (levels of commitment) × 3 (readiness for role transition) matrix illustrating this complexity (Moreland & Levine, 1984). The matrix distinguishes cases in which the group and the individual (a) have the same or different decision criteria for a role transition, (b) have the same or different commitment levels, and (c) are mutually unready, differentially ready, or mutually ready for the transition. Note that every cell (except E) contains two diagrams, one above and one below the diagonal. Diagrams above the diagonal refer to the *inclusive transitions* of entry and acceptance, in which commitment must rise above a decision criterion in order for the transition to occur. Diagrams below the diagonal refer to the *exclusive transitions* of divergence and exit, in which commitment must fall below a decision criterion in order for the transition to occur. In each diagram, lines represent group or individual decision criteria, and dots represent group or individual commitment levels. It should be noted that additional diagrams could be included in some of the cells (i.e., D, H, L). Besides clarifying the factors that influence role transitions, Figure 7.2 is useful for analyzing the processes of inclusion and exclusion.

Expressed and Perceived Inclusion/Exclusion The first row of Figure 7.2 illustrates situations in which neither the group nor the individual is ready for a role transition to occur, because their commitment levels have not reached their respective decision criteria. Nonetheless, even in these situations, the group may convey inclusion or exclusion to the individual. For example, as the group's commitment level approaches its decision criterion for a role

144 SOCIAL PSYCHOLOGY OF INCLUSION AND EXCLUSION

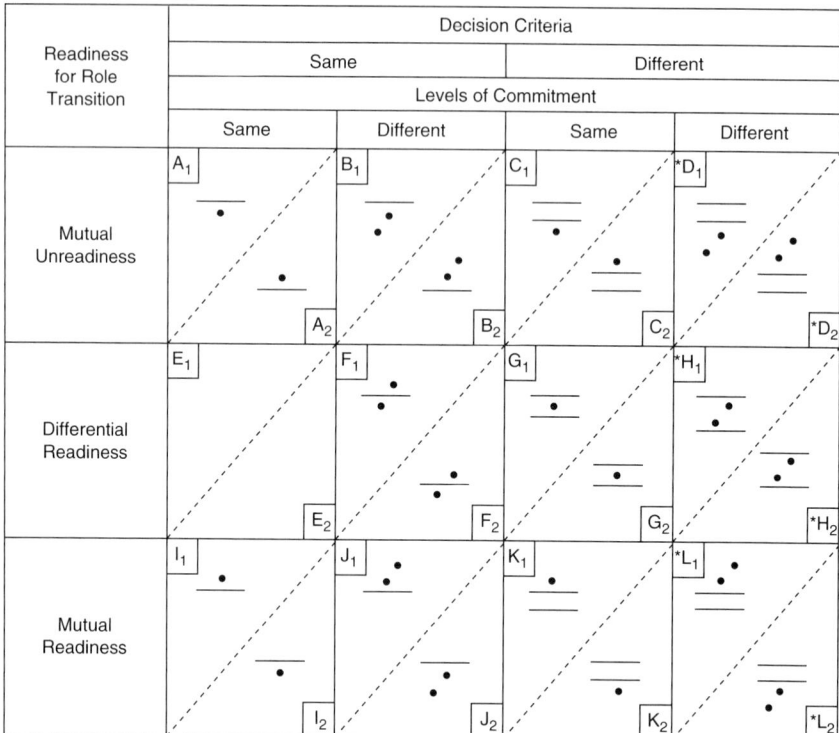

FIGURE 7.2   A typology of role transitions

Note: In the diagrams, lines represent group or individual decision criteria and dots represent group or individual commitment levels. Diagrams above the diagonals refer to the role transitions of entry and acceptance; diagrams below the diagonals refer to the role transitions of divergence and exit. In some cells (*), additional diagrams could be drawn.

transition, it will become more motivated for the transition to occur and more involved in preparing for it. When the distance between the group's commitment level and decision criterion is small, the group's motivation for the transition may be communicated, either intentionally or unintentionally, to the individual and interpreted as evidence about the group's feelings (positive in the case of inclusive transitions and negative in the case of exclusive transitions). Inclusion and exclusion may also be communicated when the distance between the group's commitment level and decision criterion is large. In these cases, the group's lack of motivation for the transition may be communicated to the individual and again interpreted as evidence about the group's feelings (negative in the case of inclusive transitions and positive in the case of exclusive transitions).

The impact of the group's inclusion/exclusion on the individual, however, may depend on more than the group's perceived motivation and preparation for a role transition. The individual's own motivation and preparation for the transition may also be important. That is, an individual who perceives the group as much more enthusiastic about an inclusive transition than he or she is may feel especially included. Conversely, an individual who perceives the group as much more enthusiastic about an exclusive transition than he or she is may feel especially excluded. How might these relative predictions play out in the first row of Figure 7.2? They are irrelevant to Cells A1 and A2, because the group and the individual share a common decision criterion and are equally committed to one another. In the remaining inclusive transition cells (B1, C1, and D1), the individual should feel *included* to the extent that the distance between the group's commitment level and decision criterion is smaller than the comparable distance for him or her. In the remaining exclusive transition cells (B2, C2, and D2), the individual should feel *excluded* to the extent that the distance between the group's commitment level and decision criterion is smaller than the comparable distance for him or her.

The second row of Figure 7.2 illustrates situations in which either the group or the individual (but not both) is ready for a role transition to occur. Here, one party's commitment level has reached its decision criterion, whereas the other party's has not. In these cases, the party whose commitment has reached its decision criterion will try to initiate the role transition. Thus, a group that is ready for entry or acceptance will communicate inclusion to the individual, whereas a group that is ready for divergence or exit will communicate exclusion. The degree of inclusion/exclusion will vary as a function of the group's eagerness for the transition, which in turn depends on how much its commitment exceeds its decision criterion for inclusive transitions and falls below its criterion for exclusive transitions.

Again, however, the individual's motivation for the transition may be important. As predicted above, an individual who perceives the group as much more enthusiastic about an inclusive transition than he or she is may feel especially included. Conversely, an individual who perceives the group as much more enthusiastic about an exclusive transition than he or she is may feel especially excluded. How might these relative predictions play out in the second row of Figure 7.2? They are irrelevant to Cells E1 and E2, because differential readiness cannot occur if both parties have identical commitment levels and decision criteria. In the remaining inclusive transition cells (F1, G1, and H1), predictions depend on which party desires the role transition. If the group desires the transition and the individual does not, then the individual should feel *included* to the extent that the distance between the group's commitment level and decision criterion is large and the distance between his or her own commitment level and decision criterion is large. However, if the individual desires the transition and the group does not, then the individual should feel *excluded* to the extent that both distances are large. In the remaining exclusive transition cells (F2, G2, and H2), predictions also depend on which party desires the role transition. If the group desires the transition and the individual does not, then the individual should feel *excluded* to the extent that both distances are large. However, if the individual desires the transition and the group does not, then the individual should feel *included* to the extent that both distances are large.

The third row of Figure 7.2 illustrates situations in which both the group and the individual are ready for a role transition to occur, because their commitment levels have reached their respective decision criteria. In these cases, as in those regarding differential readiness, a group that is ready for entry or acceptance will communicate inclusion to the individual, whereas a group that is ready for divergence or exit will communicate exclusion. Again, the degree of inclusion/exclusion will vary as a function of the group's eagerness for the transition, which in turn depends on how much its commitment exceeds its decision criterion for inclusive transitions and falls below its criterion for exclusive transitions.

But as before, the individual's motivation for the transition may be important. Thus, an individual who perceives the group as much more enthusiastic about an inclusive transition than he or she is may feel especially included, whereas an individual who perceives the group as much more enthusiastic about an exclusive transition than he or she is may feel especially excluded. How might these relative predictions play out in the third row of Figure 7.2? They are irrelevant to Cells I1 and I2, because the group and the individual share a common decision criterion and are equally committed to one another. In the remaining inclusive transition cells (J1, K1, and L1), the individual should feel *included* to the extent that the distance between the group's commitment level and decision criterion is larger than the comparable distance for him or her. Conversely, in the remaining exclusive transition cells (J2, K2, and L2), the individual should feel *excluded* to the extent that the distance between the group's commitment level and decision criterion is larger than the comparable distance for him or her.

Group Pressure and Individual Resistance   So far, we have focused on how expressed and perceived inclusion and exclusion are influenced by the relationships between group and individual commitment levels and decision criteria. As we suggested earlier, however, neither the group nor the individual is passive when it comes to inclusion and exclusion. The group may seek to raise or lower the individual's commitment level and/or decision criterion before, during, or after a role transition, and the individual may resist these influence attempts. We will focus on cases in which the group desires a role transition more than the individual does. In such cases, the more eager the group is for the transition, the more it will want the individual to share its enthusiasm. This should be true regardless of whether the two parties are mutually unready, differentially ready, or mutually ready for the transition, because in all three cases equal enthusiasm will produce less strain in the relationship than will differential enthusiasm. Of course, the less eager the individual is for the transition, the more he or she will resist the group's influence attempts.

Eagerness for a role transition has different determinants, depending on which row of Figure 7.2 is involved. When neither the group nor the individual is ready for the transition (first row), both parties' eagerness for the transition varies negatively with the distance between their commitment level and decision criterion. For example, the more the group's commitment to a prospective member approaches its entry criterion and the more the person's commitment to the group approaches his or her entry criterion, the more eagerly both parties will anticipate the role transition of entry. When the group is ready for the transition but the individual is not (second row), the group's eagerness for the transition varies positively with the distance between its commitment level and decision criterion, whereas the individual's eagerness varies negatively with the distance between his or her commitment level and decision criterion. For example, the more the group's commitment to a new member exceeds its acceptance criterion, the more eagerly it will anticipate the role transition of acceptance. Conversely, the more a new member's commitment to the group falls below his or her acceptance criterion, the less eagerly he or she will anticipate this transition. Finally, when both the group and the individual are ready for the transition (third row), both parties' eagerness for the transition varies positively with the distance between their commitment level and decision criterion. For example, the more the group's commitment to a marginal member falls below its exit criterion and the more the person's commitment to the group falls below his or her exit criterion, the more eagerly both parties will anticipate the role transition of exit.

What are the implications of this analysis for the group's efforts to convince the individual to share its enthusiasm for a role transition and the individual's resistance to such efforts? In all cases, the group's efforts should vary positively with its eagerness for the transition, whereas the individual's resistance should vary negatively with his or her eagerness. Thus, when neither party is ready for the transition, the group's efforts should be greater when its commitment–criterion distance is small rather than large, whereas the individual's resistance should be greater when his or her commitment–criterion distance is large rather than small. When the group is ready for the transition but the individual is not, both the group's efforts and the individual's resistance should be greater when their respective commitment–criterion distances are large rather than small. Finally, when both parties are ready for the transition, the group's efforts should be greater when its commitment–criterion distance is large rather than small, whereas the individual's resistance should be greater when his or her commitment–criterion distance is small rather than large.

The specific tactics that the group uses to convince the individual to share its enthusiasm for a role transition depend on whether an inclusive or an exclusive transition is involved. For inclusive transitions, the group will use tactics designed to raise the individual's commitment level and/or lower his or her decision criterion. Commitment-oriented tactics include delivering rewards to the individual and reducing his or her perceived alternatives, for example by derogating other groups that he or she might join (Levine et al. 1998). Criterion-oriented tactics include convincing the individual that his or her standards are too high, perhaps by demonstrating that past members with lower standards thrived in the group. For exclusive transitions, the group will use tactics designed to accomplish exactly the opposite goals, namely lowering the individual's commitment level and/or raising his or her decision criterion. These tactics are often mirror images of those mentioned above.

Differences between and within Inclusive and Exclusive Transitions

Our analysis so far has assumed that an individual's eagerness for any role transition depends solely on the distance between his or her commitment level and decision criterion for that transition. However, holding constant this commitment–criterion distance, people are probably more interested in making transitions that signal group inclusion (entry and acceptance) rather than group exclusion (divergence and exit). This is because inclusive transitions are more likely to satisfy a range of important motives than are exclusive transitions.

One such motive is the need to participate in social relationships and belong to groups (Baumeister & Leary, 1995). People can seek personalized belonging, based on their attractiveness as individuals, or depersonalized belonging, based on their attractiveness as group members (Ashforth, 2001; Hogg & Abrams, 1988). In either case, they should find inclusive transitions, which signal increased belonging, more appealing than exclusive transitions, which signal decreased belonging. A second motive that causes people to prefer inclusive over exclusive transitions is the need to control their social and physical environments (e.g., exert power over others, gain access to scarce resources). As Ashforth (2001) notes, "Role identities delimit domains of authority and expertise, thereby legitimizing control by the role occupants over certain spheres of activity" (p. 68). Given that inclusive transitions (entry and acceptance) allow new role occupants to gain increased control over their environments, whereas exclusive transitions (divergence and exit) force them to lose some control, people should be more attracted to the former than to the latter transitions. Finally, a third motive for preferring inclusive over exclusive transitions is the desire to have a positive social identity. People obtain positive social identity from belonging to valued groups (Tajfel & Turner, 1986) and, more importantly for our purposes, from playing group roles that others view as socially desirable (Rosenberg, 1981; Stryker, 1980). This latter mechanism is effective because people's sense of self depends heavily on what they believe others think of them (Cooley, 1902; Mead, 1934; see also Leary & Baumeister, 2000). Given that inclusive transitions signal movement into roles that others

generally view as desirable, whereas exclusive transitions signal movement into roles that others generally view as undesirable, the former should be more attractive than the latter (Glaser & Strauss, 1971).[1]

The fact that role transitions vary in social desirability has been recognized by many scholars interested in group processes (e.g., Allen & van de Vliert, 1984; Ashforth, 2001; Glaser & Strauss, 1971; Ruble & Seidman, 1996). The starkest portrayal of this variability can be found in discussions of status degradation and status accreditation ceremonies (e.g., Garfinkel, 1956; Rouse, 1996; Schwartz, 1979; Trice & Beyer, 1984). According to Garfinkel, status degradation ceremonies involve public denunciations, which are successful only when certain conditions are satisfied. For example, the denouncer must be seen as a group member in good standing who is enforcing communal norms, and the transgressor's act must be attributed to weakness of character. Similarly, Rouse (1996) argues that certain conditions must be satisfied in order for people with spoiled, or stigmatized, identities to undergo status elevation (accreditation). For example, the annunciator (opposite of denouncer) must be seen as a group member who previously underwent elevation and personifies communal values, and the former transgressor's suitability for elevation must be attributed to strength of character.

The distinctions between inclusive and exclusive role transitions and between status accreditation and degradation ceremonies underline a fundamental fact of group life—moving from a lower to a higher status role is quite different than moving in the opposite direction. In terms of the group socialization model discussed earlier, this suggests a profound difference between the role transitions of entry and acceptance, on the one hand, and divergence and exit, on the other. However, the existence of differences *between* inclusive and exclusive transitions does not preclude the existence of differences *within* these categories. To better understand the relationship between inclusion/exclusion and role transition, it is thus useful to consider separately the four role transitions specified by the group socialization model.

Entry Entry marks the role transition from prospective member to new member. The ceremonies that accompany entry are designed both to test and increase new members' commitment to the group. Such commitment is important because new members can threaten the group and hence may not be trusted by oldtimers. This distrust arises from oldtimers' concerns that new members lack important knowledge and skills, do not share group norms and goals, may disrupt long-standing relations within the group, and so on (Widdicombe & Wooffitt, 1990; Ziller, 1965). Entry ceremonies, by definition, represent inclusive role transitions, because the group is signaling its positive regard for new members by giving them increased status. Nevertheless, because these ceremonies vary widely in terms of how pleasant they seem to newcomers, they may sometimes appear to be more exclusive than inclusive to the people involved.

In some cases, entry ceremonies involve positive treatment of people making the transition from prospective member to new member. Examples include parties welcoming newcomers to the group, gifts of various kinds (often clothing or jewelry carrying group insignia), and offers of future aid (Lewicki, 1981). Such ceremonies, which provide unambiguous evidence of the group's positive regard for newcomers, may serve several functions for both newcomers and oldtimers (cf. Sutton & Louis, 1987). For newcomers, positive entry ceremonies provide evidence that the group's apparent enthusiasm for them during recruitment was genuine, thereby allaying any anxiety that they were allowed to join only because more attractive candidates refused to do so. Such ceremonies also may suggest to newcomers that the socialization period following entry will be mild rather than severe, which should reduce their fears about how they will perform during that period. Finally, positive ceremonies may elicit gratitude from newcomers, which will motivate them to work hard during socialization in order to merit the warm welcome they received. For oldtimers, positive entry ceremonies provide an opportunity to celebrate and unwind after what is often a grueling recruitment effort. Such ceremonies also allow oldtimers to smooth the ensuing socialization process by providing newcomers with informal information and advice. Finally, in order to increase their power in the group, oldtimers may use these ceremonies to form alliances with newcomers.

In other cases, entry ceremonies involve negative treatment of newcomers, whose experiences can range from embarrassing and mildly painful to psychologically degrading and physically dangerous (e.g., Bourassa & Ashforth, 1998; Haritos-Fatouros, 1988; Kanter, 1968; Winerip, 1997). Such ceremonies occur in many natural groups. At the mild end of the continuum is the entry ceremony endured by a new coal miner: "The second week after hiring in, I was sent with second shift timber crew to timber Number Three Unit's return air course. During a break, Henry Gibson asked me if I had been made a miner. When I replied that I had not, the men grabbed me and held me down while Henry gave me several swats with a cap board. 'O.K., now if anybody asks you if you've been made a miner, you can tell them that the timber crew made you a miner' " (Vaught & Smith, 1980, p. 169). At the harsh end of the continuum is the entry ceremony suffered by a new member of a high school wrestling team: "Over the span of a month . . . the sophomore had been spat on, hogtied, imprisoned inside a gymnasium locker, slammed into walls and held down while other players forced the handle of a plastic knife into his rectum" (Jacobs, 2000, p. 30).

It would not be surprising if new members forced to undergo highly negative entry ceremonies viewed themselves as targets of group exclusion in addition to (or perhaps instead of) group inclusion. If so, then why are such ceremonies so common? One possibility is that they produce cognitive dissonance in new members, which in turn increases their liking for and commitment to the group. Though early research was consistent with this hypothesis (Aronson & Mills, 1959; Gerard & Matthewson, 1966), later research casts doubt on it (e.g., Hautaluoma, Enge, Mitchell, & Rittwager, 1991; Lodewijkx & Syroit, 1997). Highly negative entry ceremonies may benefit the group for several other reasons, however. First, such ceremonies provide information about new members' commitment to the group and hence their trustworthiness. For example, new members who try to avoid unpleasant initiation activities or express annoyance with their treatment may be seen as having low commitment and therefore as needing substantial surveillance during socialization. Second, highly negative entry ceremonies may cause people with low commitment to withdraw from the group, thereby allowing oldtimers to avoid future problems with them. Third, such ceremonies communicate to new members how far they must go to win oldtimers' confidence and respect. The realization that they have low status and power in the group should increase their motivation to work hard during socialization. Finally, harsh entry ceremonies may foster cohesion among newcomers, which can make them more effective group members later.

Acceptance   Acceptance marks the role transition from new member to full member. As with entry, the ceremonies that accompany acceptance are designed both to test and increase members' commitment to the group. Though people who are completing socialization generally pose less threat to the group than do those who just joined, the group is nonetheless motivated to ensure that their commitment is high. Such commitment is important because full members have more responsibility for group welfare than do prospective, new, marginal, or ex-members. Like entry ceremonies, acceptance ceremonies represent inclusive role transitions, because the group is signaling its positive regard for members by giving them increased status. Nevertheless, acceptance ceremonies can also vary widely in pleasantness and therefore sometimes seem more exclusive than inclusive.

In some cases, acceptance ceremonies involve positive treatment of people making the transition from new member to full member. Some of these ceremonies are formal, such as throwing a party for the people involved, honoring them at a special ceremony, and giving them new privileges and responsibilities. Others are informal, such as congratulating them, giving them secret information about the group, including them in informal cliques, and monitoring their behavior less carefully (e.g., Feldman, 1977; Katovich & Reese, 1987). Informal acceptance ceremonies can vary in terms of their subtlety. A good example is the two-part ceremony experienced by a young bond trader, Michael Lewis, at Salomon Brothers: "And sometime in the middle of 1986, more by luck than by skill, I ceased to be a geek. I became a normal, established Salomon salesman. There was no one event that marked the change. I knew I was no longer a geek only because people stopped calling me geek and started calling me Michael, which I preferred. There is a difference between this, though, and being called Big Swinging Dick. . . . The journey from Michael to Big Swinging Dick happened almost immediately thereafter and was occasioned by a single sale" (Lewis, 1989, p. 180). Following this sale, Lewis got a phone call from another Salomon trader nicknamed the Human Piranha: " 'I heard you sold a few bonds,' he said. . . . He shouted into the phone, *That* is . . . awesome. . . . You are one Big Swinging Dick, and don't ever let anybody tell you different.' It brought tears to my eyes to hear it, to be called a Big Swinging Dick by the man who, years ago, had given birth to the distinction and in my mind had the greatest right to confer it upon me" (p. 184).

In other cases, acceptance ceremonies involve negative treatment, which can range from mild harassment to harsh punishment. At the mild end of the continuum are activities associated with Recognition Day at the Citadel, a public military academy in the United States: "Reentrance into manhood for the toddling knobs occurs on Recognition Day, when the upperclassmen force the knobs to do calisthenics until they drop, then gently lift up their charges and nurse them with cups of water. At that moment, for the first time in nine months, the older cadets call the knobs by their first names and embrace them" (Faludi, 1994, p. 79). At the harsh end of the continuum are activities conducted by a unit of the Canadian Airborne: "Approximately fifteen men (initiates) are lined up by the One Commando barrack block in Petawawa. They are passing a piece of bread to each other, on which they vomit and urinate prior to placing it in their mouths and chewing" (Winslow, 1999, p. 442; see also Nuwer, 1978; Vaught & Smith, 1980). Lest it be assumed that only males must endure painful acceptance ceremonies, it is important to note that an estimated two million African women undergo female circumcision each year during the rite of passage from childhood to adulthood (Leonard, 1996). Milder, but still degrading, acceptance ceremonies are experienced by women in other societies, such as the genital greasing suffered by "coal dust queens" (female coal miners) in the United States (Vaught & Smith, 1980). The benefits that a group obtains from negative acceptance ceremonies no doubt parallel those discussed earlier in regard to negative entry ceremonies.

Divergence   Divergence marks the role transition from full member to marginal member. Unlike entry and acceptance, divergence ceremonies represent exclusive role transitions, because the group is signaling its negative regard for members by taking status away from them. Moreover, divergence ceremonies involve a narrower range of activities than do entry or acceptance ceremonies. Although divergence ceremonies vary in negativity, they rarely have any positive features.

Several factors that may affect the severity of these ceremonies are suggested by analyses of how groups react to members who express deviant opinions (Levine, 1989; Levine & Thompson, 1996) or who exhibit disloyalty by leaving the group (Levine & Moreland, 2002). Characteristics of the individuals who are undergoing divergence are often important, including their perceived motive(s) for failing to satisfy group expectations and their status and tenure in the group. For example, individuals are likely to experience harsher divergence ceremonies when their behavior is attributed to volitional factors (e.g., lack of effort) rather than nonvolitional factors (e.g., temporary illness), because the former imply less concern for group welfare and a lower likelihood of changing in the future. Harsher divergence ceremonies are also likely when individuals have low status and short tenure in the group. There are at least three reasons for this. First, high status and long tenure earn idiosyncrasy credits (Hollander, 1958), which allow individuals to deviate from group norms. Second, groups resist labeling people with high status and long tenure as marginal members, because doing so forces other members to question their criteria for bestowing status and threatens their social identity (cf. Marques, Abrams, Paez, & Hogg, 2001). Finally, people with high status and long tenure have the potential to make substantial contributions to the group if they can be resocialized, so other members may not want to alienate them through harsh divergence ceremonies.[2]

Other factors affecting the severity of divergence ceremonies involve characteristics of the group. These include how well the group is performing and how adequately it is staffed (Barker, 1968). For example, groups that are performing poorly may have harsher divergence ceremonies than groups that are performing well, because the former groups feel more threatened by inadequate performance on the part of full members and hence are more motivated to discourage that kind of behavior. For similar reasons, divergence ceremonies may be harsher in understaffed than in adequately staffed groups. Because understaffed groups are likely to perform worse than adequately staffed groups, they should feel more threatened by full members who perform inadequately, which should cause them to develop harsher divergence ceremonies as a disincentive for this behavior. In addition, adequately staffed groups, which are vulnerable to problems if even a few full members perform poorly, may use harsher divergence ceremonies than overstaffed groups, which contain potential replacements for full members who fail to pull their weight.

Divergence ceremonies can vary from informal to formal and from mildly to strongly negative (Adler & Adler, 1995; Akerstrom, 1986; Lois, 1999; Trice & Beyer, 1984). In many ways, divergence ceremonies are the mirror opposites of acceptance ceremonies. They can involve such diverse experiences as being demoted in rank, having one's privileges and responsibilities reduced, receiving less secret information about the group, being excluded from informal cliques, and having one's behavior monitored more carefully.[3]

Exit Exit marks the role transition from marginal member to ex-member. Like divergence, exit ceremonies represent exclusive role transitions that vary in negativity, but rarely have positive features.[4] The factors that influence the harshness of divergence ceremonies (e.g., the perceived motive(s) of people who fail to satisfy group expectations; their status and tenure in the group; the group's performance; group staffing levels) probably have parallel effects on the harshness of exit ceremonies.

Although exit ceremonies are in many ways the mirror opposites of entry ceremonies, they differ in that groups sometimes try to hide their responsibility for the exit of marginal members, in contrast to their typical claims of responsibility for the entry of new members. Efforts to hide group responsibility for exit may derive from sympathy for marginal members' plight (based on their past contributions to the group), fear that they will retaliate against the group if they are publicly humiliated, and/or concern that outsiders will think poorly of the group if it admits that some of its members are inadequate. A variety of informal tactics can be used to hide (or at least obscure) the fact that the group is actively engaged in exit. These include eliminating the individual's responsibilities, convincing him or her to resign quietly, providing a generous severance package, allowing a grace period prior to exit, supporting the individual's explanation for why he or she is leaving ("I want to spend more time with my family and explore new challenges"), and facilitating the individual's movement into other groups (e.g., by providing inflated letters of recommendation) (Levine et al., 1998).

Of course, groups do not always worry about the feelings of marginal members and instead employ harsh, public exit ceremonies (e.g., Adler & Adler, 1995; Trice & Beyer, 1984). Such ceremonies are most likely when marginal members have violated important group norms and thereby raised doubts about what makes the group distinctive and valuable in the eyes of its members (and perhaps also nonmembers). In such cases, groups often take swift and decisive action to signal that they do not tolerate certain kinds of behavior, because failure to do so can bring severe criticism from both insiders and outsiders (witness the recent denunciations of the Catholic Church hierarchy for failing to expel priests who engaged in sexual behavior with minors) (cf. Iannaccone, 1994). During harsh exit ceremonies, the identities of marginal members are destroyed, and they are placed symbolically, as well as physically, outside the group (cf. Garfinkel, 1956). A dramatic example of this is "bone pointing," as practiced by Australian aborigines (Sarbin & Allen, 1968). In describing how victims of this ceremony are treated, Cannon (1942) noted that "the community contracts; all people who stand in kinship relation with him withdraw their sustaining support. This means that everyone he knows—all his fellows—completely change their attitudes towards him and place him in a new category. . . . The organization of his social life has collapsed and, no longer a member of a group, he is alone and isolated" (pp. 173–174). Harsh exit ceremonies can have positive consequences for the group, including increased solidarity and enhanced social identity resulting from members' joint reaffirmation of group norms. In contrast, such ceremonies often have negative consequences for ex-members, including stress, reduced self-esteem, loneliness, and feelings of powerlessness (Moreland & Levine, 1982; Williams, 2001). In extreme cases, such as bone pointing, the heightened autonomic arousal that ex-members experience can even lead to death (Sarbin & Allen, 1968).

CONCLUSIONS

In this chapter, we argued that the management of group composition necessarily involves the inclusion and exclusion of members. We suggested that inclusion/exclusion occurs via role transitions that signal the movement of individuals through several phases of group membership. The role transitions of entry (when prospective members become new members) and acceptance (when new members become full members) are inclusive, in that individuals move toward the core of the group and gain status. In contrast, the role transitions of divergence (when full members become marginal members) and exit (when marginal members become ex-members) are exclusive, in that individuals move away from the core of the group and lose status. After distinguishing cases in which groups and individuals are mutually unready, differentially ready, or mutually ready for a role transition, we discussed factors that affect (a) group expression and individual perception of inclusion/exclusion in the context of role transitions and (b) group pressure for role transitions and individual resistance to such pressure. Finally, we discussed differences between and within inclusive and exclusive role transitions and considered each of the four transitions (entry, acceptance, divergence, and exit) separately. An important hallmark of our analysis is the contention that inclusion/exclusion varies in intensity as individuals move closer to and further from the group's core. According to this view, it is simplistic to think of people as simply being "in" or "out" of the group.

Though our analysis generates several interesting predictions about inclusion and exclusion, it does not provide a complete account of this complex and fascinating phenomenon. One issue that warrants future consideration is whether groups express inclusion/exclusion outside the context of role transitions. It could be argued that inclusion/exclusion is inextricably tied to role transitions, because a group's positive or negative behavior toward an individual reflects its commitment to the person, which in turn influences its desire for the person to undergo an inclusive or exclusive role transition in the future. However, this may not always be the case. If there are very large gaps between the group's and the individual's commitment levels and respective decision criteria for a role transition, for example, then inclusion/exclusion may be expressed and perceived as simple liking/disliking, with no assumption (on the part of either the group or the individual) that the behavior has implications for the transition. In addition, if a particular role transition is impossible (e.g., because a full member has so much power that others would never consider using divergence as a sanction for norm violation), then behavior toward the individual will probably not be intended or perceived as signaling the likelihood of an upcoming transition. Finally, if the group has little interest in conducting a particular role transition (e.g., a "closed" group that does not accept new members—Ziller, 1965), then its behavior toward an individual will not have implications for the occurrence of that transition.

Another issue that deserves attention is how the inclusion/exclusion process differs when groups deal with multiple individuals (subgroups), rather than single individuals. It has been suggested, for example, that newcomers who enter a group alone experience more stress than do those who enter with others and that groups find it easier to socialize individuals than subgroups (Moreland & Levine, 1982). If so, then groups should have an easier time producing any role transition when individuals rather than subgroups are involved, because individuals will acquiesce to group pressure whereas subgroups will exert counter pressure. This implies that individuals are more likely to be targets of both inclusion and exclusion ceremonies than are subgroups. Moreover, even if an individual and a subgroup undergo the same transition, the hedonic impact of this transition (i.e., perceived inclusion/exclusion) may be higher for the individual, because he or she feels more personal responsibility for the group's reaction.

ACKNOWLEDGMENT

Preparation of this chapter was supported by Army Research Institute Contract DASW01-00-K-0018. The views, opinions, and/or findings contained in this paper are those of the authors and should not be construed as an official Department of the Army position, policy, or decision. Correspondence should be addressed to John M. Levine, 516 LRDC Bldg., 3939 O'Hara Street, University of Pittsburgh, Pittsburgh, PA 15260 USA. Email: jml@pitt.edu

NOTES

1. Although other motives and attributes of role transitions can affect the desire to leave one role and enter another (Ashforth, 2001), those discussed here seem most likely to influence preferences for inclusive versus exclusive transitions.
2. These predictions are applicable when high-status, long-tenure members are violating relatively unimportant norms. If there is clear evidence they are violating important norms, then they are at more, rather than less, risk for harsh divergence ceremonies (cf. Levine, 1989).
3. As we noted briefly in describing the group socialization model, marginal members who have experienced divergence can sometimes regain full membership by undergoing convergence, which is a kind of status accreditation ceremony. Moreover, when maintenance has a predetermined, or normative, length, divergence is expected and signals the beginning of a natural separation

between the group and the individual. In this paper, we focus on unexpected divergence, which is a troubling development for the two parties.
4. Exit is the most complicated role transition, because it can also occur during (a) the investigation and socialization phases of group membership, if the group's and the individual's commitment levels fall to their respective exit criteria, and (b) any of the first four membership phases, even though the group's and the individual's commitment levels remain above their respective exit criteria, if group factors (e.g., downsizing) or individual factors (e.g., illness) force the person to leave (Moreland & Levine, 1982; see also Ashforth, 2001, and Ebaugh, 1988). Moreover, like divergence, exit is sometimes expected, signaling a natural separation between the group and the individual. In this paper, we focus on the departure of marginal members who have undergone (unsuccessful) resocialization, as depicted in Figure 7.1.

REFERENCES

Adler, P. A., & Adler, P. (1995). Dynamics of inclusion and exclusion in preadolesent cliques. *Social Psychology Quarterly, 58*, 145–162.

Akerstrom, M. (1986). Outcasts in prison: The cases of informers and sex offenders. *Deviant Behavior, 7*, 1–12.

Allen, V. L., & van de Vliert, E. (1984). *Role transitions: Explorations and explanations*. New York: Plenum Press.

Aronson, E., & Mills, J. (1959). The effect of severity of initiation on liking for a group. *Journal of Abnormal and Social Psychology, 59*, 177–181.

Ashford, S. J., & Taylor, M. S. (1990). Adaptation to work transitions: An integrative approach. In G. R. Ferris & K. M. Rowland (Eds.), *Research in personnel and human resources management* (Vol. 8, pp. 1–39). Greenwich, CT: JAI Press.

Ashforth, B. E. (2001). *Role transitions in organizational life: An identity-based perspective*. Mahwah, NJ: Erlbaum.

Barker, R. G. (1968). *Ecological psychology*. Stanford, CA: Stanford University Press.

Baumeister, R. F., & Leary, M. R. (1995). The need to belong: Desire for interpersonal attachments as a fundamental human motivation. *Psychological Bulletin, 117*, 497–529.

Bourassa, L., & Ashforth, B. E. (1998). You are about to party *Defiant* style: Socialization and identity onboard an Alaskan fishing boat. *Journal of Contemporary Ethnography, 27*, 171–196.

Cannon, W. B. (1942). "Voodoo" death. *American Anthropologist, 44*, 169–181.

Cooley, C. H. (1902). *Human nature and the social order*. New York: C. Scribner's Sons.

Ebaugh, H. R. F. (1988). *Becoming an EX: The process of role exit*. Chicago, IL: University of Chicago Press.

Faludi, S. (1994, September 5). The naked citadel. *The New Yorker*, 62–81.

Feldman, D. C. (1977). The role of initiation activities in socialization. *Human Relations, 30*, 977–990.

Garfinkel, H. (1956). Conditions of successful degradation ceremonies. *American Journal of Sociology, 61*, 420–424.

Gerard, H. B., & Mathewson, G. C. (1966). The effect of severity of initiation on liking for a group: A replication. *Journal of Experimental Social Psychology, 2*, 278–287.

Glaser, B. G., & Strauss, A. L. (1971). *Status passage*. Chicago, IL: Aldine Atherton.
Haritos-Fatouros, M. (1988). The official torturer: A learning model for obedience to the authority of violence. *Journal of Applied Social Psychology, 18*, 1107–1120.
Hautaluoma, J. E., Enge, R. S., Mitchell, T. M., & Rittwager, F. J. (1991). Early socialization into a work group: Severity of initiations revisited. *Journal of Social Behavior and Personality, 6*, 725–748.
Hogg, M. A., & Abrams, D. (1988). *Social identifications: A social psychology of intergroup relations and group processes*. London: Routledge.
Hollander, E. P. (1958). Conformity, status, and idiosyncrasy credit. *Psychological Review, 65*, 117–127.
Iannaccone, L. R. (1994). Why strict churches are strong. *American Journal of Sociology, 99*, 1180–1211.
Jacobs, A. (2000, March 5). The violent cast of hazing in schools mirrors society, experts say. *New York Times*, p. 30.
Kanter, R. M. (1968). Commitment and social organization: A study of commitment mechanisms in utopian communities. *American Sociological Review, 33*, 499–517.
Katovich, M. A., & Reese, W. A., II. (1987). The regular: Full time identities and memberships in an urban bar. *Journal of Contemporary Ethnography, 16*, 308–343.
Leary, M. R., & Baumeister, R. F. (2000). The nature and function of self-esteem: Sociometer theory. In M. P. Zanna (Ed.), *Advances in experimental social psychology* (Vol. 32, pp. 1–62). San Diego, CA: Academic Press.
Leonard, L. (1996). Female circumcision in southern Chad: Origins, meaning, and current practice. *Social Science and Medicine, 43*, 255–263.
Levine, J. M. (1989). Reaction to opinion deviance in small groups. In P. B. Paulus (Ed.), *Psychology of group influence* (2nd ed., pp. 187–231). Hillsdale, NJ: Erlbaum.
Levine, J. M., Choi, H.-S., & Moreland, R. L. (2003). Newcomer innovation in work teams. In P. B. Paulus & B. Nijstad (Eds.), *Group creativity: Innovation through collaboration* (pp. 202–224). Oxford, UK: Oxford University Press.
Levine, J. M., & Moreland, R. L. (1985). Innovation and socialisation in small groups. In S. Moscovici, G. Mugny, & E. Van Avermaet (Eds.), *Perspectives on minority influence* (pp. 143–169). Cambridge, UK: Cambridge University Press.
Levine, J. M., & Moreland, R. L. (1991). Culture and socialization in work groups. In L. B. Resnick, J. M. Levine, & S. D. Teasley (Eds.), *Perspectives on socially shared cognition* (pp. 257–279). Washington, DC: American Psychological Association.
Levine, J. M., & Moreland, R. L. (1994). Group socialization: Theory and research. In W. Stroebe & M. Hewstone (Eds.), *European review of social psychology* (Vol. 5, pp. 305–336). New York: John Wiley & Sons.
Levine, J. M., & Moreland, R. L. (1999). Knowledge transmission in work groups: Helping newcomers to succeed. In L. L. Thompson, J. M. Levine, & D. M. Messick (Eds.), *Shared cognition in organizations: The management of knowledge* (pp. 267–296). Mahwah, NJ: Erlbaum.
Levine, J. M., & Moreland, R. L. (2002). Group reactions to loyalty and disloyalty. In S. R. Thye & E. J. Lawler (Eds.), *Group cohesion, trust and solidarity: Advances in group processes* (Vol. 19, pp. 203–228). Oxford, UK: Elsevier Science.
Levine, J. M., Moreland, R. L., & Choi, H.-S. (2001). Group socialization and newcomer innovation. In M. A. Hogg & R. S. Tindale (Eds.), *Blackwell handbook of social psychology: Group processes* (pp. 86–106). Oxford, UK: Blackwell.

Levine, J. M., Moreland, R. L., & Ryan, C. S. (1998). Group socialization and intergroup relations. In C. Sedikides, J. Schopler, & C. A. Insko (Eds.), *Intergroup cognition and intergroup behavior* (pp. 283–308). Mahwah, NJ: Erlbaum.

Levine, J. M., & Thompson, L. L. (1996). Conflict in groups. In E. T. Higgins & A. W. Kruglanski (Eds.), *Social psychology: Handbook of basic principles* (pp. 745–776). New York: Guilford Press.

Lewicki, R. J. (1981). Organizational seduction: Building commitment to organizations. *Organizational Dynamics, 10,* 5–21.

Lewis, M. (1989). *Liar's poker.* New York: Penguin Books.

Lodewijkx, H. F. M., & Syroit, J. E. M. M. (1997). Severity of initiation revisited: Does severity of initiation increase attractiveness in real groups? *European Journal of Social Psychology, 27,* 275–300.

Lois, J. (1999). Socialization to heroism: Individualism and collectivism in a voluntary search and rescue group. *Social Psychology Quarterly, 62,* 117–135.

Louis, M. R. (1980). Surprise and sense making: What newcomers experience in entering unfamiliar organizational settings. *Administrative Science Quarterly, 25,* 226–251.

Marques, J. M., Abrams, D., Paez, D., & Hogg, M. A. (2001). Social categorization, social identification, and rejection of deviant group members. In M. A. Hogg & R. S. Tindale (Eds.), *Blackwell handbook of social psychology: Group processes* (pp. 400–424). Oxford, UK: Blackwell.

Mead, G. H. (1934). *Mind, self, and society.* Chicago, IL: University of Chicago Press.

Moreland, R. L., & Levine, J. M. (1982). Socialization in small groups: Temporal changes in individual-group relations. In L. Berkowitz (Ed.), *Advances in experimental social psychology* (Vol. 15, pp. 137–192). New York: Academic Press.

Moreland, R. L., & Levine, J. M. (1984). Role transitions in small groups. In V. L. Allen & E. van de Vliert (Eds.), *Role transitions: Explorations and explanations* (pp. 181–195). New York: Plenum Press.

Moreland, R. L., & Levine, J. M. (1988). Group dynamics over time: Development and socialization in small groups. In J. E. McGrath (Ed.), *The social psychology of time: New perspectives* (pp. 151–181). Thousand Oaks, CA: Sage.

Moreland, R. L., & Levine, J. M. (1989). Newcomers and oldtimers in small groups. In P. B. Paulus (Ed.), *Psychology of group influence* (2nd ed., pp. 143–186). Hillsdale, NJ: Erlbaum.

Moreland, R. L., & Levine, J. M. (2001). Socialization in organizations and work groups. In M. E. Turner (Ed.), *Groups at work: Theory and research* (pp. 69–112). Mahwah, NJ: Erlbaum.

Moreland, R. L., & Levine, J. M. (2002). Socialization and trust in work groups. *Group Processes and Intergroup Relations, 5,* 185–202.

Moreland, R. L., & Levine, J. M. (2003). Group composition: Exploring similarities and differences among group members. In M. A. Hogg & J. Cooper (Eds.), *The Sage handbook of social psychology* (pp. 367–380). London: Sage.

Moreland, R. L., Levine, J. M., & Cini, M. A. (1993). Group socialization: The role of commitment. In M. A. Hogg & D. Abrams (Eds.), *Group motivation: Social psychological perspectives* (pp. 105–129). New York: Harvester Wheatsheaf.

Moreland, R. L., Levine, J. M., & Wingert, M. L. (1996). Creating the ideal group: Composition effects at work. In E. Witte & J. H. Davis (Eds.), *Understanding group behavior: Small group processes and interpersonal relations* (Vol. 2, pp. 11–35). Mawah, NJ: Erlbaum.

Nicholson, N. (1984). A theory of work role transitions. *Administrative Science Quarterly, 29*, 172–191.

Nuwer, H. (1978). Dead souls of Hell week. *Human Behavior, 7*, 53–56.

Rosenberg, M. (1981). The self-concept: Social product and social force. In M. Rosenberg & R. H. Turner (Eds.), *Social psychology: Sociological perspectives* (pp. 593–624). New York: Basic Books.

Rouse, T. P. (1996). Conditions for a successful status elevation ceremony. *Deviant Behavior, 17*, 21–42.

Ruble, D. N., & Seidman, E. (1996). Social transitions: Windows into social psychological processes. In E. T. Higgins & A. W. Kruglanski (Eds.), *Social psychology: Handbook of basic principles* (pp. 830–856). New York: Guilford Press.

Sarbin, T. R., & Allen, V. L. (1968). Role theory. In G. Lindzey & E. Aronson (Eds.), *The handbook of social psychology* (Vol. 1, pp. 488–567). Reading, MA: Addison-Wesley.

Schein, E. H. (1971). The individual, the organization, and the career: A conceptual scheme. *Journal of Applied Behavioral Science, 7*, 401–426.

Schneider, B. (1987). The people make the place. *Personnel Psychology, 40*, 437–453.

Schwartz, W. (1979). Degradation, accreditation, and rites of passage. *Psychiatry: Journal for the Study of Interpersonal Processes, 42*, 138–146.

Stryker, S. (1980). *Symbolic interactionism: A social structural version*. Menlo Park, CA: Benjamin/Cummings.

Sutton, R. I., & Louis, M. R. (1987). How selecting and socializing newcomers influences insiders. *Human Resource Management, 26*, 347–361.

Tajfel, H., & Turner, J. C. (1986). The social identity theory of intergroup behavior. In S. Worchel & W. G. Austin (Eds.), *Psychology of intergroup relations* (2nd ed., pp. 7–24). Chicago, IL: Nelson-Hall.

Trice, H. M., & Beyer, J. M. (1984). Studying organizational cultures through rites and ceremonials. *Academy of Management Review, 9*, 653–669.

Trice, H. M., & Morand, D. A. (1989). Rites of passage in work careers. In M. B. Arthur, D. T. Hall, & B. S. Lawrence (Eds.), *Handbook of career theory* (pp. 397–416). New York: Cambridge University Press.

Van Gennep, A. (1960). *The rites of passage* (M. B. Vizedom & G. L. Caffee, Trans.). Chicago, IL: University of Chicago Press. (Original work published 1908)

Van Maanen, J., & Schein, E. H. (1979). Toward a theory of organizational socialization. *Research in Organizational Behavior, 1*, 209–264.

Vaught, C., & Smith, D. L. (1980). Incorporation and mechanical solidarity in an underground coal mine. *Sociology of Work and Occupations, 7*, 159–187.

Wanous, J. P., & Colella, A. (1989). Organizational entry research: Current status and future directions. *Research in Personnel and Human Resources Management, 7*, 59–120.

Widdicombe, S., & Wooffitt, R. (1990). "Being" versus "doing" punk: On achieving authenticity as a member. *Journal of Language and Social Psychology, 9*, 257–277.

Williams, K. D. (2001). *Ostracism: The power of silence*. New York: Guilford Press.

Winerip, M. (1997, October 12). The beauty of beast barracks. *New York Times Magazine*, 46–53, 62, 64, 95.

Winslow, D. (1999). Rites of passage and group bonding in the Canadian Airborne. *Armed Forces and Society, 25*, 429–457.

Ziller, R. C. (1965). Toward a theory of open and closed groups. *Psychological Bulletin, 64*, 164–182.

8

When Bad Becomes Good (and Vice Versa): Why Social Exclusion Is Not Based on Difference

DOMINIC ABRAMS, GEORGINA RANDSLEY DE MOURA, PAUL HUTCHISON, and G. TENDAYI VIKI

The chapter describes our work on the subjective group dynamics model. The model proposes that whether deviant group members attract positive or negative reactions depends on the implications of their actions or attitudes for the validity of ingroup norms. As differences between ingroups and outgroups become more important, members also become more likely to endorse or reject specific individuals from either group that uphold ingroup norms. Therefore, some "pro-norm" ingroup deviants are likely to be tolerated, whereas other "anti-norm" ingroup deviants are likely to be rejected. The direction, rather than magnitude of deviance drives decisions to exclude or include them. We describe evidence that reactions to deviants serve to sustain social identity of group members and to sustain positive ingroup stereotypes. Developmental evidence suggests that these reactions are a relatively sophisticated form of ingroup bias, which may allow people to include and exclude others apparently as individuals, when in fact the reactions are group-serving.

INTRODUCTION AND OVERVIEW

The capacity of groups for intolerance is well known (Hewstone, Rubin, & Willis, 2002). Traitors are rarely tolerated for long, and vengeance is often brutal. For example, members of criminal organizations such as the mafia have been known to torture and kill ingroup members that violate accepted codes of conduct. Historically, western societies have also been known to marginalize and exclude certain people from partaking in the benefits of being members of the society. Homosexual or homeless people have historically been marginalized or socially excluded on the basis of their "deviant" social status. However, this capacity for groups to dehumanize and demonize their members (see Leyens et al., 2001) is only part of the story. In other ways, groups are, and have to be, open to new ideas, new directions, and even the inclusion of outsiders. These qualities permit groups to survive, adapt, and grow (see Caporael & Brewer, 2000; Kurzban & Leary, 2001; Moscovici, Mugny, & van Avermaet, 1985). The ideas presented in this chapter derive from a program of research exploring the subjective group dynamics model (Abrams, Marques, Randsley de Moura, Hutchison, & Bown (2004); Marques & Páez, 1994; Marques, Páez, & Abrams, 1998). We propose that social inclusion or exclusion of individuals within groups is substantially affected by intergroup context and may not depend so much on the objective magnitude or nature of their differences from others within their group. Thus, social inclusion and exclusion are often phenomena that need to be understood in terms of intergroup relations rather than interpersonal relationships or personal characteristics of individuals. This chapter describes some key aspects of the model, and introduces several areas to which it can be applied.

We begin by considering the criteria that group members may use to judge deviants. We propose that the intergroup context shapes the way group norms are perceived and defended, and that the social identity approach to intergroup relations provides a useful way of understanding the reasons for this. We propose that people use judgments and evaluations of individual group members to sustain the prescriptive norms of their ingroup. We describe some of our work on the "black sheep effect" and related patterns, which shows that differences in evaluations of normative and deviant members within groups co-occur with intergroup differentiation. Intragroup differentiation increases when intergroup relationships are more salient, are competitive, and attract higher identification among their members. When people value ingroups over outgroups as a whole they then favor other individuals from either group that endorse the value of the ingroup. We describe some research demonstrating that this more subtle form of ingroup bias follows a developmental sequence, which implies the development of a "theory of group mind" during childhood. The developmental changes provide a sociocognitive basis for the acceptance or rejection of people based on their endorsement of ingroup norms.

Group members are particularly sensitive to the direction in which others deviate, rating antinormative deviance as more atypical than pronormative deviance. Evaluations are not based on extremity or the actual behavior of deviant members, but on the extent to which the deviant helps to validate the ingroup norm relative to other members of the same group. Moreover, the presence of antinormative deviants may provoke efforts to validate the ingroup norm by strengthening, rather than weakening, a positive ingroup stereotype. Therefore, by isolating antinorm deviants from the ingroup, the norms of the group are both clarified and strengthened. Similarly by isolating outgroup antinorm deviants (i.e., those who endorse ingroup norms) from the outgroup, the distance between groups is sustained while the superiority of the ingroup is supported. Finally, we consider whether, and under what conditions, certain group members, specifically leaders, may be given license to deviate without inviting exclusion from their group members.

DEVIANCE WITHIN GROUPS

For a group to exist, and to be entitative, there must be a perception of unity at some level (see Campbell, 1958; Yzerbyt, Judd, & Corneille (2004). Sherman, Hamilton, and Lewis (1999) proposed that, "members of highly entitative groups will perceive greater differentiation from outgroups and thus show a greater degree of ingroup bias in perceptions and interpretations of events . . . [In addition] . . . entitative ingroups should be seen as having more power to do good things and to achieve positive goals . . . highly entitative groups are more likely to develop clear group norms" (p. 102). It follows that the presence of deviant group members might undermine group entitativity and thus evoke strong reactions from other group members. Moreover, for groups to define and achieve their goals they rely on compliance and cooperation among their members. Dissent or diversity may potentially derail the group's plans and call into question the premises on which it acts. Challenges to the group's ethos may be met with strong criticism and even overt hostility. For example, in the UK, a Labour member of parliament, George Galloway, was excluded from membership of the Labour Party for depicting the war with Iraq as unjust and illegal. A civil servant weapons inspector, David Kelly, was apparently driven to commit suicide after having shared with journalists his doubts about the government's evidence of Iraqi weapons of mass destruction.

We follow the classic ideas proposed by Festinger and others in holding that people depend on social consensus to achieve a subjectively valid sense of reality, particularly social reality. When groups show disunity there are counterveiling pressures to sustain consensus (e.g., Asch, 1952; Boyanowsky & Allen, 1973; Festinger, 1950; Hogg & Hains, 1998; Janis, 1982; Levine, 1989; Sherif, 1936). Given that so much may be at stake, psychologically and sometimes materially, it is not surprising that group members tend to conform to group norms and may pressurize other members of the group to do likewise (see Berkowitz & Howard, 1959; Davis & Witte, 1996; Schachter, 1951; Shaw, 1976). In an effort to maintain or support this social reality, deviant people may then be socially excluded from the benefits afforded to nondeviant ingroup members.

In general terms it is likely that members who deviate more extremely are likely to attract more attention from the rest of the group (cf. Mullen, 1991). However, not all dimensions are likely to be equally important to judgments of group members. For example, a business meeting to discuss the sales pitch for a new product may include a set of people that is diverse in terms of language, culture, nonverbal behavior and political attitudes. However, the group may care little about these variations because none are relevant to the group's goal, which is to sell the product. Diversity within the group may have no bearing on the value of the group's goals—the belief that what the group is doing or stands for is valid and worthwhile and reflects positively on its members.

What factors may influence relevance of deviance for the group? One important factor is the intergroup context. The social identity approach (e.g., Hogg & Abrams, 1988; Tajfel & Turner, 1979) holds that groups and intergroup relationships affect perception and behavior through the process of social categorization. When social identity is salient, category-based features will be attributed to all category members, thereby minimizing individual differences within categories, and maximizing intercategory differences (e.g., Abrams & Hogg, 1990; Hogg & Abrams, 1988; Tajfel, 1974; Tajfel & Turner, 1979; see also Brewer, 1988; Fiske & Neuberg, 1990). Self-Categorization Theory (SCT) strengthens this idea. SCT considers two aspects of the fit between individuals and social categories, comparative and normative fit (Oakes, 1996; Oakes, Turner, & Haslam, 1991). According to SCT, perceptions of group members are determined by a metacontrast, which can be approximated mathematically as a ratio of intragroup differences versus intergroup differences (Hogg & McGarty, 1990; Oakes, Haslam, & Turner, 1994; Turner, Hogg, Oakes, Reicher, & Wetherell, 1987). This contrast produces abstract prototypes that represent the positions (e.g., on an attitude continuum) that best capture differences between the ingroup and outgroup to the detriment of intracategorical differences.

How do people make sense of a situation in which categorization fits well, but particular individuals differ markedly from their fellow group members? One possibility is that deviants may be overlooked or disregarded under the operation of the metacontrast principle, particularly when the categories are highly salient. Another possibility is that deviants are simply reclassified (e.g., a former ingroup member is now classified as an outgroup member). Alternatively, the presence of the deviant may prompt a reassessment of the way all people are classified and may invoke a different dimension for categorization, reflecting a revised intergroup context (see Abrams, 1996, 1999; Spears, Oakes, Ellemers, & Haslam, 1997; Turner & Oakes, 1997). These responses would improve the fit between the social categorization in use and the characteristics of the people being categorized (Oakes et al., 1991, 1994). This outcome would be psychologically satisfying to the extent that it would clarify intergroup boundaries (see Hogg, 1993). However, if the existing categorizations are highly meaningful, and deviants are not, or *cannot be*, disregarded or recategorized, it might be inevitable that their presence would alter the clarity of distinctions between the groups. A possible cognitive response could be to assimilate the group prototype toward the position held by the deviant, a process that would likely depend on the extremity of deviance (e.g., Kunda & Oleson, 1997). However, in many situations adapting the group norm to take account of a specific group member may be difficult, undesirable, or unwarranted. Thus, the problem for other group members is how to deal with the deviant without imperiling the group's norms.

SUBJECTIVE GROUP DYNAMICS

The subjective group dynamics model (SGD) Marques, Páez, & Abrams, 1998; Marques, Abrams, Páez, & Hogg, 2001) follows social identity theory's tenet that group members wish to ensure that ingroups have higher value than relevant outgroups. It also adopts the presumption from SCT that the categorization process is largely driven by a search for meaning and reduction of uncertainty (e.g., Hogg, 2000). Therefore people are motivated to ensure the validity of a subjective sense of reality that is defined and shared by the ingroup (Abrams, 1990, 1992; Abrams & Hogg, 1988, 2001; Hogg, 2001a; Marques & Páez, 1994). This certainty is strengthened to the extent that self and ingroup are seen as sharing a common set of norms and values (e.g., Turner, 1991; see also Cadinu & Rothbart, 1996; Krueger & Clement, 1996). The SGD model proposes that people generally strive to confirm ingroup reality. To achieve this, group members should resist evidence that weakens the validity of ingroup norms, and accept evidence that confirms those norms. In sum, group members have two related motives; to maximize and sustain positive intergroup distinctiveness whilst also maximizing and sustaining the relative validity of prescriptive ingroup norms. The SGD model holds that these motives are satisfied through parallel and complementary processes of *inter*group differentiation and *intra* group differentiation (Marques, Abrams, Páez, & Taboada, 1998).

Ingroup superiority may often be achieved through category differentiation, whereby the ingroup is favored globally over the outgroup (see Mullen, Brown, & Smith, 1992). However, validation of ingroup norms often depends on making distinctions within groups to determine which individual members either reinforce or undermine those norms. The SGD model assumes that judgments of individual group members remain essentially depersonalized, that is, they are framed with reference to group norms and stereotypes. The intergroup and intragroup processes operate in conjunction so that it becomes possible, rather than paradoxical, that group members favor the ingroup over the outgroup as a whole, while also preferring particular outgroup members over particular ingroup members.

Bases for Differentiation—Descriptive and Prescriptive

To develop this idea, Marques, Abrams et al. (1998) distinguished between denotative and prescriptive norms. Denotative norms provide the descriptive criteria for categorization and are thus relevant to the metacontrast principle, based on comparative and normative fit, as defined in SCT. Denotative norms are perceived as essential for, inherent in, or entirely indicative of category membership. For example, physical appearance provides clear sets of attributes associated with, and largely diagnostic of, race. Ingroup bias may result from a category membership inference that is based on denotative characteristics alone. In many instances, category membership is likely to be perceived as inextricably linked to denotative norms, such that category ascriptions can be made immediately from a person's adherence to these norms. It seems likely that denotative norms are often applied nonconsciously or at least relatively unreflectively. However, people may devote conscious attention to denotative norms when there is a high degree of initial ambiguity regarding category memberships (e.g., Abrams, 1990, 1996; Abrams & Brown, 1989; Abrams & Masser, 1998), when it is important to ensure that no outgroup members are categorized as ingroup members (Yzerbyt, Castano, Leyens, & Paladino, 2000), when perceivers are prejudiced (Blascovich, Wyer, Swart, & Kibler, 1997), when they need to preserve cognitive closure (Kruglanski & Webster, 1996), or when they want to avoid expressing prejudice (Monteith, Sherman, & Devine, 1998; Plant & Devine, 1998). Norms that denote category membership may be strongly associated with judgments, but they are not the sole basis for evaluation of ingroup and outgroup members.

The SGD model holds that group members are vigilant about deviation from norms that are prescriptive of values, attitudes, and behavior for their own and other groups. Whereas denotative norms are indicative of group membership, prescriptive norms relate to the validity of the group's social standing. A simple illustration of the denotative/prescriptive distinction may clarify this point. Soccer teams sometimes have to wear different colored outfits, depending on the colors of the home team. The fans need to know how the colors indicate the membership of the team, and ingroup bias is determined by the category membership denoted by those colors rather than the colors themselves. In contrast, ingroup prescriptive norms are that fans should cheer when their team performs well. Upholding consensus for prescriptive ingroup norms provides a way of ensuring that the positive evaluation of the ingroup is subjectively valid (see Abrams & Hogg, 1988; Hogg & Abrams, 1993; McGarty, 1999).

Ingroup and outgroup norms differ in many situations (e.g., in the Champion's League, English people should support Manchester United, Spanish people should support Real Madrid). However, there are also norms and standards which are not oppositional, but which are still very important for ingroup members (see Forsyth, 1990). For example, ingroups may desire to embody generic societal, cultural or moral norms to a greater extent than outgroups (e.g., to be law abiding, to work hard, to be loyal, to be attractive, etc.). This line of reasoning is compatible with evidence that people are liable to project their ingroup attributes more than outgroup attributes onto superordinate groups (Mummendey & Wenzel, 1999). It is also consistent with research showing that the ingroup is usually accorded a more human essence than outgroups (Leyens et al., 2001). Group members' aspiration that the ingroup has superior standing on these generically valued attributes requires some validation—instances that confirm such perceptions. In sum, both oppositional and generic norms can take on a *prescriptive* character.

Inclusive and exclusive reactions to particular group members will depend on whether they appear to be an ingroup or outgroup member *and* whether their behavior undermines or validates the ingroup prescriptive norm. Evaluations of group members may also depend on backward processing (see Marques, Abrams, Paez, & Hogg, 2001), a form of counterfactual thinking that occurs when observed events run counter to expectations (Miller & Prentice, 1996). In these situations, people generate a specific frame of reference that accounts for the counterintuitive event, and they construct, online, a standard of comparison relevant to that particular context (Kahneman & Miller, 1986). Deviants violate normative expectancies, and this makes prescriptive norms highly salient as standards against which to judge ingroup and outgroup behavior. These judgments reflect the evaluative consequences of group members' characteristics and behavior for the ingroup and hence for the social self. Ingroup members attend to prescriptive norms so as to ensure consensus on criteria for positive ingroup evaluation. The value of ingroup consensus is often made all the more real when a member breaks ranks or deviates from the group norms (e.g., Holtz & Miller, 1985; Miller, Gross, & Holtz, 1991). Salient variations from prescriptive norms are therefore very likely to induce active regulation of the subjective image of the group. Specifically, because group members are motivated to preserve the subjective validity of their group's norms, they will wish to correct or remove challenges to that norm within the group, and to gather evidence from outside the group to bolster the ingroup norm.

A relatively untested aspect of the SGD model is based on Abrams (1990, 1994, 1996, 1999) Social Self-Regulation (SSR) model. This holds that specific goals or standards for group members can be determined by several variables, including the nature of the intergroup context (e.g., competitive vs. co-operative intergroup relations), group members' motivation to sustain a positive identity, their skills and ability to enact certain behaviors, and anticipated responses from a potential audience. Nonadherence to a group goal may occur either because of failure to regulate action or because of disruption. In either case, if group membership remains important, members are likely to engage in corrective action that diverges from routine forms of intergroup differentiation and intragroup conformity (e.g., diverges from a simple rule of favoring ingroup members over outgroup members).

There is a variety of direct and indirect evidence that self-regulation processes can be engaged to influence intergroup and intragroup behavior (e.g., Abrams, 1985; Abrams & Brown, 1989; Bodenhausen & Macrae, 1998; Monteith, et al., 1998; Plant & Devine, 1998; see also Reicher, Spears, & Postmes, 1995; Spears, 2001). We believe that social self-regulation processes underpin reactions to ingroup and outgroup deviance because maintenance of ingroup standards is a means of validating the standards that are used to regulate the self. Therefore, when social identity is salient or important, one aspect of group members' self-regulation is the regulation of the *group's* adherence to group standards. The presence of a deviant group member indicates that a group is failing to sustain its norms and values. This is likely to require group members to stop and think, to select actions consciously and strategically, so as to sustain the ingroup norm. Specifically, evaluations of such deviants should depend on whether the deviant's behavior provides a source of validation for ingroup norms, either directly or by undermining outgroup norms in relative terms.

Evidence: Responses to Ingroup and Outgroup Deviance

People tend to evaluatively upgrade attractive ingroup members and downgrade unattractive ingroup members, as compared to analogous outgroup members (for a review, see Marques & Páez, 1994). This phenomenon has been labeled the "black sheep effect" (Marques, Yzerbyt, & Leyens, 1988). The black sheep effect occurs even when individuals show a strong overall preference for the ingroup (Marques, Robalo, & Rocha, 1992), and the effect is larger when individuals identify with the ingroup (Biernat, Vescio, & Billings, 1999; Branscombe, Wann, Noel, & Coleman, 1993; Hutchison, Abrams, & Viki, 2002). It arises either when perceivers judge members singly (Marques et al., 1988), or when they directly compare normative and deviant members from the same group, or two members from different groups (Marques & Yzerbyt, 1988). The black sheep effect emerges when differences between group members are relevant to the maintenance of positive ingroup valence or to intergroup distinctiveness. The effect represents one manifestation of the operation of subjective group dynamics. Similar patterns of evaluation occur when group members deviate in terms of their attitudes rather than their attractiveness or likeability (for reviews, see Abrams et al., 2004; Marques, Abrams et al., 2001; Marques & Páez, 1994). Moreover, the effects are magnified when the ingroup's status is threatened or insecure (Marques, Abrams, & Serôdio, 2001; see also Christian, Hutchison, & Abrams, 2003).

Negative evaluations of deviant group members should not be taken to imply that the group members would always want to evict the deviant from the group. Different methods may be used to sustain ingroup norms. For example, Marques et al. (2001, Experiment 1) found that when the ingroup norm was undermined, participants reported higher willingness to persuade deviant targets to change their opinion in a forthcoming discussion. In Experiment 2, the black sheep effect emerged most clearly when the ingroup lacked normative uniformity. Once again participants were most willing to influence deviant individuals to change their opinion when the ingroup norm was potentially undermined by low ingroup uniformity. The Marques et al. (2001) studies illustrate that norm-reinforcing responses may not only take the form of derogatory judgments but also willingness to reintegrate deviants. Norm reinforcement emerges more strongly when the validity of a relevant ingroup norm is endangered by lack of perceived ingroup consensus. In addition, the studies showed that norm-reinforcing responses emerge primarily where deviants are deemed to be ingroup members, rather than in interpersonal or in outgroup settings.

The Relationship Between Intergroup and Intragroup Differentiation and Social Identity

According to the SGD model, phenomena such as the black sheep effect result from people's desire to sustain valued differences between groups. Therefore, differentiation between categories as a whole should be accompanied, and validated by prescriptive norm differentiation among members within groups. In a series of studies, Marques, Abrams, et al. (1998) showed that differentiation between and within groups may both arise in the same situation. A minimal (bogus) criterion was used to assign participants to different social categories (e.g., "X" and "Y"). They were informed of the norms associated with each category and were asked to evaluate the groups as a whole, and four "normative" members and one deviant member from either the ingroup or the outgroup. Participants judged the ingroup as a whole more favorably than the outgroup (denotative norm differentiation), and they *also* upgraded members whose responses were closer to the *ingroup* norm and derogated members whose responses were opposed to this norm, irrespective of whether these were ingroup or outgroup members (prescriptive norm differentiation). In subsequent experiments we found this pattern was more extreme when the prescriptive norm was made more salient, and when participants felt accountable to ingroup rather than outgroup members. Finally, we found that evaluations of group members were related to participants' identification with the ingroup. Those who initially identified more strongly with the ingroup favored individuals from *either* group who provided relatively greater support for the ingroup norm. In turn, those who engaged in more prescriptive norm differentiation subsequently showed greater increases in identification. Taken together, this evidence is consistent with the idea that people selectively evaluate members within groups in a way that sustains their ingroup norm and their social identity.

The Development of Subjective Group Dynamics—A Theory of Group Mind?

Previously, we have argued that the motivation to favor the ingroup over the outgroup also motivates the upgrading of normative relative to deviant ingroup members. However, the latter phenomenon seems likely to require a more sophisticated understanding of intergroup relationships. Before people can make distinctions among group members they need to understand the relevant criteria for judgment. In turn, this involves an appreciation of the consensual value of prescriptive norms that uphold the ingroup's validity. Intragroup differentiation involves distinguishing among group members in terms of their adherence to group-related attributes. It is not simply a matter of treating each group member as an individual.

One way to investigate the idea that subjective group dynamics are a sophisticated aspect of intergroup bias is to examine intergroup and intragroup judgments made by children of different ages. Abrams, Rutland, Cameron, and Marques (2003) conducted a study in the context of a summer play scheme for children. Children attending these schemes were drawn from a range of different schools, and thus effectively were in a new ad-hoc group, much like the children in the summer camp studies conducted by Sherif (e.g., Sherif & Sherif, 1953). We used the fact that a number of different schemes operated in the region to present children aged 6–7 years or 10–11 years with statements that were ostensibly made by ingroup members or by outgroup members.

Children first evaluated each group as a whole. Regardless of age children showed bias in favor of their own play scheme. Next, children were presented with the statements. Two group members made normative statements, which simply involved praising the play scheme that they attended. A third group member was a deviant who praised their own play scheme but also praised the other play scheme. Manipulation checks established that children of all ages did perceive the normative targets to be typical and the deviant to be less typical of the group. Younger children favored ingroup targets over outgroup, but did not differentiate significantly between normative and deviant targets. In contrast, older children favored the normative ingroup target over the deviant ingroup target, and favored the deviant outgroup target over the normative outgroup target. Thus, only the older children displayed the pattern we expect when subjective group dynamics are operating. Of equal importance was that evaluative differentiation among the targets was significantly related to global ingroup bias.

A further test of the development of subjective group dynamics was conducted by Abrams, Rutland and Cameron (2003). In that study, nearly 500 children aged between 5 and 12 years were presented with statements made by supporters of their own (England) or an outgroup (Germany) soccer team during the World Cup Soccer championships in 2002. As in the play scheme study, children of all ages showed significant global intergroup bias, but intragroup differentiation increased significantly with age, as did the relationship between intragroup bias and intergroup bias. Moreover, in the soccer study we measured group identification. It emerged that identification became more strongly related to intragroup differentiation with age. Finally, both of these studies revealed a further link in the chain between intergroup and intragroup

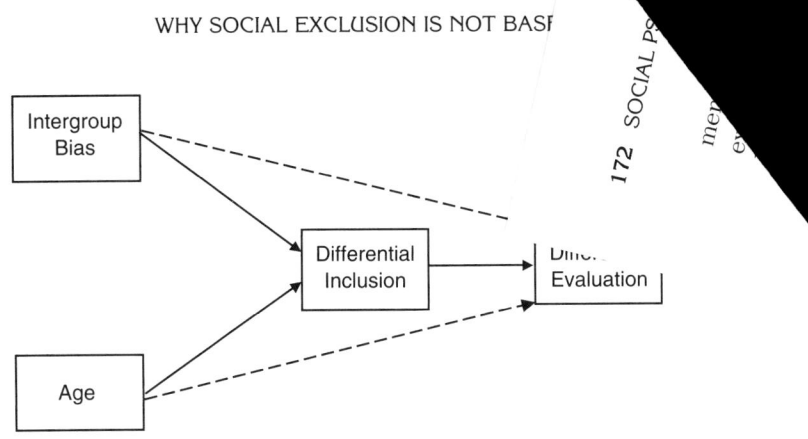

FIGURE 8.1   Development of subjective group dynamics in children

Note: All arrows depict significant relationships between variables in results from studies involving children aged 6–7 and 10–11 (Abrams, Rutland, Cameron, & Marques, 2003) and aged 5–12 (Abrams, Rutland, & Cameron, 2003). Broken lines depict paths that are mediated significantly by differential inclusions.

processes. The extent to which children favored ingroup normative members over deviant members, and the reverse pattern for outgroup members, was associated with the extent to which they recognized how acceptable each target would be to other ingroup and outgroup members (measured on an index we called differential inclusion). As shown in Figure 8.1, we found that differential inclusion mediated the effects of age on differential evaluation of the group members. In summary, the development of subjective group dynamics appears to be contingent on a developing understanding of how group dynamics operate in an intergroup context. We conjecture that this development is akin to the emergence of a "theory of mind" (Perner, Leekam & Wimmer, 1987; Perner, Ruffman & Leekam, 1994) but at the group level—a "theory of group mind." We are currently investigating whether this is associated with cognitive and social perspective taking abilities, and whether it is limited to particular types of group membership.

These two developmental studies challenge conventional ideas that older children's increasing cognitive sophistication leads them away from strong or blatant intergroup biases (see Aboud, 1988). Instead, we find that older children become more discerning about who, within both the ingroup and the outgroup, should be evaluated highly. Rather than showing a simple blanket prejudice in favor of the ingroup, they endorse individuals whose attitudes provide relative validation of the ingroup's positive status or position. Second, these studies suggest that whereas global intergroup bias may be a relatively basic response to salient social categorization, the linkage of intergroup bias to intragroup bias is a more subtle, and perhaps more powerful, aspect of the way group members sustain their own group's advantages. By reserving criticism for deviant ingroup members, and allowing praise for deviant outgroup members who implicitly or explicitly acknowledge the ingroup's value, it is possible to avoid censure for being biased against members of the outgroup, while bolstering the ingroup's position. Thus the social control of group members may operate through the potential sanctions that are in place if they undermine prescriptive ingroup norms. The targets of these sanctions are likely to vary depending on the relative vulnerability of ingroup norms at particular times. Thus, although individual children may be victimized or rejected by others, it may well be that the locus of these forms of rejection is the norm, not the person. As a result, resolutions to problems such as bullying and victimization in school may reside at least as much in understanding the intergroup context and group norms as in the particular behavior of specific individual victims or perpetrators.

Deviant Derogation as Stereotype Maintenance

The research presented so far shows that reactions to deviant ingroup members serve an identity maintenance function. Those members whose behavior or characteristics present the greatest threat to the integrity or value of the ingroup consistently attract the most negative and extreme evaluations (see also Yzerbyt, Castano, Leyens, & Paladino, 2000), and invite efforts to change their position. Hutchison and Abrams (2003) suggested that the reactions to undesirable ingroup members might function in other ways to protect the ingroup stereotype (see also Marques & Páez, 1994). Hutchison and Abrams (2003) examined the impact of a clearly undesirable ingroup member on participants' perceptions of their groups. Psychology students who differed in their level of ingroup identification rated "psychologists" on a series of pretested positive and negative stereotypical characteristics before and after reading information about a desirable (e.g., competent, ethical) or undesirable (e.g., incompetent, unethical) psychologist. In line with previous findings, high identifiers were more positive than low identifiers in their evaluation of a desirable ingroup member but were more negative than low identifiers in their evaluation of an undesirable ingroup member (see also Branscombe et al., 1993). Moreover, high identifiers expressed a more positive ingroup stereotype after, compared to before, reading about an undesirable ingroup member. They also expressed a more positive ingroup stereotype than high identifiers who read about a desirable ingroup member. In contrast, low identifiers' stereotypes were relatively unaffected by the target manipulation. This pattern of intragroup evaluations is consistent with Marques and Páez's (1994) suggestion that in derogating undesirable ingroup members, people would attempt to protect the ingroup stereotype by separating the good representatives from the "black sheep". Further support for this conjecture is provided by recent research showing that, relative to low identifiers, high identifiers tend to perceive undesirable exemplars as less typical of the ingroup (Castano, Paladino, Coull, & Yzerbyt, 2002a), are more concerned with erroneously including outgroup members in the ingroup

(Castano, Yzerbyt, Bourguignon, & Seron, 2002b), and will expend more cognitive resources to psychologically exclude undesirable members from the ingroup (Coull, Yzerbyt, Castano, Paladino, & Leemans, 2001).

A second study (Hutchison, 2003) examined effects of identification with the ingroup on university students' reactions to a positive or negative ingroup member. Participants first read a series of statements supposedly made by a target student who expressed either a positive (i.e., friendly, welcoming) or negative (i.e., unfriendly, hostile) attitude toward other students at the same university. They evaluated the target and rated the impact of the target on the image of the group. They then rated the group on a series of positive and negative stereotypical attributes. Relative to low identifiers, high identifiers were more positive in their evaluation of a desirable ingroup member, but were more negative in their evaluation of an undesirable ingroup member. Moreover, relative to low identifiers, high identifiers believed that the image conveyed by the desirable target was more positive for the image of the ingroup, but that the image conveyed by the undesirable target was more negative for the image of the ingroup. A control condition was included to examine the stereotype of the group when no target information was provided. Low identifiers' stereotypes were relatively unaffected by the target manipulation. However, higher identifiers who read about a negative group member estimated that fewer students had negative stereotypical characteristics and more had positive characteristics than those who read about a positive group member, as shown in Figure 8.2.

These findings show that the presence of deviant ingroup members provokes reactions with contrasting valence at the intragroup and intergroup levels. Among people who identify highly with the group, an individual deviant ingroup member is more strongly derogated and is perceived to convey a negative image of the group, while at the same time the positive stereotype of the group becomes reinforced or bolstered. Thus, it seems that deviants serve as exemplars from which the group norm can be contrasted, consistent with the idea of backward processing, described above.

Pro-Norm and Anti-Norm Deviance

Much of the research described above concerned judgments of ingroup and outgroup deviants who were different from the norms of both groups. However, it did not address the specific questions of whether evaluative differentiation between normative and deviant members reflects either the magnitude and/or the particular direction, of deviance. In common with social identity and self-categorization theories, the SGD model assumes that groups have normative *direction*. It may be difficult for group members to know the precise normative position for their group, but they may be relatively sure about the directions in which their group's norms differ from those of relevant other groups. It follows that deviation may be judged in terms of its perceived departure from the group's normative direction rather than objective or absolute differences from the norm.

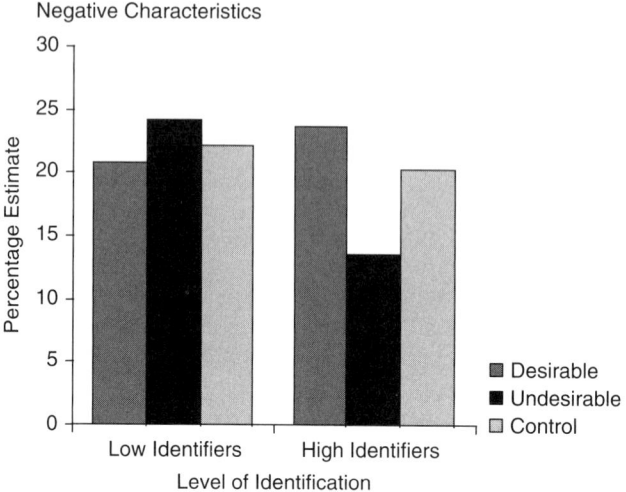
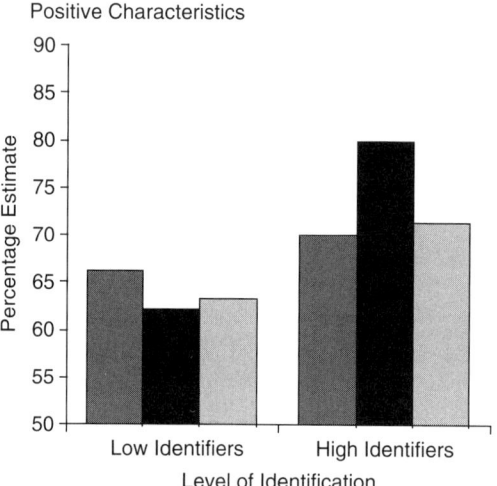

FIGURE 8.2 Negative and positive stereotyping of the ingroup following exposure to a desirable, undesirable or no ingroup target

In an intergroup context, members who deviate towards the opposing group (who we label "anti-norm" deviants) should be perceived as more atypical than those who deviate away from the opposing group (who we label "pro-norm" deviants, see Abrams, Marques, Bown, & Henson, 2000), because anti-norm deviants pose a greater contrast with the normative direction of the group. Anti-norm deviants may sometimes be members who adopt positions that are broadly moderate, and pro-norm deviants may sometimes be extremists or fanatics when judged in a wider context (e.g., Haslam, Oakes, McGarty, Turner, & Onorato, 1995). However, this will not always be true, and must depend upon that wider context. For example, members of the UK Labour Party who strongly support joining the Euro currency (a pro-norm position in line with the direction of Labour Party policy) would clearly not be judged as extremists by members of countries that have already joined.

The SGD model predicts that deviance that potentially undermines ingroup norms should attract hostile reactions. Conversely, if objective deviance potentially validates ingroup norms, it is likely to attract positive evaluations. For this reason group members may be tolerant, or even approving, of deviants whose differences from other group members mean they can contribute positively to the subjective validity of the group norm. To investigate this possibility we extended our research paradigm to distinguish the two types of deviance. The normative direction taken by anti-norm deviance *undermines* or rejects the group's position, and may imply relative validation of the norms of opposing groups. The direction taken by pro-norm deviance, in contrast, *validates* and supports the group's aims or ethos and may enhance its distinctiveness relative to opposing outgroups (Abrams et al., 2000). Two studies examined reactions to anti- and pro-norm deviants and normative members when intergroup context was implicit. A further two studies examined reactions when the intergroup context was made more explicit.

Abrams et al. (2000, Experiment 1) asked teenage participants to evaluate people from their own gender group who were ostensibly being considered for promotion in an organization. Candidates were depicted as all being very similar in levels of competence, intelligence, politeness, and other features. One candidate was much more feminine, and another was much more masculine than the remaining (normative) candidates. The magnitude of deviation from the norm was objectively equivalent for both the highly feminine and the highly masculine candidate, and these differences were subsequently reported accurately by participants. Participants regarded themselves as significantly more similar to the normative candidates than to either of the deviant candidates. However, despite the objective equivalence in the magnitude of deviance by the anti- and pro-norm candidates, participants rated the pro-norm target as having more in common with the group. The normative candidates were rated as more attractive than the pro-norm and anti-norm candidates, but the pro-norm candidate was also rated as more attractive than the anti-norm candidate. Thus, although pro-norm deviants were disliked, they were tolerated more than anti-norm deviants, consistent with the idea that ingroup pro-norm deviants were less undermining of ingroup norms.

A further study (Abrams, Marques, Bown, & Dougill, 2002, Experiment 1), examined reactions to deviance in a commercial banking organization. Employees in a major UK offshore bank read descriptions of behavior by other ingroup workers. All participants read about a normative worker. Half the participants also read about an anti-norm deviant who was critical of the organization, refused to do overtime work, and so forth. The other participants read about a pro-norm deviant who was obsessed with supporting the organization, and chose to work additional hours, recruit new members, and so forth. As in Abrams et al.'s (2000) Experiment 1, evaluations of the anti-norm deviant were significantly more negative than those of the pro-norm deviant, even though they were both perceived as being equally different from the ingroup norm. Moreover, more negative evaluations of deviants were significantly associated with prior identification with the organization. Taken together, Abrams et al. (2000, Experiment 1) and Abrams et al. (2002, Experiment 1) suggest that when distinguishing among ingroup members, people are equally able to detect the magnitude of pro-norm and anti-norm deviance, but they reserve their most negative evaluative reactions for anti-norm deviants.

Turning to an explicitly intergroup context, Abrams et al. (2000, Experiment 2) focused on British psychology students' attitudes about the number of asylum seekers that should be allowed entry to Britain each year. Participants read the results of national surveys that ostensibly had been conducted among psychology students or customs and immigration officers. They were informed (accurately) that psychology students wanted no change in the percentage of asylum seekers allowed to remain in Britain, but that immigration officers advocated a reduction in the numbers granted asylum by 30%. Participants then viewed responses to several of the survey items by six respondents, ostensibly either from a Psychology Survey or from a Customs Officers Survey. Four target group members were normative in their opinions, one was pronormative and the other was antinormative. Across conditions and types of deviant the mathematical difference between normative and deviant targets was kept constant. Moreover, the anti-norm target in the ingroup and outgroup conditions actually expressed an identical attitude (i.e., that there should be a 15% reduction in the numbers of asylum seekers allowed to remain in Britain).

As in our previous studies, participants were accurate when asked to report the actual opinion position espoused by each target member. However, unlike the results from the implicit intergroup context studies, pro-norm deviants were judged to be equally typical of their group as the four normative members. Only the anti-norm members were viewed as being atypical. This suggests that judgments of typicality were made with reference to how much the target helps to validate prescriptive norms, and not with reference to statistical typicality. In the intergroup context of the study it seems reasonable to suppose that typicality judgments reflected *prototypicality* as defined by the metacontrast ratio in SCT (e.g., Haslam, et al., 1995). In line with the typicality ratings, evaluations of ingroup normative members and ingroup pro-norm deviants were more positive than evaluations of ingroup anti-norm deviants. The reverse pattern was obtained for outgroup targets (see Figure 8.3). Indeed, the outgroup anti-norm deviant was evaluated more positively than the ingroup

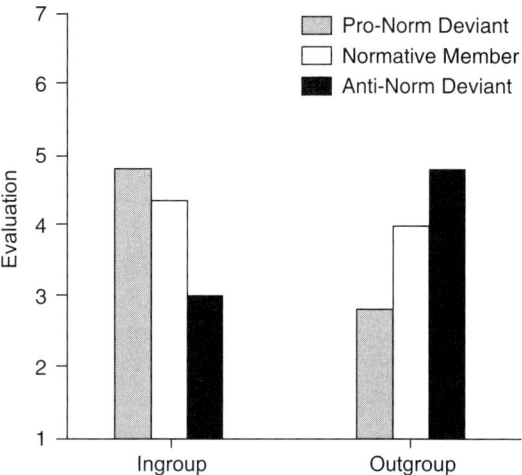

FIGURE 8.3 Favorability to pro-norm, normative, and anti-norm group members as a function of group membership

Source: Abrams, Marques et al. (2000, Experiment 2).

anti-norm deviant, even though both targets expressed identical attitudes. Finally, the more that participants identified with the ingroup the more strongly they favored deviants that validated, as compared with deviants that undermined, the ingroup norm, regardless of whether the deviants were members of the ingroup or the outgroup.

Abrams et al. (2002, Experiment 2) conducted an analogous study in the context of the University of Kent's policy for admission of students from outside Europe ("Overseas Students"). British universities charge a higher level of tuition fees to students from outside Europe, but accordingly they try to provide some advantages for these students, including privileged access to accommodation on campus and related schemes. Pilot studies confirmed that both groups of students did not object to the status quo. However, the normative direction among overseas students was that further privileges would be justified. The normative direction among British students was that a reduction in privileges for Overseas students would be appropriate. Participants were then presented with statements, ostensibly taken from the pilot study, made by three targets from each group about University policy for future cohorts of Overseas students. From each group one target expressed the normative opinion for the group, one expressed an anti-norm position and the other expressed a pro-norm position. In fact, the anti-norm ingroup target and a pro-norm outgroup target expressed identical attitudes (more privileges for future members of the outgroup), that were equally divergent from the current norm (maintain the status quo). Conversely, the pro-norm ingroup and the anti-norm outgroup targets also expressed identical attitudes (fewer privileges for future members of the outgroup).

Consistent with Abrams et al. (2000, Experiment 2) anti-norm deviants were rated as significantly more atypical than normative members and pro-norm members. Typicality ratings of normative and pro-norm members did not differ. Thus, despite potentially strong demand characteristics to distinguish among all six targets on a single continuum, perceived typicality followed a principle of *relative* normativeness, or prototypicality, independent of the actual attitude position expressed and independent of objective similarities among targets. This is consistent with the idea that typicality judgments are attributable to prototypicality defined in the intergroup context, and not to absolute differences among targets or to whether the positions adopted by the target are ingroup validating per se.

The pattern of evaluations was also consistent with that found by Abrams et al.'s (2000) Experiment 2. The pro-norm ingroup deviant was evaluated more positively than the normative member, and both were evaluated more positively than the anti-norm deviant. The reverse pattern was obtained for outgroup targets; evaluations of the pro-norm ingroup and anti-norm outgroup deviant were equally positive. Moreover, differential evaluations of the pro- and anti-norm deviants were strongly associated with the extent to which participants rated the two types of deviants as differing in typicality.

Across the Abrams et al. (2000, 2002) studies the evidence converges to show that as group membership becomes more salient (i.e., as the context becomes more explicitly intergroup), people may engage in more intragroup differentiation in terms of prescriptive norms. Anti-norm deviants are judged to be more atypical of their group than equally divergent pro-norm deviants. For ingroup targets, anti-norm deviants are evaluated very negatively, but pro-norm deviants are often evaluated similarly to normative members (in an intragroup setting) or even more favorably than normative members (in an intergroup setting). Evaluations of particular group members reflect the extent to which they help to validate rather than undermine the normative direction of the group, and hence sustain social identity. In line with this, differential evaluations in favor of ingroup validating targets within the ingroup and the outgroup are associated with higher group identification. An interesting question concerns the conditions under which ingroup anti-norm deviants are likely to be ousted by group members, or indeed whether outgroup deviants might be invited to join the ingroup.

Deviant Leadership A further direction of our research has been to examine the moderating effects of the intragroup context on evaluations of group members. We have used the leadership role as one variant of the intragroup context and we have examined how deviant group members are evaluated when members hold a leadership position compared to when they do not.

This work also draws upon social identity research on leadership and normative prototypicality (e.g., Haslam, 2001; Hogg, 2001b). Although it is arguable that leaders cannot be socially excluded, it is still a possibility. For example, the recent changes in Iraq clearly indicate that a person who is a leader in one intergroup context (e.g., Saddam Hussein during the war), can be viewed as a deviant and be socially excluded in another context (e.g., Saddam Hussein after the war). Thus, the focus on group leaders further emphasises our argument that social exclusion or inclusion is not based just on the characteristics of the individual but rather on the intergroup context in which these characteristics are manifested.

Hogg (2001b) argues that the most prototypical group member will generally emerge as group leader. For example, Hogg, Hains, and Mason (1998) found that participants selected leaders who they perceived to be significantly more prototypical than other group members. It also seems that the link between normative prototypicality and leadership emergence is enhanced when prototypes are internalized to the self-concept (social identity). For example, Hains, Hogg, and Duck (1997) found that participants who identified highly with their ingroup rated a (randomly assigned) leader as more effective when they had been previously informed that the leader was prototypical of their ingroup. Overall, we interpret Hogg's (2001b) social identity theory of leadership as holding that leadership accrues from prototypicality. Thus, the prototypical member is both the most included (psychologically) and the one who is most desired as leader.

Other research suggests an alternative (or additional) process may be operating with group leaders, whereby leadership confers prototypicality. For example, Fielding and Hogg (1997) found that the longer a group member held the leadership position the more prototypical they were perceived to be. It seems reasonable to suppose that the presence of a leader may increase the sense that the group has purpose, direction, and perhaps entitativity. Not only are leaders likely to be perceived as more prototypical than other members, it is also possible that they establish a focal point that makes the group prototype concrete, and this may support the subjective reality of the group. For example, Randsley de Moura and Abrams (2001a) found that the presence of a normative leader increased the perceived entitativity of the group.

Leaders may also be given scope to deviate from group norms and to redefine the goals or values of their group (see Hollander, 1958). Haslam and his colleagues examined reactions to non-prototypical group leaders (e.g., Haslam & Platow, 2001; Haslam et al., 2001). For example, Haslam et al. (2001) suggested that perceived leader charisma may depend on whether a leader affirms ingroup identity. They conducted a study examining whether the leader role may attract increased perceived charisma if the organization's outcomes show a positive turnaround rather than a decline. They found that the leader was perceived as more charismatic when their prior behavior had been even-handed or identity affirming, rather than identity negating. Furthermore, even-handed leaders were perceived as more charismatic following a positive turnaround, and identity-affirming behavior protected leaders from negative reactions following a decline.

In Haslam and Platow's (2001) study participants viewed a video recording of an ingroup student leader discussing a decision to nominate union board members for a prize. The leadership manipulation was devised so that in the discussion the leader either appeared to be "identity-affirming" (ingroup favoring), "even-handed," or "identity negating" (outgroup favoring) in their nominations. While the leader was judged to be the fairest in the even-handed condition, the support for the leader was greatest when the leader was ingroup favoring.

Platow and van Knippenberg (2001) varied the prototypicality and behavior of ingroup leaders and found similar results regarding non-prototypical leaders. To manipulate leader prototypicality, participants viewed information demonstrating two overlapping distributions for the ingroup and the outgroup. They were then informed about a leader who was in the centre of the ingroup's distribution ("normative"), or a leader in the tail away from the outgroup's distribution ("outlier"), or in the tail towards the outgroup norm ("outgroup bordering"). To manipulate leader behavior, participants were informed about the leader's allocation of a mix of enjoyable and boring tasks to an anonymous ingroup member and to an anonymous outgroup member. Based on SCT it was predicted that non-prototypical leaders would need to demonstrate ingroup favoring behavior to secure endorsement. Results confirmed that endorsement for the outgroup bordering (anti-norm deviant) leader was high when that leader demonstrated ingroup favoritism but significantly lower when the leader demonstrated outgroup favoritism.

The research into leadership and prototypicality suggests that non-prototypical group leaders are particularly interesting because of the conflict they create between their group norm and their own opinion/preference. These leaders often face difficult decisions and are likely to be vulnerable to criticism from other group members. Based on the SGD model, several interesting research questions arise from the research outlined above. For example, we wondered whether the pattern of evaluations and reactions to non-prototypical leaders has anything to do with leadership at all. In the studies outlined above (Haslam et al., 2001; Platow & van Knippenberg, 2001), the targets were already labeled as leaders. No comparable non-leaders were presented. Moreover, all targets were ingroup members. Therefore, it is not possible to determine whether the effects of prototypicality were unique to the leadership role and/or unique to ingroup judgments. Using the SGD model as a theoretical framework, we directly tested the question of whether non-prototypical group leaders are evaluated differently from non-prototypical group members who are not group leaders.

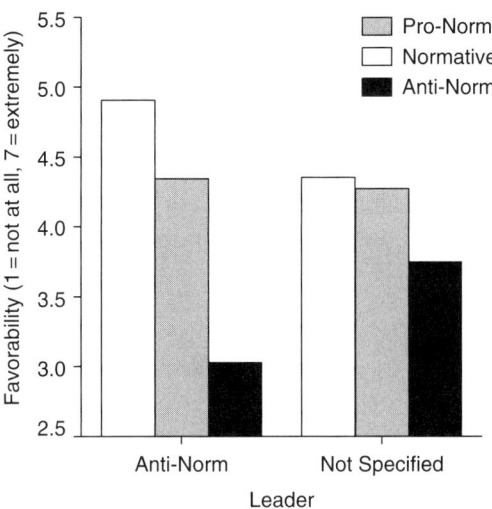

FIGURE 8.4   Favorability Ratings of Ingroup Targets as a Function of Leadership

Source: Randsley de Moura & Abrams, 2001b.

Randsley de Moura and Abrams (2001b) used the asylum attitudes paradigm from Abrams et al. (2000), in which participants viewed pro-norm, normative and anti-norm targets from either the ingroup or the outgroup. Participants were either told that the anti-norm target was the leader of the group, or participants were told that there was a leader but not which member it was. When an ingroup anti-norm deviant was specified as the leader, we found greater intragroup differentiation between targets than when no leader was specified. Specifically, as shown in Figure 8.4, the ingroup anti-norm target was downgraded and the ingroup pro-norm target was upgraded relative to the control condition. This evidence suggests that current leaders who undermine group norms are likely to attract strongly negative reactions from group members, as compared with reactions to similarly deviant nonleaders. That is, having broken ranks with the group, leaders may be more vulnerable to rejection than other deviant members.

We were also interested in whether prospective anti-norm leaders might be afforded greater leeway to define the group norm in relation to *future* activities, perhaps because they are judged to be more prototypical than similarly anti-norm nonleaders. Accordingly, Randsley de Moura and Abrams (2002a) used the asylum paradigm again, and manipulated leadership by telling participants either that the anti-norm target had been selected to be a future leader or merely that one of the targets would be a leader, without specifying which one. We found that future leadership in the hands of an anti-norm target reduced the participants' ratings of typicality for pro-norm targets. We also found that anti-norm targets were perceived more favorably when they were specified as leaders compared to when they were not. This seems consistent with the conferral hypothesis, suggesting that being a *future* leader may offset potential criticism of anti-norm targets (Randsley de Moura, & Abrams, 2002a; 2002b; 2003). This raises interesting questions about the capacity of leaders to shape and shift group norms rather than being at the mercy of social control processes typically associated with subjective group dynamics. For example, the recent history of successive leadership battles in the Conservative Party in Britain suggests that leaders are often elected with a mandate to set a "new" agenda or manifesto, but tolerance for new leaders may not be sustained if they fail to reflect the norms of the group (e.g., strong Euro-scepticism, traditional values). In such a situation, the leaders may be ejected from their positions of power and excluded from the leadership group while they languish on the backbenches of parliament.

CONCLUSIONS

The SGD model holds important implications for the management of deviance and diversity within society. People who are rejected by groups are not necessarily their most deviant members in objective terms. Quite extreme forms of (pro-norm) deviance may be tolerated by groups, and may be regarded as relatively normal. This may hold the key to phenomena such as group extremity shifts, groupthink, and polarization (Abrams, Wetherell, Cochrane, Hogg, & Turner, 1990; Janis, 1982; Turner, Wetherell, & Hogg, 1989), whereby a group's norms may become increasingly extreme under the influence of pro-norm deviants. As groups become more extreme, their "moderate" (i.e., anti-norm) members may lose the ear of the group, be vilified and either conform or be rejected. Thus, for all kinds of group decisions it may be that voices of reason— those who countenance the views of outgroups, for example, may be disregarded, coerced into conformity, and seen as vindicating the group's norm. These phenomena suggest that policy makers who are concerned with issues of social exclusion should consider the situation in not just terms of the "victim" and the excluders, but also the intergroup context. A consideration of subjective group dynamics processes could be useful in contexts such as school, organizations with multiple teams, the management of sports fans, and those working to establish communities that include diverse groups. Under some circumstances, despite apparently tolerant attitudes towards particular outgroup individuals, forcing groups together may result in a hardening of intergroup norm differences, and a resistance to change rather than integration and tolerance.

ACKNOWLEDGMENT

The authors acknowledge grants from the Economic and Social Research Council (R42200034207, R000223087, R451265070 and R000230401), which supported some of the research reported in this chapter.

REFERENCES

Aboud, F. E. (1988). *Children and prejudice*. Oxford, England: Blackwell.
Abrams, D. (1985). Focus of attention in minimal intergroup discrimination. *British Journal of Social Psychology, 24*, 65–74.
Abrams, D. (1990). How do group members regulate their behavior? An integration of social identity and self-awareness theories. In D. Abrams & M. A. Hogg (Eds.), *Social identity theory: Constructive and critical advances* (pp. 89–112). London and New York: Harvester Wheatsheaf and Springer-Verlag.
Abrams, D. (1992). Processes of self-identification. In G. Breakwell (Ed.), *Social psychology of identity and the self-concept* (pp. 57–99). San Diego: Academic Press.
Abrams, D. (1994). Social self-regulation. *Personality and Social Psychology Bulletin, 20*, 473–483.
Abrams, D. (1996). Social identity, self as structure and self as process. In W. P. Robinson (Ed.), *Social groups and identities: Developing the legacy of Henri Tajfel* (pp. 143–167). Oxford: Butterworth-Heinemann.
Abrams, D. (1999). Social identity, social cognition, and the self: The flexibility and stability of self-categorization. In D. Abrams & M. A. Hogg (Eds.), *Social identity and social cognition* (pp. 197–230). Malden, MA: Blackwell.
Abrams, D. & Brown, R. J. (1989). Self-consciousness and social identity: Self-regulation as a group member. *Social Psychology Quarterly, 52*, 311–318.
Abrams, D. & Hogg, M. A. (1988). Comments on the motivational status of self-esteem in social identity and intergroup discrimination. *European Journal of Social Psychology, 18*, 317–334.
Abrams, D. & Hogg, M. A. (1990). An introduction to the social identity approach. In D. Abrams & M. A. Hogg (Eds.), *Social identity theory: Constructive and critical advances* (pp. 1–9). London and New York: Harvester Wheatsheaf and Springer-Verlag.
Abrams, D. & Hogg, M. A. (2001). Collective Identity: Group Membership and Self-Conception. In M. A. Hogg and S. Tindale (Eds.), *Blackwell handbook of social psychology: Group processes* (Vol. 3, pp. 425–461).
Abrams, D. & Masser, B. (1998). Context and the social self-regulation of stereotyping: Perception, judgment and behaviour. In R. S. Wyer (Ed.), *Advances in social cognition* (Vol. 11, pp. 53–68). Hillsdale, NJ: Erlbaum.
Abrams, D., Rutland, A., & Cameron, L. (2003). The development of subjective group dynamics: Children's judgments of normative and deviant ingroup and outgroup individuals. *Child Development, 74*, 1840–1856.
Abrams, D., Marques, J. M., Bown, N., & Dougill, M. (2002). Anti-norm and pro-norm deviance in the bank and on the campus: Two experiments on subjective group dynamics. *Group Processes and Intergroup Relations, 5*, 163–182.

Abrams, D., Marques, J. M., Bown, N., & Henson, M. (2000). Pro-norm and anti-norm deviance within and between groups. *Journal of Personality and Social Psychology, 78*, 906–912.

Abrams, D., Marques, J. M., Randsley de Moura, G., Hutchison, P., & Bown, N. J. (2004). The maintenance of entitativity: A subjective group dynamics approach. In V. Y. Yzerbyt, C. M. Judd, & O. Corneille (Eds.), *The psychology of group perception: Contributions to the study of homogeneity, entitativity, and essentialism* (pp. 361–381). Philadelphia PA: Psychology Press.

Abrams, D., Rutland, A., Cameron, L., & Marques, J. M. (2003). The development of subjective group dynamics: When ingroup bias gets specific. *British Journal of Developmental Psychology, 21*, 155–176.

Abrams, D., Wetherell, M., Cochrane, S., Hogg, M.A., & Turner, J. C. (1990). Knowing what to think by knowing who you are: Self-categorization and the nature of norm formation, conformity, and group polarization. *British Journal of Social Psychology, 29*, 97–119.

Asch, S. (1952). *Social psychology.* New York: Prentice Hall.

Berkowitz, L. & Howard, R. (1959). Reaction to opinion deviates as affected by affiliation need and group member interdependence. *Sociometry, 22*, 81–91.

Biernat, M., T., Vescio, T. K., Billings, L. S. (1999). Black sheep and expectancy violation: Integrating two models of social judgements. European *Journal of Social Psychology, 29*, 523–542.

Blascovich, J., Wyer, N. A., Swart, L. A., & Kibler, J. L. (1997). Racism and racial categorization. *Journal of Personality and Social Psychology, 72*, 1364–1372.

Bodenhausen, G. & Macrae, C. N. (1998). Stereotype activation and inhibition. In R. S. Wyer (Ed.), *Advances in social cognition* (Vol. 11, pp. 1–52). Hillsdale, NJ: Erlbaum.

Boyanowsky, E. & Allen, V. (1973). Ingroup norms and self-identity as determinants of discriminatory behavior. *Journal of Personality and Social Psychology, 25*, 408–418.

Branscombe, N. R., Wann, D. L., Noel, J. G., & Coleman, J. (1993). Ingroup or outgroup extremity: Importance of the threatened social identity. *Personality and Social Psychology Bulletin, 19*, 381–388.

Brewer, M. B. (1988). A dual process model of impression formation. In T. K. Srull & R. S. Wyer (Eds.), *Advances in social cognition* (Vol. 1, pp. 1–36). Hillsdale, NJ: Erlbaum.

Cadinu, M. R. & Rothbart, M. (1996). Self-anchoring and differentiation processes in the minimal group setting. *Journal of Personality and Social Psychology, 70*, 661–677.

Campbell, D. T. (1958). Common fate, similarity, and other indices of the status of aggregates of persons as social entities. *Behavioral Science, 3*, 14–25.

Caporael, L. R. & Brewer, M. B. (2000). Metatheories, evolution, and psychology: Once more with feeling. *Psychological Inquiry, 11*, 23–26.

Castano, E., Paladino, M-P., Coull, A., & Yzerbyt, V. Y. (2002a). Protecting the ingroup stereotype: Ingroup identification and the management of deviant ingroup members. *British Journal of Social Psychology, 41*, 365–385.

Castano, E., Yzerbyt, V., Bourguignon, D., & Seron, E. (2002b). Who may enter? The impact of ingroup identification on ingroup/outgroup categorization. *Journal of Experimental Social Psychology, 38*, 315–322.

Christian, J. N., Hutchison, P., & Abrams, D. (2003). *Deviance and Sanctioning in Low and High Status Groups*. Paper presented at the British Psychological Society Social Section Conference, London School of Economics, September 10–12.

Coull, A., Yzerbyt, V. Y., Castano, E., Paladino, M-P., & Leemans, V. (2001). Protecting the ingroup: Motivated allocation of cognitive resources in the presence of threatening ingroup members. *Group Processes and Intergroup Relations, 4*, 327–339.

Davis, J. & Witte, E. (1996). *Understanding group behavior: Consensual action by small groups* (Vol. 2) Mahwah, NJ: Erlbaum.

Festinger, L. (1950). Informal social communication. *Psychological Review, 57*, 271–282.

Fielding, K. S. & Hogg, M. A. (1997). Social identity, self-categorisation, and leadership: A field study of small interactive groups. *Group Dynamics: Theory, Research and Practice, 1*, 39–51.

Fiske, S. T. & Neuberg, S. L. (1990). A continuum of impression formation, from category-based to individuating processes: Influences of information and motivation on attention and interpretation. In M. P. Zanna (Ed.), *Advances in Experimental Social Psychology* (Vol. 23, pp. 1–74). San Diego: Academic Press.

Forsyth, D. R. (1990). *Group dynamics*. Pacific Grove, CA: Brookes/Cole.

Hains, S. C., Hogg, M. A., & Duck, J. M. (1997). Self-categorization and leadership: Effects of group prototypicality and leader stereotypicality. *Personality and Social Psychology Bulletin, 23*, 1087–1100.

Haslam, S. A. (2001). *Psychology in organizations: The social identity approach*. London: Sage.

Haslam, S. A., Oakes, P. J., McGarty, C., Turner, J. C., & Onorato, R. (1995). Contextual changes in the prototypicality of extreme and moderate outgroup members. *European Journal of Social Psychology, 25*, 509–530.

Haslam, S. A. & Platow, M. J. (2001). The link between leadership and followership: How affirming social identity translates vision into action. *Personality and Social Psychology Bulletin, 27*, 1469–1479.

Haslam, S. A., Platow, M. J., Turner, J. C., Reynolds, K. J., McGarty, C., Oakes, P. J., et al. (2001). Social identity and the romance of leadership. The importance of being seen to be "doing it for us". *Group Processes and Intergroup Relations, 4*, 191–205.

Hewstone, M., Rubin, M. & Willis, H. (2002). Intergroup bias. *Annual Review of Psychology, 53*, 575–604.

Hogg, M. A. (1993). Group cohesiveness: A critical review and some new directions. *European Review of Social Psychology, 4*, 85–111.

Hogg, M. A. (2000). Subjective uncertainty reduction through self-categorization: A motivational theory of social identity processes. *European Review of Social Psychology, 11*, 223–256.

Hogg, M. A. (2001a). Social categorization, depersonalization, and group behavior. In R. S. Tindale and M. A. Hogg (Eds.), *Blackwell handbook of social psychology, (Vol 3): Group processes*. (pp 56–85). Oxford: Blackwell.

Hogg, M. A. (2001b). A social identity theory of leadership. *Personality and Social Psychology Review, 5*, 184–200.

Hogg, M. A. & Abrams, D. (1988). *Social identifications: A social psychology of intergroup relations and group processes*. London: Routledge.

Hogg, M. A. & Abrams, D. (1993). Towards a single-process uncertainty-reduction model of social motivation in groups. In D. Abrams & M. A. Hogg (Eds.), *Group motivation: Social psychological perspectives* (pp. 173–190). London: Harvester Wheatsheaf.

Hogg, M. A. & Hains, C. S. (1998). Friendship and group identification: A new look at the role of cohesiveness in group think. *European Journal of Social Psychology, 28*, 323–341.

Hogg, M. A., Hains, S. C. & Mason, I. (1998). Identification and leadership in small groups: Salience, frame of reference, and leader stereotypicality effects on leader evaluations. *Journal of Personality and Social Psychology, 75*, 1248–1263.

Hogg, M. A. & McGarty, C. (1990). Self-categorization and social identity. In D. Abrams & M. A. Hogg (Eds.), *Social identity theory: Constructive and critical advances* (pp. 10–27). London and New York: Harvester Wheatsheaf and Springer-Verlag.

Hollander, E. P. (1958). Conformity, status and idiosyncrasy credit. *Psychological Review, 65*, 117–127.

Holtz, R. & Miller, N. (1985). Assumed similarity and opinion certainty. *Journal of Personality and Social Psychology, 48*, 890–898.

Hutchison, P. (2003). *Motivational processes in stereotype change: Examining factors that moderate the impact of "deviant" group members on stereotypes*. Unpublished doctoral dissertation, University of Kent.

Hutchison, P. & Abrams, D. (2003). Ingroup identification moderates stereotype change in reaction to ingroup deviance. *European Journal of Social Psychology, 33*.

Hutchison, P, & Abrams, D., & Viki, G. T. (2002). *Social Identification, Social Attraction, and Reactions to Deviant In-Group Members*. Paper presented at the Society of Australasian Social Psychologists 8th Annual Meeting, Adelaide, Australia, 25–28 April.

Janis, I. L. (1982). *Groupthink* (2nd ed.). Boston: Houghton Mifflin.

Kahneman, D. & Miller, D. T. (1986). Norm theory: Comparing reality to its alternatives. *Psychological Review, 93*, 136–153.

Krueger, J. & Clement, R. W. (1996). Inferring category characteristics from sample characteristics: Inductive reasoning and social projection. *Journal of Experimental Psychology General, 125*, 52–68.

Kruglanski, A.W. & Webster, D. M. (1996). Motivated closing of the mind: "Seizing" and "freezing." *Psychological Review, 103*, 263–283.

Kunda, Z. & Oleson, K. C. (1997). When exceptions prove the rule: How extremity of deviance determines the impact of deviant examples on stereotypes. *Journal of Personality and Social Psychology, 72*, 965–979.

Kurzban, R. & Leary, M. R. (2001). Evolutionary origins of stigmatization: The functions of social exclusion. *Psychological Bulletin, 127*, 187–208.

Levine, J. M. (1989). Reactions to opinion deviance in small groups. In P. B. Paulus (Ed.), *Psychology of group influence* (pp. 187–231). Hillsdale, NJ: Erlbaum.

Leyens, J.-P., Rodriguez Perez, A., Rodriguez Torres, R., Gaunt, R., Paladino, M. P., Vaes, J., Demoulin, S. (2001). Psychological essentialism and the differential attribution of uniquely human emotions to ingroups and outgroups. *European Journal of Social Psychology, 31*, 395–411.

Marques, J. M., Abrams, D., Páez, D., & Hogg, M. A. (2001). Social categorization, social identification, and rejection of deviant group members. In M. A. Hogg & R. S. Tindale (Eds.), *Blackwell handbook of social psychology (Vol. 3): Group Processes*. Oxford: Blackwell.

Marques, J. M. Abrams, D., Páez, D., & Martinez-Taboada, C. (1998). The role of categorization and ingroup norms in judgments of groups and their members. *Journal of Personality and Social Psychology, 75(5)*, 976–988.

Marques, J. M., Abrams, D., & Serôdio, R. G. (2001). Being better by being right: Subjective group dynamics and derogation of ingroup deviants when generic norms are undermined. *Journal of Personality and Social Psychology, 81*, 436–447.

Marques, J. M. & Páez, D. (1994). The "black sheep effect": Social categorization, rejection of ingroup deviates, and perception of group variability. In W. Stroebe & M. Hewstone (Eds.), *European Review of Social Psychology* (Vol. 5, pp. 38–68), Chichester, England: Wiley & Sons.

Marques, J. M. Páez, D., & Abrams, D. (1998). Social identity and intragroup differentiation as subjective social control. In S. Worchel, J. F. Morales, D. Páez, & J. -C. Deschamps (Eds.), *Social identity: International perspectives* (pp. 124–142). London, England: Sage.

Marques, J. M. Robalo, E. M., & Rocha, S. A. (1992). Ingroup bias and the black sheep effect: Assessing the impact of cognitive-motivational and informational antecedents of judgmental extremity towards ingroup members. *European Journal of Social Psychology, 22*, 331–352.

Marques, J. M. & Yzerbyt, V. Y. (1988). The black sheep effect: Judgmental extremity towards ingroup members in inter- and intra-group situations. *European Journal of Social Psychology, 18*, 287–292.

Marques, J. M. & Yzerbyt, V. Y., & Leyens, J. -Ph. (1988). Extremity of judgments towards ingroup members as a function of ingroup identification. *European Journal of Social Psychology, 18*, 1–16.

McGarty, C. (1999) *Categorization in social psychology*. London: Sage.

Miller, D. T. & Prentice, D. A. (1996). The construction of social norms and standards. In E. T. Higgins & A. W. Kruglanski (Eds.), *Social psychology: Handbook of basic principles* (pp. 789–829). New York: The Guilford Press.

Miller, N., Gross, S., & Holtz, R. (1991). Social projection and attitudinal certainty. In J. Suls & T. A. Wills (Eds.), *Social comparison: Contemporary theory and research* (pp. 177–209). Hillsdale, NJ: Lawrence Erlbaum Associates.

Monteith, M. J., Sherman, J. W., & Devine, P. G. (1998). Suppression as a stereotype control strategy. *Personality and Social Psychology Review, 2*, 63–82.

Moscovici, S., Mugny, G., & van Avermaet, E. (Eds). (1985) *Perspectives on minority influence*. Cambridge: Cambridge University Press.

Mullen, B. (1991). Group composition, salience, and cognitive representations: The phenomenology of being in a group. *Journal of Experimental Social Psychology, 27*, 297–323.

Mullen, B., Brown, R., & Smith, C. (1992). Ingroup bias as a function of salience, relevance, and status: An integration. *European Journal of Social Psychology, 22*, 103–122.

Mummendey, A. & Wenzel, M. (1999). Social discrimination and tolerance in intergroup relations: Reactions to intergroup difference. *Personality and Social Psychology Review, 3*, 158–174.

Oakes, P. J. (1996). The categorization process: Cognition and the group in the social psychology of stereotyping. In W. P. Robinson (Ed.), *Social groups and identities: Developing the legacy of Henri Tajfel* (pp. 95–120). Oxford: Butterworth-Heinemann.

Oakes, P. J., Haslam, S. A., & Turner, J. C. (1994). *Stereotypes and social reality*. Oxford: Blackwell.

Oakes, P. J., Turner, J. C., & Haslam, S. A., (1991). Perceiving people as group members: The role of fit in the salience of social categorizations. *British Journal of Social Psychology, 30*, 125–144.

Perner, J., Leekam, S. R., & Wimmer, H. (1987). Three-year olds' difficulty with false belief: The case for a conceptual deficit. *British Journal of Developmental Psychology, 5*, 125–137

Perner, J., Ruffman, T., & Leekam, S. R. (1994). Theory of mind is contagious: You catch it from your sibs. *Child Development, 65*, 1224–1234.

Plant, E. A. & Devine, P. G. (1998). Internal and external motivation to respond without prejudice. *Journal of Personality and Social Psychology, 75*, 811–832.

Platow, M. J. & van Knippenberg, D. (2001). A social identity analysis of leadership endorsement: The effects of leader ingroup prototypicality and distributive intergroup fairness. *Personality and Social Psychology Bulletin, 27*, 1508–1519.

Randsley de Moura, G. & Abrams, D. (2001a). *Subjective Group Dynamics: Testing the Role of Intra- and Intergroup Context*. Paper presented at British Psychological Society Centenary Annual Conference, March 28–31, Glasgow, United Kingdom.

Randsley de Moura, G. & Abrams, D. (2001b, July 18–20). *Subjective Group Dynamics: Examining the Role of the Intragroup Context*. Paper presented at the British Psychological Society Social Psychology Section Conference, Surrey, United Kingdom.

Randsley de Moura, G. & Abrams, D. (2002a, June 26–29). *Does leadership role alone enhance trust in a non-prototypical group member?* Poster presented at the 13th General Meeting of the European Association of Experimental Social Psychology, San Sebastián, Spain.

Randsley de Moura, G. & Abrams, D. (2002b, September 11–13). *Subjective Group Dynamics: Investigating the Role of the Intragroup Context*. Paper presented at the British Psychological Society Social Psychology Section Conference, Huddersfield, United Kingdom.

Randsley de Moura, G. & Abrams, D. (2003). *Does Leadership Role Change Perceptions of Deviant Group Members?* Paper presented at the British Psychological Society Annual Conference, Bournemouth, United Kingdom, March 13–15.

Reicher, S. D., Spears, R., & Postmes, T. (1995). A social identity model of deindividuation phenomena. *European Review of Social Psychology, 6*, 161–198.

Schachter, S. (1951). Deviation, rejection and communication. *Journal of Abnormal and Social Psychology, 46*, 190–207.

Shaw, M. E. (1976). *Group dynamics: The psychology of small group behavior*. New York: McGraw-Hill.

Sherif, M. (1936). *The psychology of social norms*. New York: Harper & Row.

Sherif, M. & Sherif, C.W. (1953). *Groups in harmony and tension: an integration of studies of intergroup relations*. Oxford, England: Harper & Brothers.

Sherman, S. J., Hamilton, D. L., & Lewis, A. (1999). Perceived entitativity and the social identity value of group memberships. In D. Abrams & M. A. Hogg (Eds.), *Social identity and social cognition* (pp. 80–110). Malden, MA: Blackwell.

Spears, R. (2001). The interaction between the individual and the collective self: Self-categorization in context. In C. Sedikides and M. B. Brewer (Eds.), *Individual self, relational self, collective self* (pp. 171–198). Philadelphia: Psychology Press.

Spears, R., Oakes, P. J., Ellemers, N., & Haslam, S. A. (Eds.). (1997). *The social psychology of stereotyping and group life*. Oxford: Blackwell.

Tajfel, H. (1974). Social identity and intergroup behaviour. *Social Science Information, 13*, 65–93.

Tajfel H. & Turner, J. C. (1979). An integrative theory of intergroup conflict. In W.G. Austin & S. Worchel (Eds.), *The social psychology of intergroup relations* (pp. 33–47). Monterey, CA: Brookes/Cole.

Turner, J. C. (1991). *Social influence*. Milton, Keynes: Open University Press.

Turner, J. C., Hogg, M. A., Oakes, P. J., Reicher, S. D., & Wetherell, M. S. (1987). *Rediscovering the social group: A self-categorization theory*. Oxford: Blackwell.

Turner, J. C. & Oakes, P. J. (1997). The socially structured mind. In C. McGarty & S. A. Haslam (Eds.), *The message of social psychology* (pp. 355–373). Oxford: Blackwell.

Turner, J. C., Wetherell, M. S., & Hogg, M. A. (1989). Referent informational influence and group polarization. *British Journal of Social Psychology, 28*, 135–147

Yzerbyt, V. Y., Judd, C. M., & Corneille, O. (Eds.) (2004). *The psychology of group perception: Contributions to the study of homgeneity, entitativity and essentialism*. Philadelphia PA: Psychology Press.

Yzerbyt, V. Y., Castano, E., Leyens, J-P., & Paladino, M-P. (2000). The primacy of the ingroup: The interplay of entitativity and identification. In W. Stroebe & M. Hewstone (Eds.), *European Review of Social Psychology* (Vol. 11, pp. 257–296). Chichester, UK: Wiley.

Yzerbyt, V., Castano, E., Leyens, J-P., & Paladino, M-P. (2000). The primacy of the ingroup: The interplay of entitativity and identification. *European Review of Social Psychology, 11*, 257–295.

9

Fringe Dwellers: Processes of Deviance and Marginalization in Groups

MICHAEL A. HOGG, KELLY S. FIELDING, and JOHN DARLEY

A discussion is provided of the variety of forms taken and functions played by deviance and marginalization, and of the variety of causes of and reactions to deviance. We then elaborate a model, based on the social identity perspective, of marginalization in groups. There are three variables. (a) Direction: *whether the deviation from the prototype is towards the outgroup or away from the outgroup, (b)* Motivation: *whether members' dominant motivation is subjective uncertainty reduction or group and self-enhancement, and (c)* Behavior: *whether the deviate attributes his or her deviance to self or to the group. Some preliminary evidence is discussed.*

Groups can be cruel to their members. They pick on specific individuals to torment, ostracize, or use as scapegoats for the group's shortcomings; exiling these poor souls to the margins of the group, casting them out of the group altogether, or treating them as if they no longer exist (e.g., Williams, 2001). Why do groups do this? Why do groups treat fellow members in ways that are often harsher than the way they treat members of outgroups? What is it about the interactions between group dynamics and needs, and the characteristics and actions of specific group members that cause them to be treated in this way? We suggest that this is an important and underexamined question in the context of a modern social psychology that emphasizes that groups are supposed to provide shelter, support, and a collective sense of self for their members; groups are supposed to bring people together to work interdependently to achieve shared goals; groups are supposed to provide people with a sense of belonging.

In this chapter we discuss some examples of what we will call "manifestations of marginalization," in order to present a model of the conditions under which group members are accepted/included or rejected/excluded by the group (see Fielding, 2002; Hogg & Hornsey, in press). The model is derived from the social identity approach (for a recent overview see Hogg, 2003) augmented by staffing theory and a perspective drawn from thinking on attributional accounts and excuses. Briefly, we propose that group members who are peripheral (i.e., poor matches to the group prototype, non-normative) as opposed to those central to the group (i.e., good matches to the group prototype, highly normative) have the potential to be marginalized. How and when this potential is realized is moderated by the degree and nature of identity threat experienced by the group, the motivational goals of group members, the actual behavior of the peripheral member, and the accounts the peripheral member gives for his or her actions. It is also affected by the extent to which diversity (of views, practices, and identities) is a core aspect of group life and of self-definition as a group member.

SOME FORMS OF MARGINALIZATION

Exclusion as a Last Resort

The social psychology of groups has traditionally focused on pressures towards uniformity within the group. The group provides a social comparative frame of reference within which people orient and co-ordinate their perceptions, beliefs, attitudes, and feelings. Groups bring people together and replace diversity and extremity with uniformity and moderateness (e.g., Festinger, 1950; Shaw, 1976; Sherif, 1936). Contained within this view, however, is recognition that groups do have fringe members whom the group tries hard to socialize so that they conform to the group's norms (Schachter, 1959; also Levine & Moreland, 1994). The group only gives-up and excludes these people from membership if extensive socialization attempts fail. From this perspective, members are not intentionally marginalized as a first resort; on the contrary the group tries very hard to include them, and excludes them from membership only if all socialization attempts fail (see Darley, 2001).

According to staffing theory, one factor that has a significant impact on the group's tendency to exclude members is the relationship between how large the group needs to be to perform its functions and the number of candidates available and willing to be members of the group (e.g., Wicker, 1968). Where the pool of potential members is small compared to the necessary size of the group, rejection of members may threaten the group's existence, and thus more effort is made to resocialize deviants. In groups in which many potential recruits are clamoring for membership, there is less necessity to retain members, and indeed group distinctiveness may actually be served by rejecting existing marginal members in favor of admitting newer members who will be closer to the group prototype.

Another factor that may be important is the extent to which deviation, deviance, dissent, and internal criticism is considered a valued quality of the group. Where these properties are valued then deviates, dissenters, and critics are less likely to be ejected and may actually be celebrated (e.g., Hornsey, Oppes, & Svensson, 2002; McAuliffe, Jetten, Hornsey, & Hogg, 2003). Deviation and dissent may be considered to lend the group a distinctive identity.

As the above comments recognize, groups are often task-oriented; they exist to get things done, and such groups must contain the mix of talents that enables them to fulfill their tasks. For example, one important function of many groups is decision-making. There is evidence that decision-making groups that embrace diverse views and diverse subgroups function better than groups that are overly homogeneous in terms of attitudes, positions, and demographic characteristics. For example, attitudinal diversity within a decision-making group can protect against groupthink (e.g., Postmes, Spears, & Cihangir, 2001; Stasser, Stewart, & Wittenbaum, 1995), and demographic diversity within an organization can provide the organization with valued resources (e.g., Brewer, 1996). Generally, there is evidence that unshared information predicated perhaps on the presence of diverse subgroups can benefit overall group functioning (e.g., Larson, Foster-Fishman, & Keys, 1994; for reviews see Tindale, Kameda, & Hinsz, 2003; Wittenbaum & Stasser, 1996). There is also evidence that internal criticism of a group's culture or operations can promote positive group change (e.g., Hornsey et al., 2002), and that dissent created by minorities within groups can be beneficial, largely through its impact on creativity and innovation (e.g., Nemeth & Owens, 1996; Nemeth & Staw, 1989; Nemeth & Wachtler, 1983).

However, although exclusion can be detrimental to groups and social identity, processes of marginalization and exclusion remain common, one might say dominant, features of group life.

Traitors and Revisionists

Sometimes group members can behave in ways that invite marginalization and ultimate ejection from the group. Members can intentionally betray the group, by practising treachery or acting as a stalking horse for a despised outgroup. They can also intentionally try to destroy the group by introducing a schism (e.g., Sani & Reicher, 2000, also see below) or acting as revisionists. These behaviors are often viewed as a profound betrayal of loyalty and group trust. Since loyalty and a sense that you can trust your fellow members to act in the group's best interests lie at the core of group life (e.g., Tyler & Blader, 2000), betrayal of these expectations is a cardinal violation that invites severe punishment by the group. People who are disloyal in this way are usually marginalized and often ejected or excluded from the group. At the level of the Nation, disloyalty often results in execution, sometimes very gruesome public execution.

There is another side to this. Groups that want to marginalize and ultimately eject or exterminate certain individuals or subgroups often engage in creative rhetoric and elaborate campaigns of vilification and persecution in order to successfully label these unsuspecting individuals as evil traitors, deviants, unbelievers, revisionists, and so forth (e.g., Stalin's purges, the Spanish Inquisition).

Deviant Identities

Group members may sometimes intentionally seek a deviant or marginal identity. There are many reasons why this might occur. People who do this may simply be trying to exit the group. However, others may not actually wish to leave the group, but may feel a lack of distinctiveness within the group. According to Brewer's (1991) optimal distinctiveness theory people seek a balance between feeling included within a collective and feeling distinctive. If the sense of inclusion is overly satisfied then they seek distinctiveness either as individuals or through subgroup identification. Individual eccentricity or membership of a marginal subgroup would clearly reinstate optimal distinctiveness in an overly homogeneous and inclusive group. How the larger group reacts will depend on the extent to which the group is able to accommodate diversity as part of it's defining features (cf. Niedenthal & Beike, 1997; Roccas & Brewer, 2002; Wright, Aron, & Tropp, 2002).

One particular case of people intentionally seeking a marginal or deviant identity is the case of adolescent delinquency. Emler and his colleagues (Emler & Hopkins, 1990; Emler & Reicher, 1995) have suggested that delinquency, particularly among boys, is strategic behavior designed to establish and manage a favorable reputation among groups of peers. Consistent with this view is the fact that delinquent behavior is usually a group activity that occurs in public, thus satisfying its identity-confirming function. Children are particularly prone to choosing a delinquent identity within their peer group if they find it difficult to meet the high standards of academic achievement that are set for their peer group at school.

Another reason why members may seek a deviant identity within a group is in order to transform the group, or steer it in new directions. This is particularly likely to happen if a subgroup of people becomes dissatisfied with what the group has become. Such a subgroup may split off from the main group, causing a schism. For example the schism in Islam between the Sunni majority and Shii minority, which hinges on who should have ruled after the death of Muhammad in 632. The schism, which continues to this day, first came to a head in 656 in a civil war that pitched Muslim against Muslim.

Schisms are best documented in ideological groups such as religions, cults, political parties, artistic movements, scientific doctrines, schools of thought, and so forth (e.g., Liebman, Sutton, & Wuthnow, 1988). According to Sani and Reicher (1998, 1999, 2000; also see Reicher & Hopkins, 2001) a sudden change in the group's defining properties, what it stands for, its prototype, represents a significant identity threat to the group's members. They feel the group is no longer what it used to be. This produces identity threat, self-conceptual uncertainty, and a sense of self-conceptual impermanence and instability.

Those who are taken off guard by this change suddenly feel uncertain about how, and whether, they fit into the new group. To resolve this problem they can try to reestablish the group's original identity through discussion, persuasion, and negotiation. Or, particularly if they consider the group to be intolerant of dissent, unable to embrace diverse views, and inclined towards marginalization of dissenting individuals, they can split into a separate subgroup that is in conflict with the rest of the group. The group is now a marginal subgroup within the larger group, and it has a specific mission to transform the larger group so that it reconfigures itself around the subgroup's new vision for the larger group.

This is a clear case of minority social influence. The subgroup is a marginal minority within the larger majority group, and it will need to pursue minority influence tactics (e.g., promulgating a diachronically and synchronically consistent message) in order to produce latent social influence in the majority, leading ultimately to sudden conversion of the majority (e.g., Moscovici, 1980; Mugny, 1982; Nemeth, 1986; see Martin & Hewstone, 2003).

Black Sheep

Within groups, specific deviant individuals are evaluatively marginalized, and sometimes rejected, from the group. The group creates a class of stigmatized individuals within its boundaries. This process has most systematically been analyzed by Marques and his colleagues through their work on the "black sheep" effect (e.g., Marques & Páez, 1994; Marques & Yzerbyt, 1988; Marques, Yzerbyt, & Leyens, 1988; also see Marques, Abrams, Páez, & Hogg, 2001), and subsequent work on subjective group dynamics.

Marques and colleagues argue that ingroup members who are considered to be only marginally prototypical of the group are liked less as group members than prototypically central members. This differential is accentuated under high salience, so that marginal members may be strongly disliked and entirely rejected as deviants or "black sheep." By being a-prototypical, particularly in a direction that leans towards a salient outgroup, a marginal ingrouper is considered deviant and jeopardizes the distinctiveness and prototypical clarity and integrity of the ingroup. This may threaten the valence of the group, but it also introduces the threat of uncertainty. Thus, fellow ingroupers, especially those for whom uncertainty is particularly threatening, will emphatically reject the deviant in order to consolidate a clear prototype to which they can assimilate themselves through self-categorization (cf. Marques, Abrams, & Serôdio, 2001).

More recently, Marques and Abrams and colleagues have proposed a subjective group dynamics model that outlines the general processes underlying responses to a-prototypical group members. This model is framed by a social identity approach and argues that evaluations of normative and deviate group members are motivated by the need to maintain a positively distinctive ingroup identity. Accordingly, group members who invalidate the ingroup position by violating group norms or undermining the legitimacy of the ingroup's superior status will be rejected. Consistent with this perspective it has been found that group members who were outgroup normative were derogated more than group members who were ingroup normative (Marques, Abrams, Paez, & Martinez-Taboada, 1998). In another study ingroup members were derogated more when their attitudes were in the direction of the outgroup than the ingroup position (Abrams, Marques, Bown, & Henson, 2000). Moreover, ingroup deviates were also downgraded more in contexts where there was a lack of ingroup uniformity (Marques et al., 2001). These studies suggest that subjective rejection of deviates is a mechanism that allows group members to maintain certainty about the validity of ingroup standards and thus the superiority of ingroup identity.

Leaders

The black sheep effect focuses on the treatment of group members who are marginally prototypical or entirely a-prototypical; people who deviate from the group prototype. These are people who are genuine fringe dwellers from the perspective of the rest of the group. In contrast, people who are highly prototypical occupy center-stage and bathe in the spotlight of consensual positive regard from the rest of the group. These members are popular; they are consensually liked as group members (Hogg, 1993). They are highly influential and, according to the social identity analysis of leadership, in high salience groups with which members identify strongly they tend to occupy leadership positions or be endorsed as effective leaders (Hogg, 2001a; Hogg & van Knippenberg, 2003).

Although leaders may appear at first sight to be the antithesis of marginalized members, the social identity analysis of leadership identifies a paradox (Hogg, 2001b). Where groups are confronted by external threat to entitativity and valence, and members cannot readily leave, identification can be very strong and the group can be very cohesive and normatively consensual. Under these circumstances, members pay close attention to prototypicality, and thus leadership processes rest heavily on how prototypical the leader is perceived to be. These conditions, if they persist for long, furnish the leader with substantial power, and drive a wedge between leader(s) and followers.

Being a highly prototypical leader of a tightly cohesive group with which members identify very strongly endows the leader with the appearance of being very effective and having substantial leadership charisma and power. The fundamental attribution error (Ross, 1977), or correspondence bias (Gilbert & Malone, 1995), then encourages these qualities to be internally attributed to enduring dispositional properties of the leader; the leader is viewed as charismatic, a "great person." In this way the leader is gradually viewed as "other," as different from and better than the rest of the group. The common empathic bond, based on shared group membership, between leader and followers is severed and a deep status-based intergroup schism is gradually created between leader (or leadership clique) and followers. There is now great power distance (Mulder, 1977) between leader and followers, and the leader has significant reward power over the followers. Together these encourage discrimination against the followers (Ng, 1996; Sachdev & Bourhis, 1985), and leadership by coercion.

The relationship between leader(s) and followers is now, effectively, an intergroup relationship in which status differences are vast and consensual. Rather than enjoying popularity and inclusion as a group member, the leader is now often disliked and feared and excluded from group life. An atmosphere of distrust, cronyism, and rivalry pervades the group, and there is a sense that the leader's position is no longer legitimate. Although the leader still has great influence over group life, s/he is affectively marginalized.

Leaders are also relevant to marginalization in another way. It is often leaders who identify and target deviants, and orchestrate the entire process of marginalization. Leaders who feel that their prototypicality is under threat, have the resources to redefine the prototype in a self-serving manner to prototypically marginalize contenders and prototypically centralize self. This can be done by accentuating the existing ingroup prototype, by pillorying ingroup deviants, or by demonizing an appropriate outgroup. Generally all three tactics are used, and the very act of engaging in these tactics is often viewed as further evidence of effective leadership (e.g., Reicher & Hopkins, 1996).

Finally, leaders can marginalize members in a less extreme way that stems from the normal pressures of leadership that involve managing and communicating with a large number of subordinates. According to leader–member exchange (LMX) theory leaders often differentiate among subordinates, favoring some over others by developing more rewarding interpersonal relations with some than with others (Graen & Uhl-Bien, 1995). As a human resource management strategy in busy organizations this is often unavoidable, and necessary for effective leadership. The result is that some members occupy a more marginal role in the group than others. The social identity analysis of leadership (e.g., Hogg, 2001a; Hogg & van Knippenberg, 2003) suggests that in salient groups this personalized leadership style may be less favorably evaluated by followers, and thus less effective, than a more depersonalized style in which all members are treated equally as group members (e.g., Hogg & Martin, 2003;

Hogg, Martin, & Weeden, 2004). The implication is that marginalization by the leader may be more acutely felt in high than in low salience groups. However, in such groups it is possible that subordinates who consider themselves to be highly prototypical may seek preferential treatment and welcome less preferential treatment for marginal members.

POSITIVE AND NEGATIVE DEVIANCE

Our discussion of forms of marginalization indicates that most research focuses on "negative" deviates. Generally speaking, negative deviates are group members who are dislikable because they contribute negatively or do not contribute positively to group evaluation, or who are a-prototypical in a way that inclines them towards the salient outgroup and thus positions them close to the intergroup boundary. This is the traditional arena of deviance research.

However, our previous discussion of leadership suggests that highly prototypical members can sometimes be marginalized. This raises the broader issue of "positive" deviates; group members who are a-prototypical but in evaluatively favorable ways; for example, overachievers or high flyers. On the one hand overachievers should be socially unattractive because they are a-prototypical, but on the other hand they should be socially attractive because the group can bask in their reflected glory (e.g., Burger, 1985; Cialdini, Borden, Thorne, Walker, Freeman, & Sloan, 1976; Cialdini & de Nicholas, 1989; Sigelman, 1986; Snyder, Lassegard, & Ford, 1986; Wann, Hamlet, Wilson, & Hodges, 1995). There is some evidence that people are evaluatively particularly harsh on overachievers who suffer a setback or experience a fall (e.g., Feather, 1994), but this research does not differentiate between overachievers who are members of a salient ingroup and those who are not. What seems to be called for is an integrative model of reactions to deviance that deals with both negative and positive deviance within the same analytic framework.

Motivational Model of Group Responses to Deviance

What we propose here is a social identity model of reactions to deviance, that articulates with Marques and Abrams's subjective group dynamics model (e.g., Marques et al., 2001), but which places a greater emphasis on motivational processes. We suggest that the reaction of a group to deviance is influenced by the type of deviance, the behavior of the deviate, and the motivational goals of the group and its members.

Social Identity Motivations Social identity processes (e.g., Hogg & Abrams, 1988; Tajfel & Turner, 1986; Turner, Hogg, Oakes, Reicher, & Wetherell, 1987) come into play when group membership is psychologically salient, such that people categorize themselves and others in terms of the contextually salient groups (see Hogg, 2003, for a recent overview). Under these circumstances ingroup members, including self, are depersonalized in terms of the contextually salient ingroup prototype; that is, perception, attitudes, feelings, and behavior are governed by the ingroup prototype rather than by idiosyncratic qualities or interpersonal relations.

There are two motivational processes associated with social identity phenomena: self-enhancement and uncertainty reduction (Hogg, 2000). Groups provide people with a sense of self, a social identity, that evaluates self more or less favorably, and that prescribes one's perceptions, attitudes, feelings, and behaviors, and also how other people will treat one. As such, people are motivated to belong to groups that mediate a positive sense of self, and groups that provide one with a sense of certainty about who one is, how one should behave, and how others will react. If positive self-evaluation and self-certainty are threatened, then people and the groups they belong to will take action to respond to the threat.

Self-evaluation may be threatened if the group's relative status or valence is threatened. Such a threat may come from direct intergroup comparisons, or from having members who lower the valence of the group. Clearly, one response to valence threat of this kind is to distance oneself and the group from marginal members who lower the valence of the group; such members may be marginalized and rejected. Self-certainty may be threatened if the group's entitativity is reduced and/or if the group prototype becomes too fuzzy and complex. Such a threat may come from various forms of internal normative conflict, or from the presence of members who are simply highly a-prototypical. One response to certainty or entitativity threat is to purge the group of a-prototypical members by marginalizing and rejecting them.

Motivational Model of Responses to Deviance
Building on these motivational considerations, we can construct a model of how different forms of deviance may be reacted to. There are two dimensions to the model: a functional dimension and a social attribution dimension.

The *functional dimension* relates motivation to the type of deviance. Where solidarity, consensual prototypicality and prototype clarity are particularly important to the group, perhaps due to entitativity threat, group members are motivationally oriented toward uncertainty reduction. Under these circumstances *any* a-prototypical member will pose a threat to the group; negative deviates (those who occupy fringe positions oriented toward the relevant outgroup prototype—marginal members) and positive deviates (those who occupy fringe positions oriented away from the relevant outgroup prototype—extreme members) alike. Both types of deviates are dysfunctional for the group and will be evaluatively downgraded and marginalized. Marginalization reclaims entitativity and prototype clarity, and thus reduces subjective uncertainty.

Where group valence and status are particularly important to the group, due to valence and status threat, group members are motivationally oriented towards self-enhancement through positive group evaluation. Under these circumstances negative deviates (marginal members) pose a greater threat to the group than do positive deviates (extreme members). Marginal members occupy a position in the group that has low valence because it is more closely associated with the evaluatively relatively negative outgroup prototype. Marginalization and rejection of these people will improve the valence of the group. In contrast, extreme members occupy a position in the group that has high valence because it is more remote from the evaluatively negative outgroup prototype. Marginalization and rejection of these people would not improve the valence of the group; they are functional for the group, and would be upgraded as they contribute to a favorable redefinition of ingroup identity.

This analysis can be rephrased. Negative deviates (marginal members) are always marginalized because they threaten both the entitativity and the valence of the group. Positive deviates (extreme members) are sometimes marginalized but sometimes included too, because although they threaten entitativity they actually enhance valence.

The *social attribution dimension* recognizes that marginalization processes will be influenced by what deviates actually do; in particular how they account for their deviant behavior to the ingroup. Here we draw on a substantial literature on "accounts" for social action and the ways that the meanings of social actions can be negotiated by the actors involved. We suggest that when people who exhibit socially positive deviant behavior offer accounts of the deviant behavior that allows the behavior to be "owned" by the group, the deviate will be favorably evaluated. This would be the case, for example, if the high scorer on an athletic team modestly attributed her scoring behavior to the supporting contributions of the other team players rather than her own personal ability. This works best when the deviate has had little personal history of overachievement. A long history of overachievement is less plausibly attributed, by the actor or the group, externally to the group; personal talent is a more plausible explanation (cf. the fundamental attribution error or correspondence bias; Gilbert & Malone, 1995; Ross, 1977).

In cases in which the positively deviant behavior is not framed by the performer in ways that can be "owned" by the group, the performer may well attract negative evaluations. This would be likely where the deviate took full personal credit for the behavior without acknowledging the group's support (i.e., "boasted"), or where the deviate had a long personal history of overachievement (i.e., was an enduring deviate). The group then faces a choice. If the performance of the high achiever is sufficiently valuable to the group, the high achiever will, for instrumental reasons, probably not be expelled from the group, but will be marginalized and derogated within the group.

A quite different dynamic would be expected for negative deviates. People who fail to perform their tasks on problems important to the group have a rather grimmer attributional problem to solve. Negative deviates who try to attribute their negative deviance, their failure, to the group as a whole are likely to be strongly rejected as they are blaming the group for their own low valence performance. However, negative deviates who attribute their deviance to themselves, not the group, are less likely to be strongly rejected as they are not blaming the group for their low valence marginal position on the dimension in question; they are taking personal responsibility.

The accounts that negative deviates offer for their poor performance or prototypically marginal behavior can make a considerable difference to the group's reactions to them; in some initially counterintuitive ways. If one has failed the group once, it may be better to have done so because of some momentary loss of motivation rather than low ability— "I wasn't really trying." However, if the failures will continue, it may be better to frame them as coming from low ability at the task, rather than a long term lack of motivation to do what the group needs to have done. A person who repeatedly is not motivated to do what the group needs done is one who is signaling a quite negative attitude toward the group, inviting derogation or expulsion. Admitting low ability on one task is particularly possible if the group has multiple tasks to do, and the person in question is able to make high ability contributions on other tasks that are critical to group life.

Figure 9.1 describes the types of group responses that are likely to occur when positive or negative deviates externally or internally attribute their deviance under conditions of entitativity or valence threat.

		Entitativity Threat		Valence Threat	
		Personal attribution	Group attribution	Personal attribution	Group attribution
Deviance	Positive	Exclusion	Exclusion	Exclusion	Strong inclusion
	Negative	Exclusion	Strong exclusion	Exclusion	Strong exclusion

FIGURE 9.1 Group reactions to deviates as a function of type of deviation (positive vs. negative), deviate behavior (personal vs. group attribution), and group threat (entitativity vs. valence)

Empirical Tests Two recent studies have tested aspects of this model. In the first study ($N = 61$) (Fielding, 2002) participants' identity as Australians was made salient prior to them being presented with a media article describing an Australian Olympic athlete. Previous research has shown that sporting achievement is an important dimension of Australian identity (Feather, Volkmer, & McKee, 1991), and therefore sporting achievement at the Olympic level is clearly a form of positive deviance. The motivations of group members were varied by threatening either the valence or the distinctiveness of Australian identity. Threatening the positive valence of Australian identity was expected to focus participants on self-enhancement, and thus motivate them to try to restore the positive image of their group (cf. Branscombe & Wann, 1994; Doosje, Ellemers, & Spears, 1995). A threat to the distinctiveness of Australian identity, in contrast, was expected to focus participants on reducing uncertainty by reestablishing a clear ingroup prototype. Checks on this manipulation showed that it was successful. Participants perceived Australian identity as less positive in the valence than the distinctiveness threat condition and as less distinctive in the distinctiveness than the valence threat condition. After reading the media article describing the positive deviate, participants evaluated the prototypicality and overall favorability of the positive deviate. Identification as an Australian was also measured.

When group members were motivated by self-enhancement motives it was expected that they would evaluate positive ingroup deviates favorably regardless of the deviates' level of perceived prototypicality. In this context it is the achievement of the positive deviate that is paramount for satisfying participants' motivational goal. In contrast, the prototypicality of the positive deviate should be critical when group members were motivated to restore ingroup distinctiveness. Regardless of whether the positive deviate can contribute to a favorable ingroup image, if they are not judged as prototypical group members they do little to satisfy the predominant motivation.

Consistent with this reasoning a significant interaction between group threat and the perceived prototypicality of the positive deviate emerged $F(1, 57) = 7.28, p < .01$. When participants were motivated by self-enhancement needs (the valence threat condition) the perceived prototypicality of the positive deviate did not influence evaluations $F(1, 57) = 2.89, p = .094$. However, when participants were motivated by a need to reestablish a distinct and clear prototype (the distinctiveness threat condition), the positive deviate who was perceived to be highly prototypical was evaluated more favorably than the positive deviate who was perceived as low in prototypicality, $F(1, 57) = 29.93, p < .001$ (see Figure 9.2). This pattern also emerged on the measure of Australian identification $F(1,57) = 4.17, p < .05$. When motivated by self-enhancement needs the prototypicality of the positive deviate did not influence how strongly participants identified as Australian (low prototypicality $M = 7.03$, high prototypicality $M = 7.14$; $F < 1$). However, when motivated by the need to reestablish

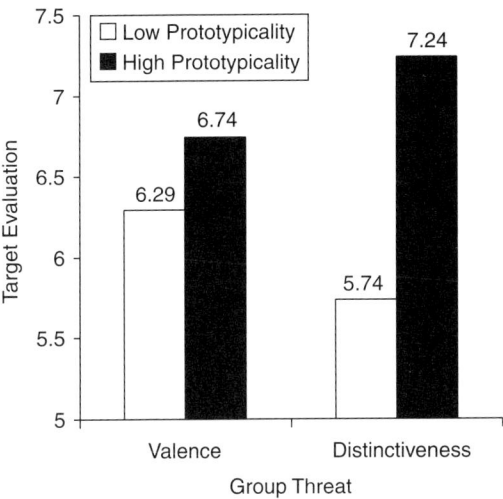

FIGURE 9.2 Evaluation of the positive deviate as function of group threat and the positive deviate's perceived prototypicality

group distinctiveness participants identified more strongly as Australian when the positive deviate was perceived to be highly prototypical ($M = 7.59$) than low in prototypicality ($M = 6.16$), $F(1, 57) = 9.67, p < .01$).

The social attribution aspect of the model has also been tested ($N = 62$) (Fielding, Hogg, & Annandale, in press). Participants' identity as University of Queensland students was made salient and they were presented with media articles describing two ingroup (own university) or two outgroup (other university) positive deviates. One of the positive deviates had won a national academic prize and the other had won a national sporting competition. The attribution style of the positive deviates was manipulated. The positive deviates either attributed their success solely to their own hard work (personal attribution) or they attributed their success, at least in part, to their university (group attribution).

As expected, the interaction between target's group membership and attribution style was significant, $F(1, 55) = 4.65, p < .05$. The ingroup positive deviates who made group attributions for their success were evaluated more favorably than the ingroup positive deviates who made personal attributions for their success, $F(1, 55) = 5.76, p < .05$, whereas evaluations of the outgroup positive deviates were not influenced by attribution style ($F < 1$; see Figure 9.3). This pattern was again reflected in group perceptions. Whereas the attribution style of the outgroup positive deviates did not affect perceptions of group homogeneity (personal attribution $M = 5.07$, group attribution $M = 5.16; F < 1$), group members perceived greater group homogeneity when the ingroup positive deviate made group attributions ($M = 5.67$) rather than

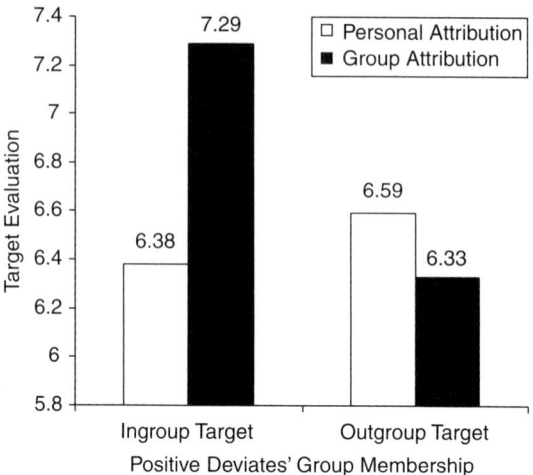

FIGURE 9.3 Evaluations of positive deviates as a function of the positive deviates' group membership and attribution style

personal attributions ($M = 4.25$, $F(1, 58) = 7.09$, $p < .01$) suggesting an attempt to embrace a positive ingroup identity.

Taken together these studies highlight the idea that responses to extreme or marginal group members are not uniform but rather depend on the way in which these extreme group members impact on identity concerns (cf. Schmitt, Silvia, & Branscombe, 2000).

CONCLUSION

The aim of this chapter has been to sketch out a framework for understanding how groups respond to members who deviate from the group prototype and are thus nonnormative in certain respects. Our analysis rests on the social identity perspective, and places the motivational orientation of group members center-stage in how members react to deviates. The three key variables were (a) whether the deviation from the prototype is toward the outgroup (negative deviance) or away from the outgroup (positive deviance), (b) whether members' dominant motivation is subjective uncertainty reduction (promoted by a threat to group entitativity and prototype clarity) or group and self-enhancement (prompted by a threat to group valence), and (c) whether the deviate attributes his or her deviance to self or to the group.

In general, deviance leads to exclusion, marginalization and various forms of rejection from the group. This is most pronounced for negative deviates, particularly those who try to attribute their deviance to the group, and is probably least pronounced for positive deviates who attribute their deviance to themselves, under conditions of valence threat. The only condition under which there is a high probability that the group will include and welcome a deviate is when the group is under valence threat, and the deviate is a positive deviate who attributes his or her deviance to the group.

Although this analysis still requires a full program of empirical investigation, we reported two studies that provide some support. There are, however, many implications of this analysis. One implication concerns the conditions that foster tolerance, or celebration, of diversity within groups. Diversity is all about genuine acceptance and inclusion of non-prototypical members within a larger group. This issue has many manifestations. When do nations or organizations accept rather than marginalize racial and ethnic minorities? When do peer groups accept people with disabilities? When do decision-making groups accept members with different views? We have all, from time to time, been in situations where we have felt marginalized by a group because we challenge their tidy consensual orthodoxy.

Our analysis suggests that genuine acceptance of diversity is difficult to achieve, because deviation always threatens entitativity and almost always threatens valence. However, there is one set of circumstances that should encourage tolerance, even celebration of diversity. That is, when a group's status or valence is threatened, and a deviate member or subgroup that employs a group attribution deviates in a favorable direction away from the outgroup (i.e., it is a positive deviate or an overachiever). For example, an organization is more likely to embrace a minority if the minority is considered highly competent at an organization-defining task, the minority packages its advantage in terms of the supportive context of the organization, and the organization's prestige and status is under threat. All aspects of this dynamic are of course subject to strategic packaging of information. A progressive majority subgroup could present the situation as described. However, a reactionary subgroup could reconstruct the status quo as one where the threat was more to do with entitativity, solidarity, and homogeneity, and one where the minority attributes its advantage to its own essential skills that cannot be shared with and have not been developed by the organizational context.

ACKNOWLEDGMENTS

Some of the ideas presented in this chapter are developed from a paper by Michael Hogg, John Darley, and Kelly Fielding, which was presented in Dominic Abrams and Michael Hogg's symposium on *Social inclusion and exclusion: Intergroup and intragroup processes*, at the annual meeting of the Society of Experimental Social Psychology, Atlanta, October 19–21, 2000.

Michael Hogg would like to acknowledge funding from the Australian Research Council, and from the Portugese Science and Technology Foundation (FCT), Ministry of Science, which has helped to support various aspects of this research.

REFERENCES

Abrams, D., Marques, J. M., Bown, N., & Henson, M. (2000). Pro-norm and anti-norm deviance within and between groups. *Journal of Personality and Social Psychology, 78*, 906–912.

Branscombe, N. R., & Wann, D. L. (1994). Collective self-esteem consequences of outgroup derogation when a valued social identity is on trial. *European Journal of Social Psychology, 24*, 641–657.

Brewer, M. B. (1991). The social self: On being the same and different at the same time. *Personality and Social Psychology Bulletin, 17*, 475–482.

Brewer, M. B. (1996). Managing diversity: The role of social identities. In S. Jackson & M. Ruderman (Eds.), *Diversity in work teams*(pp. 47–68). Washington, D.C.: American Psychological Association.

Burger, J. M. (1985). Temporal effects on attributions for academic performances and reflected-glory basking. *Social Psychology Quarterly, 48*, 330–336.

Cialdini, R. B., Borden, R. J., Thorne, A., Walker, M. R., Freeman, S., & Sloan, L. R. (1976). Basking in reflected glory: Three (football) field studies. *Journal of Personality and Social Psychology, 34*, 366–375.

Cialdini, R. B., & de Nicholas, M. E. (1989). Self-presentation by association. *Journal of Personality and Social Psychology, 57*, 626–631.

Darley, J. (2001). Social comparison motives in ongoing groups. In M. A. Hogg, & R. S. Tindale (Eds.), *Blackwell handbook of social psychology* (pp. 334–351). Oxford, UK: Blackwell.

Doosje B., Ellemers, N., & Spears, R. (1995). Perceived intragroup variability as a function of group status and identification. *Journal of Experimental Social Psychology, 31*, 410–436.

Emler, N., & Hopkins, N. (1990). Reputation, social identity and the self. In D. Abrams & M. A. Hogg (Eds.), *Social identity theory: Constructive and critical advances* (pp. 113–130). London: Harvester Wheatsheaf.

Emler, N., & Reicher, S. D. (1995). *Adolescence and delinquency: The collective management of reputation*. Oxford, UK: Blackwell.

Feather, N. T. (1994). Attitudes towards high achievers and reactions to their fall: Theory and research concerning tall poppies. *Advances in Experimental Social Psychology, 26*, 1–73.

Feather, N. T., Volkmer, R., & McKee, I. (1991). Attitudes towards high achievers in public life: Attributions, deservingness, personality and affect. *Australian Journal of Psychology, 43*, 85–91.

Festinger, L. (1950). Informal social communication. *Psychological Review, 57*, 271–282.

Fielding, K. S. (2002). *Reactions to deviance: A social identity analysis of over- and underachievement in groups.*Unpublished doctoral dissertation, University of Queensland, Australia.

Fielding, K. S., Hogg, M. A., & Annandale, N. (in press). Reactions to positive deviance: Social identity and attribution dimensions. *Group Processes and Intergroup Relations*.

Gilbert, D. T., & Malone, P. S. (1995). The correspondence bias. *Psychological Bulletin, 117*, 21–38.

Graen, G. B., & Uhl-Bien, M. (1995). Relationship-based approach to leadership: Development of leader–member exchange (LMX) theory of leadership over 25 years: Applying a multi-level multi-domain approach. *Leadership Quarterly, 6*, 219–247.

Hogg, M. A. (1993). Group cohesiveness: A critical review and some new directions. *European Review of Social Psychology, 4*, 85–111.

Hogg, M. A. (2000). Subjective uncertainty reduction through self-categorization: A motivational theory of social identity processes. *European Review of Social Psychology, 11*, 223–255.

Hogg, M. A. (2001a). A social identity theory of leadership. *Personality and Social Psychology Review, 5*, 184–200.

Hogg, M. A. (2001b). From prototypicality to power: A social identity analysis of leadership. In S. R. Thye, E. J. Lawler, M. W. Macy, & H. A. Walker (Eds.), *Advances in group processes* (Vol. 18, pp. 1–30). Oxford, UK: Elsevier.

Hogg, M. A. (2003). Social identity. In M. R. Leary & J. P. Tangney (Eds.), *Handbook of self and identity* (pp. 462–479). New York: Guilford.

Hogg, M. A., & Abrams, D. (1988). *Social identifications: A social psychology of intergroup relations and group processes.* London: Routledge.

Hogg, M. A., & Hornsey, M. J. (in press). Self-concept threat and differentiation within groups. In R. J. Crisp & M. Hewstone (Eds.), *Multiple social categorization: Processes, models, and applications*. New York: Psychology Press.

Hogg, M. A., & Martin, R. (2003). Social identity analysis of leader–member relations: Reconciling self-categorization and leader–member exchange theories of leadership. In S. A. Haslam, D. van Knippenberg, M. J. Platow, & N. Ellemers (Eds.), *Social identity at work: Developing theory for organizational practice* (pp. 139–154). New York: Psychology Press.

Hogg, M. A., Martin, R., & Weeden, K. (2004). Leader–member relations and social identity. In D. van Knippenberg & M. A. Hogg (Eds.), *Leadership and power: Identity processes in groups and organizations* (pp. 18–33). London: Sage.

Hogg, M. A., & van Knippenberg, D. (2003). Social identity and leadership processes in groups. In M. P. Zanna (Ed.), *Advances in experimental social psychology* (Vol. 35, pp. 1–52). San Diego, CA: Academic Press.

Hornsey, M. J., Oppes, T., & Svensson, A. (2002). "It's OK if we say it, but you can't": Responses to intergroup and intragroup criticism. *European Journal of Social Psychology, 32*, 293–307.

Larson, J. R., Jr., Foster-Fishman, P. G., & Keys, C. B. (1994). Discussion of shared and unshared information in decision-making groups. *Journal of Personality and Social Psychology, 67*, 446–461.

Levine, J. M., & Moreland, R. L. (1994). Group socialization: Theory and research. *European Review of Social Psychology, 5*, 305–336.

Liebman, R. C., Sutton, J. R., & Wuthnow, R. (1988). Exploring the social sources of denominationalism: Schisms in American Protestant denominations, 1890–1980. *American Sociological Review, 53*, 343–352.

Marques, J. M., Abrams, D., Páez, D., & Hogg, M. A. (2001). Social categorization, social identification, and rejection of deviant group members. In M. A. Hogg & R. S. Tindale, (Eds.), *Blackwell handbook of social psychology: Group processes* (pp. 400–424). Oxford, UK: Blackwell.
Marques, J. M., Abrams, D., Páez, D., & Martinez-Taboada, C. (1998). The role of categorization and in-group norms in judgments of groups and their members. *Journal of Personality and Social Psychology, 75*, 976–988.
Marques, J. M., Abrams, D., & Serôdio, R. (2001). Being better by being right: Subjective group dynamics and derogation of in-group deviants when generic norms are undermined. *Journal of Personality and Social Psychology, 81*, 436–447.
Marques, J. M., & Páez, D. (1994). The "black sheep effect": Social categorization, rejection of ingroup deviates and perception of group variability. *European Review of Social Psychology, 5*, 37–68.
Marques, J. M., & Yzerbyt, V. Y. (1988). The black sheep effect: Judgmental extremity towards ingroup members in inter- and intra-group situations. *European Journal of Social Psychology, 18*, 287–292.
Marques, J. M., Yzerbyt, V. Y., & Leyens, J. -P. (1988). The black sheep effect: Extremity of judgements towards in-group members as a function of group identification. *European Journal of Social Psychology, 18*, 1–16.
Martin, R., & Hewstone, M. (2003). Social influence processes of control and change: Conformity, obedience to authority, and innovation. In M. A. Hogg & J. Cooper (Eds.), *The Sage handbook of social psychology* (pp. 347–366). London: Sage.
McAuliffe, B. J., Jetten, J., Hornsey, M. J., & Hogg, M. A. (2003). Individualist and collectivist group norms: When its OK to go your own way. *European Journal of Social Psychology, 33*, 57–70.
Moscovici, S. (1980). Toward a theory of conversion behavior. In L. Berkowitz (Ed.), *Advances in experimental social psychology* (Vol. 13, pp. 209–239). New York: Academic Press.
Mugny, G. (1982). *The power of minorities*. London: Academic Press.
Mulder, M. (1977). *The daily power game*. Leiden, The Netherlands: Martinus Nijhoff Social Sciences Division.
Nemeth, C., (1986). Differential contributions of majority and minority influence. *Psychological Review, 93*, 23–32.
Nemeth, C., & Owens, P. (1996). Making work groups more effective: The value of minority dissent. In M. A. West (Ed.), *The handbook of workgroup psychology* (pp. 125–141). Chichester, UK: Wiley.
Nemeth, C., & Staw, B. M. (1989). The tradeoffs of social control and innovation in groups and organizations. In L. Berkowitz (Ed.), *Advances in experimental social psychology* (Vol. 22, pp. 175–210). San Diego, CA: Academic Press.
Nemeth, C., & Wachtler, J. (1983). Creative problem solving as a result of majority vs. minority influence. *European Journal of Social Psychology, 13*, 45–55.
Ng, S. H. (1996). Power: An essay in honour of Henri Tajfel. In W. P. Robinson (Ed.), *Social groups and identities: Developing the legacy of Henri Tajfel* (pp. 191–214). Oxford, UK: Butterworth-Heinemann.
Niedenthal, P. M., & Beike, D. R. (1997). Interrelated and isolated self-concepts. *Personality and Social Psychology Review, 1*, 106–128.

Postmes, T., Spears, R., & Cihangir, S. (2001). Quality of decision making and group norms. *Journal of Personality and Social Psychology, 80*, 918–930.

Reicher, S. D., & Hopkins, N. (1996). Seeking influence through characterising self-categories: An analysis of anti-abortionist rhetoric. *British Journal of Social Psychology, 35*, 297–311.

Reicher, S. D., & Hopkins, N. (2001). *Self and nation*. London: Sage.

Roccas, S., & Brewer, M. B. (2002). Social identity complexity. *Personality and Social Psychology Review, 6*, 88–109.

Ross, L. (1977). The intuitive psychologist and his shortcomings. In L. Berkowitz (Ed.), *Advances in experimental social psychology* (Vol. 10, pp. 174–220). New York: Academic Press.

Sachdev, I., & Bourhis, R. Y. (1985). Social categorization and power differentials in group relations. *European Journal of Social Psychology, 15*, 415–434.

Sani, F., & Reicher, S. D. (1998). When consensus fails: An analysis of the schism within the Italian Communist Party (1991). *European Journal of Social Psychology, 28*, 623–645.

Sani, F., & Reicher, S. D. (1999). Identity, argument and schisms: Two longitudinal studies of the split in the Church of England over the ordination of women to the priesthood. *Group Processes and Intergroup Relations, 2*, 279–300.

Sani, F., & Reicher, S. D. (2000). Contested identities and schisms in groups: Opposing the ordination of women as priests in the Church of England. *British Journal of Social Psychology, 39*, 95–112.

Schachter, S. (1959). *The psychology of affiliation*. Stanford, CA: Stanford University Press.

Schmitt, M. T., Silvia, P. J., & Branscombe, N. R. (2000). The intersection of self-evaluation maintenance and social identity theories: Intragroup judgment in interpersonal and intergroup contexts. *Personality and Social Psychology Bulletin, 26*, 1598–1606.

Shaw, M. E. (1976). *Group dynamics* (2nd ed.). New York: McGraw-Hill.

Sherif, M. (1936). *The psychology of social norms*. New York: Harper.

Sigelman, L. (1986). Basking in reflected glory revisited: An attempt at replication. *Social Psychology Quarterly, 49*, 90–92.

Snyder, C. R., Lassegard, M. -A., & Ford, C. E. (1986). Distancing after group success and failure: Basking in reflected glory and cutting off reflected failure. *Journal of Personality and Social Psychology, 51*, 382–388.

Stasser, G., Stewart, D. D., & Wittenbaum, G. (1995). Expert roles and information exchange during discussion: The importance of knowing who knows what. *Journal of Experimental Social Psychology, 31*, 244–265.

Tajfel, H., & Turner, J. C. (1986). The social identity theory of intergroup behavior. In S. Worchel & W. Austin (Eds.), *Psychology of intergroup relations* (pp. 7–24). Chicago: Nelson-Hall.

Tindale, R. S., Kameda, T., & Hinsz, V. B. (2003). Group decision-making. In M. A. Hogg & J. Cooper (Eds.), *The Sage handbook of social psychology*. London: Sage.

Turner, J. C., Hogg, M. A., Oakes, P. J., Reicher, S. D., & Wetherell, M. S. (1987). *Rediscovering the social group: A self-categorization theory*. Oxford, UK: Blackwell.

Tyler, T. R., & Blader, S. L. (2000). *Cooperation in groups: Procedural justice, social identity, and behavioral engagement*. Philadelphia, PA: Psychology Press.

Wann, D. L., Hamlet, M. A., Wilson, T. M., & Hodges, J. A. (1995). Basking in reflected glory, cutting off reflected failure, and cutting off future failure: The importance of group identification. *Social Behavior and Personality, 23*, 377–388.

Wicker, A. W. (1968). Undermanning, performances, and students' subjective experiences in behavior settings of large and small high schools. *Journal of Personality and Social Psychology, 10*, 25–261.

Williams, K. D. (2001). *Ostracism: The power of silence.* New York: Guilford.

Wittenbaum, G. M., & Stasser, G. (1996). Management of information in small groups. In J. L. Nye & A. M. Brower (Eds.), *What's social about social cognition* (pp. 3–28). Thousand Oaks, CA: Sage.

Wright, S. C., Aron, A., & Tropp, L. R. (2002). Including others (and groups) in the self: Self-expansion and intergroup relations. In J. P. Forgas & K. D. Williams (Eds.), *The social self: Cognitive, interpersonal, and intergroup perspectives* (pp. 343–363). New York: Psychology Press.

10

Delinquency: Cause or Consequence of Social Exclusion?

NICHOLAS EMLER and STEPHEN REICHER

Our argument is that involvement in delinquency is reinforced by feelings of exclusion from the law's protection. We develop this argument documenting how children's early unanimity concerning the benevolence of authority gives way by early adolescence to increasingly divided views. Moreover, this division strongly predicts delinquent conduct, and delinquency itself appears to offer a substitute to those who feel excluded by the official system; it provides both "self help" justice and the basis for protection against victimization by establishing a dangerous reputation. We consider the ways in which formal educational, cognitive development, and direct experience of both procedural fairness and the reliability or otherwise of legal protection shape attitudes towards authority, and then go on to examine how a sense of exclusion among some young people is reinforced by the inter-group character of adolescent-police relations. Finally, we examine options for intervention and their capacity to overcome rather than confirm young offenders' feelings of exclusion from the formal system.

INTRODUCTION: SOCIAL INCLUSION, OR THE BENEFITS OF CLUB MEMBERSHIP

We do not intend to linger for long over definitions but it is helpful to begin with what it means to be socially *in*cluded. People join clubs because membership delivers certain desired benefits. Some people also join particular civil societies for similar reasons. And although most of us do not make this kind of deliberate choice—birth gives us membership in one such "club" and we tend to retain this exclusive membership throughout our lives—we might expect to enjoy benefits of membership just as deliberate joiners do. Let us push the analogy a little bit further: what is on the list of benefits for full members? It includes a variety of services collectively organized and delivered through the apparatus of the state, and relating to such matters as education, health, transport, and housing. Politics, legislation, case law, international treaties and conventions, all continually reinterpret, refine and, more often than not, add to the list. Certainly, the contemporary citizen of this and many other countries expects and probably derives a much wider range of benefits from membership than would have been the case even one or two centuries ago. In this chapter, however, we are concerned with just one area of benefit, albeit of a particularly basic and ancient kind: the protection of individual rights and freedoms through a system of laws and means for their enforcement.

The basic character and value of such benefits is, for example, central to the argument developed by Hobbes in Leviathan: one should submit to a sovereign authority because one will then enjoy the protection of this authority. It also forms a theme in Icelandic sagas dating back to the eleventh century. Individuals who forfeited this protection, who quite literally became "outlaws," could be deprived of their property, beaten, and put to death by any of the surviving membership, who themselves need fear no legal reprisal. This raises four perhaps rather obvious points. First, historically there has been change, for the most part progressive, in definitions of who should benefit from these protections. Formally, not only are all citizens equal but these protections also apply to any person currently in the country, citizen or not. Second, the rights and freedoms to which these protections apply are far more detailed, extensive, and precisely defined than they were for an eleventh century Icelander. Third, both the means and the effectiveness with which these protections are provided have been transformed over the centuries. The fourth point is that the rights of protection are linked to duties and obligations, although the linkage in contemporary Britain is quite different to—and much less direct than—that in Iceland nine hundred years ago.

If social inclusion entails the protection of the law, what about social *exclusion*? Again we have a couple of obvious points to make. The first is that no one is excluded formally from legal protection. The second is that there is a wide gulf between principle and practice. Our interest lies in the nature of that gulf. For a moment, let us specify the nature of the benefits a little further. If one enjoys the protection of the law then one's legally defined rights should be defended by whatever range of means the state has put in place against possible violation. There is, for example, a popular if somewhat misplaced belief that policemen patrolling the streets, whether on foot, in cars, on horseback or on bikes, deter criminal action against our homes and persons. Street lighting, speed humps, and security cameras may also afford us some measure of protection. And of course, there are other deterrent measures provided by systems of inspection, monitoring, and auditing. But when deterrence fails, we supposedly enjoy a second line of protection, namely police pursuit of our victimizers and redress for our injuries and legitimate grievances through the courts. If these are the protections—the benefits of social inclusion—what is the nature of the gulf between principle and practice?

It needs to be said first, although it is not central to our story (but also not irrelevant), that no system for delivering legally guaranteed rights of protection has ever or will ever work perfectly. The more important point is whether the system works with the same level of imperfection for everyone. It does not. Social exclusion here can be defined in two ways, in terms of the risk of being a victim, which is to say having one's legally guaranteed rights and freedoms violated, and in terms of lack of effective legal redress when any one of those rights and freedoms is violated. Exclusion of the first kind is the rather better documented. Membership of four broad social categories increases the risk of victimization. These are the categories defined by age, sex, social class, and ethnicity; there are of course other relevant categories including just about any minority.

Children are more likely to be victims of crime than adults. Males are in general more likely to be victims than females. On the other hand, those of middle-class background are less likely to be victims of crime than those of working-class background. The same is true for the ethnic majority in this country. Whether precisely the same pattern exists with respect to legal redress we cannot say, though we are fairly confident that the social class effect would be found (cf. Black, 1983). The middle classes, by virtue of various advantages, have always been more effective at securing any benefits provided by the state, and there is no reason to expect that effective legal remedy in the event of victimization will be the exception.

This preamble has now brought us close to the substance of this chapter, the relationship between social exclusion and delinquency. Our thesis in brief is that delinquency is linked to, and to a degree sustained by, a sense among those involved of social exclusion and alienation from authority. Young people involved in delinquency lack faith in the impartiality and legitimacy of teachers, police officers, and court officials. They are not optimistic that, should they become the victims of others, these authorities will intervene on their behalf. In this context, delinquent action serves a number of purposes. It communicates to peers that the actor stands opposed to "the system." It claims the support and solidarity of others who are likewise opposed in living a life on the margins. It also provides an alternative system of protection, both by warning would-be assailants that they are dealing with a "hard case" and by serving as direct redress should anyone be foolish enough to ignore these warnings.

We do not intend to idealize or romanticize delinquent action as heroic self-help justice by the deprived and dispossessed. Nor do we want to suggest that it is an effective alternative to the protection of the law, because patently it is not. The point rather lies in what young people perceive or believe to be the case. And we do wish to raise questions about "solutions" to adolescent criminality that effectively operate as self-fulfilling prophecies, confirming those young people's beliefs that they are socially excluded.

WHAT CHILDREN BELIEVE ABOUT VICTIMIZATION AND ABOUT AUTHORITY AS A REMEDY

Young children are routinely the victims of other children—their siblings, other children at the child-minder's, in the nursery or play group, in the street and in school—other children who hit them, take away their toys and sweets, rip their clothes and damage their possessions. In these respects childhood is a hazardous time. Some research (e.g., Tremblay, 2000) suggests that early childhood, around two years, is the peak age for violence, and the most frequent targets are other children. Over this same period children also learn about one important weapon against these hazards. Parents, playgroup supervisors, teachers, and others responsible for their care intervene to stop fights, restore property to its rightful owners, enforce fair shares, and replace broken possessions. But adults are not perfect instruments of justice and many children develop another strategy of redress; they are not above a bit of retribution which, depending on their physical attributes, may or may not work in their favor.

What do children make of these options? Piaget's (1932) classic studies of children's moral judgment reveal some of the picture. Piaget characterized the views of younger children, by which he meant those below six to seven years of age, as "heteronomous." He found that younger children seem to be in awe of the power and omniscience of adults. Adults are invariably right and capable of putting things to rights. Malefactors are always punished and if not by adults then by natural forces. Whether because these views are so regularly contradicted by experience or because better insight into the workings of human agency and natural causes renders them implausible, they are progressively abandoned. As children age they become increasingly aware of adults' limitations and are diminishingly inclined to see justice as immanent in nature. On the other hand, and contrary to some interpretations of his evidence (e.g., Durkin, 1961), Piaget's (1932) data show a clear trend towards and not away from belief in the legitimacy of retaliation as a response to victimization. It is also worth noting, however, that Piaget found a striking sex difference here. The trend was evident only among boys.

Asked about authorities outside the family or school, young children's views are understandably vaguer. Take their views of the police. Much of what is currently known about early childhood beliefs in this area has come from studies of political socialization (e.g., Hess & Torney, 1967). Political scientists have been interested in young children's attitudes to the police because these are among the first attitudes formed about what are in effect representatives of the institutional system of government. But the police are significant for another reason in this period of life. Police officers are likely to provide young children with their first concrete experience of a hierarchy of power and authority to which their own parents are subject.

In the policeman the child encounters a power outside the family to which even parents are subordinate. Through observation of police cars, of behavior at traffic lights, bus stops, parking meters and traffic signs, of the conversation of other children and adults, and of the mass media, the child learns that in connection with the policeman certain rules and decisions of external authority should be accepted. As the police are an instrument of political power and represent governmental authority the child in fact becomes conditioned to political authority. (Stacey, 1978, p. 8)

Stacey's observations bring out an important point about the formation of attitudes in childhood: these attitudes are shaped by direct experiences which crucially include the way that people around them, such as their parents, act and react in relation to legal authority, but also by the way these people talk about such matters, and by what children observe in television images either as fiction or as news reporting. One might suppose therefore that the conclusion to which children come would depend on the content of these influences. Thus if parents are particularly defiant, disrespectful or critical of legal authority, or if media representations are routinely negative, will these children not themselves develop rather negative views of the police and other representatives of authority? Exceptional conditions, such as when the police are widely regarded and experienced in a community as the repressive representatives of an occupying power, as in Apartheid South Africa, Palestinian communities under Israeli occupation, and some ethnic minority communities in a dominant white culture (Greenberg, 1970), may be associated with such effects. Otherwise, however, the most conspicuous quality of young children's attitudes to authority is their highly positive tone. This characteristic precludes a straightforward explanation of children's attitudes as products of social learning.

Six-to-seven-year olds, typically the youngest children to have been included in studies of political and legal socialization (cf. Hess & Torney, 1967; Easton & Dennis, 1969) regard police officers as good, kind, all-knowing, all-powerful, and infallible. The youngest children in Hess and Torney's American survey, for example, viewed policemen as more omniscient than their fathers, their government and even the Supreme Court. The same research shows, however, that young children idealize all forms of authority, not just policemen. They emphasize the benevolent character of all the apparently powerful figures who populate their worlds, including kings and queens, presidents and prime ministers. Easton and Dennis (1969) interpreted these idealized views of authority in two ways. First, because children are weak and vulnerable relative to adults and therefore dependent upon their good will and protection, they have a defensive need to see powerful figures as benign and protective. This suggests that as children grow and in the process become stronger and less dependent, their defensive needs in these respects become correspondingly weaker and their attitudes in consequence should become less idealized. As we shall see, this prediction is borne out.

Second, according to Easton and Dennis, there is a transfer of a positive image of parental authority to other forms of authority outside the family. This accords with a psychoanalytic interpretation of socialization (cf. Adorno Frenkel-Brunswik, Levinson, & Sanford, 1950) but not with the evidence. Research indicates very little relation between attitudes toward parental authority and attitudes to other forms of authority (e.g., Amorso & Ware, 1983; Burwen & Campbell, 1957). Easton and Dennis themselves only found evidence for this kind of transfer with respect to perceptions of power; children who saw their fathers as powerful were also more likely to see other figures of authority as powerful.

Another interpretation of children's attitudes to legal authorities such as the police is that these are strongly shaped by the limited intellectual powers of young children and associated limitations in their capacity to understand and analyze social relations and social institutions. Thus the most crucial determinant of young children's attitudes may be their perception that the police are powerful and, on the basis of their direct experience, apparently even more powerful than their parents. Piaget 's (1932) studies of children's moral judgments revealed a tendency that has been confirmed many times since (Lickona, 1976): in the minds of young children "powerful" equals "good."

This interpretation leads us to expect that as intellectual sophistication grows so do attitudes change, and indeed it is consistent with what we know about the development of attitudes toward authorities from early childhood onwards. Initially these are on the one hand predominantly positive but on the other they possess very little content. Children's beliefs about the police, for example, emphasize their benevolent character ("they do good things, help people"), but lack functional detail; the same children have little if any notion of precisely what police officers do or what the nature and scope of their powers or duties are beyond the vague idea that they catch criminals.

From this starting point two major kinds of change occur in views of authority. First, the early moral absolutism described by Piaget declines. In purely evaluative terms, beliefs become progressively less idealized and less positive with increasing age. This trend characterizes some authorities rather more than others, however. Hess and Torney (1967) found, for example, that American children were strongly inclined to regard the policeman as a source of willing and benevolent assistance and this positive view did not decline as rapidly as it did with respect to political figures, with whom the idea of a personal and supportive relationship faded rapidly. On the other hand they found with age a steadily declining belief in the omniscience of policemen, a declining view of the police as hard working and a steeply declining belief in the infallibility of policemen.

The second kind of change relates to the content of beliefs. In parallel with and partly producing the evaluative changes is a growing insight into the role and functions of both legal regulation of behavior and legal authorities. The majority view of the law's function remains that it is to keep people safe, but the emphasis on its punitive and behavioral control function declines while emphasis on its importance in running the country increases. There is a similar shift in view about the role of the police from the position that this is primarily one of catching law-breakers to the view that this includes helping people in trouble and enforcing obedience to the law. There is also a sharp decline in the perceived punitive powers of the police among children from eight years onwards.

Developments in attitudes and beliefs about particular kinds of authority figure need to be seen in the context of a developing appreciation of the nature of formal or institutional authority as such. On the one hand, between the ages of 6 and 12, children acquire an intuitive understanding of some of the basic principles underlying and common to all systems of institutional authority, such as notions of hierarchy, of formally defined spheres of jurisdiction and explicit limits on powers, and of impartiality and impersonality (cf. Emler, Ohana, & Moscovici, 1987; Emler, 1992). On the other, agents of authority come to be identified as part of the formal mechanisms and institutions for regulating social relationships so that attitudes to particular kinds of authority figure become integrated into attitudes about formal or institutional authority more generally.

Childhood attitudes and beliefs about legal and political authority have often been characterized as personalized (e.g., Easton & Dennis, 1969), meaning both that children see institutions in terms of particular people representing them and that they fail to differentiate between the particular occupants of official positions on the one hand, and the roles or positions themselves on the other (Furth, 1980). As teenagers this is one important distinction they begin to make more clearly and explicitly. This enables them to separate out the formal criteria that are supposed to govern the functions and activities of police officers or other officials and evaluate these as general principles without confusing these with judgments of the behavior of particular office holders. At the same time they become capable of evaluating individual behavior against the standards provided by these formal criteria. Thus they may simultaneously conclude that impartiality in the exercise of authority is a fundamental and highly desirable principle and also that some individuals are partial and biased in the exercise of their powers. Or they may conclude that a system of legal regulation is morally desirable but also that the current system is corrupt and ineffective. Hence, the observation that attitudes to authority become less positive with increasing age must be qualified somewhat; beliefs become more differentiated with the result that attitudes can vary across the different belief elements.

If one source of the development of attitudes and beliefs about authority is intellectual growth, another is very likely to be experience of formal education.

Emler, Ohana, and Moscovici (1987) found that children between 6 and 10 years were far more sophisticated in their understanding of the nature of formal authority in this setting than other research has indicated them to be with respect to formal institutions of which they have much less direct experience. Similarly Cullen (1987) found that although 8- and 11-year olds were better than 5-year olds at recognizing legitimate authority figures in a structured authority situation, the 5-year olds demonstrated more insight when the context given was the school. This led Cullen to conclude that from their first year in school, children are able to establish realistic and functional notions of authority at least in this directly experienced context.

To conclude this section, early in life children cope with the hazards and experience of victimization through a combination of direct action and recourse to the protection of adults. To begin with they are disposed to believe that they enjoy the benevolent protection of adult authority but progressively develop views of the operation of authority that are both increasingly differentiated, particularly with respect to principle versus practice, and increasingly qualified as to its perfect effectiveness and fairness in practice. But do they also come to feel systematically excluded from its protection? That is the question to which we now turn.

THE EMERGENCE OF INDIVIDUAL AND GROUP DIFFERENCES IN ATTITUDES

If adolescence sees further significant developments of the individual's insight into the nature and functions of formal authorities, this period is also important for the emergence of clear differences between individuals in their attitudes. More specifically, the views of some young people become significantly more negative and critical than those of others (cf. Clark & Wenninger, 1964; Gibson, 1967; Greenberg, 1970; Waldo & Hall, 1970). A first point to make here is that although there have been studies specifically concerned with adolescents' attitudes toward the police (e.g., Gibson, 1967), it has also become clear that these attitudes do not exist in isolation. Rather they form part of an individual's views about institutional authority in general. Hence, those teenagers who express the most negative views about the police are likely to be the same teenagers who voice the most negative views about other figures and forms of institutional authority. Rigby and Rump (1979), for example, found that teenagers' attitudes to various authority sources including teachers, the police, the army, and the law, were positively intercorrelated (cf. also Amorso & Ware, 1983; Murray & Thompson, 1985; Rigby, Schofield, & Slee 1987).

We have argued (e.g., Reicher and Emler, 1985) that such correlational patterns reflect the fact that formal authority constitutes a coherent entity for adolescents. We defined the domain of formal authority in Weberian terms as legal-rational authority (cf. Weber, 1947). Weber proposed that in any social group authority is accepted to the degree that it is perceived by the members of that group to be legitimate. He went on to specify three basic types of legitimacy: charismatic, traditional, and legal-rational. He argued that the third form would assume the most significance in the modern world. It is the authority system of the bureaucracy, in which "obedience is owed to the legally established impersonal order. It extends to the persons exercising the authority of office under it only by virtue of the formal legality of their commands and only within the scope of authority of the office" (Weber, 1947, p. 328).

Four distinguishing features of legal-rational authority were identified by Weber. The first was that all positions of authority exist within a rationally organized hierarchy, an institution or formal organization, and have no legitimacy except in terms of their positions in this system. The second was that each position always has specific, explicit, formally defined, and limited spheres of jurisdiction; authority is rationally distributed. The third was that holders of such authority can legitimately exercise this authority only in accordance with formally defined, impersonal, and impartial criteria and not in the service of personal interests. Finally, office holders have formally defined duties and obligations, which are likewise distinct from their personal inclinations.

As noted above, by the beginning of adolescence there is some insight into the principles of this kind of authority system. Thus, in adolescence, the various representatives of institutional authority—teachers, police officers, and other officials of the state—are in adolescence increasingly likely to be judged and evaluated in terms of these common underlying principles. We were able to confirm the existence of generalized attitudes to formal authority in a study of the views of 14–15-year old males and females on a range of issues relating to the exercise of police powers, obligations of obedience to authority, willingness to uphold the law and to defend the law, and the purpose and benefits of rules, regulations, and laws (Reicher & Emler, 1985).

This study also revealed something about the content of attitudes to formal authority. A factor analysis of responses generated four interpretable factors. The first, labeled "alienation from the institutional system," was defined by pragmatic attitudes to rules and regulations ("ignore them if you can get away with it") combined with beliefs that commitment to the system provided no personal benefits. The second factor, identified as "absolute priority of rules and authorities," was defined by attitudes towards recommendations of unconditional compliance. The third, "bias versus impartiality of authorities," was expressed in terms of views about the extent of bias in laws and regulations and in the manner of their enforcement. Finally, a factor of "relationship to rules and authority" reflected views about the general desirability of a rule system. A development of this work in a study of Italian teenagers has confirmed the existence of an additional factor relating to the perceived effectiveness of institutional authority as a system for regulating social behavior, protecting rights, and resolving grievances (Palmonari & Rubini, 1999). A similar factor emerged in work by Nelsen, Eisenberg, and Carroll (1982) in the United States, though in this latter case it was defined more by views about the likelihood of lawbreakers being caught and punished.

There is also evidence that female adolescents have more positive attitudes to formal authority than do males. We found a significant difference of this kind (Reicher & Emler, 1985) and later replicated this finding in three separate samples: one of university students, one of 15–17-year olds and one of 12–14-year olds (Emler & Reicher, 1987). We found additionally that these sex differences were most marked with respect to views about the impartiality of the police and the law. More generally, sex differences in attitudes to authority have been replicated with a sample of 12–16-year olds (Emler & Reicher, 1995), and in a study of 4,800 16- and 18-year olds in Britain (Banks et al., 1992). Finally, Torney (1971) found that such sex differences were already apparent in childhood though they become more exaggerated with age.

There have been few studies of other possible group differences in attitudes to authority (Greenberg, 1970, is an exception) even though there has been much speculation that adolescents belonging to disadvantaged ethnic minorities or from economically deprived backgrounds will be more suspicious, distrustful, and critical of all forms of state authority than members of dominant social groups. In fact, in the large-scale study referred to above (Banks et al., 1992) attitudes to authority proved to be barely related to social class background.

To conclude this section, a division of attitudes toward legal authority and its representatives becomes increasingly apparent during adolescence. On the one side are those who have confidence in the legal system to treat them fairly and protect their interests. On the other are young people who feel distrustful of this system, and have little confidence that it provides meaningful protection. In effect, they feel excluded from the organized system of protection, conflict resolution, and grievance procedures represented by the law. In the following sections we consider successively, behavior associated with these feelings, their possible sources, and what might effectively be done to overcome the sense of exclusion and its possible consequences.

Attitudes and Behavior

The attitudes of young people toward formal authorities are correlated with their conduct. The less positive a young person's views about authority, the more likely is that individual to ignore regulations, defy authority, and break laws. A series of studies have now confirmed this link whether behavior is measured in terms of officially recorded offences (West & Farrington, 1977; Levy, 2001) or self-reported misbehavior (Brown, 1974b; Emler & Reicher, 1987, 1995; Heaven, 1993; Reicher & Emler, 1985). Brown (1974b) found that the reported noncompliance of a sample of American adolescents, aged between 11 and 18, was inversely related to the positiveness of their views about the law and the police. Interestingly, the strength of the relationship varied with the salience of law where this was defined as the extent to which individuals thought about whether different kinds of behavior involved a violation of the law; the greater the salience of law, the stronger the association between attitudes and conduct. A potential weakness of this study, however, is that it is based on a wide age range, 11–17. It is known that both delinquency levels and attitudes to the law change over this age range, raising the possibility that the correlations reflect the effect of age rather than any direct relation between attitudes and behavior. This alternative was ruled out in the study by Reicher and Emler (1985); almost all of the respondents were aged 14. Their scores on a self-report measure of delinquent and antisocial behavior correlated 0.79 with scores on a measure of attitudes to institutional authority.

Although this association between attitudes and behavior is not entirely surprising, its true significance may not be immediately apparent. First, it indicates that respect for the law and its representatives is not an unconscious habit or reflex which happens to be poorly developed in some individuals but a reasoned choice drawing upon the beliefs and attitudes that individuals hold about the legal system and its representatives, and about their own obligations toward this system. Second, consider another finding from the Reicher and Emler (1985) study: Not only did females express more positive views of authority and, as expected, report lower levels of involvement in delinquent activities, but this sex difference in conduct was entirely "explained", in the statistical sense, by the sex difference in attitudes. In other words, the attitudes are not merely a correlate of conduct, they are intrinsic and integral to a pattern of reactions that also includes the manner in which young people behave with respect to legal obligations. In particular, young people who break the law regard themselves as excluded from the protection of a biased system that is loaded against them.

Adolescent delinquency has one further striking feature relevant to our argument. It is overwhelmingly a group activity and thus a relatively public activity (Emler & Reicher, 1995). In this it also therefore symbolizes or expresses something. It is the behavioral expression of alienation from formal authority. The question we need to address is why some young people should feel, more than others, excluded from the system of legal protection.

EDUCATION AS A FORMATIVE EXPERIENCE

One explanation for differences in attitudes invokes the different experiences young people have in formal education. It is possible that participation in a process of formal schooling not only provides children with insights into the way in which formal authority is supposed to work but also shapes their attitudes to the way it works in practice. The close association between attitudes to authority in the school and attitudes to other kinds of institutional authority (e.g., Amorso & Ware, 1983; Reicher & Emler, 1985) might be taken as support for the argument that attitudes in this area are formed first of all in that context of which young people have the most extensive direct experience, namely the school, and that attitudes formed here are then generalized to other kinds of formal authority, most obviously to that sphere in which the police are seen to operate. More specifically, these attitudes may be shaped by the outcomes young people experience in school.

In adolescence, differences in educational performance are likely to receive increasingly explicit attention and to have increasingly significant consequences for the ways in which individuals are publicly identified and labeled. Whereas in childhood distinctions might be made between slower and faster learners, the language in which these differences are discussed implies that the slower children could eventually catch up. In the early teens the labeling shifts toward more explicit references to success and failure. Depending on the local terminology, they may be "streamed" (Hargreaves, 1967) according to ability with implications for their probable final level of achievement, or placed on different curricula "tracks" (Kelly, 1975; Wiatrowski, Hansell, Massey, & Wilson, 1982) leading to quite different educational destinations. Streaming, curriculum tracking, and other arrangements are also partly responses to the organizational problems posed by the large populations of individual secondary schools; cohorts have to be divided into smaller, teachable units, but such divisions are seldom if ever random and carry messages about the public evaluation of individual pupils. And, in whatever way academic success and failure is marked in schools, as the end of compulsory schooling looms one of its central purposes: it both produces and legitimizes inequality (Jencks, 1972).

What then is the effect on those identified and labeled as relative failures by the educational system? One view is that these young people either temporarily or more permanently lose their stake in the conventional system and feel free to reject the values with which it has become associated (Hirschi, 1969). To the extent that the school is associated for young people with the system of institutional authority, then those who are labeled educational failures also become alienated from this system.

The close association between lack of success in school and involvement in criminal activities as an adolescent is well established, whether educational success is measured by years of high-school education, grades, number of examinations entered, or attainment in public examinations (e.g., Hargreaves, 1967; Kelly, 1975; Reiss & Rhodes, 1961; West & Farrington, 1977). There is also a close association between success in school and positive attitudes to authority (Emler & St. James, 1990, 1994). What is less clear is whether educational attainment is the independent variable in these patterns of empirical association (cf. Liska & Reed, 1985). That is, these correlations could be interpreted as indicating that young people continue to obey the law, show respect for authority, and hold positive views about the police to the extent that they continue to do well in the education system and correspondingly that their conduct and beliefs become more negative to the extent that they fail. But this is not the only interpretation that is consistent with the evidence.

It is also entirely possible that individuals do well in a system of formal education precisely because they have a positive orientation to the kind of authority which operates within it, and do badly because they have a negative orientation to this kind of authority. It is after all plausible that doing well in school depends on one's willingness to defer to the authority of teachers, accept the rules and regulations of the classroom, and generally accommodate to the requirements of a bureaucratic regime (cf. Danziger, 1971; Jencks, 1972) and plausible that to the extent one finds such authority irksome one's relations with this institution will be rather less fruitful, quite independently of one's ability.

Willis's classic ethnographic study of working class "lads" (Willis, 1977) provides strong support for such a position. He shows that such boys see school as a con, they believe that however much effort they put in, they will remain at the bottom of the pile and hence spend their time messing around rather than working hard. The irony is that this becomes a self-fulfilling prophecy: educational failure leads on to working class jobs for the "lads." It is important to note that this process does not depend upon their own experience of discrimination and failure in the educational system, but rather their experience of the fate of others like them—parents, older siblings, neighbors and other acquaintances. What they are rejecting is not particular teachers or particular schools but rather the school system, or, to be more precise, the idea that working hard and complying will lead to personal advancement. It follows that a rejection of the school will be associated with ostentatious rejection of compliance. These are arguments we have developed elsewhere (Emler & Reicher, 1995) and which we will return to later.

For now, though, we need to consider an obvious objection to this general line of argument—namely that educational attainment is largely a function of ability while adolescent delinquency is also correlated with ability (cf. Rutter & Giller, 1983), and that this latter association is more consistent with the view that educational failure creates a rupture with authority than the reverse. The responses to these objections are that differences in ability explain only a proportion of the variance in educational attainment (Jencks, 1972, for example, concludes that it explains considerably less than half the variance), and that there remains some argument about the existence and importance of a relationship between ability or IQ on the one hand and anti-authority behavior and attitudes on the other. Some studies report no relationship between delinquency and IQ (e.g., Menard & Morse, 1984; Tarry, 2001), while others report a negative, if not particularly strong relationship (e.g., Lynham, Moffitt, & Stouthamer-Loeber, 1993). Deciding on this question does have profound implications of our understanding of the roots of attitudes to authority. Finally, Emler & St. James (1994) found that attitudes to authority in early adolescence predicted variance in subsequent educational attainment over and above that predicted by cognitive measures.

COGNITIVE DEVELOPMENT AND ORIENTATION TO AUTHORITY

Brown (1974a) argued that two specific kinds of intellectual change in adolescence influence the young person's orientation toward the law. First, the perceived likelihood of punishment for noncompliance declines from late childhood. Kohlberg (1984) found that children begin from a position in which they analyze moral problems on the assumption that lawbreakers are always punished but then abandon this as they recognize that punishment and indeed detection does not always follow an offence. Brown suggested that this growing recognition of the uncertainty of punishment combined with concurrently growing desires for autonomy and independence, desires that cause constraint to be resented, lead adolescents initially to become less willing to comply with laws and regulations. He also pointed out that across the period of adolescence insight into the functions and purposes of laws continues to evolve (cf. Adelson, Green, & O'Neill, 1969).

Brown's own research shows that hypothetical willingness to comply with a range of laws changes between the ages of 11 and 17 but that these changes do not follow identical trends for all laws; the precise pattern depends upon the nature of the law in question. His interpretation of this pattern is that varying levels of willingness to comply with law are partly due to the capacity to appreciate the social benefits of different kinds of laws. In some cases these benefits are obvious and straightforward, in other cases a more sophisticated notion of social life is required to appreciate what the relevant benefits might be. This sophistication develops gradually and continues to grow throughout the period of adolescence. As a result, willingness to comply with the law declines initially and then gradually grows again as it is extended to an increasingly wider range of laws. What is true for perception of the social benefits of laws may well also be true for perception of the positive functions of a police force. These too require sufficient intellectual insight to comprehend the role the police play in modern society.

There are, however, two difficulties with this way of interpreting attitude differences. One is that not all intellectually sophisticated analyses of the social functions of law, institutional authority, or police forces conclude that these are entirely beneficial to the innocent (cf. Box, 1983). The second difficulty is more serious. Brown's interpretation could provide part of the explanation for the curvilinear relation between age and respect for the law; crime is above all a phenomenon of adolescence and most of those involved as adolescents do not continue a life of crime into adulthood. But if cognitive changes are at work here they do not so readily explain why there should also be differences in attitudes and behavior *within* groups of young people of the same age and at the same cognitive level; yet such differences are well established (Emler & Reicher, 1995). One source of clues about the origins of these differences is to be found in the *content* of young people's beliefs about institutional authority.

THE PROCEDURAL FAIRNESS OF AUTHORITY SYSTEMS

We have seen that belief in the infallibility of police officers declines with age. Belief in the invariable fairness of the law suffers a similar decline. In effect, there seems to be a growing general awareness with age of the imperfections of legal systems. The strict application of the law sometimes produces injustices. Officials do occasionally make mistakes and treat people unfairly. Policemen are not all invariably honest. Some may even be racially prejudiced, corrupt or willing to fake evidence against suspects. This awareness may have some effect of weakening support for the police and the rule of law. The critical question, however, is why some adolescents become more convinced than others that policemen and others in authority over them are dishonest, unnecessarily brutal, or biased and partial in the way they treat people and why they develop a more skeptical view of authority in general.

A possibility is that whereas the general trend toward skepticism and even a degree of cynicism about those in authority reflects the cumulative effects of media reporting of the system's imperfections and failures and possibly even gossip about others' bad experiences, the more rapid growth of cynicism and disenchantment among some individuals is a function of their own direct and personal experiences in encounters with authority. Support for this explanation comes for the work of Tyler (1990, 1997). Tyler examined the experiences of a sample of American adults in their dealings with the legal system, and specifically in dealings in which they had been suspected of or charged with some offence. One dimension of these experiences considered by Tyler was the favorableness to the individual of the outcome of the legal process. Another was the perceived procedural fairness of the process.

There are a number of dimensions to legal procedures that are open to evaluation in terms of their fairness; Leventhal (1980) has suggested six: representativeness, consistency, suppression of bias, accuracy, correctability, and ethicality. Tyler's own measures of procedural fairness drew on these definitions. His data indicated that compliance with the law was a function of the perceived legitimacy of legal authorities. Perceived legitimacy was in its turn unrelated to the favorableness of past outcomes of legal procedures. But it was related to the perceived fairness of those procedures. Tyler concluded on the basis of this and other studies that personal experience of legal procedures as fair is a particularly important determinant of their acceptance as legitimate.

There is another interesting dimension to this work. As Tyler and his colleagues have shown (Lind & Tyler, 1988; Tyler & Lind, 1992), one of the ways in which fairness relates to compliance is through its effects on group relationships. We tend to see those who treat us fairly as "one of us" whereas those who treat us unfairly are liable to be dismissed as part of another group—the "other" who stands against us. Thus those who see the law (or other formal authorities) as unfair will see themselves as standing outside the law, with all that this entails. This dimension is something we will pick up later on.

One interesting implication of this is that experience of failure in the educational system need not alienate adolescents from the system, *provided they believe their failure was fairly determined*. Conversely, adolescents do not need to experience failure or to have had actual evidence of unfair treatment or even to anticipate personal mistreatment in order to be alienated from the system. However it comes about, whether by what has happened to them, what they think will happen to them, or what they see happening to others; what is crucial is how adolescents perceive the legitimacy of school and other authorities.

But can this analysis be generalized beyond the kind of adult sample studied by Tyler? Its applicability to children and adolescents requires that they too have some notion of what constitutes fair procedures for allocating rewards or punishments or for determining guilt or innocence, and it requires that they regard procedural fairness as important. Up to the present there has been very little research which has directly examined young people's notions of or concern with procedural fairness. A study by Fry and Corfield (1983) confirms what many parents must recognize: Children are capable of making judgments about the procedural fairness of decisions affecting them in the home (cf. also Gold, Darley, Hilton, & Zanna, 1984). Emler, Ohana, and Moscovici (1987) found that children as young as ten also have well-developed notions about what constitute fair decision making procedures in the school though Demetriou and Charitides (1986) have also found that conceptions of procedural justice continue to develop in sophistication at least up to the age of seventeen. But is there any evidence that young people differ in their personal experience—either direct or vicarious—of the procedural fairness of authorities inside or outside the school?

Again the amount of relevant evidence is limited but it does point to significant variations in experience of procedural unfairness. Negative attitudes to authority have regularly been found to relate to reported personal experience of unfair treatment (Reicher & Emler, 1985; Emler & Reicher, 1987). Thus such attitudes are strongly associated with reports of being picked upon unfairly by teachers or police officers. Recall that, in the study of attitudes to authority by Reicher and Emler (1985), perceived bias versus impartiality of authorities emerged as a distinct factor. Moreover, scores on this factor were strongly correlated with self-reported defiance of the law.

Equally, our interview studies with adolescents (Emler & Reicher, 1995) suggest that delinquents characteristically see the whole system, rather than specific teachers, as being biased against them. Even at the age of 13, most believe that they will be either unemployed or in a menial job when they leave school. They believe that, whatever claims are made for education, they will remain at the bottom of the pile however good they are. In part this can be linked to the experiences of those around them. Many of our delinquents came from sink estates where, at the time, adult unemployment was as high as 70 or 80%. Their older siblings and cousins and those of their friends were generally unemployed after leaving school, irrespective of whether they had conformed or rebelled. If those like them had not benefited from school, why should things be any different for themselves? Perhaps if they had come from one of the better parts of town or grown up speaking in a posher accent, their chances would have been far better. In short they have an abiding sense that authority offers promises in bad faith: Why then should they keep up their end of the bargain when authorities won't keep theirs?

Hence there are two questions that need to be addressed in future research. First, are reported experiences of being a victim of unfair procedures related to objective evidence of unfair treatment? Are certain categories of young people—males as compared to females, members of ethnic minorities, those with working class origins—objectively more likely to be discriminated against by teachers, harassed by the police, or denied a fair hearing by the courts? Alternatively are individual members of such categories more likely to experience unwelcome official attention because they are in fact more often involved in mischief and mayhem? Second, how do young people come to estimate their future chances and hence make investments in the present based upon the promise of outcomes that are not yet known? How do they decide whether to work hard and defer to those in authority at the age of 13 and 14 when they will not know if it was worth it until they are at least 16 or 17? To what extent are they influenced by the experiences of others, and whose experiences do they anticipate will foreshadow their own fate? This, of course, is the great dilemma of all contracts and particularly a dilemma when the contract determines the rest of one's life.

The Uncertain Protection of the Law

Adelson's (1971) work on young people's insight into the functions of law suggests a further influence on their attitudes to legal authority. Adelson noted that while children perceive the function of the law and of legal authorities primarily in terms of constraint, adolescents are increasingly aware of their protective functions. That is, they come progressively to see that the functions of the law include the protection of individuals and their rights. However, the personal experiences of young people may differ as to the effectiveness with which these functions operate in practice and in relation to their own rights. As we have seen, young people differ in their beliefs about the effectiveness of the legal system (Nelsen et al., 1982; Palmonari & Rubini, 1999). Moreover, this is not just a matter of differing views about the certainty of punishment for offenders but also about effective protection of one's own legal rights and effective prosecution of one's own persecutors.

How do young people cope with the risk of being victimized by others or for that matter the reality of being a victim, should this occur? The approved option is to seek the protection of the law and to seek redress for one's grievances through legal procedures. In practice, not only are legal protection and redress uncertain but these uncertainties are unevenly socially distributed and are perceived to be so. Moreover, it is not just that certain social groups by virtue of their habits of behavior more routinely put themselves at risk of being victimized, although this may be a factor. We know, for example, that adolescent girls are less likely to be the victims of crimes involving violence than are adolescent boys (cf. Mawby, 1980) and this may well be in part because boys are more often in public places without the protective company of adults than are girls of the same age and thus are more available targets for such aggression.

Black (1983) has argued that the law is relatively unavailable to persons with grievances when those persons are of low status—and this is likely to include those who are young, members of ethnic minorities, and socioeconomically disadvantaged. One might also imagine that this is often the position of children who experience physical abuse at the hands of their parents or guardians: No one intervenes to provide them with effective protection. If it is indeed the case that some groups find that the law is relatively unavailable for either protection or redress one consequence which might be anticipated is cynicism about and distrust of those who represent the law for failing to deliver on its obligations. Emler and Reicher (1995) found that some adolescents would consistently report that teachers, policemen, and others in authority were not interested in their problems.

One effect of this experience is to encourage pursuit of alternative grievance procedures and alternative methods of self-protection. Black (1983) suggests that much of the conduct regarded and treated as criminal in contemporary society is in fact motivated by a concern to resolve grievances. It is, in Black's terms, a form of "self-help" justice. Emler and Ohana (1992) found that 6–10-year olds would frequently recommend that victims should take matters into their own hands rather than relying on those in authority to put things right. Moreover, there was no indication that this was simply an immature stage of social problem solving. And, consistent with Black's argument about the social distribution of law's availability, children of working class backgrounds were more likely to recommend this "self-help" approach than middle-class children. We found (Emler & Reicher, 1995) that a regular theme in young people's views about their social lives was the idea of defending oneself and settling one's own grievances by direct action. These adolescents did not see the police as their natural allies in the protection of their rights and even took some pride in their capacity and willingness to protect themselves. A more recent study (Stouthamer-Loeber, Loeber, Homish, & Wei, 2001) found that young people maltreated by members of their own household were subsequently more likely than children not treated in this way to become involved in delinquency involving authority conflict.

Finally on this point, we have elsewhere argued (Emler & Reicher, 1995) that a delinquent pattern of behavior may provide another form of protection for those who have no confidence in the formal system. One product of delinquent behavior can be a reputation within a community as a person inclined to direct and violent retaliation and so dangerous to offend.

Of course, if this process begins with unequal treatment by the authorities it does not end there, for such treatment initiates a dynamic process which exacerbates social exclusion. Thus, once people feel rejected by "the law" or "the system," then as we have seen previously they begin to view themselves as "outlaws." It then becomes a point of honor not to call on the authorities, for to do so would admit dependence on an outgroup. Indeed, to invoke the law against a fellow outlaw—to use the outgroup against ingroup members (at one level an aggressor may be categorized with an outgroup, a rival gang perhaps, but at a more abstract level representatives of the law become the salient outgroup)—is just about the ultimate sin. The opprobrium heaped up "grasses" and "stool-pigeons" is well known. What is more, anyone relying on the authorities to fight their corner risks losing their own reputation for retaliatory capacity. Thus even if they won redress with the law's help they could open themselves to greater attack in the future.

Over time, then, those who are rejected by authorities begin to reject authority. They might start down the path to delinquency by being refused full rights and resources, but in time come to spurn even such things as are on offer. In part, this is an individual decision, but as we have argued, it is also a collective issue; there is honor among delinquents. And delinquency is a group, much more than it is a solitary, activity. There are norms and values, processes of conformity and compliance, of intra- and inter-group relations which affect their behavior as much as for the members of any group. Groups do offer both mutual protection among members and a group-based reputation. But the group context suggests further sources of differentiated attitudes to legal authorities.

InterGroup Relations: The "System" as Outgroup

The cumulative effects of a set of experiences—being abused by parents or other adults, being subjected to unfair procedures, whether of moral or intellectual evaluation, being labeled a failure, being accorded little or no effective protection or redress for grievances, seeing brothers and sisters on the dole or in dead-end jobs—all these could contribute to a sense of exclusion and feelings of antagonism toward the sources of these experiences. However, a further dimension, which is added in adolescence, is that these may become shared experiences in such a way that the antagonism is amplified.

Two points may be made here. First, the social lives and activities of young people typically revolve around peer groups and these groups closely reflect their views about authority. Those teenagers who are most hostile to authority tend to associate with peers who share their opinions. One interpretation of this is that the views themselves are elaborated within the peer group (cf. Granic & Dishion, 2003) and reflect the norms of the particular group to which they belong. If young people whose inclinations are initially on the negative or critical side are more disposed to associate with one another than with more positively inclined adolescents, the effects of this "differential association" will be to polarize attitudes even further in a negative direction.

The second point concerns the consequences of these differentiated patterns of association for direct contacts with authority. This is relevant in several senses. Consider contacts with police officers. First, the police officer is acting as a member of an organized social category rather than as an individual. Second, police–youth encounters often involve several young people at a time (the same two points of course apply to encounters in the classroom). Of particular interest here is the process whereby an interaction between the police and an individual young person may develop in such a way as to bring in peers who are essentially bystanders and hence escalate into a larger and more conflictual encounter. Some insights can be gained here from work on the development of conflict between crowds and the police (Reicher, 1996; Stott & Reicher, 1998). Reicher describes how the police may come to perceive a collection of different individuals or groupings as if they were a homogenous whole and how, as a corollary, police responses to the actions of specific individuals may be generalized to all those defined as belonging to the category. From the point of view of those on the receiving end of this action, this may be experienced as unjustified and illegitimate (prompting anger and resistance) and may indeed have the effect of developing the common categorization that the police assumed in the first place.

In addition, because the emergent *collective* response confirms the police's original construction of the homogeneity of the crowd (and hence the scale of its threat), further police responses against the crowd as a whole are, from the police point of view, regarded as legitimate (thereby contributing to the escalation of conflict). If, as seems likely, similar processes are at work in police–youth interactions, it becomes clearer why these might often escalate with adolescent bystanders "recruited" into an encounter in which both the young people and the police adopt increasingly confrontational styles (cf. Piliavin & Briar, 1964).

It is also easy to see how these actions may be taken as confirming the participants' perceptions of one another; while the initial characterization of the situation by the police as one of a group causing trouble would be confirmed, so too would the young people's construction of the police as an arbitrarily intrusive force.

The ingroup/outgroup dimension to encounters between those in authority and adolescents is reinforced in various ways. First, there may be a perceived conflict of goals (e.g., having fun, getting high, messing about, sorting out one's troubles aggressively, accessing adult privileges, versus keeping the peace, preventing fights, enforcing status laws, etc.) and the co-occurrence of other category differences (child versus adult, ethnic minority versus White official). Second, as various studies (e.g., Hunter, Stringer, & Watson, 1991; Taylor & Jaggi, 1974) indicate, group membership can bias attribution to produce conflicting interpretations of ingroup and outgroup actions. Hunter et al. for example found that acts of lethal aggression were interpreted either as legitimate retaliation or as evidence of moral depravity depending on whether the authors of the acts were in-group or out-group members.

Finally, and more generally, these inter-group conflicts can come to be imbued with great symbolic meaning as young people and those in authority contest rights to adopt particular lifestyles, use various public and institutional spaces in particular ways, and so forth. It is striking that the majority of school exclusions are triggered by issues of this kind rather than by conduct presenting a serious danger to others (Parsons & Howlett, 1996). The corollary of this is that much delinquency may be understood not so much as a response to intergroup divisions but as a symbolic means of signaling how one sees the intergroup relations and where one stands within them. To be more concrete, delinquent acts are perhaps the clearest possible way of indicating that you see authority as opposed to you and hence that you are opposed to authority. Moreover, such acts of exclusion from the formal social order are signals of eligibility for inclusion in groups that oppose the social order. Thus, in our work, we find that young people who act in delinquent ways may want to hide their own authorship of specific actionable misdemeanors from the authorities, but they certainly want the authorities to realize they are noncompliant. However, when it comes to their peers, they advertise, exaggerate, and brag about flouting rules and laws and they realize that failure to offend (or squeamishness about the offending of others) could lead to marginalization or even ejection from their peer groups (Emler & Reicher, 1995, see also Reicher & Levine, 1994).

INFORMAL SOCIAL EXCLUSION

By now it should be clear that there is a rich and complex relationship between social exclusion and delinquent action. On the one hand social exclusion can be seen as an antecedent of delinquency—or rather, delinquency arises in part as a reaction to the perception that authorities are not neutral and this is but one more aspect of their illegitimacy. On the other hand, delinquent action is not simply an inchoate reaction to an unfair world, but rather it is a meaningful way of navigating one's path through such a world. Delinquency is a practical way of protecting oneself if one cannot rely on the protection of others. It is also a way of communicating one's disdain of the system and hence claiming membership among like-minded others. The danger is that these various factors become mutually reinforcing: that the perception of exclusion becomes a self-fulfilling prophecy. We argue that, whether this happens or not is not simply down to young people themselves, it is also down to the general institutional practices which structure their world and also down to the specific institutional responses to delinquency.

We have argued elsewhere that conduct is subject to extensive informal social control and that adolescent delinquency needs to be understood at least in part in terms of the way that such control operates, or fails to operate, for some young people (Emler & Reicher, 1995; see also Braithwaite, 1993, Sampson & Laub, 1993, for closely related arguments). In effect, adolescents most involved in delinquency are also relatively cut off from relations with more law-abiding teenagers and with adults outside the immediate family. This informal social exclusion has at least two potentially important effects. It shifts the balance of informal social pressure away from respect for the law and towards its violation, and the potency of such pressure is well documented (cf. Asch, 1956; Milgram, 1964). It also isolates them from alternative and more positive readings of the nature of legal authority.

The exclusivity of the delinquent peer group may be in part self-chosen. But it is also a product of limited opportunity, for example, as created by the streaming practices of secondary schools. It is also a response to exclusion from alternative patterns of association. In the longer run alienation from formal authority further reinforces informal social exclusion. Those who are most alienated are the most likely to leave formal education at the first opportunity and the least likely to find employment afterwards (Emler & St. James, 1994). And those outside either of these two social institutions have dramatically lower rates of informal social contact than their peers who are in employment, or education (Emler, 2000).

The point here is that the subjective sense of social exclusion may be an important component in an explanation of delinquency, but it will not get us very far unless we investigate its relation to the reality of social exclusion. However alienated individuals may be from the system, their actions are governed not only by internal dispositions but also by external constraints. Those young people who feel most excluded from the formal protection of legal and educational authorities are in reality most excluded from the kinds of social relations that normally operate to constrain lawbreaking and antisocial behavior. Thus if we are serious about addressing juvenile lawbreaking we need to address the informal social exclusion that enables it.

LIMITING THE SENSE OF EXCLUSION: WHAT WORKS?

Before we can investigate what works to limit the perception and the reality of exclusion, we need to say a little more about the nature of these perceptions and realities. Note, in our conclusion to the previous section, we referred to social exclusion in relative, not absolute terms: those who feel *most* excluded are in reality *most* excluded. It is important to bear this in mind because otherwise it is easy to get a false impression of the issues we confront. Delinquents may feel and be more excluded than nondelinquents, especially from relations with teachers, schools, policemen, employers, and so on. However they are not completely excluded from relations with those who frown on delinquent activity and they are eager not to offend in ways that would disrupt those relations.

Two very clear findings came out of our interviews with delinquent and nondelinquent youth (Emler & Reicher, 1995). The first is that the delinquents were as close to their parents as nondelinquents and, while they might brag of their misdemeanors to their peers, they didn't want their parents to know what they got up to. The second is that nearly all the delinquents aspired to some form of employment and they didn't want their prospects to be sullied by any sort of criminal record. Thus, at around the age of 15 when misdemeanors are less likely to be discounted as youthful indiscretion and are more likely to mark the individual for life, many of our erstwhile offenders decided that the balance of profit and loss had shifted so as to make delinquent action far less appealing.

This may go some way toward explaining what is possibily the single most striking aspect of delinquency and the single most effective way of stopping it. There is a delinquent bulge. Offending rates tail off dramatically around the age of 15 or 16. The best cure for delinquency is to grow older. New commitments to employers and mortgage companies and wives and children, new forms of social inclusion, combine to end the delinquent phase. Hence, when discussing how to address delinquency we must first ask what might best stop young people develop a sense of social exclusion. Second, we must avoid forms of action which impede the process of social reinclusion. Let us consider the two in reverse order.

Whenever a response to juvenile offending is considered, it is of the utmost importance to ask what it will do to future prospects for social integration: How will it affect the family lives, the employment prospects, or the social networks of those involved? Our concern is that, all too often, the prospects are nothing but negative and that temporary exclusion is made permanent. Incarceration and punitive responses, whether separately or in combination have precisely this effect, and with consequences that are entirely predictable from the foregoing analysis. That is to say, these responses strengthen the sense of exclusion, confirming the validity of initial beliefs, and do nothing to reduce reoffending rates, if anything actually increasing them (Lipsey, 1995). We propose, in effect, that the consequences described by labeling theorists as "secondary deviance," and extensively demonstrated in research, are mediated by the effects of punitive responses upon the sense of exclusion.

By contrast, responses which seek to reintegrate offenders into the communities they have offended against, to get them to confront the impact of their acts upon their victims and, by taking the perspective of those victims, to develop a relationship with them, seem to us altogether more fruitful and indeed this is backed up by the results of a variety of projects (Strang, Barnes, Braithwaite, & Sherman, 1999). It is no coincidence that this process, sometimes called restorative justice from the perspective of the victim, is also termed reintegrative shaming from the perspective of the offender. Lest anyone dismiss such approaches as "mollycoddling" it is, perhaps, worth relating an anecdote told to us by someone involved in the 1980s policy of giving delinquents a "short sharp shock." The offenders rather enjoyed the tough physical regime and they came out leaner, fitter criminals. If they found anything difficult it was talking to the psychologists about their thoughts, their concerns, and their feelings!

Let us now turn to how we might stop people from developing a sense of exclusion from authorities and from the institutional world in the first place. One promising approach would appear to be offered by those explicit attempts to improve relations between school pupils and the police. There have been hosts of liaison programs, which introduce police officers into classrooms in the hope of challenging negative images of authority. Yet they seldom deliver the hoped-for benefits (Griffiths, 1982; Hopkins, Hewstone, & Hanzi, 1992). Data concerning pupils' perceptions of the visiting schools liaison officers (SLOSs) shed some light on this failure. When asked to rate these officers, pupils rated them less as aggressive, racist, rude, or strict and as more friendly and fair (Hewstone, Hopkins, & Routh, 1992). This pattern suggests that the failure of the contact program cannot simply be explained in terms of their dislike of these individual officers. Rather the problem seemed to be that these relatively positive evaluations did not generalize to the police in general (a common problem of intergroup contact programs—see Hewstone & Brown, 1986). Interviews with school children involved in the project suggested that the failure was bound up with the feeling that the dynamics surrounding their contact within the school were so different from those associated with contacts on the street as to make them irrelevant for their evaluation of the police as a whole.

There are, however, other factors which could affect the success or otherwise of a liaison or contact program. Thus, does the program focus upon relevant belief content? The implications of research already examined is that being nice, approachable, or friendly are less relevant than persuading by argument and example that police officers and others in authority are honest, unprejudiced, respectful of the rights and dignities of individuals, not bullies, willing and able to protect young people against victimization, disposed to pursue their legitimate grievances, and above all, committed to fair and impartial procedures in the administration of justice. There is a simple but profound point here that is of relevance not only to initiatives concerning relations of young people with the police but to any and all attempts to address perceptions of the social order and feelings of social exclusion. It is not enough to work on the level of personal relations if one wants to change structural perceptions and it is not enough to present an affable face if one's practices remain disrespectful. What really counts is the structure of relations between young people and societal institutions. It is at this level that initiatives need to operate. With this in mind, let us consider what that might mean in terms of the school–student relationship. However in doing so, let us stress that our aim is to use the issue of legitimacy as a perspective from which to ask questions about educational practices rather than to suggest definitive answers.

It is possible to address this relationship in terms of what happens before, during, and after young people enter the more formally structured world of secondary education. The importance of before has to do with whether students enter the institution on equal terms. If they see themselves as inherently disadvantaged and hence preselected for failure then their sense of legitimacy of and commitment to school authorities is already handicapped. That is why early interventions are so important when they can demonstrate that educational support is equally available to all. This extends to the provision of nursery education which has been shown to have important benefits at a number of levels, including subsequent delinquency (Berreuta-Clement, Schweinhhart, Barnett, Epstein, & Weikart, 1984; Yoshikawa, 1994).

Within the secondary school system itself, it is possible to interrogate a number of domains. The first, and most obvious, concerns the treatment of students by teachers. Are certain categories of student accorded more or less respect and impartiality by teachers, a factor which has a major impact on attitudes to authority (Gouviea-Pereira, Vala, Palmonari, & Rubini, 2003)? One possible influence upon this is school size: in a small institution it is easier to include everybody and to ensure that some people are not allowed to disappear (Barker, 1968). Yet British secondary schools are characteristically very large with numbers in excess of 1,500. A second factor is the structure of the curriculum. While project and continuous assessment work may have many educational merits, these may also disadvantage those whose parents cannot afford books, computers, trips to relevant sites, or whatever. The potential cost of such inequalities needs to be kept in mind and factored into any assessment of the pros and cons of such practices. The same goes for the content of the syllabus: who is rendered visible or invisible by it, whose experiences are addressed or ignored? The relationship of such issues to attitudes towards authority and toward delinquency is yet another important area of investigation.

Last, but very far from least, what prospects exist for students once they leave school? Do they believe that they are in with a good chance of a place at University or a decent job—for, as we have argued, the belief that they have no such chances is one of the things most likely to corrode their relationship with authority and hence increase their endorsement of delinquent action. What is more, when it actually comes to leaving school, a job or a university place is one of the strongest means of achieving social inclusion (cf. Lipsey, 1995) even for erstwhile rebels and hence for ensuring the "delinquent phase" comes to an end. Once again, these are costs which need to be considered when governments think about a range of policies from University tuition fees to job creation.

CONCLUSIONS: KEEPING THINGS IN PERSPECTIVE

Having focused upon the development of negative views about formal authority and upon the various forces which contribute to such developments, some correctives are in order. The first is that a majority of young people retain a broadly positive view of the police and the legal system even if they abandon the exaggerated idealization typical of childhood. One might say that their views are more balanced and realistic, their support more qualified and conditional.

The second is that juvenile troublemaking and lawbreaking have many other direct and indirect sources, including family poverty and poor parenting (cf. Farrington & West, 1990; Patterson, 1986). It would be quite inappropriate to imply that delinquency is entirely a consequence of a breakdown in relations with authority. On the other hand, it is tempting for those in authority to regard their own treatment of juveniles as no more than a reaction to juvenile misbehavior; that is, their actions are the dependent variables, to be explained by the lawlessness of some youth. Labeling theorists have encouraged the view that legal system and offender behavior are interdependent (Archer, 1985) and we believe it is more productive to recognize that the influences can run in both directions.

The third is to reiterate a point made earlier, but one whose importance cannot be overestimated. The great majority who were delinquent in their early teens will cease being delinquent by their mid- to late-teens as they begin to look for a job or begin to form a family. In the case of delinquency at least, time is generally a great healer. The least one can ask of any proposed ways of dealing with delinquency is that they do not interfere with this process. If they do, they will not only be useless, they will be worse than useless. If there is one clear message to come out of our work and out of this chapter, that is it. Insofar as delinquency can be related to social exclusion then beware of intervening in ways that make temporary forms of exclusion more permanent. Once that is accepted, perhaps it will be possible to develop more positive interventions which make it less likely that young people will feel excluded in the first place.

These will not be easy interventions, or quick interventions, or cheap interventions. That is why their success is not just a matter of psychological understanding. The critical factor in whether they happen or not is a political vision and a political will that can rise above short-term political expediency.

REFERENCES

Adelson, J. (1971). The political imagination of the young adolescent. *Daedalus, 100*, 1031–1050.

Adelson, J., Green, B., & O'Neil, R. (1969). Growth of the idea of law in adolescence. *Developmental Psychology, 1*, 327–332.

Adorno, T. W., Frenkel-Brunswik, E., Levinson, D. J., & Sanford, R. N. (1950). *The authoritarian personality.* New York: Harper & Row.

Amorso, D. M., & Ware, E. E. (1983). Youth's perception of police as a function of attitudes towards parents, teachers and self. *Canadian Journal of Criminology, 25*, 191–199.

Archer, D. (1985). Social deviance. In G. Lindzey & E. Aronson (Eds.), *Handbook of social psychology* (Vol. 2, 3rd ed.) New York: Random House.

Asch, S. (1956). Studies of independence and conformity: A minority of one against a unanimous majority. *Psychological Monographs, 7*(9) (Whole No. 416).

Banks, M., Bates, I., Breakwell, G., Bynner, J., Emler, N. Jamieson, L., & Robrts, K. (1992). *Careers and identities.* Milton Keynes: Open University Press.

Barker, R. G. (1968). *Ecological psychology.* Stanford CA: Stanford University Press.

Berreuta-Clement, J. R., Schweinhhart, L. J., Barnett, W. S., Epstein, A. S., & Weikart, D. P. (1984). *Changed lives: The effects of the Perry preschool program on youths through age 19.* Ypsilanti, MI: High/Scope Press.

Black, D. (1983). Crime as social control. *American Sociological Review, 48*, 34–45.

Box, S. (1983). *Power, crime and mystification.* London: Tavistock.

Braithwaite, J. (1983). Shame and modernity. *British Journal of Criminology, 33*, 1–17.

Brown, D. (1974a). Cognitive development and willingness to comply with law. *American Journal of Political Science, 18*, 583–594.

Brown, D. (1974b). Adolescent attitudes and lawful behaviour. *Public Opinion Quarterly, 38*, 96–106.

Burwen, L., & Campbell, D. T. (1957). The generality of attitudes towards authority and nonauthority figures. *Journal of Abnormal and Social Psychology, 54*, 24–31.

Clark, J. P., & Wenninger, E. P. (1964). The attitude of juveniles towards the legal institution. *Journal of Criminal Law, Criminology and Political Science, 55*, 482–489.

Cullen, J. L. (1987). Relating to authority in the elementary school years. *Child Study Journal, 17*, 227–238.

Danziger, K. (1971). *Socialization.* Harmondsworth: Penguin.

Demetriou, A., & Charitides, L. (1986). The adolescent's construction of procedural justice as a function of age, formal thought and sex. *International Journal of Psychology, 21*, 333–353.

Durkin, D. (1961). The specificity of children's moral judgments. *Journal of Genetic Psychology*, 98, 3–14.
Easton, D., & Dennis, J. (1969). *Children in the political system: Origins of political legitimacy*. New York: McGraw-Hill.
Emler, N. (1992). Childhood origins of beliefs about institutional authority. *New Directions for Child Development*, 56, 65–77.
Emler, N. (2000). Social structures and individual lives: Effects of participation in the institutions of family, education and work. In J. Bynner & R. K. Silbereisen (Eds.), Adversity and challenge in life in the new Germany and in England. London: MacMillan Press.
Emler, N., & Ohana, J. (1992). Réponses au prejudice: Representations sociales enfantines. *Bulletin de Psychologie*, 45, 223–231.
Emler, N., Ohana, J., & Moscovici, S. (1987). Children's beliefs about institutional roles: A cross-national study of representations of the teacher's role. *British Journal of Educational Psychology*, 57, 26–37.
Emler, N., & Reicher, S. (1987). Orientations to institutional authority in adolescence. *Journal of Moral Education*, 16, 108–116.
Emler, N., & Reicher, S. (1995). *Adolescence and delinquency: The collective management of reputation*. Oxford: Blackwell.
Emler, N., & St. James, A. (1990). Staying at school after sixteen: Social and psychological correlates. *British Journal of Education and Work*, 3, 60–70.
Emler, N., & St. James, A. (1994). Carriers scolaires et attitudes envers l'authorité formelle. *L'Orientation Scolaire et Professionelle*, 23, 355–367.
Farrington, D.P., & West, D. J. (1990). The Cambridge study of delinquent development. In S. A. Mednick & A. E. Baert (Eds.), *Prospective longitudinal research: An empirical basis for the primary prevention of psychosocial disorder*. Oxford: Oxford University Press.
Fry, P. S., & Corfield, V. K. (1983). Children's judgements of authority figures with respect to outcome and procedural fairness. *Journal of Genetic Psychology*, 143, 241–250.
Furth, H. G. (1980). *The world of grown ups*. New York: Elsevier.
Gibson, H. B. (1967). Self reported delinquency among schoolboys and their attitudes to the police. *British Journal of Social and Clinical Psychology*, 3, 190–195.
Gold, L. J., Darley, J. M., Hilton, J. L., & Zanna, M. P. (1984). Children's perceptions of procedural justice. *Child Development*, 55, 1752–1759.
Gouviea-Pereira, M., Vala, J., Palmonari, A., & Rubini, M. (2003). School experience, relational justice and legitimation of institutional authorities. *European Journal of Psychology of Education*, 28, 309–325.
Granic, I., & Dishion, T. (2003). Deviant talk in adolescent friendships: A step toward measuring a pathogenic attractor process. *Social Development*, 12, 314–334.
Greenberg, E. (1970). Black children and the political system. *Public Opinion Quarterly*, 34, 333–345.
Griffiths, C. T. (1982). Police school programs: The realities of the remedy. *Canadian Journal of Criminology*, 24, 329–340.
Hargreaves, D. H. (1967). *Social relations in a secondary school*. London: Routledge.
Heaven, P. (1993). Personality predictors of self-reported delinquency. *Personality and Individual Differences*, 14, 67–76.

Hess, R. D., & Torney, J. V. (1967). *The development of political attitudes in children*. New York: Aldine.

Hewstone, M., & Brown, R. J. (1986). Contact is not enough: An intergroup perspective on the contact hypothesis. In M. Hewstone & R. Brown (Eds.), *Contact and conflict in intergroup encounters*. Oxford: Blackwell.

Hewstone, M., Hopkins, N., & Routh, D. (1992). Cognitive models of stereotype change I: Generalisation and subtyping in young people's views of the police. *European Journal of Social Psychology, 22*, 219–234.

Hirschi, T. (1969). *Causes of delinquency*. Berkeley, CA: University of California Press.

Hopkins, N., Hewstone, M., & Hantzi, A. (1992). Police-school liaison and young people's image of the police: An intervention evaluation. *British Journal of Psychology, 83*, 203–220.

Hunter, J., Stringer, M., & Watson, R. P. (1991). Intergroup violence and intergroup attributions. *British Journal of Social Psychology, 30*, 261–266.

Jencks, C. (1972). *Inequality*. Harmondsworth: Penguin.

Kelly, D. H. (1975). Status origin, track position and delinquent involvement. A self-report analysis. *Sociological Quarterly, 16*, 264–271.

Kohlberg, L. (1984). *The psychology of moral development: Vol 2. Essays on moral development*. New York: Harper & Row.

Leventhal, G. S. (1980). What should be done with equity theory? New approaches to the study of fairness in social relationships. In K. Gergen, M. Greenberg, & R. Willis (Eds.), *Social exchange*. New York: Plenum.

Levy, K. (2001). The relationship between adolescent attitudes towards authority, self concept, and delinquency. *Adolescence, 36*, 333–346.

Lickona, T. (1976). Research on Piaget's theory of moral development. In T. Lickona (Ed.), *Moral development and behavior: Theory, research and social issues*. New York: Holt, Rinehart, & Winston.

Lind, E. A., & Tyler, T. R. (1988). *The social psychology of procedural justice*. New York: Plenum.

Lipsey, M. (1995). What do we learn from 400 research studies on the effectiveness of treatment with juvenile delinquents? In J. McGuire (Ed.), *What works? Reducing reoffending*. Chichester: Wiley.

Liska, A. E., & Reed, M. D. (1985). Ties to conventional institutions and delinquency: Estimating reciprocal effects. *American Sociological Review, 50*, 547–560.

Lynham, D., Moffitt, T., & Stouthamer-Loeber, M. (1993). Explaining the relation between IQ and delinquency: Class, race, test motivation, school failure, or self-control? *Journal of Abnormal Psychology, 102*, 187–196.

Mawby, R. (1980). Sex and crime: The results of a self-report study. *British Journal of Sociology, 31*, 525–543.

Menard, S. & Morse, B. J. (1984). A structuralist critique of the IQ-delinquency hypothesis: Theory and evidence. *American Journal of Sociology, 89*, 1347–1378.

Milgram, S. (1964). Group pressure and action against a person. *Journal of Abnormal and Social Psychology, 69*, 137–143.

Murray, C., & Thompson, F. (1985). The representation of authority: An adolescent viewpoint. *Journal of Adolescence, 8*, 217–229.

Nelsen, E. A., Eisenberg, N., & Carroll, J. L. (1982). The structure of adolescents' attitudes towards law and crime. *Journal of Genetic Psychology, 140*, 47–58.

Palmonari, A., & Rubini, M. (1999). *A Psychosocial Approach to the Study of Orientation to Formal Authority*. Paper presented at XII General Meeting of EAESP. Oxford (6–11 July).
Parsons, C., & Howlett, K. (1996). Permanent exclusion from school: A case where society is failing its children. *Support for Learning, 11*, 109–112.
Patterson, G. R. (1986). Performance models for anti-social boys. *American Psychologist, 44*, 105–111.
Piaget, J. (1932). *The moral judgement of the child*. London: Routledge.
Piliavin, I. & Briar, S. (1964). Police encounters with juveniles. *American Journal of Sociology, 70*, 206–214.
Reicher, S. (1996). The Battle of Westminster: Developing the social identity model of crowd behaviour in order to deal with the initiation and development of collective conflict. *European Journal of Social Psychology, 26*, 115–134.
Reicher, S., & Emler, N. (1985). Delinquent behaviour and attitudes to formal authority, *British Journal of Social Psychology, 3*, 161–168.
Reicher, S., & Levine, M. (1994). On the consequences of deindividuation manipulations for the strategic communication of self: identifiability and the presentation of social identity. *European Journal of Social Psychology, 24*, 511–524.
Reiss, A. J., & Rhodes, A. L. (1961). The distribution of juvenile delinquency in the social class structure. *American Sociological Review, 26*, 720–732.
Rigby, K., & Rump, E. (1979). The generality of attitude to authority. *Human Relations, 32*, 469–487.
Rigby, K., Schofield, P., & Slee, P. (1987). The similarity of attitudes towards personal and impersonal types of authority among adolescent school children. *Journal of Adolescence, 10*, 241–253.
Rutter, M. & Giller, H. (1983). *Juvenile delinquency: Trends and perspectives*. Harmondsworth: Penguin.
Sampson, R. J., & Laub, J. H. (1993). *Crime in the making: Pathways and turning points through life*. Cambridge MA: Harvard University Press.
Stacey, B. G. (1978). *Political socialization in Western society*. London: Edward Arnold.
Stouthamer-Loeber, M., Loeber, R., Homish, L., & Wei, E. (2001). Maltreatment of boys and the development of disruptive and delinquent behaviour. *Development and Psychopathology, 13*, 941–955.
Strang, H., Barnes, G., Braithwaite, J., & Sherman, L. (1999). *Experiments in Restorative Policing: A Progress Report on the Canberra Reintegrative Shaming Experiments (RISE)*, from http://www.aic.gov.au/rjustice.
Stott, C., & Reicher, S. (1998). Crowd action as inter-group process: Introducing the police perspective. *European Journal of Social Psychology, 28*, 509–530.
Tarry, H. (2001). *The role of moral reasoning in delinquency*. Unpublished doctoral thesis, Oxford University.
Taylor, D. M., & Jaggi V. (1974). Ethnocentrism and causal attribution in a S. Indian context. *Journal of Cross Cultural Psychology, 5*, 162–171.
Torney, J. V. (1971). Socialization of attitudes towards the legal system. *Journal of Social Issues, 27*, 137–154.
Tremblay, R. E. (2000). The development of aggressive behaviour during childhood: What have we learned in the past century? *International Journal of Behavioral Development, 24*, 129–141.

Tyler, T. (1990). *Why people obey the law*. New Haven, CN: Yale University Press.
Tyler, T. (1997). The psychology of legitimacy: A relational perspective on voluntary deference to authorities. *Personality and Social Psychology Review, 1*, 323–345.
Tyler, T. R., & Lind, E. A. (1992). A relational model of authority in groups. *Advances in Experimental Social Psychology, 25*, 115–191.
Waldo, G. P., & Hall, N. E. (1970). Delinquency potential and attitudes towards the criminal justice system. *Social Forces, 49*, 291–298.
Weber, M. (1947). *The theory of social and economic organisation*. New York: Free Press.
West, D. J., & Farrington, D. P. (1977). *The delinquent way of life*. London: Heinemann.
Wiatrowski, M. D., Hansell, S., Massey, C. R., & Wilson D. L. (1982). Curriculum tracking and delinquency. *American Sociological Review, 47*, 151–160.
Willis, P. (1977). *Learning to labour*. London: MacMillan.
Yoshikawa, H. (1994). Prevention as cumulative protection: Effects of early family support and education on chronic delinquency and its risks. *Psychological Bulletin, 115*, 28–54.

Section III

Intergroup Inclusion and Exclusion

11

Social Inclusion and Exclusion: Recategorization and the Perception of Intergroup Boundaries

JOHN F. DOVIDIO, SAMUEL L. GAERTNER,
GORDON HODSON, MELISSA A. HOULETTE, and
KELLY M. JOHNSON

Attraction and prejudice are fundamentally related to defining who is included in one's own group (a "we") and who is excluded (a "they"). In this chapter, we posit that understanding the processes that underlie the development of intergroup biases can help guide strategies to reduce biases. In particular, in the Common Ingroup Identity Model, we propose that if members of different groups are induced to conceive of themselves more as a single, superordinate group rather than as separate groups, attitudes toward former outgroup members will become more positive through processes involving pro-ingroup bias. Moreover, increasing the salience of a superordinate identity while maintaining the salience of a subgroup identity (i.e., emphasizing a dual identity) can also reduce bias, but the effectiveness of this strategy is moderated by group status and social values. Data, reported in this chapter, from laboratory studies and field experiments offer converging evidence for the model.

Intergroup inclusion and exclusion have critical implications for one's attitudes toward others. Attraction and prejudice are fundamentally related to social categorization and to the perception of intergroup boundaries—boundaries that define who is included in one's own group (a "we") and who is excluded (a "they"). Upon social categorization, people favor ingroup members in terms of evaluations, attributions, material resources, helping, and social support. Thus, changing the nature of intergroup inclusion and exclusion can have important consequences for interpersonal and intergroup relations. Building on research demonstrating the importance of social categorization in creating and maintaining bias, in this chapter we explore the implications of the Common Ingroup Identity Model (Gaertner & Dovidio, 2000; Gaertner, Dovidio, Anastasio, Bachman, & Rust, 1993). According to this model, if members of different groups are induced to recategorize themselves as a superordinate group rather than as two separate groups, then intergroup prejudice, stereotyping, and discrimination will be reduced through the extension of pro-ingroup bias to former outgroup members.

In this chapter we first review theoretical and empirical evidence of the role of social categorization in reducing bias. We next examine, with data from laboratory studies, field experiments, and surveys involving a range of different types of groups, the fundamental power of recategorizing former outgroup members as members of the ingroup—that is, changing the nature of exclusion and inclusion—for reducing intergroup bias. Then, we explore differences in orientations of majority and minority group members to the different forms of recategorization and social inclusion, in particular identification with a super-ordinate group or a dual identity, and illustrate evidence relating to this aspect of the Common Ingroup Identity Model. We conclude by considering the practical and theoretical implications of these data.

THE ROLE OF SOCIAL INCLUSION AND EXCLUSION IN INTERGROUP BIAS

Social categorization is a fundamental aspect of human functioning and perception. With respect to functioning, humans are social animals, relying on select others for interdependent activity and co-operation that have both short- and long-term survival benefits. Group membership is a key element in this activity. Co-operation and other forms of assistance ultimately benefit the provider if others are willing to reciprocate. To the extent that opportunities for reciprocation are greater within than across groups, social categorization thus provides a basis for achieving the benefits of cooperative interdependence while minimizing risk or excessive costs.

Because of the importance of identifying group membership, one universal facet of human perception essential for efficient functioning is the ability to sort people, spontaneously and with minimum effort or awareness, into a smaller number of meaningful categories (Brewer, 1988; see also Fiske, Lin, & Neuberg, 1999). Given the centrality of the self in social perception, social categorization further involves a basic distinction between the group containing the self, the ingroup, and other groups, the outgroups—between the "we's" and the "they's" (see Social Identity Theory, Tajfel, & Turner, 1979; Self-Categorization Theory, Turner, Hogg, Oakes, Reicher, & Wetherell, 1987).

This distinction of social inclusion and exclusion has a profound influence on social perception, affect, cognition, and behavior. Perceptually, when people or objects are categorized into groups, actual differences between members of the same category tend to be minimized (Tajfel, 1969) and often ignored in making decisions or forming impressions, while between-group differences tend to become exaggerated (Abrams, 1985; Turner, 1985). Emotionally, people spontaneously experience more positive affect toward other members of the ingroup than toward members of the outgroup (Otten & Moskowitz, 2000), particularly toward those ingroup members who are most prototypical of their group (Hogg & Hains, 1996). Cognitively, people retain more information in a more detailed fashion for ingroup members than for outgroup members (Park & Rothbart, 1982), have better memory for information about ways in which ingroup members are similar to and outgroup members are dissimilar to the self (Wilder, 1981), and remember less positive information about outgroup members (Howard & Rothbart, 1980). And behaviorally, people are more helpful toward ingroup than toward outgroup members (Dovidio et al., 1997), and they work harder for groups identified as ingroups (Worchel, Rothgerber, Day, Hart, & Butemeyer, 1998). In contrast, when ingroup–outgroup social categorization is salient, people tend to behave in a more greedy and less trustworthy way toward members of other groups than if they were reacting to each other as individuals (Insko et al., 2001).

The process of social categorization, however, is not completely unalterable. Categories are hierarchically organized, with higher-level categories (e.g., nations) being more inclusive of lower level ones (e.g., cities or towns). By modifying a perceiver's goals, motives, perceptions of past experiences, and expectations, as well as factors within the perceptual field and the situational context more broadly, there is opportunity to alter the level of category inclusiveness that will be most influential in a given situation. This malleability of the level at which impressions are formed is important because of its implications for altering the way people think about members of ingroups and outgroups, and consequently about the nature of intergroup relations.

Because categorization is a basic process that is fundamental to intergroup bias, social psychologists have targeted this process as a starting point to begin to improve intergroup relations. In the next section we explore how the forces of categorization can be harnessed and redirected toward the reduction, if not the elimination, of intergroup bias.

REDUCING INTERGROUP BIAS

Since the mid-20th century, the Contact Hypothesis (Allport, 1954; see also Pettigrew, 1998) has represented the primary strategy for reducing intergroup bias and conflict. This hypothesis proposes that for contact between groups to reduce bias successfully, certain prerequisite features must be present. These characteristics of contact include equal status between the groups, cooperative (rather than competitive) intergroup interaction, opportunities for personal acquaintance between the members (especially with those whose personal characteristics do not support negative stereotypic expectations), and supportive norms by authorities within and outside of the contact situation (Pettigrew, 1998). Research in laboratory and field settings generally supports the fundamental importance of these conditions for achieving improved intergroup relations (see Pettigrew & Tropp, 2000).

Recent research, however, has moved beyond specifying what conditions moderate the reduction of bias to understanding what underlying processes, such as those involving social categorization, may be involved (see Pettigrew, 1998). From the social categorization perspective, the issue to be addressed is how intergroup contact can be structured to alter inclusive–exclusive collective representations of others. Two of the approaches that have been proposed involve decategorization and recategorization. Decategorization refers to influencing whether people identify themselves primarily as group members or as distinct individuals on the dimension proposed by Tajfel and Turner (1979; see also Brewer, 1988; Brewer & Miller, 1984; Fiske et al., 1999). Recategorization, in contrast, is not designed to reduce or eliminate categorization, but rather to structure a definition of group categorization at a higher level of category inclusiveness in ways that reduce intergroup bias and conflict (Allport, 1954, p. 43; see Gaertner & Dovidio, 2000).

In each case, reducing the salience of the original inclusive–exclusive group boundaries is expected to decrease intergroup bias. With decategorization, group boundaries are degraded, inducing members of different groups to conceive of themselves and others as separate individuals (Wilder, 1981) and encouraging more personalized interactions. When personalized interactions occur, people "attend to information that replaces category identity as the most useful basis for classifying each other" (Brewer & Miller, 1984, p. 288), and thus category-based biased are reduced.

With recategorization as proposed by the Common Ingroup Identity Model (Gaertner & Dovidio, 2000; Gaertner et al., 1993), inducing members of different groups to conceive of themselves as a single, more inclusive superordinate group rather than as two completely separate groups produces attitudes toward former outgroup members that become more positive through processes involving pro-ingroup bias. That is, the processes that lead to favoritism toward ingroup members would now be directed toward former outgroup members as they become redefined from exclusive to inclusive categories.

The decategorization and recategorization strategies and their respective means of reducing bias were directly examined in a laboratory study (Gaertner, Mann, Murrell, & Dovidio, 1989). In this experiment, members of two separate laboratory-formed groups were induced through various structural interventions (e.g., seating arrangement) either to decategorize themselves (i.e., conceive of themselves as separate individuals) or to recategorize themselves as one superordinate group. Supporting the proposed value of altering the level of category inclusiveness, these changes in the perceptions of intergroup boundaries reduced intergroup bias. Furthermore, as expected, these strategies reduced bias in different ways. Decategorizing members of the two groups reduced bias by decreasing the attractiveness of former ingroup members. In contrast, recategorizing ingroup and outgroup members as members of a more inclusive group reduced bias by increasing the attractiveness of the former outgroup members. Consistent with Self-Categorization Theory, "the attractiveness of an individual is not constant, but varies with the ingroup membership" (Turner, 1985, p. 60).

In the next section, we present support for the Common Ingroup Identity Model and the effects of recategorization. In addition, we discuss the value of a "dual identity" in which original group identities are maintained but within the context of a superordinate identity.

The Common Ingroup Identity Model

In the Common Ingroup Identity Model (see Figure 11.1), we outline specific potential antecedents and outcomes of direct or symbolic intergroup contact, as well as identify possible mediating social categorization processes. In particular, we hypothesize that the different types of intergroup interdependence and cognitive, perceptual, linguistic, affective, and environmental factors can either independently or in concert alter individuals' cognitive representations of the

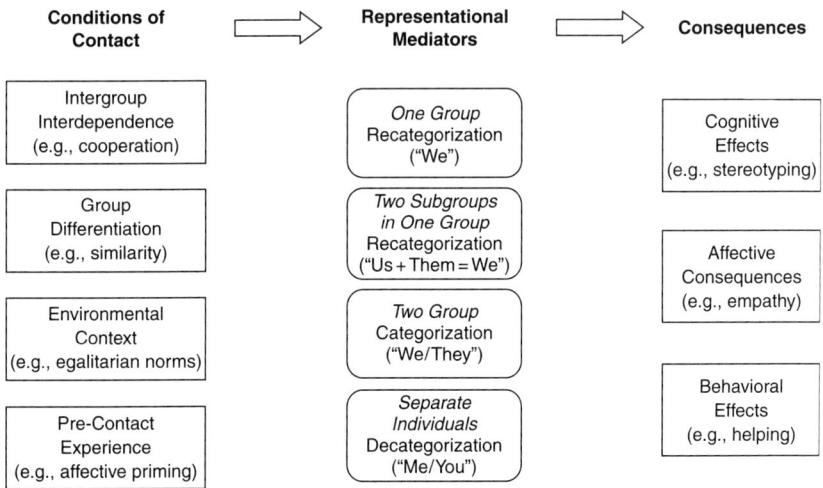

FIGURE 11.1 The common ingroup identity model

aggregate. These resulting cognitive representations (i.e., one group, two subgroups within one group, two groups, or separate individuals) are then proposed to produce specific cognitive, affective, and overt behavioral consequences (listed on the right). Thus, the causal factors listed on the left (which include features specified by the Contact Hypothesis) are proposed to influence people's cognitive representations of the memberships (center) that in turn mediate the relationship, at least in part, between the causal factors (on the left) and the cognitive, affective, and behavioral consequences (on the right). In addition, we propose that a common ingroup identity can be achieved by increasing the salience of existing a common superordinate memberships (e.g., a school, a company, a nation) or by introducing factors (e.g., common goals or shared fate) that are perceived to be shared between the original groups.

Once outgroup members are perceived as ingroup members, it is proposed that they would be accorded the benefits of ingroup status. There would likely be more positive thoughts, feelings, and behaviors (listed on the right) toward these former outgroup members by virtue of their recategorization as ingroup members. These more favorable impressions of outgroup members are not likely to be finely differentiated, at least initially (see Mullen & Hu, 1989). Rather, we propose that these more elaborated, personalized impressions can soon develop within the context of a common identity because the newly formed positivity bias is likely to encourage more open communication and greater self-disclosing interaction between former outgroup members. Thus, as proposed by Pettigrew (1998; see also Hewstone, 1996), the nature of intergroup contact can influence group representations in different ways sequentially across time. We suggest that, over time, a common identity can lead to decategorization and encourage personalization of outgroup members and thereby initiate a second route to achieving reduced bias.

Within this model, we also acknowledge that the development of a common ingroup identity does not necessarily require each group to forsake its less inclusive group identity completely. As Brewer (2000) noted, individuals belong simultaneously to several groups and possess multiple potential identities. These identities, under some circumstances and for some people (e.g., particularly minority group members), may also be salient simultaneously. For instance, with respect to immigrant minority groups, Berry (1984) presented four forms of cultural relations in pluralistic societies that represent the intersection of "yes–no" responses to two relevant questions: (a) Are the original cultural identity and customs of value to be retained? (b) Are positive relations with the larger society of value, to be sought? These combinations reflect four adaptation strategies for intergroup relations: (a) integration, when cultural identities are retained and positive relations with the larger society are sought; (b) separatism, when original cultural identities are retained but positive relations with the larger society are not sought; (c) assimilation, when cultural identities are abandoned and positive relations with the larger society are desired; and (d) marginalization, when cultural identities are abandoned and are not replaced by positive identification with the larger society.

Although this framework has been applied primarily to the ways in which immigrants acclimate to a new society (van Oudenhoven, Prins, & Buunk, 1998), we have argued that it can be adapted to apply to intergroup relations between majority and stigmatized minority groups more generally (see Dovidio, Gaertner, & Kafati, 2000). Substituting the separate strengths of the subgroup and subordinate group identities for the answers to Berry's (1984) two questions, the combinations map onto the four main representations considered in the Common Ingroup Identity Model: (a) different groups on the same team (subgroup and superordinate group identities are high, like integration); (b) different groups (subgroup identity is high and superordinate identity is low, like separatism); (c) one overall group (subgroup identity is low and superordinate group identity is high, like assimilation); and (d) separate individuals (subgroup and superordinate group identities are low, like marginalization).

Thus, as depicted by the "subgroups within one group" (i.e., a same team or dual identity) representation, we believe that it is possible for members to conceive of two groups as distinct units within the context of a superordinate identity. When group identities are highly salient or are central to members' functioning, it may be undesirable or impossible for people to relinquish these group identities or, as perceivers, to become "colorblind" and truly ignore intergroup distinctions. Indeed, demands to forsake these group identities or to adopt a colorblind ideology would likely arouse strong reactance and result in especially poor intergroup relations. If, however, people continued to regard themselves as members of different groups but all playing on the same team or as part of the same superordinate entity, intergroup relations between these subgroups would be more positive than if members only considered themselves as separate groups. This aspect of the Common Ingroup Identity Model is compatible with, although not identical to, other models that propose that maintaining the salience of intergroup distinctions can be important for producing generalized and longer-term reductions in intergroup bias (Hewstone & Brown, 1986).

In the next part of this section, we briefly review empirical tests of the Common Ingroup Identity Model that focus on the benefits, in terms of improving intergroup attitudes and fostering organizational commitment, of recategorizing formerly excluded group members into an inclusive ingroup identity. After that, we examine the differences in responses between majority and minority groups and the potential role of a dual identity in reducing bias.

Intergroup Bias   Among the antecedent factors proposed by the Common Ingroup Identity Model (listed on the left of Figure 11.1) are the features of contact situations (Allport, 1954) that are necessary for intergroup contact to be successful (e.g., interdependence between groups, equal status, egalitarian norms). From our perspective, cooperate interaction may enhance positive evaluations of outgroup members and reduce intergroup bias, at least in part, by transforming interactants' representations of the memberships from two groups to one group.

In one test of this hypothesis, we conducted an experiment that brought two 3-person laboratory groups together under conditions designed to vary independently: (a) the members' representations of the aggregate as one group or two groups through manipulation of the contact situation and (b) the presence or absence of intergroup cooperate interaction (Gaertner, Mann, Dovidio, Murrell, & Pomare, 1990). The interventions designed to emphasize common group membership through structural changes in the contact situation (e.g., integrated vs. segregated seating; a new group name for all six participants vs. the original group names) and to encourage cooperate interaction (joint evaluation and reward vs. independent outcomes) both reduced intergroup bias. Moreover, they did so through the same mechanism. Contextual features emphasizing common "groupness" and joint outcomes each increased one-group representations (and reduced separate-group representations), which in turn related to more favorable attitudes toward original outgroup members and lower levels of bias. Consistent with the Common Ingroup Identity Model, more inclusive, one-group representations *mediated* the relationship between the interventions and the reduction of bias.

The advantage of this experimental design is that interdependence preceded changes in participants' representations of the aggregate from two groups to one group and also changes in intergroup bias. In addition, because the representations of the aggregate were manipulated in the absence of interdependence, the development of a one-group representation preceded changes in intergroup bias. Thus, we can be confident about the directions of causality in this study. In other experiments we have manipulated structural aspects of intergroup contact situations, such as segregated or integrated seating, and found that these manipulations directly influenced group representations and, ultimately, intergroup bias (see Gaertner & Dovidio, 2000). These studies provide convergent evidence for a clear sequence of events and identification of causal relations.

An additional laboratory study (Houlette & Gaertner, 1999) explored the effects of varying the degree of inclusiveness of a superordinate identity on intergroup bias between three-person groups of liberals and conservatives. The recategorization manipulation emphasized members' common affiliation with groups varying in inclusiveness: with their ad hoc six-person laboratory work group, their identity as University of Delaware students, or their common national citizenship (i.e., United States). Greater inclusiveness of the common superordinate entity (i.e., from the six-person work group to national citizenship) related to higher levels of identification and to lower levels of intergroup bias.

These findings thus provide additional experimental evidence of the effectiveness of interventions designed to emphasize common group membership for reducing intergroup bias.

In a subsequent series of studies we utilized survey techniques under more naturalistic circumstances to examine the impact of common group identity for a range of types of intergroup bias. Participants in these studies included students attending a multiethnic high school (Gaertner, Rust, Dovidio, Bachman, & Anastasio, 1996), banking executives who had experienced a corporate merger involving a wide variety of banks across the United States (Bachman, 1993), and college students who are members of blended families whose households are composed of two formerly separate families trying to unite into one (Banker & Gaertner, 1998).

These studies offer converging support for the hypothesis that the features specified by the Contact Hypothesis reduce intergroup bias, in part, because they transform members' representations of the memberships from separate groups to one more inclusive group. Consistent with the role of an inclusive group representation that is hypothesized in the Common Ingroup Identity Model, across all three studies (a) conditions of intergroup contact that were perceived as more favorable predicted lower levels of intergroup bias, (b) more favorable conditions of contact predicted more inclusive (one group) and less exclusive (different groups) representations; and (c) more inclusive representations mediated lower levels of intergroup bias and conflict (see Gaertner, Dovidio, Nier, Ward, & Banker, 1999).

Thus far, we have reported consistent evidence across a range of laboratory experiments and field studies demonstrating that encouraging a common, one-group representation can reduce negative intergroup affective reactions and bias. Additional evidence, consistent with our model, indicates that the development of a common ingroup identity can also influence behavioral orientations, such as institutional commitment.

Commitment Both individually and socially, organizational commitment can have important consequences in terms of retention and productivity (Milliken & Martin, 1996). To explore the applicability of the Common Ingroup Identity Model to these issues, we have examined data relating to feelings of racial/ethnic stigmatization and institutional commitment among White, Black, and Hispanic faculty members in academic psychology departments (Niemann & Dovidio, 1998) and among Black and White college students (Dovidio, Gaertner, Niemann, & Snider, 2001). With respect to faculty commitment, we hypothesized that stronger feelings of a common group identity would predict higher levels of job satisfaction and mitigate the effects of feelings of racial/ethnic stigmatization among faculty of color. Supportive of this hypothesis, common group identity (feelings of equality and belonging) correlated positively with job satisfaction for minorities. Feelings of racial/ethnic stigmatization correlated negatively with job satisfaction. Moreover, as expected, inclusive group representations mediated the relation between stigmatization and job satisfaction.

Complementing these results, in a study of Black and White college students attending a midwestern state university (Dovidio et al., 2000, 2001), we found that feelings of a common ingroup identity—"feeling part of the university community"—reduced the negative impact of perceived discrimination on their satisfaction with and commitment to their university. These effects were particularly strong for minority group members (see also Brewer, von Hippel, & Gooden, 1999). Taken together, these findings indicate that developing a common group identity can help counteract the effects of stigmatization that produce racial and ethnic differences in satisfaction.

In summary, with respect to the development of an inclusive one-group identity, across a range of experiments and surveys we have found consistent support for the critical mediating role of more inclusive and less exclusive group representations on intergroup affect, intergroup bias, and behavioral orientations in a variety of intergroup contexts. In the next section we consider how the different types of recategorized inclusive representations, one group and same team (i.e., dual identity), can influence the orientations of minority and majority group members.

Recategorization and a Dual Identity

Hewstone (1996) has argued that, at a practical level, interventions designed to create a common, inclusive identity (such as equal status contact) may not be sufficiently potent to "overcome powerful ethnic and racial categorizations on more than a temporary basis" (p. 351). Moreover, at a theoretical level based on the assumptions of Social Identity Theory (Tajfel & Turner, 1979), introducing equal status interventions in intergroup contact situations may produce a threat to the integrity of members' separate group identities and needs for group distinctiveness. Consequently, in an effort to reestablish positive and distinctive group identities, members of such equal status interacting groups may maintain relatively high levels of intergroup bias (Brown & Wade, 1987) or even show increased levels of bias (Dovidio, Gaertner, & Validzic, 1998).

However, recategorization into a single, undifferentiated group (a one-group representation) is only one form considered in the Common Ingroup Identity Model. As we explained earlier, recategorization can also take the form of a dual identity (a "different groups working together on the same team" representation) in which superordinate and subgroup identities are simultaneously salient. Establishing a common superordinate identity while maintaining the salience of subgroup identities may be particularly effective because it permits the benefits of a common ingroup identity to operate without arousing countervailing motivations to achieve positive distinctiveness. Moreover, this type of recategorization may be particularly effective when people have strong allegiances to their original groups. In this respect, the benefits of a dual identity may be particularly relevant to interracial and interethnic group contexts. Among people of color in particular, the development of a dual identity, in terms of a bicultural or multicultural identity (consistent with an ideal of pluralistic integration), may not only improve intergroup relations and reduce their own biases but may also contribute to social adjustment, psychological adaptation, and overall well-being (LaFromboise, Coleman, & Gerton, 1993).

Majority and Minority Group Perspectives As our previous work has shown, emphasis on a common superordinate identity can improve intergroup attitudes and relations in significant ways. Other research also reveals that in naturalistic settings White people's stronger identification with a superordinate, national group (i.e., the United States) related to greater support for policies supporting minority groups (i.e., affirmative action) within the superordinate category (Smith & Tyler, 1996, Study 1).

Among people of color, even when racial or ethnic identity is strong, perceptions of a superordinate connection enhance interracial trust and acceptance of authority within an organization. Huo, Smith, Tyler, and Lind (1996) surveyed White, Black, Hispanic, and Asian employees of a public-sector organization. Identification with the organization (superordinate identity) and racial/ethnic identity (subgroup identity) were independently assessed. Regardless of the strength of racial/ethnic identity, respondents who had a strong organizational identity perceived that they were treated fairly within the organization, which in turn was correlated with favorable attitudes toward institutional authority. Huo et al. (1996) concluded that having a strong identification with a superordinate group can redirect people from focusing on their personal outcomes to concerns about "achieving the greater good and maintaining social stability" (pp. 44–45), while also maintaining important racial and ethnic identities. We found converging evidence in our multiethnic high school survey study (Gaertner et al., 1996), which we introduced earlier. Supportive of the role of a dual identity, students who described themselves as *both* American and as a member of their racial or ethnic group had less bias toward other groups in the school than did those who described themselves only in terms of their subgroup identity. Thus, even when subgroup identity is salient, the simultaneous salience of a common ingroup identity is associated with lower levels of intergroup bias.

Although these findings suggest the value of developing a dual identity as an alternative to a one-group representation for improving intergroup attitudes and the behavioral orientations of minority group members, we caution that the effectiveness of a dual identity may be substantially moderated by the nature of the intergroup context. In contrast to the consistent, significant effect for the one-group representation across the multiethnic high school (Gaertner et al.,

1996), banking executive (Bachman, 1993), and stepfamily (Banker & Gaertner, 1998) studies described in the previous section, the role of the dual identity measure functioned differently across the three intergroup settings. First, more favorable conditions of contact predicted a stronger dual identity in the high school setting but a weaker dual identity in both the corporate merger and stepfamily settings. Second, a stronger sense of a dual identity was related to less bias in the high school study but to more bias in the corporate merger study and to more conflict within the stepfamily study (see Gaertner et al., 1999).

One potential factor that might moderate the effectiveness of a dual identity is the "cultural ideal" of the social entity. That is, the greater the correspondence of the representation to the values that people have for the social entity (e.g., society, university, multiethnic high school, or family), the more likely this representation will be the primary mediator of lower levels of bias. For example, among the student population of the multiethnic high school, comprised predominantly of minority students, the same-team, dual-identity representation was a significant mediator of more positive reactions to outgroup members. In contrast, within the context of a corporate merger, in which maintaining strong identification with the earlier subgroup might threaten the primary goal of the merger, and within the context of a blended family, in which allegiance to one's former family can be diagnostic of serious problems, a one-group representation would be expected to be—and is—the most important mediator of positive intergroup relations. We explore this possibility further in the next section.

Dual Identity and Group Values

Although identification with a common group identity can have beneficial effects for both majority and minority group members, it is still important to recognize that members of these groups also have different perspectives (Islam & Hewstone, 1993). These different perspectives can shape perceptions of and reactions to the nature of the contact. Whereas minority group members often tend to want to retain their cultural identity, majority group members favor the assimilation of minority groups into one single culture (a traditional "melting pot" orientation)—a process that reaffirms and reinforces the values of the dominant culture. Van Oudenhoven et al. (1998), for instance, found in the Netherlands that Dutch majority group members preferred an assimilation of minority groups (in which minority group identity was abandoned and replaced by identification with the dominant Dutch culture), whereas Turkish and Moroccan immigrants most strongly endorsed integration (in which they would retain their own cultural identity while also valuing the dominant Dutch culture). With samples in the United States, we have found that White college students most prefer the one group, assimilation approach, whereas racial and ethnic minorities favor a "same team," pluralistic integration model.

Furthermore, as we suggested about factors that influence the effectiveness of a dual identity, these preferred types of intergroup relations for majority and minority groups, a one-group representation for Whites and same-team representation for people of color, appear to differentially mediate the consequences of intergroup contact for the different groups (see Dovidio et al., 2000). For White college students, more positive perceptions of intergroup contact related to stronger perceptions of students consisting of one group, different groups on the same team, and separate individuals, as well as to weaker perceptions of different groups. However, when considered simultaneously, only the one-group representation mediated commitment to the university. Conditions of contact also significantly predicted each of the representations for students of color, but the mediating representation was different. In contrast to the pattern for Whites, the different groups on the same-team representation, and not the one-group representation, mediated commitment to the university. In general, these effects were stronger for people higher in racial ethnic identification, both for Whites and students of color. Thus, recategorized representations—but different ones—were critical mediators of institutional commitment for White and students of color. Additional analyses, using intergroup attitudes as the outcome measure of interest, rather than commitment to the university, produce a generally similar pattern of results. The one-group representation was the strongest predictor of positive attitudes toward minorities for Whites, whereas the same-team representation was the strongest predictor of positive attitudes toward Whites among students of color.

Complementing the above findings for White and students of color a study by Johnson, Gaertner and Dovidio (2001) found that, within a sample predominantly of White students, status moderates the relationship between a dual identity and bias. Among low and high status university students (i.e., regular students and students in the prestigious Honors Program, respectively), who expected to perform the same tasks within a superordinate workgroup, the relationship between perceptions of the aggregate as two subgroups within a group (a dual identity) and bias depended upon the status of the group. For low status, regular students, higher perceptions of a dual identity significantly predicted less bias, whereas for higher status honors students a stronger dual identity predicted greater bias.

We obtained further evidence indicating the importance of a group ideal for cultural relations and the effectiveness of a dual identity for reducing bias in another study, in which we investigated the extent to which exposure to a single outgroup member can generalize to more positive attitudes toward the outgroup as a whole. In particular, in this experiment (Dovidio, Gaertner, & Johnson, 1999), White college students from Colgate University first read a campus newspaper article and then viewed a videotape that portrayed a Black student who had experienced a serious illness that had caused them academic difficulties. The presentation of the Black student, a confederate, was designed to make a positive impression. After the initial presentation of the confederate, an interviewer asked on the videotape, "And how do you see yourself?" The response was constructed to reflect one of the four representations outlined in the Common Ingroup Identity Model: (a) "I see myself primarily as a Colgate student" (one group), (b) "I see myself primarily as a Black person" (different group), (c) "I see myself primarily as a Black Colgate student [or a Colgate student who is Black]" (dual identity), or (d) "I see myself primarily as a unique individual" (separate individuals). Because this response followed the main introduction to the student, we expected that it would have little effect on the evaluation of and attitudes toward this student. It did not; across all of the conditions, White participants responded to the person equivalently favorably. Our hypothesis, though, was that this information would affect the generalization of this positive response to other members of the group as a whole.

The results of this study provide further evidence that the effectiveness of a dual identity is critically moderated by the social context and cultural values. In this case, the manipulation based on a one-group representation, which was most compatible with an assimilation ideology, was the most effective strategy for White college students. Attitudes toward Blacks in general were significantly less prejudiced and more favorable when the Black student described himself or herself solely in terms of common university membership than in the other three conditions. Attitudes in the other three conditions—dual identity, different groups, and separate individuals—did not differ from one another.

Mummendey and Wenzel (1999) suggest a specific mechanism that may be involved in determining the relative effectiveness of interventions designed to produce one-group or dual identity representations—relative prototypicality. They propose that, when a common, superordinate identity is salient, people tend to overestimate the extent to which their own group's norms, values, and standards are prototypical of the superordinate category relative to the extent to which other group's norms, values, and standards are prototypical. When the standards of one's own group are perceived to represent those of the superordinate category, the standards of other groups will be seen as nonnormative and inferior. As a consequence, bias results. It is further possible that a salient subgroup identity, which can increase the strength of projection of beliefs, values, and norms (Mullen, Dovidio, Johnson, & Copper, 1992), can exacerbate the effects of relative protypicality when the superordinate group identity is also salient. Thus, even though strong racial identities, alone or in the form of a dual identity, may be initially beneficial, particularly for minorities (LaFromboise et al., 1993), the adoption of a single, inclusive identity might be the primary predictor of reductions in bias over time and across situations, particularly in organizations, such as traditionally White colleges, in which assimilation is the dominant ideal.

Supportive of this reasoning, we investigated in a longitudinal study the *changes* that occurred in the attitudes of minority college students over an academic year as a function of group representations. In particular, 37 minority students (representing about half the sample described earlier; see also Dovidio et al., 2000), were surveyed, first at the beginning of the academic year and then again within six weeks before the end of the academic year. Students were asked about their perceptions of the favorability of intergroup contact on campus, their representations of racial and ethnic groups on campus (one group, different subgroups on the same team, different groups, and separate individuals), and attitudes toward Whites on campus.

Consistent with the results for the larger sample reported earlier, in the initial survey, more favorable conditions of intergroup contact predicted more positive attitudes toward Whites ($r = .66$), and the same-team representation was the primary mediator of the relation between conditions of contact and these attitudes. The favorability of initial contact also significantly predicted positive attitudes toward Whites at the end of the year, but the magnitude of this effect was more modest ($r = .32$). To examine mediation effects longitudinally, we next examined in sets of multiple regression analyses the effects of perceptions of initial contact on each of the cognitive, group representations at the end of year, controlling for the representation at the beginning of the year. Of these, initial favorability of contact significantly predicted the subsequent one-group representation ($beta = .39$), two-group representation ($beta = -.49$), but not the subsequent same-team representation ($beta = .14$), nor the separate individuals representation ($beta = -.10$). Finally, we tested the effect of initial perceptions of contact and the initial representational mediators on attitudes toward Whites at the end of the year, having controlled for attitudes toward Whites at the beginning of the year. In this analysis, consistent with the hypothesized mediation, initial contact no longer significantly predicted attitudes toward Whites ($beta = .04, p = .85$). In addition, the only significant predictor was the one-group representation ($beta = .46, p < .03$). The effects were not significant for the different-groups ($beta = -.30, p = .11$), same-team ($beta = -.35, p = .15$), and separate-individuals ($beta = .04, p = .85$) representations. We note, however, that the same-team representation, despite its initial association with positive intergroup attitudes, tended (like the different-groups representation) to be negatively related to subsequent changes in positive attitudes toward Whites. Overall, these findings suggest that, whereas a same-team representation may *initially* relate to positive outcomes such as favorable intergroup attitudes, it is an inclusive one-group representation that primarily facilitates *subsequent increases* in favorable intergroup attitudes.

SUMMARY AND CONCLUSIONS

In this chapter, we propose that by understanding the processes that underlie the development of intergroup biases, these forces can be redirected to reduce prejudice and discrimination. We have argued that discrimination and bias fundamentally involve the social categorization of others in inclusionary and exclusionary ways. Categorizing people as members of one's own group (the ingroup) and other groups (outgroups) automatically initiates biases that produce and maintain more positive attitudes, stereotypes, and actions toward ingroup than toward outgroup members. Strategies for reducing bias, therefore, can productively be targeted at encouraging the recategorization of others in more inclusionary ways. According to the Common Ingroup Identity Model, if members of different groups are induced to conceive of themselves more as a single, superordinate group rather than as two separate groups, attitudes toward former outgroup members will become more positive through processes involving pro-ingroup bias. In general, data from laboratory studies, field experiments, and surveys including a range of different types of groups offer converging evidence in support of the model. Moreover, our findings suggest that diverse microlevel interventions such as intergroup contact, the jigsaw classroom (Aronson & Patnoe, 1997), and cooperative learning (Johnson & Johnson, 2000) may operate, at least in part, through the common mechanism of creating more inclusive group representations.

Our research also has relevance to macrolevel interventions, such as policies based on colorblind or multicultural perspectives (Jones, 1997). In colorblind approaches (e.g., equal opportunity legislation), race and ethnicity are considered irrelevant attributes in forming impressions and in making decisions, and emphases are placed on individual merit or on a single collective identity (e.g., national identity). In contrast, multicultural approaches (e.g., bilingual education or affirmative action) explicitly recognize race and ethnicity and tailor actions to address the unique historical circumstances and contemporary needs of members of particular groups.

Within our model, recategorization can take the form of identification with a single superordinate identity, in which subgroup identities are ignored (as in a colorblind approach), or a dual identity (such as by a "different groups working together on the same team" representation), in which superordinate and subgroup identities are both salient (as in a multicultural approach). However, the relative effectiveness of these representations for reducing bias may be critically influenced by group values that give priority to a one-group or a dual-identity representation. For instance, because of the importance of racial and ethnic identities among minority group members, these priorities may systematically differ for minority and majority group members. We have found that Whites most prefer assimilation (reflecting a one-group identity), whereas racial and ethnic minorities favor pluralistic integration (involving a dual-identity or same-team representation). Thus interventions that work effectively for the majority group (e.g., emphasis on a single, assimilated, colorblind entity) may be ineffective or counterproductive for minority group members. For racial and ethnic minorities, strategies that deny the value of their culture and traditions may not only be perceived as less desirable but also as threatening to their personal and social identity. Thus, efforts to create a single superordinate identity, although well intentioned, may threaten one's social identity, which in turn can intensify intergroup bias and conflict—at least initially.

Our research, however, further highlights the importance of distinguishing between initial reactions and the processes involved with changing attitudes over time. In particular, we found that whereas a dual identity may be important to adjustment (e.g., positive intergroup attitudes and university commitment) during the early stages of minority students' college careers, the strength of an inclusive, one-group representation is a better and more direct predictor of their longer-term adjustment later in their careers. Because people have different needs, goals, and objectives with increasing experience in group and intergroup contexts, the processes facilitating positive relations may systematically shift over time. As a consequence, as Pettigrew (1998) and Hewstone (1996) have proposed, different types of representations, including decategorization as well as the different forms of recategorized representations can, over time, play complementary roles in the reduction of intergroup biases. Thus, at both practical and theoretical levels, it will be valuable for work to move from questions of which type of process, decategorization, or recategorization into a single or a dual group identity, is the most effective strategy at any given point in time, to understanding the shifting and complementary nature of these processes for different people at different times.

ACKNOWLEDGMENT

Preparation of this chapter was supported by NIMH Grant MH 48721 to the first two authors.

REFERENCES

Abrams, D. (1985). Focus of attention in minimal intergroup discrimination. *British Journal of Social Psychology, 24*, 65–74.

Allport, G. W. (1954). *The nature of prejudice.* Cambridge, MA: Addison-Wesley.

Aronson, E., & Patnoe, S. (1997). *The jigsaw classroom.* New York: Longman.

Bachman, B. A. (1993). *An intergroup model of organizational mergers.* Unpublished doctoral dissertation, Newark, DE: University of Delaware.

Banker, B. S., & Gaertner, S. L. (1998). Achieving stepfamily harmony: An intergroup-relations approach. *Journal of Family Psychology, 12*, 310–325.

Berry, J. W. (1984). Cultural relations in plural societies. In N. Miller & M. B. Brewer (Eds.), *Groups in contact: The psychology of desegregation* (pp. 11–27). Orlando, FL: Academic Press.

Brewer, M. B. (1988). A dual process model of impression formation. In T. S. Srull & R. S. Wyer (Eds.), *Advances in social cognition: Vol. I: A dual process model of impression formation* (pp. 1–36). Hillsdale, NJ: Erlbaum.

Brewer, M. B. (2000) Reducing prejudice through cross-categorization: Effects of multiple social identities. In S. Oskamp (Ed.), *Reducing prejudice and discrimination* (pp. 165–183). Hillsdale, NJ: Erlbaum.

Brewer, M. B., & Miller, N. (1984). Beyond the contact hypothesis: Theoretical perspectives on desegregation. In N. Miller & M. B. Brewer (Eds.), *Groups in contact: The psychology of desegregation* (pp. 281–302). Orlando FL: Academic Press.

Brewer, M. B., von Hippel, W., & Gooden, M. P. (1999). Diversity and organizational entity: The problem of entrée after entry. In D. A. Prentice & D. T. Miller (Eds.), *Cultural divides: Understanding and overcoming group conflict* (pp. 337–363). New York: Russell Sage Foundation.

Brown, R. J., & Wade, G. (1987). Superordinate goals and intergroup behavior: The effect of role ambiguity and status on intergroup attitudes and task performance. *European Journal of Social Psychology, 17,* 131–142.

Dovidio, J. F., Gaertner, S. L, & Johnson, J. D. (1999, October). *New directions in prejudice and prejudice reduction: The role of cognitive representations and affect.* Symposium paper presented at the annual meeting of the Society for Experimental Social Psychology, St. Louis, MO.

Dovidio, J. F, Gaertner, S. L., & Kafati, G. (2000). Group identity and intergroup relations: The Common In-Group Identity Model. In S. R. Thye, E. J. Lawler, M. W. Macy, & H. A. Walker (Eds.), *Advances in group processes* (Vol. 17, pp. 1–34). Stamford, CT: JAI Press.

Dovidio, J. F., Gaertner, S. L., Niemann, Y. F., & Snider, K. (2001). Racial, ethnic, and cultural differences in responding to distinctiveness and discrimination on campus: Stigma and common group identity. *Journal of Social Issues, 57,* 167–188.

Dovidio, J. F., Gaertner, S. L., & Validzic, A. (1998). Intergroup bias: Status, differentiation, and a common in-group identity. *Journal of Personality and Social Psychology, 75,* 109–120.

Dovidio, J. F., Gaertner, S. L., Validzic, A., Matoka, K., Johnson, B., & Frazier, S. (1997). Extending the benefits of re-categorization: Evaluations, self-disclosure and helping. *Journal of Experimental Social Psychology, 33,* 401–420.

Fiske, S. T., Lin, M., & Neuberg, S. L. (1999). The continuum model: Ten years later. In S. Chaiken & Y. Trope (Eds.), *Dual process theories in social psychology* (pp. 231–254). New York: Guilford.

Gaertner, S. L., & Dovidio, J. F. (2000). *Reducing intergroup bias: The Common Ingroup Identity Model.* Philadelphia, PA: The Psychology Press.

Gaertner, S. L., Dovidio, J. F., Anastasio, P. A., Bachman, B. A., & Rust, M. C. (1993). The common ingroup identity model: Recategorization and the reduction of intergroup bias. In W. Stroebe & M. Hewstone (Eds.), *European review of social psychology* (Vol. 4, pp. 1–26). New York: John Wiley & Sons.

Gaertner, S. L., Mann, J. A., Murrell, A. J., & Dovidio, J. F. (1989). Reduction of intergroup bias: The benefits of recategorization. *Journal of Personality and Social Psychology, 57,* 239–249.

Gaertner, S. L., Mann, J. A., Dovidio, J. F., Murrell, A. J., & Pomare, M. (1990). How does cooperation reduce intergroup bias? *Journal of Personality and Social Psychology, 59,* 692–704.

Gaertner, S. L., Dovidio, J. F., Nier, J., Ward, C., & Banker, B. (1999). Across cultural divides: The value of a superordinate identity. In D. A. Prentice & D. T. Miller

(Eds.), *Cultural divides: Understanding and overcoming group conflict* (pp. 173–212). New York: Russell Sage Foundation.

Gaertner, S. L., Rust, M. C., Dovidio, J. F., Bachman, B. A., & Anastasio, P. A. (1996). The Contact Hypothesis: The role of a common ingroup identity on reducing intergroup bias among majority and minority group members. In J. L. Nye & A. M. Brower (Eds.), *What's social about social cognition?* (pp. 230–260). Newbury Park, CA: Sage.

Hewstone, M. (1996). Contact and categorization: Social psychological interventions to change intergroup relations. In C. N. Macrae, C. Stangor & M. Hewstone (Eds.), *Foundations of stereotypes and stereotyping* (pp. 323–368) New York: Guilford.

Hewstone, M., & Brown, R. J. (1986). Contact is not enough: An intergroup perspective on the "Contact Hypothesis." In M. Hewstone & R. Brown (Eds.), *Contact and conflict in intergroup encounters* (pp. 1–44). Oxford, UK: Basil Blackwell.

Hogg, M. A., & Hains, S. C. (1996). Intergroup relations and group solidarity: Effects of group identification and social beliefs on depersonalized attraction. *Journal of Personality and Social Psychology, 70,* 295–309.

Houlette, M., & Gaertner, S. L. (1999).The Common Ingroup Identity Model: Effects of inclusiveness of common ingroup identity and subgroup salience on ingroup bias. Unpublished data. Department of Psychology, University of Delaware, Newark, DE.

Howard, J. M., & Rothbart, M. (1980). Social categorization for in-group and out-group behavior. *Journal of Personality and Social Psychology, 38,* 301–310.

Huo, Y. J., Smith, H. H., Tyler, T. R., & Lind, A. E. (1996). Superordinate identification, subgroup identification, and justice concerns: Is separatism the problem. Is assimilation the answer? *Psychological Science, 7,* 40–45.

Insko, C. A., Schopler, J., Gaertner, L., Wildschut, T., Kozar, R., Pinter, B., Finkel, E. J., Brazil, D. M., Cecil, C. L., & Montoya, M. R. (2001). Interindividual-intergroup discontinuity reduction through the anticipation of future interaction. *Journal of Personality and Social Psychology, 80,* 95–111.

Islam, M. R., & Hewstone, M. (1993). Dimensions of contact as predictors of intergroup anxiety, perceived outgroup variability and outgroup attitude: An integrative model. *Personality and Social Psychology Bulletin, 19,* 700–710.

Johnson, D. W., & Johnson, R. T. (2000). The three Cs of reducing prejudice and discrimination. In S. Oskamp (Ed.), *Reducing prejudice and discrimination* (pp. 239–268). Hillsdale, NJ: Erlbaum.

Johnson, K. M., Gaertner, S. L., & Dovidio, J. F. (2001). The effect of equality of job assignment on ingroup identity and bias for low and high status groups. Unpublished data, Department of Psychology, University of Delaware, Newark, DE.

Jones, J. M. (1997). *Prejudice and racism* (2nd ed.). New York: McGraw-Hill.

LaFromboise, T., Coleman, H. L. K., & Gerton, J. (1993). Psychological impact of biculturalism: Evidence and theory. *Psychological Bulletin, 114,* 395–412.

Milliken, F. J., & Martins, L. L. (1996). Searching for common threads: Understanding the multiple effects of diversity in organizational groups. *Academy of Management Review, 21,* 402–433.

Mullen, B., Dovidio, J. F., Johnson, C., & Copper, C. (1992). Ingroup–outgroup differences in social projection. *Journal of Experimental Social Psychology, 28,* 422–440.

Mullen, B., & Hu, L. T. (1989). Perceptions of ingroup and outgroup variability: A meta-analytic integration. *Basic and Applied Social Psychology, 10*, 233–252.

Mummendey, A., & Wenzel, M. (1999). Social discrimination and tolerance in intergroup relations: Reactions to intergroup difference. *Personality and Social Psychology Review, 3*, 158–174.

Niemann, Y. F., & Dovidio, J. F. (1998). Relationship of solo status, academic rank, and perceived distinctiveness to job satisfaction of racial/ethnic minorities. *Journal of Applied Psychology, 83*, 55–71.

Otten, S., & Moskowitz, G. B. (2000). Evidence for implicit evaluative in-group bias: Affect-based spontaneous trait inference in a minimal group paradigm. *Journal of Experimental Social Psychology, 36*, 77–89.

Park, B., & Rothbart, M. (1982). Perception of out-group homogeneity and levels of social categorization: Memory for the subordinate attributes of in-group and out-group members. *Journal of Personality and Social Psychology, 42*, 1051–1068.

Pettigrew, T. F. (1998). Intergroup contact theory. *Annual Review of Psychology, 49*, 65–85.

Pettigrew, T. F., & Tropp, L. R. (2000). Does intergroup contact reduce prejudice? Recent meta-analytic findings. In S. Oskamp (Ed.), *Reducing prejudice and discrimination* (pp. 93–114). Hillsdale, NJ: Erlbaum.

Smith, H. J., & Tyler, T. R. (1996). Justice and power: When will justice concerns encourage the advantaged to support policies which redistribute economic resources and the disadvantaged to willingly obey the law? *European Journal of Social Psychology, 26*, 171–200.

Tajfel, H. (1969). Cognitive aspects of prejudice. *Journal of Social Issues, 25*(4) 79–97.

Tajfel, H., & Turner, J. C. (1979). An integrative theory of intergroup conflict. In W. G. Austin & S. Worchel (Eds.), *The social psychology of intergroup relations* (pp. 33–48). Monterey, CA: Brooks/Cole.

Turner, J. C. (1985). Social categorization and the self-concept: A social cognitive theory of group behavior. In E. J. Lawler (Ed.), *Advances in group processes* (Vol. 2, pp. 77–122). Greenwich, CT: JAI Press.

Turner, J. C., Hogg, M. A., Oakes, P. J., Reicher, S. D., & Wetherell, M. S. (1987). *Rediscovering the social group: A self-categorization theory*. Oxford, UK: Basil Blackwell.

van Oudenhoven, J. P., Prins, K. S., & Buunk, B. (1998). Attitudes of minority and majority members towards adaptation of immigrants. *European Journal of Social Psychology, 28*, 995–1013.

Wilder, D. A. (1981). Perceiving persons as a group: Categorization and intergroup relations. In D. L. Hamilton (Ed.), *Cognitive processes in stereotyping and intergroup behavior* (pp. 213–257). Hillsdale, NJ: Erlbaum.

Worchel, S., Rothgerber, H., Day, E. A., Hart, D., & Butemeyer, J. (1998). Social identity and individual productivity with groups. *British Journal of Social Psychology, 37*, 389–413.

12

Intergroup Contact in a Divided Society: Challenging Segregation in Northern Ireland

MILES HEWSTONE, ED CAIRNS, ALBERTO VOCI,
STEFANIA PAOLINI, FRANCES McLERNON,
RICHARD J. CRISP, ULRIKE NIENS, and JEAN CRAIG

This chapter focuses on a particular kind of social exclusion, religious segregation, that is fundamental to understanding sectarian conflict in Northern Ireland. This chapter deals with the nature, extent, processes, and consequences of cross-community or intergroup contact that occurs in this setting, despite segregation. The chapter considers six central issues: (a) the historical and social background to the political violence in Northern Ireland; (b) the extent of segregation, its causes and consequences; (c) the theoretical background to the "contact hypothesis" and its relevance for, and application in, Northern Ireland; (d) major findings from our research programme; (e) policy implications of our research; and (f) general conclusions that can be drawn and areas where future work is still needed.

> We all had bigotry in us. It was a part of the tradition of all of us, on all sides. The point is to get the conditions in place to be able to let go of that.
> (David Trimble, former First Minister of Northern Ireland;
> *New York Times Magazine*, December 12, 1999)

After hundreds of years of conflict, and decades of paramilitary terrorism, a series of ceasefires in the 1990s by paramilitary groups on both sides in Northern Ireland led, eventually, to the Belfast Agreement, signed on Friday, April 10, 1998. This agreement received the support of 71% of the Northern Irish electorate in a referendum which in turn led to the setting up of a local assembly and a power-sharing government, embracing all the major political parties. (The assembly has collapsed at the time of writing this chapter; however, there are strong hopes that it will soon be restored.) One of many aims of the Good Friday Agreement was to create an "inclusive society" (Robinson, 2003); a society that would turn its back on sectarian violence between Catholics and Protestants, and in which people would "firmly dedicate ourselves to the achievement of reconciliation, tolerance, and mutual trust, and to the protection and vindication of the human rights of all." (Article 2 of The Agreement). In this chapter we will focus specifically on exclusion in the form of the religious segregation that lies at the heart of Northern Irish society and, we argue, its problems.

Our primary interest in this chapter, indeed in the extensive research programme on which it is based, is to study the nature of *intergroup contact* in Northern Ireland. This chapter unfolds in six parts. First, we review briefly the historical and social background to the political violence in Northern Ireland; second, we review evidence for the extent of segregation in Northern Ireland, and touch on its causes and consequences; third, we consider the "contact hypothesis" and its relevance for, and application in, Northern Ireland; fourth, we review major findings from our own continuing research programme; fifth, we consider policy implications of our work; finally, we draw some conclusions and outline areas where future work is still needed.

A BRIEF BACKGROUND TO SECTARIAN CONFLICT IN NORTHERN IRELAND

Although the conflict in Ireland can be traced back to roots that were in place before the 16th century Protestant Reformation in Western Europe (see McLernon, Cairns, Lewis, & Hewstone, 2003), we refer primarily to the modern history here. The Treaty of 1921 partitioned the island of Ireland into two sections: the predominantly Protestant six counties of the north, which remained an integral part of the United Kingdom, and the mainly Catholic twenty-six counties of the south which separated from the United Kingdom, and became known as "The Free State" (later the Republic of Ireland). Since that time, significant violence has occurred, with Irish Republican Army (IRA) campaigns in the 1920s, 1940s, and 1950s. The latest and most sustained period of violence began in the late 1960s when claims by the Catholic population of Protestant discrimination in jobs, education, housing, and local elections led to a civil rights campaign which quickly escalated into violence, resulting in the deployment of British troops to try to restore order, and the imposition of direct rule from London (see Bowyer Bell, 1993; Holland, 1999; Whyte, 1990).

There has been considerable debate about the causes of, and possible solutions to, what is called, colloquially and euphemistically, "The Troubles" (McGarry & O'Leary, 1995).[1] The conflict in Northern Ireland is most easily understood as a struggle between those who wish to see Northern Ireland remain part of the United Kingdom (Protestants/Unionists/Loyalists) and those who wish to see the reunification of the island of Ireland (Catholics/Nationalists/Republicans) underpinned by historical, religious, political, economic, and psychological elements. A large majority of "Protestants" are "Unionists"; and most "Catholics" are "nationalists". The advantages of the religious classification are that it is (almost) all-inclusive, seems to correspond more precisely "to the realities as perceived by individuals" (Whyte, 1990, p. 20), and that it was used by Rose (1971) in his pioneering survey on social attitudes in Northern Ireland, which has become the baseline for many subsequent comparisons. The vast majority of people in Northern Ireland also identify with being Catholic or Protestant, "Green" or "Orange", categories that are starkly divided, with few social categories cross-cutting the religious dimension (Cairns & Mercer, 1984). As the writer Dervla Murphy put it:

The average Northern Ireland citizen is born either Orange or Green. His whole personality is conditioned by myth and he is bred to live the sort of life that will reinforce and protect the myth for transmission to future generations. Moreover, these myths are used daily to justify distrust and resentment of "the other side." (Murphy, 1978, p. 188)

A mystery for "outsiders" to the conflict is how religious group membership is ascertained, given that the two groups do not differ physically. There is, in fact, a large literature on what is colloquially referred to as "telling" or distinguishing Catholics from Protestants (Burton, 1978; Cairns, 1980, 1987; Darby, 1986; Jenkins, 1982; see Whyte, 1990). Seamus Heaney referred to this as:

> Manoeuvring to find out name and school,
> Subtle discrimination by addresses
> With hardly an exception to the rule
> That Norman, Ken and Sidney signalled Prod
> And Seamus (call me Sean) was sure-fire Pape.
> ("*Whatever You Say, Say Nothing*," 1975)

A complex interplay of cues is used, including name, face, dress, demeanour, residence, education, language, and iconography. Cairns (1980) found that students reported principally using area, school name, appearance, and speech.

Today it is estimated that 44% of the Northern Irish population is Roman Catholic and 53% is Protestant (Northern Ireland Census, December 2002) with those not wishing to state a denomination comprising the rest of the population. Identification with one of the two religious communities has been shown to play an important role in the maintenance of the conflict in Northern Ireland (Cairns, 1982; Trew & Benson, 1996). Indeed church membership and attendance in Northern Ireland have historically been very high: membership and weekly attendance rates of 87% and 62%, respectively, in Northern Ireland, are much higher than in Great Britain, 66% and 14% (see Cairns, 1991; Cairns & Darby, 1998).

Yet, we must emphasize that, although religion is widely perceived as a cause of The Troubles, our use of the terms "Catholic" and "Protestant" to identify conflicting groups is as much ethnic and political as religious. Northern Ireland seems to illustrate Dean Swift's view, "We have just enough religion to make us hate, and not enough to make us love one another." (quoted by McCreary, 1975). Thus Cairns and Darby (1998) considered religion to be the least important of many plausible causes of the conflict, a claim supported by some of our own research that measured religiosity (using the "Attitudes toward Christianity" scale; see Francis, 1993) and correlated it with various measures. Among Protestant students at the University of Ulster ($N = 175$), we detected only small, but significant, correlations ($p < .05$), positive in the case of outgroup "forgiveness" ($r = .18$), but negative in the case of "contact with outgroup friends" ($r = -.18$). Church affiliation is important, however, because it "spills over" into other social activities (Whyte, 1990).

Over the last 30 years, the violence in Northern Ireland has been sporadic and confined to particular areas at any one time. Yet with over 3,600 deaths since 1969, the impact of The Troubles has been marked on the closely-knit urban and rural areas of Northern Ireland, an area with a population of only 1.7 million (see, e.g., Fay, Morrissey, & Smyth, 1999; McKittrick, Kelters, Feeney, & Thornton, 1999). Of the deaths, the vast majority (2,000 plus) have been civilians (including members of terrorist groups from both communities) while the remainder have been members of the security forces, that is, the police (formerly named the Royal Ulster Constabulary, RUC, now named the Police Service of Northern Ireland, PSNI), the British Army, and its associated locally recruited militia (the Ulster Defence Regiment, UDR). Detailed analyses of patterns of deaths (see Fay et al., 1999; McKittrick et al., 1999; Morrissey & Smyth, 2002; Smyth, 1998; White, 2001) show that the dead have been predominantly male and young, from urban locations (especially Belfast and Derry/Londonderry; Mitchell, 1979; Poole & Douherty), and Catholic rather than Protestant (death rates per 1,000 of 2.5 vs. 1.9).

Deaths are, of course, only one index of the conflict. *The Cost of the Troubles Study* (see Fay et al., 1999; Smyth, 1998) estimates some forty to fifty thousand people have been injured by The Troubles—suffering blindness, loss of hearing, disfigurement, and amputations—injuries which impact on "secondary victims" in families permanently damaged by the severe injury of a close relative or loved one. These deaths and injuries rendered some of the population "psychiatric casualties" of the conflict, while a much greater proportion suffered from milder forms of stress (see Cairns, Wilson, Gallagher, & Trew, 1995; Harbison & Harbison, 1980). The impact of The Troubles has also been felt particularly by young children and adolescents (see Cairns, 1987, 1996), who are particularly likely to have had their political outlook influenced by growing up amidst widespread violence and conflict (Hayes & McAllister, 2002).

Hayes and McAllister (2002) argue that exposure to violence contributes in two ways to the intractability of the conflict. First, so many people have been victims of violence, "directly" (e.g., being a victim of a violent event, and perhaps suffering injury) or "indirectly" (e.g., having a family member or close relative killed or injured). This has meant that The Troubles have left "most families touched in some way" (Cairns & Darby, 1998, p. 754). Second, exposure to violence is associated with public support for paramilitary groups. Indirect experience of violence is associated with increased sympathy for paramilitary groups. In contrast, personal experience of violence is associated with decreased sympathy for loyalist paramilitary groups among Protestants, but with increased sympathy for republican groups among Catholics.

RELIGIOUS SEGREGATION IN NORTHERN IRELAND

A crucial characteristic of Northern Irish society that helps explain many aspects of the conflict is the extreme degree to which the two religious communities are segregated (Cairns & Hewstone, 2002; Knox & Hughes, 1994; Murtagh, 2002; Whyte, 1990). Even though segregation is not the cause of intergroup conflict, it plays a major role in establishing and maintaining conflict between communities; it also exacerbates conflict by increasing mutual ignorance (Whyte, 1990). Hamilton (1995) suggested a "cyclical and interdependent" (p. 1) effect between segregation and violence. Three types of segregation have received most attention: residential (Poole, 1982; Poole & Doherty, 1996), personal and marital (e.g., Gallagher & Dunn, 1991), and educational (Darby et al., 1977; Gallagher, 1989; McClenaghan, Cairns, Dunn, & Morgan, 1996), although other types of segregation (e.g., at work, sport, and leisure) have been identified as well (Niens, Cairns, & Hewstone, 2003). We review, briefly, the literature on these main types of segregation, and attitudes toward mixing in each domain, as a prelude to examining the literature on actual intergroup or cross-community contact.

Residential Segregation

Catholics and Protestants have been residentially segregated, in both urban and rural areas, since long before the outbreak of The Troubles (Smyth, 1995). Whyte (1990) estimated that about 35–40% of the population live in completely segregated neighbourhoods, which means that more than 50% of the population live in mixed neighbourhoods (see also Boyle & Hadden, 1994). Residential segregation can also reinforce other forms of segregation, as Boal

(1969) showed: Catholics in Clonard (98% Catholic) and Protestants in Shankhill (99% Protestant), two contiguous areas of Belfast, tended to read different newspapers, support different football teams, patronize different shops, send their children to different schools, and have totally different kinship networks.

Segregated housing often covaries with relatively deprived working-class areas in Northern Ireland (as in Catholic Falls Road and Protestant Shankill areas in Belfast), whereas middle- and upper-class residential areas are often more mixed. There has been a slight increase in segregated living from Rose's (1971) study to more recent research (Cairns & Hewstone, 2002; Gallagher & Dunn, 1991; Niens et al., 2003), especially following periods of political violence. As Boal, Murray, and Poole (1976) pointed out, the functions of segregation include provision of a base for self-defence, avoidance of embarrassing contacts with unfriendly outsiders, preservation of a way of life, and a base from which to attack enemies. There is, in short, safety in segregation, and residential segregation increased as a direct result of large population movements in response to intimidation, as families moved from religiously mixed areas into safe havens dominated by their coreligionists.

Personal and Marital Segregation

Approximately 55% of Protestants and 75% of Catholics report that "all or most" of their friends are of the same religion as themselves (a consistent result in surveys from 1968 to 1998; see Cairns & Hewstone, 2002). Craig and Cairns (1999) found that 50% of their interviewees did not have any outgroup friends before the age of 15, and if they had outgroup friends from an early age, it was usually a neighbour. Other studies have, however, reported that cross-community friendships do exist (e.g., McClenahan et al., 1996), but Trew (1986) argued that they function only as long as certain issues are not mentioned (in Seamus Heaney's famous line, "whatever you say, say nothing").

So-called "mixed marriages" account for, at minimum, 4–5% of marriages (Cairns & Hewstone, 2003; Gallagher & Dunn, 1991; Moxon-Browne, 1983; Rose, 1971) and at maximum, between 9–10% (Niens et al., 2003; Northern Ireland Life and Times Survey, 1998). Whatever the level of intermarriage in Northern Ireland, however, Whyte (1990) argued that it "bridged no gaps" because one partner, usually the husband, cut off all ties with his own kin. People in mixed relationships are frequently targeted; some like Mrs Elizabeth O'Neill, the 3,293rd person to die in The Troubles, paying for it with their life (see *The Guardian*, June 7, 1999).

Educational Segregation

Both primary and secondary education are highly segregated (Gallagher, 1995, estimates that 97% of school-age children in Northern Ireland attend denominational schools; and Cairns and Hewstone, 2001, report that over 90% of children attend either a Catholic or a Protestant school at *both* elementary and secondary level). As Whyte (1990) points out, the mere fact of separate education allows prejudice and stereotypes to flourish (see Murray, 1985, on segregated schooling).

Support for this school system comes from both communities, even though in surveys the majority of the population claims they would support integrated education (see Hughes & Carmichael, 1998) or would, at least, like to see some mixing between pupils from different schools (see Boal, Keane, & Livingstone, 1997). There are some Integrated Schools (Smith, 1995), which involve pupils from both sides of the community. Numbers have risen from 1989, when about 1,400 pupils went to 10 integrated schools. Today there are 50 such schools, comprising 18 Integrated Second Level Colleges, and 32 Integrated Primary Schools; in addition there are 13 Integrated Nursery Schools, most of which are linked to Primary schools. However, the integrated sector still educates a tiny proportion of the total pupil population (ca. 16,000 pupils, representing 5% of the total school-going population; see Niens et al., 2003; Smith, 2001), and its growth is opposed by some church and community leaders on both sides of the divide (Cornell, 1994).

Segregation sustains conflict by creating a social climate that fosters mutual ignorance and suspicion (Gallagher, 1995), but it should be emphasized that total segregation does not exist (Cairns & Hewstone, 2002; Poole, 1982). Whyte (1990) characterized the Catholic and Protestant communities as being "deeply but not totally divided" (p. 16). Therefore, unlike some other apparently intractable conflicts, the potential for contact between members of the two communities exists in many areas (Cairns & Darby, 1998; Trew, 1986). For example, in the cities, even where working-class housing areas in particular are more highly segregated, people often travel out of their own area to work, thus increasing the potential for contact in the work place. Thus we argue that because of the extensive segregation in Northern Irish society, intergroup contact matters; and despite the segregation, it occurs. But it is also now well established that any attempts at positive community relations get thwarted by political violence (Cairns & Hewstone, 2002), and Robinson (2003) reports an increased preference for working and living apart over the last seven years.

THE CONTACT HYPOTHESIS AND ITS ROLE IN NORTHERN IRELAND

The "Contact Hypothesis"

In its simplest form, the contact hypothesis (Allport, 1954; Hewstone & Brown, 1986; Pettigrew, 1986) proposes that bringing together individuals from opposing groups "under optimal conditions" (Pettigrew & Tropp, 2000) can reduce prejudice and improve intergroup relations. Allport (1954) suggested these positive effects were most likely if four conditions were met. First, there should be equal status among the groups who meet, or at least among the individuals drawn from different groups, who meet. Second, the situation in which intergroup contact occurs should require co-operation between groups or offer common goals to both groups. Third, co-operation between the groups involved should be encouraged. Lastly, the contact situation should be legitimized through institutional support. Allport influenced research for the next 50 years and also had a profound impact on social policy in many countries (see Miller & Brewer, 1984; Pettigrew & Tropp, 2000; Schofield & Eurich-Fulcer, 2001).

More recently, attention has turned to understanding both *mediational* ("how" does contact work?) and *moderational* ("when" does contact work?) questions regarding intergroup contact (see Baron & Kenny, 1986; Hewstone, 1996; Voci & Hewstone, 2003). Pettigrew's (1998) optimistic review of recent research on co-operative intergroup contact, supplemented by meta-analytic support (Pettigrew & Tropp, 2000), pointed to our increased knowledge of the *mediating* processes by which contact can reduce bias. Pettigrew (1998) has highlighted the importance of positive affective processes in explaining what makes contact effective, and there is evidence that contact is associated with reduced "intergroup anxiety" (Islam & Hewstone, 1993). Stephan and Stephan (1985) proposed that intergroup anxiety stems mainly from the anticipation of negative consequences for oneself during contact. Some of the major antecedents of intergroup anxiety may be minimal previous contact with the outgroup, the existence of large status differentials, and a high ratio of outgroup to ingroup members. Both Islam and Hewstone (1993) and Greenland and Brown (1999), showed that anxiety mediates the relation between quality of contact, as predictor, and negative outgroup affect and intergroup bias, as outcomes (see also Stephan, Diaz-Loving, & Duran, 2000; Stephan & Stephan, 2000). From their meta-analysis, Pettigrew and Tropp (under review) concluded that approximately 21% of the effect of contact reducing prejudice was mediated by contact also reducing anxiety.

Because of the correlational nature of much of this research, we should be cautious in interpreting these data in causal terms, that is, concluding that contact causes reduced anxiety, which causes changes in outcomes (see Paolini, Hewstone, Voci, Harwood & Cairns, in press). To draw such conclusions, longitudinal or experimental research is required, both of which are still relatively scarce in the contact literature in general (Pettigrew & Tropp, 2000) and in the intergroup anxiety literature in particular (exceptions are Greenland & Brown, 1999, Study 2; Levin, van Laar, & Sidanius, 2003). While we believe it makes good sense to argue that contact leads to reduced intergroup anxiety, intergroup anxiety is also likely to lead to contact avoidance (Plant & Devine, 2003; Wilder, 1993). Indeed Levin et al.'s (2003) longitudinal study found evidence for reciprocal effects; cross-group ethnic friendship during college predicted reduced intergroup anxiety at the end of college, but intergroup anxiety at the end of the first year of college also predicted reduced cross-group friendship at the end of college.

Complementing Pettigrew's (1998) review, which focused on mediators of contact, recent research has accumulated evidence that group salience is a key *moderator* of the effect of intergroup contact on criterion variables (Hewstone, 1996; Hewstone, Rubins & Willis, 2002). Evidence has accrued that the salience of group boundaries should be maintained during contact, to promote generalization across members of the target outgroup (Brown, Vivian, & Hewstone, 1999; Hewstone, 1996). The importance of group membership salience during contact has been demonstrated both experimentally (e.g., Brown et al., 1999, Study 1; Desforges et al., 1991; Scarberry, Ratcliff, Lord, Lanieck, & Desforges, 1997; Van Oudenhoven, Groenewoud, & Hewstone, 1996; Wilder, 1984), and in correlational studies (Brown, Maras, Masser, Vivian, & Hewstone, 2001; Brown et al., 1999, Study 2). These studies provide evidence that the generalization process, from the judgments concerning single individuals to the whole outgroup, is favoured by the presence of a link between these individuals and the group. This link must, however, be made carefully, because making categories salient during contact risks reinforcing perceptions of group differences and increasing intergroup anxiety, especially where there are large status differences between groups (Ramirez & Soriano, 1993) and may be a reason why ingroup members resist outgroup contact (Fiske & Ruscher, 1993).

The most effective way to capitalize on salience for generalization but avoid intergroup anxiety seems to be to promote contact that is both "interpersonal" and "intergroup" simultaneously. For example, a typical outgroup member might disclose positive personal information (Ensari & Miller, 2001). Voci and Hewstone (2003) showed the importance of studying simultaneously one key mediator, intergroup anxiety, and one key moderator, the salience of group memberships during contact (between Italians and immigrants in Italy). As in previous studies, they found strong evidence that intergroup anxiety functions as a mediator; that is, contact has its effect on prejudice, in part, via reduced intergroup anxiety. But they also reported strong, consistent evidence that the effect of contact on prejudice was moderated by the salience of group memberships during contact. It was the combination of positive contact with individuals from the outgroup and the salience, during it, of group memberships, which led to reduced anxiety and to more positive orientations towards the outgroup in general.

Previous Work on Intergroup Contact in Northern Ireland

Catholics and Protestants do come into contact with each other, but previous research agrees that much of the contact is superficially courteous, and not of a degree to alter suspicions or change stereotypes (Cairns & Hewstone, 2002;

Niens et al., 2003; Harris, 1972; Trew, 1986). Much of this work has focused on interventions, but there is little evidence that programs have been properly evaluated. Cross-community contact seems to have been largely superficial, and methodology has been suboptimal (with a focus on interpersonal outcomes, little attention to the problem of generalizing beyond the contact setting and specific outgroup partner, and a failure to assess the quality and quantity of intergroup contact; see Harris, 1972; McClenahan et al., 1996; Trew, 1986). Yet, previous studies of cross-community contact in Northern Ireland do suggest that there is a positive association between contact and attitudes towards the religious outgroup.

AN OVERVIEW OF OUR RESEARCH ON INTERGROUP CONTACT IN NORTHERN IRELAND

In this section we review briefly the results of some of our research on intergroup contact in Northern Ireland. We organize this section under five themes: secondary analysis of archival data sets; the importance of outgroup friends; mediators and moderators of contact; direct and indirect forms of contact; and the value of contact in educational settings.

Secondary Analysis of Archival Data Sets

Our first research in this area was to conduct secondary analyses of archival survey data. Secondary analysis of data has advantages and disadvantages as a methodological tool (see Kiecolt & Nathan, 1985). A main advantage is that we make use of existing data sets, prior to collecting original data. However a main disadvantage is that our research objectives were not those of the original compilers of the survey, and indeed measures of some of the key constructs (notably the measures of contact) are suboptimal. The original random sample surveys were carried out in February–March 1989 and 1991 under the aegis of the "Northern Ireland Social Attitude Survey." The surveys used the same limited set of measures designed to explore attitudes towards intergroup contact (specifically, attitudes towards "mixing" with the other group). This is an important criterion variable, because it allows us to assess whether prior contact makes people more, or less, willing to engage in future contact with the outgroup (see, e.g., Boal et al., 1997). Measures included distal variables, education and social class, and more proximal variables, prior experience of integrated schooling and self-reported contact (see Hewstone, Cairns, Voci, Hamberger, & Niens, in press; and Hamberger, 1998, for full details on the surveys).

Education has a consistently positive effect on outgroup attitudes (see Hagendoorn & Nekuee, 1999; Pettigrew et al., 1998; Wagner & Zick, 1995).

Class is typically positively associated with both contact and tolerance (e.g., Hamberger & Hewstone, 1997; Pettigrew, 1997); moreover, middle- and upper-class residential areas are often more mixed, which again may affect people's attitudes toward, as well as their opportunity for, intergroup contact (Poole, 1982). Measures of both prior experience of integrated education and contact were quite simple (respondents were asked whether they had "ever attended a mixed or integrated school" and "about how many of your friends/relatives/neighbors [3 items] are the same religion as you"). The criterion variable was attitudes toward mixing with the outgroup (an index based on preference for mixing vs. separation in primary schools, secondary schools, where people live, where people work, people's leisure or sports activities, and people's marriages).

We computed path analyses to test whether attitudes toward mixing with the outgroup could be predicted from other measures (we developed a model for the 1989 data, which we then tested on the 1991 data set). There was support for the contact hypothesis. In all four subsamples (i.e., Catholics and Protestants, for 1989 and 1991), and partialing out the effects of the other variables (class, education, and prior experience of integrated education), only contact made a consistent, significant contribution to explaining variance in the criterion variable. Moreover, in all cases the direction of the path coefficient was positive, indicating that respondents who reported having more contact with outgroup members held a more positive attitude towards mixing with the outgroup.

The remaining four themes all arose from our own primary research. All of this research has been cross-sectional survey research, using Catholic and Protestant respondents (drawn, in all cases but one, from either the integrated University of Ulster, or sampled at random from the adult population of Northern Ireland). Our research (six surveys to date) has measured six types of variables: (a) Opportunities for contact (i.e., mixed or segregated neighbourhood and school; see Wagner, Hewstone, & Machleit, 1989). (b) Social identification with religious ingroup (measured using an adapted version of Brown et al.'s, 1986, scale). (c) Self-reported quality and quantity of contact with the religious outgroup, across different domains. (d) Potential mediators of contact (intergroup anxiety, Stephan & Stephan, 1985; outgroup perspective taking, items from Davis', 1994, Interpersonal Reactivity Index, as used by Batson et al., 1997, adapted for this particular intergroup context). (e) Potential moderators of contact ("intergroup" contact, measuring salience and awareness of group memberships, and perceived typicality of outgroup members encountered; Brown et al., 1999). (f) Criterion measures (outgroup attitudes, e.g., Wright, Aron, McLaughlin-Volpe, & Ropp's, 1997, general evaluation measure; bias, measured as the difference between ingroup and outgroup "warmth" ratings on a "feeling thermometer," see Haddock, Zanna, & Esses, 1993); outgroup trust, adapted from Brehm & Rahn's, 1997, measure; and forgiveness, a short form of the Enright Forgiveness Inventory, Subkoviak et al., 1995, adapted to measure intergroup forgiveness; or a specially developed measure of intergroup forgiveness in this context; see Hewstone et al., 2004).

The Importance of Outgroup Friends

Several recent papers have provided evidence from survey data for the special impact of cross-group friendships on reduced prejudice (see Hamberger & Hewstone, 1997; Pettigrew, 1997, 1998; Phinney, Ferguson, & Tate, 1997). Within friendship contacts, Pettigrew (1997) highlights the importance of close interaction with an outgroup member, self-disclosure, and extensive and repeated contact in a variety of social contexts. Cross-group friendships also provide access to friendship networks, which can be a major source of increasing cross-friendship friendships (see Hewstone, 1996).

In one of our surveys (Voci, Hewstone, & Cairns, in prep.) using a representative sample of the Northern Ireland population, we compared the effect of "contact in general" and "contact with friends" on three criterion measures (prejudice, outgroup trust, and forgiveness). In each case, general contact had weaker effects on criterion variables than did friendship contact. This finding supports Pettigrew's emphasis on cross-group friendships, but should not be misinterpreted. In many circumstances, it may be difficult to promote cross-group friends; this does not then render intergroup contact "ineffective." We emphasize that in much of our work, and the published literature (see Pettigrew & Tropp, under review), general contact is also a significant predictor of reduced prejudice, but friendship is typically even more so.

Mediators and Moderators of Contact

Our research has highlighted both mediators and moderators of the effect of contact on multiple criterion measures (Hewstone, Cairns, Voci, & McLernon, in prep.). Consistent with Pettigrew's (1998) argument that contact promotes tolerance via positive affective processes, we have found evidence for two affective mediators (intergroup anxiety and perspective taking).

First, there is strong and consistent evidence that contact is associated with reduced intergroup anxiety (Stephan & Stephan, 1985). We have found this effect in surveys using Catholics and Protestant as students at the University of Ulster, and in representative samples. Second, having a close outgroup friend promoted perspective taking, which made a unique contribution towards predicting outgroup attitudes, trust, and forgiveness. One of our first studies (which surveyed 16–18-year olds in 1997–8), sought to predict outgroup evaluation from evaluation of outgroup friends, anxiety, general outgroup contact, and importance attached to one's own and other's religion (Craig, Cairns,

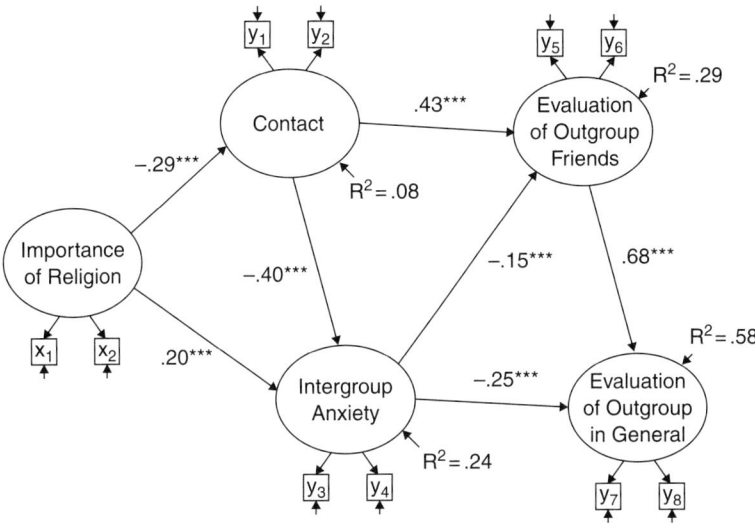

FIGURE 12.1 Estimated model of the mediating role of anxiety in the relation between contact and outgroup evaluations

Note: Numbers are standardized parameters; *** $p < .001$. Goodness-of-fit indexes: $\chi^2 (25) = 40.94$, $p = .023$; RMSEA = 0.038; SRMR = 0.024; CFI = 0.99; $N = 440$.

Hewstone, & Voci, 2002). Figure 12.1 shows the path model from an analysis using structural equation modeling (LISREL 8.3: Jöreskog & Sörbom, 1999). The effect of contact on evaluation is mediated by reduced intergroup anxiety, anxiety itself being negatively associated with evaluation. We have also found anxiety to be a mediator not only of outgroup attitudes or bias, but also perceived outgroup variability (the extent to which the members of the outgroup are seen as "all alike" or, rather, differentiated), forgiveness, and outgroup trust. Second, we have found evidence for perspective taking as a mediator. Contact with friends is associated with greater willingness to take the other community's perspective on the conflict, and this perspective taking makes a unique contribution to the prediction of prejudice, trust, and forgiveness (being only weakly correlated with anxiety).

Three of our studies (Hewstone et al., in prep.) have also provided the opportunity to test the idea that the salience of group boundaries should be maintained during contact, to promote generalization across members of the target outgroup (Brown et al., 1999; Hewstone, 1996). We showed, first, that there was a stronger association between general outgroup contact and outgroup attitudes when group memberships were salient. Thus "intergroup" contact (awareness of group memberships during contact) moderated the effect of contact on outgroup attitudes. Next, we found results consistent with the idea that contact that is "high" on both interpersonal and intergroup dimensions should be most effective. Contact with outgroup friends was associated with more positive outgroup evaluation and greater forgiveness only for respondents who reported high (vs. low) awareness of group memberships during contact. Finally, in one survey we assessed contact by asking respondents to rate a single, close friendship with an outgroup member. Although this was a very close relationship (characterized, for example, by high inclusion of the other in the self; see Aron, Aron, & Norman, 2001), it only affected generalized outgroup evaluation for those respondents who rated the salience of group memberships during contact as high.

Direct and Indirect Forms of Contact

Pettigrew (1997) suggests that a reduction ingroup prejudice might be achieved by promoting direct friendship between members of rival groups, the "direct cross-group friendship hypothesis," for which we have already reported evidence from our own research program. Wright and colleagues suggest, additionally, that such a beneficial effect might also stem from "vicarious" experiences of friendship, that is, from the knowledge of ingroup members' being friends with outgroup members, the "indirect cross-group friendship hypothesis" (Wright et al., 1997). They provided both correlational and experimental evidence in support of this hypothesis. The effect of vicarious or indirect cross-group friendship is expected to occur because three elements serve as catalysts: the positivity and friendliness of the behaviors that the outgroup member exhibits (or is assumed to exhibit) towards the ingroup member; the referent informational influence of the ingroup member, demonstrating positive intergroup attitudes and tolerant ingroup norms (Haslam, McGarty, & Turner, 1996; see also Liebkind & McAlister, 1999); and the cognitive inclusion of the target ingroup and outgroup members in the self (Smith & Henry, 1996).

Indirect friendship might have even greater potential for achieving harmonious intergroup relations than direct friendship. Wright and colleagues (1997) believe indirect friendship to be more effective and easier to implement than direct friendship. It is more effective for two reasons. First, because group membership is expected to be relatively more salient—thus facilitating generalization—to an observer not acquainted with the individuating features of the outgroup member, than to the individual directly involved in the cross-group friendship. Second, because intergroup anxiety should be weaker in vicarious experiences than in first-hand experiences, it reduces the risk of an undesired intergroup backlash. Indirect friendship is also easier to implement on a larger scale, because it can improve intergroup relations without every group member having to have intergroup friends themselves. In two correlational investigations, respondents—belonging to either majority or minority groups—who knew at least one ingroup member with an outgroup friend consistently reported weaker outgroup prejudice than did respondents without indirect friends; furthermore, the more ingroupers known to have friends in the outgroup, the weaker the prejudice (Wright et al., 1997).

We tested the indirect cross-group friendship hypothesis, with two extensions (Paolini, Hewstone, Cairns, & Voci, 2004). First, we assessed whether cross-group friendship could both reduce prejudice toward the outgroup and increase perceived outgroup variability; second, we tested whether reduced intergroup anxiety was the underlying psychological mechanism. We conducted two surveys (the first on a sample of Catholic and Protestant students at the University of Ulster, and the second on a representative sample of the Northern Ireland population) and used structural equation modeling to test the cross-group friendship effects and the mediational role of intergroup anxiety (see Figure 12.2, which shows the path model for the student sample).

In both samples, direct and indirect cross-group friendship significantly predicted weaker prejudice towards the rival community and greater perceived outgroup variability. These effects remained significant, although not large in magnitude, even when the other type of cross-group friendship was controlled for. Furthermore, an anxiety-reduction mechanism provided a common explanatory basis for both the direct and the indirect cross-group friendship effects (see also Wright et al., 1997). We expected cross-group friendship to provide examples of successful and pleasant interactions with outgroup members

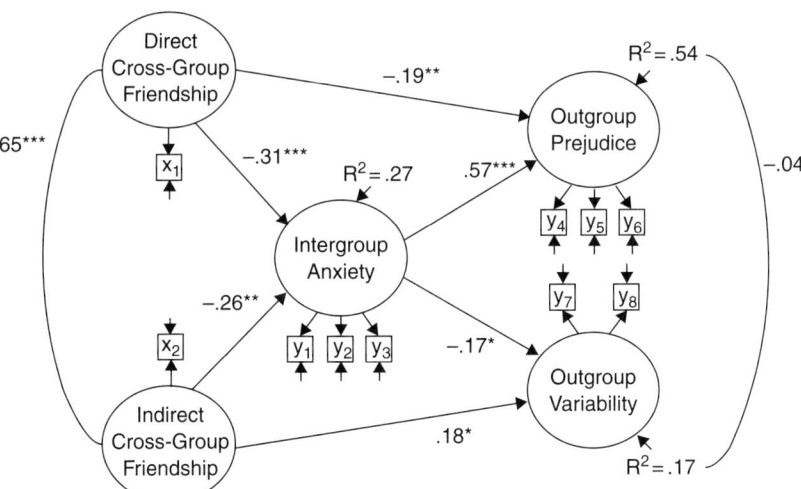

FIGURE 12.2 Estimated model of the mediating role of anxiety in the relation between direct and indirect friendships and outgroup evaluations and perceptions (Paolini et al., 2004, Study 1)

Note: Numbers are standardized parameters; * $p < .05$; ** $p < .01$; *** $p < .001$. Goodness-of-fit indexes: $\chi^2 (27) = 49.48$, $p = .005$; RMSEA = 0.049; SRMR = 0.023; CFI = 0.99; $N = 341$.

and, hence, to reduce prejudice and increase outgroup variability by means of reducing intergroup anxiety. Consistent with these predictions, analyses on both samples confirmed that having a close friend in the outgroup, or having an ingroup friend who has an outgroup friend, both reduced prejudice and increased outgroup variability by decreasing the anxiety associated with expectations that future interactions with outgroup members would be uncomfortable. Direct cross-group friendship had a direct negative effect on prejudice towards the group, while indirect cross-group friendship had a direct and positive effect on perceived outgroup variability (and on outgroup prejudice, but only in the representative sample). Moreover, both types of friendship were negatively related to intergroup anxiety, which in turn was strongly and positively associated with prejudice and negatively linked to perceived outgroup variability. Thus, full mediation of anxiety held for the relationship between direct friendship and group variability and indirect friendship and outgroup prejudice (in the student sample only). Partial mediation of anxiety held for the relationship between direct friendship and prejudice, indirect friendship and variability, and indirect friendship and prejudice (in the representative sample only).

Our theoretical model provided good fit to the data in both samples. Supplementary analyses showed that the total effect of direct cross-group friendship on prejudice was somewhat greater than the total effect of indirect cross-group friendship. The opposite pattern was true for group variability, but only in the representative sample (i.e., no difference between total effects of direct and indirect friendship seemed to hold in the student sample). The *indirect* effect that each predictor variable exerted on each of the criterion variables (i.e., *via* another variable, in this case intergroup anxiety) was also significant, although sometimes quite modest in size, confirming that each type of cross-group friendship played a significant role in predicting each type of group judgment and that intergroup anxiety was a significant mediator of both the direct and indirect friendship-to-group relationships.

The Value of Contact in Educational Settings

Given the extensive educational segregation in Northern Ireland a key practical issue is whether the promotion of contact in educational settings is of value. We end with summaries of two analyses that provide affirmative answers to this question. Both analyses are based on recent surveys of Catholic and Protestant students at the University of Ulster.

In the first study, we asked students to provide ratings of their opportunity for contact (i.e., extent to which it was a desegregated setting) and to report their actual number of outgroup friends at primary school, secondary school, and university (Cairns, Hewstone, & Voci, in prep., Study 1). The university ratings, of course, are current, whereas the school ratings are retrospective, and should therefore be treated with some caution. Then, using a structural equation model, we tried to predict current levels of ingroup bias. In the model we allowed for three main types of effect: (a) from opportunity for contact (at each education level) to contact at that level; (b) from contact at an earlier educational level to contact at the next educational level; and (c) from types of contact to bias. At each educational level, opportunity for contact predicted self-reported contact. There were also highly significant effects of primary school friends on secondary school friends, and secondary school friends on university friends. Finally, all three measures of contact were negatively associated with bias. As one might expect, current university friends had the highest impact on bias, but both university friends and secondary school friends were significant predictors of bias; friends at primary school, however, was not. We think this latter result is important for two reasons. First, it rules out an explanation in terms of participants giving socially desirable responses to all measures of contact; second, it makes sense that the current levels of bias of students in their twenties should be associated with their current outgroup friends, and the outgroup friends they had at their secondary school (11–18 years), but not with the outgroup friends they had at their primary school (5–11 years). We are not, however, denying the importance of primary school outgroup friends, because these friendships were highly predictive of secondary school outgroup friends, which themselves were significantly associated with lower levels of bias.

In the second study, we asked students to provide ratings of opportunity for contact, general outgroup contact, and contact with outgroup friends, both at home and at university (Cairns et al., in prep., Study 2). We then tested a structural equation model, with the aim of predicting current levels of ingroup bias and perceived outgroup variability. In this model we allowed for two main types of effect: (a) from opportunity to contact (separately for home and university settings); (b) from types of contact to criterion measures. Consistent with Study 1, opportunity for contact predicted self-reported contact. But general contact and contact with friends had differential impact on bias and variability, depending on the setting. General contact at home was significantly associated with bias, negatively, and outgroup variability, positively; friends at home had no impact on either criterion. At university, however, it was friends that had a highly significant negative effect on bias, and a positive effect on variability; general contact at university had no impact on either criterion. At present, we do not know what specific aspects of general and friendship contacts in the two settings are responsible for their specific effect, this is a focus of our current work. However, these data again rule out an explanation in terms of participants' giving socially desirable responses to all measures of contact, and they again highlight the value of educational contact in challenging prejudice.

Cross-community experiences of university students in Northern Ireland are likely to differ from those of the general population in several important respects, which make the university setting a particularly propitious one for an attack on sectarian attitudes. First, as noted earlier, higher levels of education are generally associated with less virulent outgroup attitudes. Second, although research suggests that intergroup contact in Northern Irish universities tends to be relatively cursory, consisting of casual rather than intimate contact, attending university undoubtedly increases most people's overall amount of contact and their opportunity for intimate contact with members of the rival community (Cairns, Gallagher, & Dunn, 1993). Swapping segregated secondary education for integrated (or, at least, desegregated) higher education ought to be a significant step. As journalist and television presenter Nick Ross, who studied in Northern Ireland, put it, "Many of my Protestant friends had not met a Catholic, and Catholics had scarcely met a Protestant, until they got to University." (*The Guardian*, March 25, 1999).

A Methodological Caveat

Notwithstanding the strong and consistent effects of contact we have reported, it is important to acknowledge that all our data are cross-sectional, and clearly need to be backed up by both more controlled and extensive experimental evidence and longitudinal results. Our research has also concentrated exclusively on explicit measures of bias, and has so far focused on anxiety as the key intergroup emotion. Our current work therefore includes longitudinal diary-based studies of contact, virtual intergroup contact via the internet, and incorporation of both implicit and explicit measures of bias, as well as more detailed analysis of intergroup emotions.

Particular care should be taken in making causal inferences from cross-sectional data when using structural equation models, as we have done (MacCullum & Austin, 2000). As these authors point out, "There is no true model . . . all models are wrong to some degree . . . the best one can hope for is to identify a parsimonious, substantively meaningful model that fits observed data adequately well" (p. 218). We have, however, increased our confidence in the reliability and generalizability of our results by following their guidelines carefully. In particular, we have conducted multiple studies with different (large) samples and measures (almost all of which have used methodologically superior "latent" rather than merely "measured" variables); we have used multiple measures of fit of our model to the covariance matrix; and we have provided careful presentation and interpretation of all our data.

Despite these limitations on our data base, there are reasons to be confident in our assertion that positive contact promotes tolerance in Northern Ireland. First, there is growing evidence from experimental and longitudinal work that the path from contact to prejudice is stronger than the reciprocal path (see Pettigrew, 1997, 1998). We have been able to test these two paths in two of our own studies; both reported results consistent with Pettigrew's.

Second, Wright and colleagues (1997) believe that the unique contribution of indirect friendship over and above direct friendship reflects the beneficial causal effect of increased friendship on reduced prejudice, rather than prejudice leading to friendship avoidance. More specifically, they argue that being less prejudiced toward an outgroup would more easily translate into one's having more friends in the outgroup than in having more ingroup friends who have outgroup friends. Hence, finding a significant effect of indirect friendship on group judgments, partialing out the effect of direct friendship, increases our confidence that friendship contact causes (reduced) prejudice and not vice-versa.

POLICY IMPLICATIONS

Northern Ireland provides an especially useful context within which to explore the contact hypothesis, because the main policy initiatives that have been pursued in order to transform the conflict have concentrated on making contact between Catholics and Protestants possible (see Cairns & Hewstone, 2002; Cornell, 1994; Hughes, 1999; Hughes & Carmichael, 1998; Niens et al., 2003; Trew, 1986).

In an attempt to transform the conflict, or at least respond to the level of segregation, various policy initiatives have been pursued, aimed at improving community relations; these schemes include government-funded holiday schemes (see Dunn, 1986; Trew, 1986) and interschool contacts with a curricular focus (Smith & Dunn, 1990). This policy has been implemented since 1987 via the Central Community Relations Unit (CCRU) whose importance can be gauged by the fact that in 1995/96 it received £5.3 m out of total Government spending for Northern Ireland on community relations of £8.4 m (Knox & Hughes, 1996). As Knox and Hughes note, CCRU has funded a wide range of community relations projects which have ranged from "Cultural Traditions" workshops which focus on cultural awareness, reconciliation groups, and groups set up in response to some particular act of political violence (Hughes, 1997). Because of the extent of segregation in education in Northern Ireland, the government introduced Education for Mutual Understanding (EMU) in 1987, which promotes cross-community school activities (see Northern Ireland Council for Educational Development, 1986). In addition, the educational authorities have funded peace education (see Dunn & Morgan, 1999) through encouraging contact between Catholic and Protestant schools, and more recently through the development of planned integrated schools. While specific goals for all these projects have been framed in generic terms they have concentrated principally on making *contact* between Protestants and Catholics possible.

Notwithstanding that much government policy is predicated on the contact hypothesis, most community-relations work has been exploratory. There is a need for evaluations that use sophisticated methodology (including multi-item measures and causal models) to test theoretical models, with attention paid to predictors, mediators, moderators, and outcomes. This is what we have sought to do in our work.

We believe that the policy implications of our work are especially evident for educational settings (as noted above). We also believe that the relatively new idea of indirect or extended contact may be an important one in a society as strictly segregated as Northern Ireland. The development of planned integrated schools, with approximately equal numbers of Catholic and Protestant pupils, teachers, and school governors (Smith, 1995), represents one of the most radical attempts to combat segregation. Critics have suggested, however, that because of the modest number of schools (and pupils) involved, integrated education is unlikely to have a major impact on Northern Irish intergroup relations. Against this pessimistic claim, our findings concerning indirect friendship raise the possibility that integrated education may be impacting intergroup relations on a wider scale than its absolute numbers would suggest, via a "ripple" effect (one person's outgroup friends also affecting the attitudes of others who are not direct friends of the outgroup member), and should therefore be encouraged. We are currently undertaking new work which explores the impact of indirect and direct forms of contact in residential areas undergoing transition from segregated to mixed communities.

CONCLUSION

This chapter has summarized the background to the intergroup conflict in Northern Ireland and reviewed the most detailed programme of research on Catholic–Protestant contact and prejudice ever undertaken. We hope to have shown that socio-psychological theory can make a contribution to a better understanding of, and hopefully ultimately resolution of, this intergroup conflict. We have focused on the potential for cross-community contact (especially, but not exclusively, contact with outgroup friends) to influence a range of measures that are crucial to intergroup relations, including outgroup attitudes and perceptions, forgiveness, and trust. We have also identified key mediators (anxiety and perspective taking) and moderators (measures of category salience during contact) that increase our understanding of why and when contact works. Given the extent of intergroup conflict in Northern Ireland over the last thirty years, we think this research provides impressive evidence for the contact hypothesis. Using standard measures of respondents' personal experience of sectarianism, we have also shown that the association between contact and criterion measures holds up even for people who have high direct and indirect experience of The Troubles (see Boal et al., 1997; Hayes & McAllister, 2002), or who live in neighborhoods that have suffered especially from sectarian violence (see Hewstone et al., in press).

Finally, we have sought to spell out the policy implications of our research. We believe that the consistent pattern of our results provides strong support for continuing contact schemes in the educational and community relations sectors in Northern Ireland. Specifically, those schemes need to promote contact under conditions that lower anxiety and increase perspective taking, while ensuring that participants are still aware of their own and others' group memberships. Done in this way, intergroup contact can mount an effective challenge to social exclusion.

ACKNOWLEDGMENTS

We gratefully acknowledge the financial support of the Central Community Relations Unit, the Templeton Foundation, and the Russell Sage Foundation, without which much of this research would not have been possible, and thank M. Poole for his help in assigning scores for the neigbourhood violence index referred to. Miles Hewstone wishes to express his gratitude to the Center for Advanced Study in the Behavioral Sciences, Stanford; his time as a Fellow there provided him with the opportunity to plan much of this work, and read up on the literature. He gratefully acknowledges financial support provided by the William and Flora Hewlett Foundation. Finally, we thank the editors for their constructive comments on an earlier version. Sadly, Jean Craig died before this chapter was completed; her study was the first to measure intergroup anxiety in Northern Ireland.

NOTE

1. Although this term is now widely understood to refer to contemporary problems in Northern Ireland, it has, in fact, been used to refer to unrest in Ireland since at least 1880, and James Joyce's Ulysses (published in 1922) refers to "Times of the troubles" (Oxford English Dictionary).

REFERENCES

Allport, G.W. (1954). *The nature of prejudice.* Reading, MA: Addison-Wesley.

Aron, A., Aron, E. N., & Norman, C. (2001). Self-expansion model of motivation and cognition in close relationships and beyond. In G.J.O. Fletcher & M.S. Clark (Eds.), *Blackwell handbook of social psychology: Interpersonal processes* (pp. 478–501). Malden, MA. & Oxford, UK: Blackwell.

Baron, R., & Kenny, D. A. (1986). The moderator–mediator variable distinction in social psychological research: Conceptual, strategic, and statistical considerations. *Journal of Personality and Social Psychology, 51,* 1173–1182.

Batson, C. D., Sager, K., Garst, E., Kang, M., Rubchinsky, K., & Dawson, K. (1997). Is empathy-induced helping due to self-other merging? *Journal of Personality and Social Psychology, 73,* 495–509.

Boal, F. W. (1969). Territoriality on the Shankhill-Falls divide, Belfast. *Irish Geography*, 6, 30–50.

Boal, F. W., Murray, C. R., & Poole, M. A. (1976). Belfast: The urban encapsulation of a national conflict. In S. C. Clarke & J. L. Obler (Eds.), *Urban ethnic conflict: A comparative perspective* (Comparative Urban Studies Monograph no. 3, 77–13). Chapel Hill: Institute for Research in Social Science, University of North Carolina.

Boal, F. W., Keane, M. C., & Livingstone, D. N. (1997). *Them and us? Attitudinal variation among churchgoers in Belfast*. Belfast: Institute of Irish Studies, Queen's University of Belfast.

Bowyer Bell, J. (1993). *The Irish Troubles: A generation of violence, 1967–1992*. New York: St. Martin's Press.

Boyle, K., & Hadden, T. (1994). *Northern Ireland: The choice*. Harmondsworth, Middlesex: Penguin.

Brehm, J., & Rahn, W. (1997). Individual-level evidence for the causes and consequences of social capital. *American Journal of Political Science*, 41, 999–1023.

Brown, R. J., Condor, S., Mathews, A., Wade, G., & Williams, J. A. (1986). Explaining intergroup differentiation in an industrial organization. *Journal of Occupational Psychology*, 59, 273–86.

Brown, R., Maras, P., Masser, B., Vivian, J., & Hewstone, M. (2001). Life on the ocean wave: Testing some intergroup hypotheses in a naturalistic setting. *Group Processes and Intergroup Relations*, 4, 81–98

Brown, R., Vivian, J., & Hewstone, M. (1999). Changing attitudes through intergroup contact: The effects of group membership salience. *European Journal of Social Psychology*, 29, 741–764.

Burton, F, (1978). *The politics of legitimacy: Struggles in a Belfast community*. London: Routledge & Kegan Paul.

Cairns, E. (1980). The development of ethnic discrimination in young children. In J. Harbison & J. Harbison (Eds.), *Children and young people in Northern Ireland: A society under stress* (pp. 115–127). Somerset: Open Books.

Cairns, E. (1982). Intergroup conflict in Northern Ireland. In H. Tajfel (Ed.), *Social identity and intergroup relations* (pp. 277–297). London: Cambridge University Press.

Cairns, E. (1987). *Caught in the crossfire: Children and the Northern Ireland conflict*. Belfast: Appletree Press.

Cairns, E. (1991). Is Northern Ireland a conservative society? In P. Stringer & G. Robinson (Eds.), *Social attitudes in Northern Ireland* (pp. 142–151). Belfast: Blackstaff Press.

Cairns, E. (1996). *Children and political violence*. Oxford, UK & Cambridge, MA: Blackwell.

Cairns, E., & Darby, J. (1998). The conflict in Northern Ireland: Causes, consequences, and controls. *American Psychologist*, 53, 754–760.

Cairns, E., Gallagher, A. M., & Dunn, S. (1993). *Intergroup contact in a Northern Irish university setting: A report to the Central Community Relations Unit*. Coleraine: Centre for the Study of Conflict, University of Ulster.

Cairns, E., & Hewstone, M. (2002). The impact of peacemaking in Northern Ireland on intergroup behaviour. In G. Salomon, & B. Nevo (Eds.), *The nature and study of peace education* (pp. 217–28). Hillsdale, NJ: Erlbaum.

Cairns, E., Hewstone, M., & Voci, A. *The value of intergroup contact in educational settings in Northern Ireland.* Manuscript in preparation. University of Ulster.

Cairns, E. & Mercer, G. W. (1984). Social identity in Northern Ireland. *Human Relations, 37*, 1095–1102.

Cairns, E., Wilson, R., Gallgher, T., & Trew, K. (1995). Psychology's contribution to understanding conflict in Northern Ireland. *Peace and Conflict: Journal of Peace Psychology, 1*, 131–148.

Cornell, J. C. (1994). Prejudice reduction through intergroup contact in Northern Ireland: A social-psychological critique. *Conflict Quarterly, 14*, 30–47.

Craig, J. & Cairns, E. (1999). *Intergroup interaction: An investigation into its role in reducing intergroup anxiety in further education students in Northern Ireland. A Report to the Central Community Relations Unit.* Coleraine: University of Ulster.

Craig, J., Cairns, A., Hewstone, M., & Voci, A. (2002). *Young people's attitudes to and contact with members of the religious outgroup.* Unpublished manuscript, University of Ulster.

Darby, J. (1986). *Intimidation and the control of the conflict in Northern Ireland.* Dublin: Gill and Macmillan.

Darby, J., Murray, D., Batts, D., Dunn, S., Farren, S., & Harris, J. (1977). *Education and community in Northern Ireland: Schools apart?* Coleraine: The New University of Ulster.

Davis, M. H. (1994). *Empathy: A social psychological approach.* Madison, WI: Brown & Benchmark.

Desforges, D. M., Lord, C. G., Ramsey, S. L., Mason, J. A., Van Leeuwen, M. D., West, S. C., & Lepper, M. R. (1991). Effects of cooperative contact on changing negative attitudes toward stigmatized social groups. *Journal of Personality and Social Psychology, 60*, 531–544.

Dunn, S. (1986). The role of education in the Northern Ireland conflict. *Oxford Review of Education, 12*, 233–42.

Dunn, S., & Morgan, V. (1999) A fraught path—education as a basis for developing community relations in Northern Ireland. *Oxford Review of Education, 25*, 141–153.

Ensari, N., & Miller, N. (2002). outgroup must not be so bad after all: The effects of disclosure, typicality and salience on intergroup bias. *Journal of Personality and Social Psychology, 83*, 313–329.

Fay, M. T., Morrissey, M., & Smyth, M. (1999). *Northern Ireland's troubles: The human costs.* London: Pluto Press.

Fiske, S. T., & Ruscher, J. (1993). Negative interdependence and prejudice: Whence the affect? In D. Mackie & D. Hamilton (Eds.), *Affect, cognition, and stereotyping* (pp. 239–268). San Diego, CA: Academic Press.

Francis, L. J. (1993). Reliability and validity of a short scale of attitude towards Christianity among adults. *Psychological Reports, 72*, 615–618.

Gallagher, A. M. (1989). Social identity and the Northern Ireland conflict. *Human Relations, 42*, 917–935.

Gallagher, A. M. (1995). The approach of government: Community relations and equity. In S. Dunn (Ed.), *Facets of the conflict in Northern Ireland* (pp. 27–43). New York: St. Martin's Press.

Gallagher, A. M. & Dunn, S. (1991). Community relations in Northern Ireland: Attitudes to contact and integration. In P. Stringer & G. Robinson (Eds.), *Social attitudes in Northern Ireland: The first report* (pp. 7–22). Belfast: Blackstaff Press.

Greenland, K. & Brown, R. (1999). Categorization and intergroup anxiety in contact between British and Japanese nationals. *European Journal of Social Psychology, 29*, 503–521.

Haddock, G., Zanna, M. P., & Esses, V. M. (1993). Assessing the structure of prejudicial attitudes: The case of attitudes toward homosexuals. *Journal of Personality and Social Psychology, 65*, 1105–1118.

Hagendoorn, L., & Nekuee, S. (Eds.). (1999). *Education and racism: A cross-national inventory of positive effects of education on ethnic tolerance*. Aldershot, UK: Ashgate.

Hamberger, J. (1998). *Changing intergroup perceptions: A multi-methodological approach*. Unpublished doctoral dissertation, Cardiff University, UK.

Hamberger, J., & Hewstone, M. (1997). Inter-ethnic contact as a predictor of blatant and subtle prejudice: Tests of a model in four West European nations. *British Journal of Social Psychology, 36*, 173–190.

Hamilton, A. (1995, June 15). The effects of violence in Communities. *Sixth public Discussion: The effects of violence*. Central Library, June 15, 1995. University of Ulster.

Harbison, J., & Harbison, J. (Eds.). (1980). *Children and young people in Northern Ireland: A society under stress*. Somerset: Open Books.

Haslam, S. A., McGarty, C., & Turner, J. C. (1996). Salient group membership and persuasion: The role of social identity in the validation of beliefs. In J. L. Nye & A. M. Brown (Eds.), *What is social about social cognition? Research on socially shared cognition in small groups* (pp. 29–56). Thousand Oaks, CA: Sage.

Hayes, B.C., & McAllister, I. (2002). Sowing dragon's teeth: Public support for political violence and paramilitarism in Northern Ireland. *Political Studies, 49*, 901–22.

Harris, R. (1972). *Prejudice and tolerance in Ulster: A study of neighbours and strangers in a border community*. Manchester: Manchester University Press.

Hewstone, M. (1996). Contact and categorization: Social psychological interventions to change intergroup relations. In C. N. Macrae, C. Stangor, & M. Hewstone (Eds.), *Stereotypes and Stereotyping* (pp. 323–368). New York: The Guilford Press.

Hewstone, M., & Brown, R. (1986). Contact is not enough: An intergroup perspective on the contact hypothesis. In M. Hewstone, & R. Brown (Eds.), *Contact and conflict in intergroup encounters* (pp. 3–44). Oxford: Basil Blackwell.

Hewstone, M., Cairns, E., Voci, A., Hamberger, J., & Niens, U. (in press). Intergroup contact, forgiveness, and experience of "The Troubles" in Northern Ireland. *Journal of Social Issues*.

Hewstone, M., Cairns, E., Voci, A., & McLernon, A. (in prep.). *Intergroup contact and intergroup attitudes in Northern Ireland: Mediational and moderational evidence*. University of Oxford.

Hewstone, M., Cairns, E., Voci, A., McLernon, F., Niens, U., & Noor, M. (2004). Intergroup forgiveness and guilt in Northern Ireland: Social psychological dimensions of "The Troubles". In N. R. Branscombe & B. Doosje (Eds.), *Collective guilt: International perspectives* (pp. 193–215). New York: Cambridge University Press.

Hewstone, M., Rubin, M., & Willis, H. (2002). Intergroup bias. *Annual Review of Psychology, 53*, 575–604.
Holland, J. (1999). *Hope against history*. London: Hodder & Stoughton.
Hughes, J. (1997). Rerouting community relations in the wake of Drumcree. (Ulster Papers in Public Policy and Management, No. 69). Coleraine: University of Ulster.
Hughes, J. (1999). Bridging the gap: Community relations policy in Northern Ireland. Ulster (Papers in Public Policy and Management, No. 87). Belfast: University of Ulster.
Hughes, J., & Carmichael, P. (1998). Community relations in Northern Ireland: Attitudes to contact and segregation. In G. Robinson, D. Heenan, A.M. Gray, & K. Thompson (Eds.), *Social attitudes in Northern Ireland: The Seventh Report* (p. 8). Gower England, Aldershot.
Islam, M. R. & Hewstone, M. (1993). Dimensions of contact as predictors of intergroup anxiety, perceived outgroup variability, and outgroup attitude: An integrative model. *Personality and Social Psychology Bulletin, 19*, 700–710.
Jenkins, R. (1982). *Hightown rules: Growing up in a Belfast Estate*. Leicester, UK: National Youth Bureau.
Jöreskog, K. J., & Sörbom, D. (1999). LISREL 8.3: Interactive LISREL [Computer software]. Chicago: Scientific Software International.
Kiecolt, K. J., & Nathan, L. E. (1985). *Secondary analysis of survey data*. Beverly Hills, CA: Sage.
Knox, C., & Hughes, J. (1994). *Cross community contact: Northern Ireland and Israel—A comparative perspective*. (Ulster Papers in Public Policy and Management, Number 32).
Knox, C., & Hughes, J. (1996). Crossing the divide: Community relations in Northern Ireland. *Journal of Peace Research, 33*, 83–98.
Knox, C., & Hughes, J. (1997). *Ten years wasted effort?—An overview of community relations in Northern Ireland*. A Report to the Central Community Relations Unit.
Levin, S., van Laar, C., & Sidanius, J. (2003). The effects of ingroup and outgroup friendship on ethnic attitudes in college: A longitudinal study. *Group Processes and Intergroup Relations, 6*, 76–92.
Liebkind, K., & McAlister, A. L. (1999). Extended contact through peer modelling to promote tolerance in Finland. *European Journal of Social Psychology, 29*, 765–80.
MacCallum, R. C. & Austin, J. T. (2000). Applications of structural equation modeling in psychological research. *Annual Review of Psychology, 51*, 201–226.
McLenahan, C., Cairns, E., Dunn, S., & Morgan, V. (1996). Intergroup friendships: Integrated and desegregated schools in Northern Ireland. *The Journal of Social Psychology, 136*, 549–558.
McCreary, A. (1975). *Corymeela: The search for peace*. Belfast: Christian Journals Limited.
McCullough, M. E., Rachal, K. C., & Worthington, E. L. (1997). Interpersonal forgiving in close relationships. *Journal of Personality and Social Psychology, 73*, 321–336.
McGarry, J., & O'Leary, B. (1995). *Explaining Northern Ireland*. Oxford: Blackwell.

McKittrick, D., Kelters, S., Feeney, B., & Thornton, C. (1999). *Lost lives: The stories of the men, women and children who died as a result of the Northern Ireland Troubles*. Edinburgh: Mainstream.
McLernon, F., Cairns, E., & Hewstone, M. (2002). Views on forgiveness in Northern Ireland. *Peace Review, 14*, 285–290.
McLernon, F., Cairns, E., Lewis, C.A., & Hewstone, M. (2003). Memories of recent conflict and forgiveness in Northern Ireland. In E. Cairns & M. Roe (Eds.), *The role of memory in ethnic conflict* (pp. 125–143). Basingstoke: Palgrave/Macmillan.
Miller, N., & Brewer, M. B. (Eds.). (1984). *Groups in contact: The psychology of desegregation*. Orlando, FL: Academic Press.
Mitchell, J. K. (1979). Social violence in Northern Ireland. *Geographical Review, 69*, 179–201.
Morrissey, M., & Smyth, M. (2002). *Northern Ireland after the Good Friday Agreement: Victims, grievance, blame*. London: Pluto Press.
Moxon-Browne, E. (1983). *Nation, class and creed in Northern Ireland*. Aldershot, England: Gower.
Murphy. D (1978). *A place apart*. Harmondsworth: Penguin.
Murray, D. (1985). *Worlds apart: Segregated schools in Northern Ireland*. Belfast: Appletree.
Murtagh, B. (2002). *The politics of territory: Policy and segregation in Northern Ireland*. Basingstoke: Palgrave.
Niens, U., Cairns, E., & Hewstone, M. (2003). Contact and conflict in Northern Ireland. In O. Hargie & D. Dickson (Eds.), *Researching The Troubles: Social science perspectives on the Northern Ireland conflict* (pp. 123–140). Edinburgh: Mainstream.
Northern Ireland Council for Educational Development (NICED). (1986). *Education for mutual understanding: A guide*. Belfast: Stranmillis College.
Northern Ireland Life and Times Survey (1998). from http://www.qub.ac.uk/ss/csr/nilt
Paolini, S., Hewstone, M., Cairns, E., & Voci, A. (in press). Effects of direct and indirect cross-group friendships on judgments of Catholics and Protestants in Northern Ireland: The mediating role of an anxiety-reduction mechanism. *Personality and Social Psychology Bulletin*.
Paolini, S., Hewstone, M., Voci, A., Harwood, J., & Cairns, E. (2004). Intergroup contact and the promotion of intergroup harmony: The influence of intergroup emotions. In R. J. Brown & D. Capozza (Eds.), *Social identities: Motivational, emotional, cultural influences PSPB30* (pp. 770–786). Hove, UK: Psychology Press.
Pettigrew, T. F. (1986). The intergroup contact hypothesis reconsidered. In M. Hewstone & R. Brown (Eds.), *Contact and conflict in intergroup encounters* (pp. 169–195). Oxford: Basil Blackwell.
Pettigrew, T. F. (1997). Generalized intergroup contact effects on prejudice. *Personality and Social Psychological Bulletin, 23*, 173–185.
Pettigrew, T. F. (1998). Intergroup contact theory. *Annual Review of Psychology, 49*, 65–85.
Pettigrew, T. F., Jackson, J., Ben Brika, J., Lemaine, G., Meertens, R. W., Wagner, U., & Zick, A. (1998). outgroup prejudice in Western Europe. In W. Stroebe & M. Hewstone (Eds.), *European review of social psychology* (Vol. 8, pp. 241–273). Chichester, UK: J. Wiley.

Pettigrew, T. F., & Tropp, L. R. (2000). Does intergroup contact reduce prejudice? Recent meta-analytic findings. In S. Oskamp (Ed.), *Reducing prejudice and discrimination. "The Claremont Symposium on Applied Social Psychology"* (pp. 93–114). Mahwah, NJ: Lawrence Erlbaum.

Pettigrew, T. F., & Tropp, L. R. *A meta-analytic test of intergroup contact theory.* Manuscript submitted for publication.

Phinney, J. S., Ferguson, D. L., & Tate, J. D. (1997). Intergroup attitudes among ethnic minority adolescents: A causal model. *Child Development, 68*, 955–69.

Plant, E. A., & Devine, P. G. (2003). The antecedents and implications of interracial anxiety. *Personality and Social Psychology Bulletin, 26*, 709–801.

Poole, M. (1982). Religious segregation in urban Northern Ireland. In F. W. Boal & J. N. H. Douglas (Eds.), *Integration and division: Geographical perspectives on the Northern Ireland problem* (pp. 281–308). London: Academic Press.

Poole, M., & Doherty, P. (1996). *Ethnic residential segregation in Northern Ireland.* Coleraine: University of Ulster.

Ramirez, A., & Soriano, F. I. (1993). Differential patterns of intra- and interethnic interaction in minority adolescents: A causal model. *Journal of Social Psychology, 133*, 307–16.

Robinson, G. (2003). *Northern Irish communities drifting apart.* University of Ulster Report. from http://www.ulst.ac.uk/news/releases/2003/725.html

Rose, R. (1971). *Governing without consensus.* London: Faber.

Scarberry, N. C., Ratcliff, C. D., Lord, C. G., Lanieck, D. L., & Desforges, D. M. (1997). Effects of individuating information on the generalization part of Allport's contact hypothesis. *Personality and Social Psychology Bulletin, 23*, 1291–1299.

Schofield, J. W., & Eurich-Fulcer, R. (2001). When and how school desegregation improves intergroup relations. In R. Brown & S. L. Gaertner (Eds.), *Blackwell handbook of social psychology: Intergroup processes* (pp. 475–494). Malden, MA & Oxford, UK: Blackwell.

Smith, A. (1995). Education and the conflict in Northern Ireland. In S. Dunn (Ed.), *Facets of the conflict in Northern Ireland* (pp. 168–186). New York: St. Martin's Press.

Smith, A. (2001). Religious segregation and the emergence of integrated schools in Northern Ireland, *Oxford Review of Education, 27*, 559–75.

Smith, A., & Dunn, S. (1990). *Extending school links.* Coleraine: University of Ulster.

Smith, E. R., & Henry, S. (1996). An ingroup becomes part of the self: Response-time evaluation. *Personality and Social Psychological Bulletin, 22*, 635–642.

Smyth, M. (1995). Limitations on the capacity for citizenship in post cease-fire Northern Ireland. In M. Smyth & R. Moore (Eds.), *Three conference papers on aspects of segregation and sectarian division: Researching sectarianism; borders within borders; and the capacity for citizenship* (pp. 50–66). Derry/Londonderry: Templegrove Action Research.

Smyth, M. (1998). Remembering in Northern Ireland: Victims, perpetrators and hierarchies of pain and responsibility. In B. Hamber (Ed.), *Past imperfect: Dealing with the past in Northern Ireland and societies in transition* (pp. 31–49) Derry/Londonderry: INCORE, University of Ulster.

Stephan, W. G. & Stephan, C. W. (1985). Intergroup anxiety. *Journal of Social Issues, 41*, 157–175.

Stephan, W. G., & Stephan, C. W. (2000). An integrated threat theory of prejudice. In S. Oskamp (Ed.), *Reducing prejudice and discrimination* (pp. 23–46). Hillsdale, NJ: Erlbaum.

Stephan, W. G., Diaz-Loving, R., & Duran, A. (2000). Integrated threat theory and intercultural attitudes: Mexico and the United States. *Journal of Cross-Cultural Psychology, 31*, 240–249.

Subkoviak, M. J., Enright, R. D., Wu, C., Gassin, E. A., Freedman, S., Olson, L. M., et al. (1995). Measuring interpersonal forgiveness in late adolescence and middle adulthood. *Journal of Adolescence, 18*, 641–655.

Trew, K. (1986). Catholic–Protestant contact in Northern Ireland. In M. Hewstone & R. Brown (Eds.), *Contact and conflict in intergroup encounters* (pp. 93–106). Oxford: Basil Blackwell.

Trew, K., & Benson, D. (1996). Dimensions of social identity in Northern Ireland. In G. M. Breakwell & E. Lyons (Eds.), *Changing European identities* (pp. 123–143). Oxford: Butterworth-Heinemann.

Van Oudenhoven, J-P., Groenewoud, J. T., & Hewstone, M. (1996). Cooperation, ethnic salience and generalization of interethnic attitudes. *European Journal of Social Psychology, 26*, 649–661.

Voci, A., & Hewstone, M. (2003). Intergroup contact and prejudice towards immigrants in Italy: The mediational role of anxiety and the moderational role of group salience. *Group Processes and Intergroup Relations, 6*, 37–54.

Voci, A., Hewstone, M., & Cairns, A. (in prep.). *Intergroup contact in Northern Ireland as a predictor of outgroup attitudes, trust, and forgiveness*. University of Padua, Italy.

Wagner, U., Hewstone, M., & Machleit, U. (1989). Contact and prejudice between Germans and Turks: A correlational study. *Human Relations, 42*, 561–574.

Wagner, U., & Zick, A. (1995). Formal education and ethnic prejudice. *European Journal of Social Psychology, 25*, 41–56.

White, R. W. (1993). On measuring political violence: Northern Ireland, 1969 to 1980. *American Sociological Review, 58*, 575–585.

White, R.W. (2001). Social and role identities and political violence. In R. D. Ashmore, L. Jussim, & D. Wilder (Eds.), *Social identity. intergroup conflict, and conflict reduction* (pp. 133–158). New York: Oxford University Press.

Whyte, J. (1986). How is the boundary maintained between the two communities in Northern Ireland? *Ethnic and Racial Studies, 9*, 219–234.

Whyte, J. (1990). *Interpreting Northern Ireland*. Oxford: Clarendon Press.

Wilder, D. A. (1984). Intergroup contact: The typical member and the exception to the rule. *Journal of Experimental Social Psychology, 20*, 177–194.

Wright, S. C., Aron, A., McLaughlin-Volpe, T., & Ropp, S. A. (1997). The extended contact effect: Knowledge of cross-group friendships and prejudice. *Journal of Personality and Social Psychology, 73*, 73–90.

13

Cognitive Representations and Exclusion of Immigrants: Why Red-Nosed Reindeer Don't Play Games

DIANA R. RICE and BRIAN MULLEN

Ethnophaulisms, or ethnic slurs, have previously been examined as markers of the cognitive representations used in thinking about ethnic immigrants. The present chapter reports the results of new work that examines the consequences of the cognitive representations of ethnic immigrant groups as signified by the ethnophaulisms describing the groups. Specifically, we examine ethnophaulisms and their relationship to direct exclusion of immigrants through immigration quotas and naturalization laws. We also examine ethnophaulisms and their relationship to indirect exclusion of immigrants through biased visual and verbal portrayals of immigrants in children's books. The implications of these results for theoretical approaches to intergroup relations are considered.

> The other reindeer made fun of Rudolph and called him names. "Rudolph, the red-nosed reindeer," they teased over and over again until tears glistened on Rudolph's large red nose.... All the reindeer loved to play games. They played tree tag and snow slide and tumble bones. But Rudolph was never asked to play. He stood behind a pine tree and watched. He was very lonely.
>
> B.S. Hazen (1958) *Rudolph the Red-Nosed Reindeer* (pp. 2–4)

Ethnophaulisms[1] (Roback, 1944; from the Greek roots meaning "a national group" and "to disparage") are the *blason populaire*, the words used as ethnic slurs to refer to outgroups (Allen, 1983; Eisminger, 1979; Ericson, 1939; Izmirlieva & Ivanov, 1996; Joesten, 1935; Khleif, 1979;

MacMullen, 1963; Nielsen, 1979). Palmore (1962, p. 442) went so far as to state that, "it is probably safe to say that there is no known group which does not use ethnophaulisms." Even in what is sometimes caricatured as a "politically correct" cultural climate, the popular media continue to report the use of ethnophaulisms in interethnic conflicts (e.g., Associated Press, 1999, 2000, 2001, 2003; Fuquay, 2003; Peterson, 2000; Reuters, 2000, 2001). Indeed, even popular fiction uses "fictional" ethnophaulisms as a telegraphic shorthand for intergroup conflict and hostility. For example, in the film "The Matrix" (1999), the character Switch denigrates the protagonist Neo by using as an ethnophaulism the derogatory term *coppertop* referring to Neo's membership in the category of humans who are used as an energy source by the Matrix (see also the use of *skinjobs* in the film *Blade Runner* (1982), the use of *flattops* in Smith's (1974) short story "A day in the suburbs," or the use of *mudblood* in Rowling's (1999) children's book *Harry Potter and the Chamber of Secrets*).

A few studies have focused on responses to ethnophaulisms by their targets (Pankiw & Bienvenue, 1990) or by observers (Citron, Chein, & Harding, 1950; Greenberg, Kirkland, & Pyszczynski, 1988). However, a programmatic line of research over the past several years has examined the *antecedents* of the cognitive representations of ethnic immigrant groups in ethnophaulisms (Mullen 2001; Mullen & Johnson, 1993, 1995; Mullen & Rice, 2003; Mullen, Rozell, & Johnson, 2000, 2001). A more recent direction of this line of research has examined the *consequences* of the cognitive representations of ethnic immigrant groups in ethnophaulisms. This chapter summarizes the results of some of this new work examining the cognitive representations of ethnic immigrant groups and some forms of direct and indirect exclusion of those groups.

COGNITIVE REPRESENTATIONS OF ETHNIC IMMIGRANT GROUPS

Ethnophaulisms reveal how members of the receiving society think about members of ethnic immigrant groups. As Carter (1944) observed, ethnophaulisms are "collective representations which stand as symbols of the groups themselves" (p. 243; see also Mullen, 2001; Pankiw & Bienvenue, 1990). One aspect of the cognitive representation of ethnic immigrant groups is the relatively low complexity of these representations. For example, as suggested by Graumann and Wintermantel's (1989) discussion of ethnic slurs, the use of ethnophaulisms provides a gauge of prototype representation of ethnic groups: "Typing [a member of a social category] by nouns fixates the other person as a *typical* instance of a social category" (p. 192, emphasis added; see also Greenberg et al., 1988; Mullen, 2001). However, the cognitive representations of all ethnic immigrant groups are not of equally low complexity. Mullen and Johnson (1993) initiated the examination of the Scott's H statistic (Scott,

Osgood, & Peterson, 1979) derived for ethnophaulisms as a gauge of complexity in cognitive representation. In order to determine the complexity with which a particular ethnic immigrant group is represented, the ethnophaulisms used to describe that group are placed into categories derived from Allen's (1983) work on ethnophaulisms. He analyzed six mutually exclusive categories into which ethnophaulisms could be placed: physical traits, personal traits, personal names, food habits, group names, or miscellaneous. In the present context, when the set of ethnophaulisms for an immigrant group is categorized into a fewer number of categories, and most of those ethnophaulisms are clustered into one category, this renders a small Scott's H indicating low complexity in cognitive representation.

Another aspect of the cognitive representation of ethnic immigrant groups in ethnophaulisms is the extremely negative valence of some of these representations. As indicated above, the very term *ethnophaulism* literally means to disparage an ethnic group (Roback, 1944). Palmore (1962) and Roback (1944) observed that the vast majority of ethnophaulisms express some unfavorable stereotype (see also Greenberg et al., 1988; Mullen, 2001). However, the cognitive representations of all ethnic immigrant groups are not of equally negative valence. Mullen, Rozell, and Johnson (2000) initiated the examination of the valence of the ethnophaulisms applied to ethnic immigrant groups. They made "annotated" descriptions of the ethnophaulisms by noting a brief description from Allen (1983) regarding the derivation of the word. These annotated ethnophaulisms were then rated on a 1 (very negative) to 7 (very positive) scale, rendering a high degree of interjudge reliability (interjudge correlation $r = .734$; Spearman-Brown effective reliability $R = .847$). In the present context, when a given set of ethnophaulisms is relatively negative in valence, this would render an average valence that was relatively low, indicating extreme negativity in cognitive representation.

It is interesting to note that there was a consistent tendency for ethnic immigrant groups characterized by more negative ethnophaulisms also be characterized by ethnophaulisms that cluster together with less complexity, $r = .420$ (Mullen, 2001; Mullen & Rice, 2003; Mullen, Rozell, & Johnson, 2000, 2001).[2] This is analogous to the tendency for people with low cognitive complexity to respond to outgroups with more extreme negative evaluations (e.g., Ben-Ari, Keden, & Levy-Weiner, 1992; Schaller, Boyd, Yohannes, & O'Brien, 1995).

Several attributes of ethnic immigrant groups have been found to determine the complexity and the negativity of cognitive representations of ethnic immigrant groups in ethnophaulisms (Mullen, 2001; Mullen & Johnson, 1993, 1995; Mullen & Rice, 2003; Mullen et al., 2000, 2001). First, the ethnic immigrant group is, by definition, *smaller* than the receiving society into which they are immigrating. Research in anthropology (e.g., Banks, 1996; Hirschfeld, 1996) and social psychology (e.g., Biernat & Vescio, 1993, 1994; Kanter, 1977;

Mullen, 1983; Nichols, Abrams, & Mullen, 2000; Taylor, Fiske, Etcoff, & Ruderman, 1978) has considered the effects of relative group sizes on cognitive representations of race and ethnicity. According to Mullen's (1991) model of the phenomenology of being in a group, relative group sizes influence the salience, and in turn the subsequent cognitive representation, of the ingroup and the outgroup. With reference to cognitive representations in ethnophaulisms, there is a significant tendency for smaller groups to be cognitively represented with less complexity, and more negativity, in ethnophaulisms (Mullen, 2001; Mullen & Rice, 2003; Mullen et al., 2000, 2001).

Second, the ethnic immigrant group is, by definition, *unfamiliar* to the receiving society into which they are immigrating. The effects of familiarity on intergroup perception are not entirely clear. On the one hand, some researchers (e.g., Linville, 1998; Linville, Fischer, & Salovey, 1989) have argued that greater familiarity with a target group is associated with more complex cognitive representation of that target. On the other hand, several other studies have reported that greater familiarity with a target group led to greater perceived uniformity of that target group (e.g., Huddy & Virtanen, 1995; Park, Ryan, & Judd, 1992; Simon, Kulla, & Zobel, 1995; Taft, 1959) and thus to less complex cognitive representations. With reference to cognitive representations in ethnophaulisms, there is a significant tendency in our research for less familiar groups to be cognitively represented with less complexity, and more negativity, in ethnophaulisms (Mullen, 2001; Mullen et al., 2001).

Finally, the ethnic immigrant group is, by definition, *foreign* to the receiving society into which they are immigrating. Anthropological scholars have considered at great length the effects of foreignness on the cognitive representations of ethnic ingroups and outgroups (e.g., Fried, 1975; Marushiakova, 1992; Weil, 1995). With reference to cognitive representations in ethnophaulisms, there is a significant tendency for more foreign groups to be cognitively represented with less complexity, and more negativity, in ethnophaulisms (Mullen, 2001; Mullen et al., 2000).

ETHNOPHAULISMS AND EXCLUSION

The research on the antecedents of cognitions regarding ethnic immigrant groups gives rise to questions regarding the influence of these cognitions on behaviors toward these ethnic immigrant groups. For example, if we know something about the cognitive representations the receiving society uses for an ethnic immigrant group, this suggests that we may also know something about the way that group is treated by members of the receiving society. This link between how members of the receiving society *think about* ethnic immigrants and how members of the receiving society *behave toward* those ethnic immigrants is at the very core of research on intergroup relations (see an extensive discussion by Mackie & Smith, 1998).

With specific reference to cognitive representations in ethnophaulisms, several scholars who have considered the "topography" of ethnophaulisms have speculated about the role played by ethnophaulisms in subsequent exclusionary behavior aimed at the target groups. For example, in coining the term ethnophaulism, Roback (1944) posed

The question whether the various ethnophaulisms exercise an influence on the behavior of the people or whether they are merely transformers of surplus energy. My answer is that the aspersions implied do actually enter into the conduct of not only the average person, but even the outstanding man or woman who has not become immune to such prejudices. (p. 316)

Similarly, Allport (1954), Grauman (1998), and Khleif (1979) all conjectured how ethnophaulisms serve as markers for the maintenance of boundaries and the exclusion of the targeted groups. This potential link between ethnophaulisms and exclusion is poignantly illustrated in the epigram presented at the start: Referring to a social target by hurtful epithets anticipates the exclusion of that target.

A further question concerns the types of behaviors that might arise from simple, negative cognitions about an ethnic immigrant group. Some behaviors might be direct and explicit in their exclusion. That is, such behaviors might be blatant and intentional in their exclusion of ethnic immigrants. For example, simple and negative cognitions about an ethnic immigrant group might affect the rates at which immigrants are allowed entrance into a receiving society. However, other behaviors arising from the cognitions characterized by ethnophaulisms might be indirect and subtle in the way they exclude members of ethnic immigrant groups. That is, such behaviors might be subtle and unintentional in their exclusion of ethnic immigrants. For example, simple and negative cognitions about an ethnic immigrant group might affect the frequency with which immigrants are portrayed in the popular culture.

Direct Exclusion

One goal of our research was to explore the link between cognitive representation in ethnophaulisms and direct exclusion of ethnic immigrant groups. The analyses reported below examine archival data for an association between complexity and valence in cognitive representations in ethnophaulisms and various aspects of direct behavioral exclusion of ethnic immigrant groups. The direct exclusionary behaviors upon which we focused our attention were immigration quotas and naturalization rates.

This line of research was based upon a sample of 19 ethnic groups (Belgians, Dutch, English, French, Germans, Greeks, Hungarians, Irish, Italians, Norwegians, Poles, Portuguese, Russians, Scots, Spaniards, Swedes, Swiss, Turks, and Welsh). These European groups have been studied extensively in other research examining ethnophaulisms directed toward immigrant groups

(Mullen, 2001; Mullen & Johnson, 1993, 1995; Mullen & Rice, 2003; Mullen et al., 2000, 2001). A total of 15 consecutive 10-year (decade) periods were identified (from 1821–30 to 1961–70), and cognitive representation in ethnophaulism were operationalized for each group for each of these time periods. For this sample of 19 ethnic groups, cognitive representations in ethnophaulisms were operationalized as the complexity and valence of the ethnophaulisms (described above) for each of the 15 ten-year time periods. This sample of 19 European ethnic groups covered the majority of immigration to the United States during the time period under investigation: During every one of these 15 ten-year time periods, this sample of 19 ethnic groups accounted for 80–90% of all immigrants into the United States.

Immigration Quotas

The first instantiation of the exclusion of the ethnic immigrant group is represented in immigration quotas. Prevention of immigration is one of the most obvious exclusion behaviors that can be examined. It is the clear, unambiguous, and intentional exclusion of potential immigrants. The Quota Law of May 19, 1921 was passed as an emergency measure to "stem the tide of immigration," quite literally excluding (to varying degrees) ethnic immigrants from entry into the United States. The quotas established in the Quota Law of May 19, 1921 were extended by the Act of May 11, 1922, and the Immigration Act of May 26, 1924. They reified a set of immigration quotas that remained essentially unchanged until the Immigration and Naturalization Act of October 3, 1965. The 1924 Immigration Act enforced quotas that were based on 2% of the number of foreign-born people from each country that were already residing in the United States in 1890. This effectively eliminated the immigration of groups who had not begun moving into the United States prior to 1890, specifically immigrants from Southern and Eastern Europe (Takaki, 1993; for further historical overviews, see Ngai, 1999; Shapiro, 1997).

A political cartoon published in the *Providence Evening Bulletin* (1921) captures the experience of immigrants attempting to enter America despite the strict quotas. Uncle Sam uses a funnel to sift through the masses of European immigrants crossing the Atlantic Ocean. (See Figure 13.1). Very few immigrants actually make it through his funnel to land on American soil, as he actively sets a gate to prevent the immigration of newcomers from Europe. This caricature captures the then-current American sentiment that restricting immigration was both necessary and good. It is important to note that the immigrants are depicted in fairly simplistic, stereotypic ways (e.g., the clothing they wear as they pass through the funnel clearly identifies them as foreign). Thus, this political cartoon illustrates a link between cognitive representations of the ethnic groups and immigration quotas. Despite anecdotal evidence like this cartoon, to date, there has been no empirical evidence examining the link

FIGURE 13.1   Political cartoon from the *Providence Evening Bulletin*, 1921

between cognitive representations in ethnophaulisms and exclusion of ethnic immigrant groups in terms of immigration quotas. It was predicted that ethnic immigrant groups cognitively represented in ethnophaulisms characterized by less complexity and more negativity would be subjected to more restrictive immigration quotas.

The United States immigration statutes provided data on immigration quotas. Specifically, the Quota Law of May 19, 1921, the Act of May 11, 1922, and the Immigration Act of May 26, 1924 provided the numbers of ethnic immigrants from each group that were allowed entry into the United States during each year from 1921 to 1965. Thus, the data for immigration quotas was based on all 19 ethnic immigrant groups for four of the 10-year time periods (1921–30, 1931–40, 1941–50, and 1951–60).

The Scott's H and the valence for ethnophaulisms for each of the 19 European ethnic immigrant groups were correlated with the naturalization for each ethnic immigrant group. Standardized beta weights (β) were derived to gauge the independent contributions of ethnophaulism complexity and ethnophaulism valence (see Mullen, 2001; Mullen & Johnson, 1993, 1995; Mullen & Rice, 2003; Mullen et al., 2000, 2001). With reference to ethnophaulism complexity, the Scott's H statistic derived from the ethnophaulisms for 19 ethnic groups in four decades significantly predicted the immigration quotas for each ethnic group, $\bar{r} = .503$, $Z = 4.353$, $p = .0000068$ ($\bar{\beta} = .455$, $p = .0000221$). With reference to ethnophaulism negativity, the ethnophaulism valence for each ethnic group significantly predicted the immigration quotas for each ethnic group, $\bar{r} = .424$, $Z = 3.615$, $p = .000150$ ($\bar{\beta} = .315$, $p = .00201$). Thus, there is a significant tendency for the groups cognitively represented with less complexity, and more negativity, in ethnophaulisms to be less likely to be admitted into the United States.

Naturalization Rates

Another instantiation of direct exclusion of ethnic immigrant groups examined is represented in the extent to which members of those ethnic immigrant groups attained naturalized citizenship once they were allowed entrance into the United States. Naturalization brings with it most of the advantages of native-born citizenship, including the right to vote and to be elected to most public offices, access to public assistance programs, and enhanced abilities to sponsor immediate family members for immigration. Ngai (1999) and Yang (1994) have discussed at length the history of denying naturalization as a form of exclusion of ethnic immigrant groups. Takaki (1993) notes that this exclusion began as far back as 1790 with the passage of a Naturalization Act that required immigrants who desired citizenship to first be "white," and then to serve a 2-year probationary period in which time they would demonstrate their good behavior and character.

An 1899 political cartoon published in *Puck* captures the then-current perspective regarding the naturalization of ethnic immigrants. (See Figure 13.2) A disconcerted Uncle Sam sits next to a ballot box, while he examines approaching voters, who are portrayed as split in half, one part representing their "American-ness," the other representing their undeniable and inescapable ethnicity. This cartoon captures the ambivalence Americans felt regarding naturalized citizens, and helps explain why some ethnic groups were prevented from naturalizing. Again, it is important to note the simplified and stereotypic portrayal of the "ethnic" half of the immigrants (e.g., the Irish American has a pug nose and a shamrock; the Dutch American wears wooden clogs and smokes a meerschaum pipe). And it is toward this simplified, stereotypic ethnic half that Uncle Sam directs his disdain and his concern regarding naturalized immigrants voting. To date, there has been no empirical evidence examining the link between cognitive representations in ethnophaulisms and exclusion of ethnic immigrant groups in terms of naturalization rates. It was predicted that ethnic

FIGURE 13.2 A political cartoon from *Puck*, 1899

immigrant groups cognitively represented in ethnophaulisms characterized by less complexity and more negativity would evidence lower naturalization rates.

The United States Census decennial reports provided data on naturalization rates. Specifically, the United States Census decennial reports tabulated the percentage of the members of ethnic immigrant groups that became naturalized during a given decade. Thus, the data for naturalization rates was based on all 19 ethnic immigrant groups for three of the 10-year time periods (1901–10, 1911–20, and 1921–30).

With reference to ethnophaulism complexity, the Scott's H statistic derived from the ethnophaulisms for 19 ethnic groups in three decades significantly predicted the naturalization rates for each ethnic group, $\bar{r} = .449$, $Z = 3.289$, $p = .000502$ ($\bar{\beta} = .356, p = .00763$). With reference to ethnophaulism negativity, the ethnophaulism valence for each ethnic group significantly predicted the immigration quotas for each ethnic group, $\bar{r} = .358$, $Z = 2.581$, $p = .00493$ ($\bar{\beta} = .208, p = .0749$). Thus, there is a significant tendency for the groups cognitively represented with less complexity, and more negativity, in ethnophaulisms to be less likely to receive naturalized citizenship in the United States.

The analyses reported thus far document an association between cognitive representations in ethnophaulisms and various aspects of direct behavioral exclusion of ethnic immigrant groups. Both complexity and valence of cognitive representations of ethnic immigrant groups in ethnophaulisms predicted the exclusion of those groups from the receiving society. These patterns emerged across varying numbers of European ethnic immigrant groups, across various segments of the 150-year time frame previously studied, and across an array of different domains of exclusion behavior.

Indirect Exclusion

The exclusion behaviors described to this point have been direct. That is, immigration quotas and restriction of naturalization are clear, blatant, and intentional behaviors that prevent ethnic immigrants from fully participating in some aspect of the receiving country's social or political structure. However, not all exclusion behaviors must necessarily be so direct. It is possible that indirect exclusionary behaviors (unintentional, subtle) could also affect the life of the immigrant. For example, the absence of portrayals of group members from a specific ethnic immigrant group in the common culture of the receiving society might, although unintentional and indirect, still effectively exclude members of that group. Thus, a second goal of our research is to further explore the link between cognitive representations in ethnophaulisms and the indirect exclusion of ethnic immigrant groups.

One such type of indirect exclusion concerns representations of ethnic immigrant groups in media materials directed toward children. Bettelheim (1977) asserted that children's literature is one of the most potent vehicles through which children absorb their culture. There seems to be ample evidence in support of the premise that the stories and pictures to which children are exposed can exert significant and enduring effects. Consider McClelland's (1961) classic archival study linking the expression of achievement themes in the children's stories of various countries with subsequent indicators of the economic development of those countries. Similarly, in an analysis of 600 children's books, Kuethe (1966) reported a significant tendency for boy characters to be pictured owning a dog, and for girl characters to be pictured owning a cat; this pattern becomes particularly poignant in light of Poresky's (1997) subsequent demonstration that, among college-aged respondents, men whose childhood pet was a dog (and women whose childhood pet was a cat) had higher self-concept scores than men whose childhood pet was a cat (and women whose childhood pet was a dog).[3]

The area of intergroup perceptions represents a unique aspect of the influence of children's media on children's assimilation of cultural values and development of potentially lasting intergroup perceptions. The dominant culture's evaluation of ethnic groups has been shown to be related to the portrayal of these racial groups in children's books. Research by Pescosolido, Grauerholz, and Milkie (1997), demonstrated that when African American challenges to the dominant society are strongest (e.g., conflicts, protests, legal actions), African

American characters virtually disappear from American children's books. The portrayals of racial groups in children's books also have been shown to exert a significant influence on children's intergroup perceptions. For example, Lichter and Johnson (1969) studied the effects of a multi-ethnic reader in a school system with no African American students, and found that use of the multi-ethnic reader led to more positive attitudes towards African Americans among European American second-graders (see also Monson, Howe, & Greenlee, 1989). Taken together, this body of work suggests that the presentation of a target group in children's media will be determined by the way in which the dominant society views that target group. Further, it becomes clear that children absorb the lessons being taught. Therefore, stories and pictures regarding ethnic immigrant groups may be a potent arena in which to examine a relatively subtle, yet significant, form of exclusion (see also Klein, 1985).

This logic was examined by exploring the tendency for the prevailing cultural cognitive representation of European ethnic immigrant groups in America to influence the portrayal of those European ethnic immigrants to children. Two different facets of the portrayal of ethnic immigrant groups to children were examined: The portrayal of child ethnic immigrant group characters in terms of their facial characteristics and the portrayal of child ethnic immigrant group characters in terms of their speech patterns. In order to examine these aspects of indirect exclusion, the same European ethnic groups were studied, with complexity and valence of the ethnophaulisms calculated in the same way as described above.

The Portrayal of Ethnic Immigrant Children Characters' Head Size
Our research addressed two readily apparent and theoretically important facets of the portrayal of ethnic immigrant children characters in children's story books. One facet of the portrayal of ethnic immigrant children characters can be derived from pictures illustrating children's stories. Of particular interest in the present context is the theoretically interesting attribute of head size of the ethnic immigrant children characters. Head size actually conveys three intriguing elements of social information. First, prominence of a social target's face (or, "face-ism") is associated with greater perceptions of dominance, intelligence, assertiveness, and ambition (e.g., Schwartz & Kurz, 1989; Zuckerman & Kieffer, 1994). Second, larger head size has been associated with perceptions of youthfulness and cuteness (e.g., Alley, 1981; Gould, 1979). Third, larger head size has been associated with enhanced school performance and cognitive abilities (e.g., Desch, Anderson, & Snow, 1990; Tisserand, Bosma, Van Boxtel, & Jolles, 2001). Children as young as 5 years of age appear to be responsive to these effects (e.g., Gross, 1997; Nash & Harris, 1970). Thus, ethnic immigrant children characters portrayed with larger heads would seem to convey a complex constellation of positive social attributes that include dominance, cuteness, and intelligence.

Ridge's (1929) *Little Americans from many lands* provided data on the portrayal of ethnic immigrant children characters. In each of Ridge's (1929) stories, the main character is a child who is going to be emigrating to America. The plot of each story involved a child emigrating to America to escape some form of economic or familial hardship in their European country of birth. It is apparent from the compassionate spirit of these stories that the author's intent is to facilitate acceptance of ethnic immigrants by the intended childhood audience of the book. Due to the use of Ridge's (1929) book as the source of the portrayals of ethnic immigrant children characters, the time frame for these analyses was restricted to the decade from 1921 to 1930, and only the nine European ethnic immigrant groups represented in Ridge's book (Dutch, French, Germans, Irish, Italians, Norwegians, Russians, Scots, and Swedes) were included in these analyses.

Each story in Ridge (1929) began with a picture that included a full-body pictorial portrayal of the main character. The size of the head (from top to bottom, in mm) was measured in each picture, and measurements of the child's forearm were also taken in order to adjust for variations in the size of the child as portrayed in the picture. This adjusted head size measurement indicated that the pictorial portrayal of the children was generally consistent with an accurate portrayal of children, in that their heads were relatively large in comparison to the rest of their bodies.

The Scott's H statistic derived from the ethnophaulisms for each ethnic immigrant group significantly predicted the pictorial portrayal of the ethnic immigrant children characters, $r_{(7)} = .906$, $p = .000414$ ($\bar{\beta} = .901$, $p = .00105$). However, the ethnophaulism valence for each ethnic immigrant group did not significantly predict the pictorial portrayal of the ethnic immigrant children characters, $r_{(7)} = .141$, $p = .3589$ ($\bar{\beta} = .055$, $p = .3794$). Thus, children from immigrant groups that were represented with ethnophaulisms of lower complexity were portrayed as having smaller heads.

The Portrayal of Ethnic Immigrant Children Characters' Verbal Complexity

The other facet of the portrayal of ethnic immigrant children characters can be derived from what the characters say in children's stories. Of particular interest in the present context is the theoretically interesting attribute of cognitive complexity of the ethnic immigrant children characters. The verbal behavior of children has been used to gauge the cognitive complexity of children, variously labelled "quality of ideation" (Myklebust, 1965) or "linguistic maturity" (Kaldegg, 1950). Flesch's (1943, 1948) "readability index," an operational definition of this construct (which incorporates linguistic variables like the number of syllables per word and the number of words per sentence) has been shown to correlate with the mental age and the IQ scores of children (e.g., Tillman, 1969). Thus, ethnic immigrant children characters portrayed with greater verbal complexity would seem to convey the positive attributes of greater intelligence and cognitive complexity.

Ridge's (1929) book also provided data on the portrayal of the verbal complexity of the ethnic immigrant children characters. For each story, every word of dialog attributed to that ethnic immigrant child character was typed into Microsoft® Word 2000, and the Flesch Readability index was calculated as a gauge of the cognitive complexity of the children's speech. This Flesch Readability index was subtracted from 100 in order to scale this indicator in the direction of higher complexity (thus 0 = low verbal complexity and 100 = high verbal complexity). The verbal portrayal of the children was generally consistent with an accurate portrayal of children in that their language was at an elementary school level. It is interesting to note that the measurement of head size adjusted by forearm length and the verbal complexity index exhibited a strong intercorrelation, $r_{(7)} = .716, p = .0153$, indicating that the ethnic immigrant groups which were portrayed as having relatively large heads also tended to speak with relatively more complexity.

In these analyses, the Scott's H statistic significantly predicted the verbal portrayal, $r_{(7)} = .818, p = .00367$ ($\bar{\beta} = .820, p = .00688$), but the ethnophaulism valence did not significantly predict the verbal portrayal, $r_{(7)} = .060, p = .4392$ ($\bar{\beta} = -.018, p = .4702$). Thus, children from ethnic immigrant groups that were represented with ethnophaulisms of lower complexity were portrayed as talking in simpler speech.

DISCUSSION AND IMPLICATIONS FOR RESEARCH AND POLICY

The results presented above indicate that cognitive representations of a group impact behavior toward that group. Simply, the way that we think about a group affects the way that we act towards that group. What is interesting about this archival line of research is that it demonstrates that our cognitions affect both direct and indirect behaviors: Cognitive representations of an ethnic group in ethnophaulisms predicted such varied behaviors as whether group members were allowed entrance into the receiving society (direct behavior) or the apparent level of intelligence evidenced in the speech of fictional characters from that group (indirect behavior). Additional evidence supporting the link between cognitive representations in ethnophaulisms and direct exclusion (Mullen & Rice, 2003) as well as the link between cognitive representations in ethnophaulisms and indirect exclusion (Mullen, 2004) has recently been reported in the literature.

Throughout this research on cognitive representations of immigrants and exclusion, results consistently point to the complexity of cognitive representations in ethnophaulisms as rendering stronger predictions of exclusion behavior than the valence of cognitive representations in ethnophaulisms. This finding may seem counter-intuitive. At first glance, one might expect the negativity with which a group is represented to be much more important than the simplicity with which it is represented in determining actions toward a group. However, this plausible expectation is not borne out by the data. Returning to the epigram with which this chapter began, this difference between the effects of cognitive representations in ethnophaulism complexity and valence can be clearly illustrated. After all, in the grand scheme of things, being called a "red-nosed" reindeer is not that negative. Rather, it is the simplicity of the derogatory name, the fact that Rudolph is characterized only by *one* physical dimension, rather than by his many other abilities, skills, and traits, that apparently leads to his exclusion from reindeer games.

The relative difference between the complexity and valence of the representations in ethnophaulisms is important to note because efforts to improve intergroup relations often focus on the negativity with which one group views another. Children are taught not to call others "bad" names, but the "badness" of the name is more likely to be an indicator of the negativity of cognitive representations than simplicity of cognitive representations. Indeed, hate speech legislation has tended to focus on the group libel and harassment aspects of the words used, but not on the complexity of the hateful vocabulary. Such efforts to prevent negative speech toward members of other groups are entirely well intentioned, and to a certain extent, useful. This utility derives from the correlation between valence and complexity of ethnophaulisms. Because the valence and complexity of ethnophaulisms are correlated ($\bar{r} = .420$), it is plausible that increasing the valence with which a group is cognitively represented will also affect the complexity with which that group is cognitively represented. However, because the correlation is only moderate, it is also clear that addressing valence alone is insufficient to effectively eliminate or even reduce exclusion behaviors. Thus, a more important issue to address is the complexity with which one group views another. The research described here suggests that parents and educators should focus their attention on the complexity with which we view other groups. Rather than keying in on the negativity of ethnophaulisms, efforts should be directed toward fostering a deeper understanding of people from other ethnic groups and cultures. The focus should be on increasing the complexity of the cognitive representations of a group rather than on a simplistic appeal to "niceness."

One potential application of this focus on complexity rather than the valence of cognitive representations in ethnophaulisms leads to an approach to multicultural education not commonly espoused. Commonly, students are taught the "correct" names for ethnic groups (e.g., using "Polish" rather than the derogatory "Polack"). However, as indicated above, this approach does not address the complexity of the cognitive representations. Rather, one simple, albeit slightly less negative, word is substituted for another simple word. A more useful approach could entail increasing the complexity of the words used to describe members of ethnic groups. If people are forced to create new categories with new descriptors for specific ethnic groups, their cognitive representations of those groups will increase in complexity. For example, imagine an ethnic group called "Malgravian" is characterized by a relatively simple cognitive representation (two ethnophaulisms relevant to a single attribute, rendering Scott's H = 0.000). People could be taught to increase the complexity of the cognitive representation for "Malgravians" by exploring more categories, along with more subsequent characteristics within those categories for "Malgravians" in an attempt to increase the amount of information they have about that group, thereby increasing the complexity of their cognitive representations for the "Malgravians." Such a procedure might result in people having a larger number of names and categories upon which to categorize "Malgravians" (five ethnophaulisms divided among three categories, rendering Scott's H = 1.522). Mullen, Leader, and Rice (2004) have recently conducted just such an experimental investigation, with promising results.

An alternative effort to implement this reasoning begins by having people first develop cognitive representations for nonsocial targets. Mullen, Pizzuto, and Foels (2002) trained participants to focus on stimulus objects either using a simple, prototypic representation, or using a complex, exemplar representation. Specifically, participants were trained to examine drinking glasses in a way that emphasized their similarity (simple, prototypic representation) or in a way that accentuated the differences among them (complex, exemplar representation). Mullen et al. (2002) found that the way in which participants examined drinking glasses transferred to the way they later examined social targets. For example, after working with the drinking glasses, participants looked at pictures of indigenous people. Participants trained to develop prototype (or exemplar) cognitive representations of the drinking glasses were subsequently more likely to employ prototype (or exemplar) cognitive representations of the indigenous people. This intervention, focused directly on the *type* of cognitive representations used, holds promise for future work on the reduction of exclusion behaviors experienced by ethnic immigrant groups.

Another important distinction that arises from this research concerns the nature of the exclusionary behaviors. Previous research has largely focused on what is called here "direct exclusion": The intentional and blatant behaviors that prevent ethnic immigrants from participating fully in the host society. A search of recent psychological and sociological treatments of exclusion documents this fact. Examining PsycFIRST (an online database of published psychological and sociological materials) reveals a large majority of work in exclusion of immigrants focusing on direct exclusion: 54 articles relate to immigration quotas, whereas only 14 articles relate to the portrayal of immigrants to children. The foregoing research described in this chapter also examines indirect exclusion: Unintentional and somewhat subtle behaviors that prevent ethnic immigrants from participating fully in the host society. In light of this disparity in the amount of attention paid to these two types of exclusion, it is important to consider the degree to which these two types of exclusion can be predicted. A more careful examination of our research suggests that the cognitive complexity with which an immigrant group is represented is more strongly related to the indirect exclusionary behaviors than to the direct exclusionary behaviors. The complexity of cognitive representations is strongly related to indirect exclusion ($\bar{r} = .869$), whereas the complexity of cognitive representations is only moderately related to direct exclusion ($\bar{r} = .476$). Future research might well be directed to scrutinizing indirect exclusion, as it has been previously underresearched.

Policy implications arise from this distinction. Social commentaries frequently focus on the idea of "legislating morality." At one level, any of the laws that a government enforces for the safety and prosperity of its citizens can be thought of as legislating morality. Laws against murder or theft legislate moral actions. This kind of official legislation at the governmental level is important in understanding the direct exclusion of immigrants. For example, governments legislate the degree to which immigrants are allowed into a country, the equality of their employment opportunities, and the degree to which they may participate within a host society. And, as has been shown, this kind of legislation is affected by the complexity with which specific ethnic immigrant groups are represented. However, if our attention is confined to this direct, legislated exclusion, the indirect and subtle types of exclusion that are better predicted by cognitive representations are ignored. It is the subtle, indirect exclusion behavior that is most strongly related to how we think about ethnic immigrants. And it is this subtle, indirect exclusion that that may be most difficult to legislate.

The disturbing aspect of this relationship between cognitive representations of immigrant groups and indirect exclusion is twofold. First, this exclusion is subtle enough that it can be easily overlooked. Even those who make conscious efforts to include people from other ethnic groups in their social arenas might not be aware of exclusion from various media outlets. This is not typically the kind of obvious exclusion that would elicit protests or letters to public officials. It is subtle and difficult to notice. Indeed, it can occur despite good intentions. Ridge's (1929) stories were compassionate in tone and attempted to teach her readers to appreciate their new immigrant neighbors. However, her work was rife with the kind of indirect exclusion discussed above.

The second disturbing aspect of this relationship between cognitive representations and indirect exclusion is its self-perpetuating nature. This line of research indicates that simple cognitive representations can lead to indirect exclusion of ethnic immigrants in books aimed toward children. Simple cognitive representations of immigrant groups leads to portrayals of group members as simple, uncute, and unintelligent. This portrayal of members of ethnic immigrant groups unintentionally presents this image of immigrants to the children reading the books. Thus a simple cognitive representation of immigrants leads to simple, negative portrayals of these groups to children, which in turn leads to a new generation of simple cognitive representations of ethnic immigrant groups. The fact that this cyclical transmission is unintentional and subtle is disturbing indeed.

Another implication of the research described in this chapter regards the well intentioned programs frequently instituted in schools that attempt to raise multicultural awareness and understanding among students. Typically, such programs attempt to teach children that people from other cultures and ethnic backgrounds may have different customs, but that they are equally valid as the culture from which the students come. Often, such programs take the form of teaching students about children in other countries. This line of research as described above leads to several suggestions for those designing and implementing such multicultural awareness programs in schools. First, the ethnic groups represented must be carefully considered. While it is clear that the time constraints of a typical academic year may prevent educators from teaching their students about ethnic groups from every nation around the world, it is also clear that such multicultural education programs should be broader in scope than addressing only one or two groups. It is clear from this line of research that lack of familiarity with and perceived foreignness of an ethnic group lead to simpler, more negative cognitions about members from that group, thus leading to exclusion. This kind of exclusion leads to an effective invisibility of ethnic immigrant groups, and has been labeled "symbolic annihilation" (Tuchman, 1978). This invisibility has been documented for depictions of African Americans in children's books (Children's Literature Review Board, 1977; Miller, 1986; Pescosolido et al., 1997). By leaving out numerous groups, traditional multicultural education programs might be considered guilty of the indirect exclusion we have been discussing.

Also, the way in which members of immigrant groups are represented must be carefully designed and controlled. The research described in this chapter demonstrates just how subtle the exclusion of other groups can be. The representations of ethnic group members in children's books serve to create "second-hand" exemplars, based on second-hand information. Because children do not have first-hand experience with members of all ethnic immigrant groups, their knowledge base relies on books and film rather than personal contact. Linville and Fischer (1993) discussed possible effects of exposure to this second hand information, whereby simple, prototypic cognitive representations of immigrant groups are particularly resistant to change. Ethnic immigrant groups subject to the simplest cognitive representations tend to be conspicuous by their absence (see Mullen, 2004). When these ethnic immigrant groups actually are featured in children's books, they are subtly portrayed in a derogatory manner that would not serve to disconfirm the simple and negative representations of the group common at the time. In order to reduce this subtle form of exclusion, educators must pay attention to the way they represent children of different ethnic backgrounds. Simplistic versions of children from other countries will serve only to reinforce the indirect exclusion with which they have already been treated, thus reinforcing simplistic, stereotypical views. Thus, it is not enough to present information about children from different ethnic groups. The information must be calculated to present children as complex characters that are similar in stature and complexity to those of American host societies.

A reexamination of the way in which children are taught about members of ethnic immigrant groups is essential. Several recent publications have suggested that the current multicultural education movement does not adequately address the problem of preventing prejudice toward ethnic immigrants and members of ethnic groups different from the majority group (see Bigler, 1999; Van Ausdale & Feagin, 2001). Indeed, Bigler (1999) describes the research on multicultural education as characterized by a "prevalence of nonsignificant effects" (p. 691). The research described here suggests that one reason the methods used have not worked to date is that the focus has been misdirected. Rather than focusing on complexity of cognitive representations, educators have tended to focus on valence. This focus on valence is somewhat misguided. According to the results reported here, complexity of cognitive representation is more strongly related to any type of exclusion ($\bar{r} = .727$) than is valence of cognitive representation ($\bar{r} = .252$). Thus, future educational efforts should be directed toward changing the complexity of childrens' cognitive representations rather than the valence of those representations.

ACKNOWLEDGMENT

The authors would like to thank Jack Dovidio and Vicki Esses for helpful comments on an earlier draft of this chapter.

NOTES

1. At about the same time that Roback (1944) coined the term *ethnophaulism*, Ericson (1939) proposed *ecthronym* (from the Greek roots meaning "hostile" and "name") to identify the same words used as ethnic slurs to refer to outgroups. However, while Roback's term ethnophaulism gained currency, especially among linguists and sociologists, Ericson's term ecthronym is seldom used.
2. As delineated below, the results summarized here are based upon a sample of 19 European ethnic immigrant groups (Belgians, Dutch, English, French, Germans, Greeks, Hungarians, Irish, Italians, Norwegians, Poles, Portuguese, Russians, Scots, Spaniards, Swedes, Swiss, Turks, and Welsh), and a total of 15 consecutive 10-year (decade) periods, from 1821–1830 to 1961–1970.
3. The authors would like to thank Darcy Mullen for bringing these two studies to their attention.

REFERENCES

Allen, I. L. (1983). *The language of ethnic conflict: Social organization and lexical culture*. New York: Columbia University Press.

Alley, T. R. (1981). Head shape and the perception of cuteness. *Developmental Psychology, 17,* 650–654.

Allport, G. W. (1954). *The nature of prejudice*. Garden City, NY: Doubleday Anchor books.

Associated Press (4/22/1999). Boy tells how friend was killed. *Associated Press*.

Associated Press (1/4/2000). Complaint filed over "frog" slur. *Associated Press*.

Associated Press (4/28/2001). Tigers confirm fight, deny slur. *Associated Press*.

Associated Press (3/10/2003). Vanbiesbrouck quits after using racial slur. *Associated Press*.

Banks, M. (1996). *Ethnicity: Anthropological constructions*. London: Routledge.

Ben-Ari, R., Kedem, P., & Levy-Weiner, N. (1992). Cognitive complexity and intergroup perception and evaluation. *Personality and Individual Differences, 13,* 1291–1298.

Bettelheim, B. (1977). *Uses of enchantment*. New York, NY: Vintage Books.

Biernat, M., & Vescio, T. K. (1993). Categorization and stereotyping: Effects of group context on memory and social judgement. *Journal of Experimental Social Psychology, 29,* 166–202.

Biernat, M., & Vescio, T. K. (1994). Still another look at the effects of fit and novelty on the salience of social categories. *Journal of Experimental Social Psychology, 30,* 399–406.

Bigler, R. S. (1999). The use of multicultural curricula and materials to counter racism in children. *Journal of Social Issues, 55,* 687–705.

Carter, A. A. (1944). Nicknames and minority groups. *Phylon, 5*(24), 1–245.

Children's Literature Review Board (1977). Starting out right: Choosing books about Black people for young children. In D. MacCann & G. Woodard (Eds.), *Cultural conformity in books for children* (pp. 107–145). Metuchen, NJ: Scarecrow Press.

Citron, A. F., Chein, I., & Harding, J. (1950). Anti-minority remarks: A problem for action research. *Journal of Abnormal and Social Psychology, 45,* 99–126.

Desch, L. W., Anderson, S. K., & Snow, J. H. (1990). Relationship of head circumference to measures of school performance. *Clinical Pediatrics, 29,* 389–392.

Eisminger, S. (1979). A glossary of ethnic slurs in American English. *Maledicta, 3,* 153–174.

Ericson, E. E. (1939). Ecthronyms: Derisive names for various peoples. *Words, 5,* 100–103.

Flesch, R. (1943). *Marks of readable style: A study in adult education*. New York, NY: Columbia University Press.

Flesch, R. (1948). A readability yardstick. *Journal of Applied Psychology, 32,* 221–233.

Fried, M. (1975). *The notion of tribe*. Menlo Park, CA: Cummings.

Fuquay, J. (5/16/2003). LP&L chief faces profanity complaint weeks after ethnic slur. Lubbock TX: Avalanche Journal.

Gould, S. J. (1979). This view of life: Mickey Mouse meets Konrad Lorenz. *Natural History, 88,* 30–36.

Graumann, C. F. (1998). Verbal discrimination: A neglected chapter in the social psychology of aggression. *Journal for the Theory of Social Behavior, 28,* 41–61.

Graumann, C. F., & Wintermantel, M. (1989). Discriminatory speech acts: A functional approach. In D. Bar-Tal, C. F. Graumann, A. W. Kruglanski, & W. Stroebe (Eds.), *Stereotyping and prejudice: Changing conceptions.* New York, NY: Springer-Verlag.

Greenberg, J., Kirkland, S. L., & Pyszczynski, T. (1988). Some theoretical notions and preliminary research concerning derogatory ethnic labels. In G. Smitherman-Donaldson & T. A. van Dijk (Eds.), *Discourse and discrimination.* Detroit, MI: Wayne State University Press.

Gross, T. E. (1997). Children's perceptions of faces of varied immaturity. *Journal of Experimental Child Psychology, 66,* 42–63.

Hazen, B. S. (1958). *Rudolph, the red-nosed reindeer.* Racine, WI: Western.

Hirschfeld, L. A. (1996). *Race in the making: Cognition, culture, and the child's construction of human kinds.* Cambridge, MA: MIT Press.

Huddy, L., & Virtanen, S. (1995). Subgroup differentiation and subgroup bias among Latinos as a function of familiarity and positive distinctiveness. *Journal of Personality and Social Psychology, 68,* 97–108.

Izmirlieva, V., & Ivanov, P. (1996). *We Can Always Call Them Bulgarians: Anglophone Mass Media Image of Bulgaria.* Paper presented at the annual meeting of the American Association of Teachers of Slavic and Eastern European Languages, Chicago, IL.

Joesten, J. (1935). Calling names in any language. *American Mercury, 36,* 483–487.

Kaldegg, G. (1950). Substance symbolism: A study in language psychology. *Journal of Experimental Education, 18,* 331–342.

Kanter, R. M. (1977). Some effects of proportions on group life: Skewed sex ratios and responses to token women. *American Journal of Sociology, 82,* 465–490.

Khleif, B. B. (1979). Insiders, outsiders, and renegades: Toward a classification of ethnolinguistic labels. In H. Giles & B. Saint-Jacques (Eds.), *Language and Ethnic Relations.* Oxford: Pergamon Press.

Klein, G. (1985). *Reading into racism: Bias in children's literature and reading materials.* London: Routledge & Kegan Paul.

Kuethe, J. L. (1966). Perpetuation of specific schemata in literature for children. *Psychological Reports, 18,* 433–434.

Lichter, J. H., & Johnson, D. W. (1969). Changes in attitudes toward Negroes of White elementary school students after use of multiethnic readers. *Journal of Educational Psychology, 60,* 148–152.

Linville, P. (1998). The heterogeneity of homogeneity. In J. Cooper and J. Darley (Eds.), *Attribution processes, person perception, and social interaction: The legacy of Ned Jones.* Washington, DC: American Psychological Association.

Linville, P., & Fischer, G. W. (1993). Exemplar and abstraction models of perceived group variability and stereotypicality. *Social Cognition, 11,* 92–125.

Linville, P., Fischer, G. W., & Salovey, P. (1989). Perceived distributions of the characteristics of ingroup and outgroup members: Empirical evidence and a computer simulation. *Journal of Personality and Social Psychology, 57,* 165–188.

Mackie, D. M., & Smith, E. R. (1998). Intergroup relations: Insights from a theoretically integrative approach. *Psychological Review, 105*, 499–529.

MacMullen, J. (1963). Derisive ethnic names. *Western Folklore, 22*, 197.

Marushiakova, E. (1992). Ethnic identity among Gypsy groups in Bulgaria. *Journal of the Gypsy Lore Society, 2*, 95–115.

McClelland, D. C. (1961). *The achieving society*. Princeton, NJ: Van Nostrand.

Miller, J. A. (1986). Black images in American children's literature. In W. T. Moynihan, M. E. Shaner, & J. Cott (Eds.), *Masterworks of children's literature* (pp. 99–118). New York, NY: Stonehill.

Monson, D. L., Howe, K., & Greenlee, A. (1989). Helping children develop cross-cultural understanding with children's books. *Early Child Development and Care, 48*, 3–8.

Mullen, B. (1983). Operationalizing the effect of the group on the individual: A self-attention perspective. *Journal of Experimental Social Psychology, 19*, 545–559.

Mullen, B. (1991). Group composition, salience, and cognitive representations: The phenomenology of being in a group. *Journal of Experimental Social Psychology, 27*, 297–323.

Mullen, B. (2001). Ethnophaulisms for ethnic immigrant groups. *Journal of Social Issues, 57*, 457–475.

Mullen, B. (2004). Sticks and stones can break my bones, but ethnophaulisms can alter the portrayal of immigrants to children. *Personality and Social Psychology Bulletin, 30*, 250–260.

Mullen, B., & Johnson, C. (1993). Cognitive representation in ethnophaulisms as a function of group size: The phenomenology of being in a group. *Personality and Social Psychology Bulletin, 19*, 296–304.

Mullen, B., & Johnson, C. (1995). Cognitive representation in ethnophaulisms and illusory correlation in stereotyping. *Personality and Social Psychology Bulletin, 21*, 420–433.

Mullen, B., Leader, T., & Rice, D. R. (2004). *An Experimental Examination of the Effects of Ethnophaulism's Complexity on Exclusion*. Paper to be presented at the annual meeting of the Society of Personality and Social Psychology, Austin, TX.

Mullen, B., Pizzuto, C., & Foels, R. (2002). Altering intergroup perceptions by altering prevailing mode of cognitive representation: "They look like people." *Journal of Personality and Social Psychology, 83*, 1333–1343.

Mullen, B., & Rice, D. R. (2003). Ethnophaulisms and exclusion: Cognitive representation of ethnic immigrant groups and social distance. *Personality and Social Psychology Bulletin, 29*, 1056–1067.

Mullen, B., Rozell, D., & Johnson, C. (2000). Ethnophaulisms for ethnic immigrant groups: Cognitive representation of "the minority" and "the foreigner." *Group Processes and Intergroup Relations, 3*, 5–24.

Mullen, B., Rozell, D., & Johnson, C. (2001). Ethnophaulisms for ethnic immigrant groups: The contributions of group size and familiarity. *European Journal of Social Psychology, 31*, 231–246.

Myklebust, H. R. (1965). *Development and disorders of written language*. New York, NY: Grune & Stratton.

Nash, H., & Harris, D. B. (1970). Body proportions in children's drawings of a man. *Journal of Genetic Psychology, 117*, 85–90.

Ngai, M. M. (1999). The architecture of race in American immigration law A re-examination of the Immigration Act of 1924. *Journal of American History, 86*, 67–92.

Nichols, D. R., Abrams, D., & Mullen, B. (2000). *Effects of Gender Composition in Groups. I: An Integration of the Group Discussion Paradigm.* Paper presented at the meeting of the Society of Personality and Social Psychology, Nashville, TN.

Nielsen, W. A. (1979). *Acceptance of Asian Americans and Ethnophaulisms Used against Them.* Paper presented at the annual meeting of the Southwestern Sociological Association.

Palmore, E. B. (1962). Ethnophaulisms and ethnocentrism. *American Journal of Sociology, 67*, 442–445.

Pankiw, B., & Bienvenue, R. M. (1990). Parental responses to ethnic name-calling: A sociological inquiry. *Canadian Ethnic Studies, 22*, 78–98.

Park, B., Ryan, C. S., & Judd, C. M. (1992). Role of meaningful subgroups in explaining differences in perceived variability for ingroups and outgroups. *Journal of Personality and Social Psychology, 63*, 553–567.

Pescosolido, B. A., Grauerholz, E., & Milkie, M. A. (1997). Culture and conflict: The portrayal of Blacks in U.S. children's picture books through the mid- and –late-twentieth century. *American Sociological Review, 62*, 443–464.

Peterson, A. M. (6/1/2000). Wonder bread worker accuses bias. *Associated Press.*

Poresky, R. H. (1997). Sex, childhood pets and young adults' self concept scores. *Psychological Reports, 80*, 371–377.

Reuters (7/17/2000). First Lady denounces anti-Semitic charge. *Reuters.*

Reuters (3/26/2001). There were race slurs at Indian wells, says Williams sr. *Reuters.*

Ridge, M. L. (1929). *Little Americans from many lands.* New York: Samuel Gabriel Sons.

Roback, A. A. (1944). *A dictionary of international slurs.* Cambridge: Sci-Art.

Schaller, M., Boyd, C., Yohannes, J., & O'Brien, M. (1995). The prejudiced personality revisited: Personal need for structure and formation of erroneous group stereotypes. *Journal of Personality and Social Psychology, 68*, 544–555.

Schwartz, N., & Kurz, E. (1989). What's in a picture? The impact of face-ism on trait attribution. *European Journal of Social Psychology, 19*, 311–316.

Scott, W. A., Osgood, D. W., & Peterson, C. (1979). *Cognitive structure: Theory and measurement of individual differences.* Washington, DC: Winston.

Shapiro, M. J. (1997). Narrating the nation, unwelcoming the stranger: Anti-immigration policy in contemporary "America." *Alternatives, 22*, 1–34.

Simon, B., Kulla, C., & Zobel, M. (1995). On being more than just a part of the whole: Regional identity and social distinctiveness. *European Journal of Social Psychology, 25*, 325–340.

Smith, E. E. (1974). A day in the suburbs. In J. W. Milstead, M. H. Greenberg, J. D. Olander, & P. S. Warrick (Eds.), *Sociology through science fiction* (pp. 218–225). New York, NY: St. Martin's Press.

Taft, R. (1959). Ethnic stereotypes, attitudes, and familiarity: Australia. *Journal of Social Psychology, 49*, 177–186.

Takaki, R. (1993). *A different mirror: A history of multicultural America.* Boston, MA: Back Bay Books.

Taylor, S. E., Fiske, S. T., Etcoff, N. L., & Ruderman, A. J. (1978). Categorical bases of person memory and stereotyping. *Journal of Personality and Social Psychology, 36*, 778–793.

Tillman, M. H. (1969). Level of abstraction in the written compositions of children varying in intelligence and age. *Psychological Reports, 24*, 419–424.

Tisserand, D. J., Bosma, H., Van Boxtel, M. P. J., & Jolles, J. (2001). Head size and cognitive ability in nondemented older adults are related. *Neurology, 56*, 969–971.

Tuchman, G. (1978). Introduction: The symbolic annihilation of women by the mass media. In G. Tuchman, A. K. Daniels, & J. Benet (Eds.), *Hearth and home: Images of women in the mass media* (pp. 3–38). New York: Oxford University Press.

Van Ausdale, D., & Feagin, J. R. (2001). *The first r: How children learn race and racism.* Lanham, MD: Rowman & Littlefield.

Weil, S. (1995). Collective designations and collective identity among Ethiopian Jews. *Israel Social Science Research, 10*, 25–40.

Yang, P. Q. (1994). *Ethnicity and naturalization. Ethnic and Racial Studies, 17*, 593–618.

Zuckerman, M., & Kieffer, S. C. (1994). Race differences in face-ism: Does facial prominence imply dominance? *Journal of Personality and Social Psychology, 66*, 86–92.

14

Attitudes toward Immigrants and Immigration: The Role of National and International Identity

VICTORIA M. ESSES, JOHN F. DOVIDIO,
ANTOINETTE H. SEMENYA, and LYNNE M. JACKSON

In this chapter, we explore the role of national and international identity in determining attitudes toward immigrants and immigration. We begin by describing nativist versus civic/cultural definitions of national identity, and the distinction between patriotism and nationalism. We also outline two more international perspectives—internationalism and support for a world government. Next, we describe the relations between these forms of identification and attitudes toward immigrants and immigration. This includes a review of relevant literature, as well as a summary of our recent research on this topic. In the third section, we present our experimental work designed to examine strategies for improving immigration attitudes through manipulations of identity and inclusiveness. In the final section, we illustrate theoretical and practical implications, including support for Social Identity Theory and the Common Ingroup Identity Model, contributions to understanding cross-national and historical trends in immigration attitudes and policy, and development of programs to promote more positive attitudes.

National crisis and threat, such as the September 11, 2001 terrorist attacks on New York City and Washington, DC, often lead to an increased focus on national identity and renewed attachment to the nation (Citrin, Reingold, & Green, 1990; Jaret, 1999; Kosterman & Feshbach, 1989; Worchel & Coutant, 1997). At the same time, conditions of threat increase the salience of the psychological boundaries between people perceived as members of the ingroup versus members of outgroups, and narrow the psychological boundaries defining the national ingroup (Greenberg, Solomon, & Pyszczynski, 1997; Rothgerber, 1997). As a consequence, there is a decreased acceptance of "foreigners" (Citrin et al., 1990; Esses, Dovidio, & Hodson, 2002; Jaret, 1999; Stephan & Stephan, 2000).

Although there is considerable work on the effects of threat and group identification in a range of laboratory and naturalistic settings (Doosje & Ellemers, 1997), national boundaries, which are often formally permeable (e.g., through immigration) and can involve a range of cognitive and emotional connections, reflect unique and complex dynamics in people's relations to others. How exactly do national attachment and identity relate to attitudes toward "outsiders," particularly immigrants who are trying to enter the national ingroup? And what of internationalism—concern for the welfare of other nations and identification with an international community (Feshbach, 1990; Kosterman & Feshbach, 1989)? Are attachment to one's own nation and internationalism necessarily opposite ends of a continuum, or do they represent different types of identities, reflecting different aspects of an individual's overall set of multiple social identities (Brewer, 2000)? Moreover, are there factors, such as threat, that moderate the relation between these identities? For example, does increased national attachment in times of threat necessarily lead to a reduction in concern for the welfare of others, including potential immigrants? The answer to these questions may depend on the specific form that national attachment takes and how national identity is defined. In this chapter, we explore the role of national and international identity in determining attitudes toward immigrants and immigration.

The role of national and international identity in determining immigration attitudes is important at both theoretical and practical levels. At a theoretical level, Social Identity Theory (Tajfel & Turner, 1979; see also Self Categorization Theory: Turner, Hogg, Oakes, Reicher, & Wetherell, 1987) states that the social categorization of people into outgroups (different from the self) and an ingroup (which includes the self) stimulates a motivation to perceive or achieve a sense of positive group distinctiveness. This may take the form of enhancing the image, prestige, or resources available to one's own group by derogating or discriminating against outgroups. Thus, based on Social Identity Theory, we would predict that to the extent that immigrants are not included as part of the national ingroup, derogation of immigrants will occur in order to promote a positive sense of national identity. In addition, Social Identity Theory proposes that the strength of ingroup identification may moderate these effects such that individuals who highly identify with the ingroup will be particularly motivated to seek positive group distinctiveness (e.g., Branscombe & Wann, 1994; Gagnon & Bourhis, 1996; Perreault & Bourhis, 1999). This proposition suggests that high levels of national attachment may be especially associated with derogation of immigrants (see also Mummendey, Klink, & Brown, 2001).

At a practical level, it is important to understand the role of national and international identity in determining attitudes toward immigrants and immigration because at the same time that immigration levels have climbed to historically unprecedented levels (Dovidio & Esses, 2001), issues of national identity and globalization seem to be the focus of attention in many parts of the world, including North America and Europe. Indeed, the arrival of large numbers of immigrants to receiving nations can be directly associated with increased concern over national self-definition and nativist sentiments (e.g., Feagin, 1997; Jaret, 1999). Thus, the interplay between national and international identity, on the one hand, and attitudes toward immigrants and immigration, on the other, is likely to have an important influence on national and international relations in the 21st century.

We begin this chapter with a section that defines the various forms of *national* attachment and identity, including patriotism and nationalism, and civic/cultural versus nativist definitions of national identity. We also describe two *international* perspectives that an individual might take, internationalism and support for a world government. In addition to defining these terms, we describe previous research that has examined the relations among them, and their correlations with attitudes toward relevant social issues. The next section focuses more specifically on research that has examined the relations between various forms of national and international identity, on the one hand, and attitudes toward immigrants and immigration, on the other. This includes an analysis of research conducted by previous researchers and our own recent correlational research on this topic. The third section describes our attempts to improve attitudes toward immigrants and immigration through manipulations intended to influence perceptions of identity at the national and international levels and degree of inclusiveness of the ingroup. This research is informed by theory and research on the Common Ingroup Identity, which has received considerable support (see Gaertner & Dovidio, 2000). In our final section, we summarize what we have learned, and describe the implications at the level of both theory and practice.

FORMS OF NATIONAL AND INTERNATIONAL IDENTITY

National identity and attachment can take multiple forms. However, we focus on two important distinctions that have been made in the literature on national identity: (a) nativist versus civic/cultural national identity, and (b) patriotism versus nationalism (see Table 14.1). These distinctions, which are considered in the first two parts of this section, represent two different dimensions of attitudes toward one's national group and its members. The nativist versus civic/cultural distinction reflects who is defined as a legitimate member of one's national ingroup (Jones, 1997). The patriotism versus nationalism distinction reflects, given a particular definition of who is an ingroup member and who is not, differential emphasis on the affective versus cognitive bases of attachment

TABLE 14.1 Measures of National and International Identity

Nativist national identity	Belief that national identity is based on birth, kinship
Civic/cultural national identity	Belief that national identity is based on voluntary commitment to national laws and institutions
Patriotism	Affective attachment to one's nation
Nationalism	Belief in superiority of one's nation compared to others; belief in importance of promoting the welfare of one's nation above all others
Internationalism	Concern for global welfare; identification with a world community
Support for a world government	Support for a central world government or authority

to one's nation and national identity (Kosterman & Feshbach, 1989). Along with national identity, it is possible that people may also identify to different degrees and in different ways to a larger, often superordinate, entity, such as identification with an international community. In the third part of this section we thus examine measures of international identity (see Table 14.1).

Nativist and Civic/Cultural National Identity

An important factor to consider in thinking about the role of national identity in attitudes toward immigrants and immigration is exactly how the national group is construed. That is, one's definition of the national ingroup may strongly influence attitudes toward those who are trying to enter it. In an analysis of Australian Election Survey data, Jones (1997, 1999) demonstrated an important distinction between nativist versus civic/cultural beliefs about who is a member of the national ingroup (see also Pakulski & Tranter, 2000). Nativist identity is the belief that national identity is based on having been born in the country, or at least having lived there a long time, and on being a member of the dominant religion. This is closely aligned with ethno-national identity, in which national identity is defined in terms of bonds of kinship and a common ethnic heritage (Condor, 2001; Pakulski & Tranter, 2000). In contrast, civic/cultural identity is the belief that national identity is based on a voluntary commitment to the laws and institutions of the country, and on a feeling of being a member of the national group. Thus, a common political and institutional allegiance forms the basis of this national identity. The two different types of beliefs about national identity are positively, though only weakly, related ($r = .15$; Jones, 1997).

Patriotism and Nationalism

Although the terms patriotism and nationalism are sometimes used interchangeably in both academic and nonacademic domains, the distinction between them may have important implications for understanding attitudes toward other nations and their members. Patriotism is simply affection for and pride in one's nation. It may include attachment to the national ingroup and, at times, attachment to the land in which the group resides (e.g., Bar-Tal & Staub, 1997; Feshbach, 1990, 1994; Feshbach & Sakano, 1997; Hurwitz & Peffley, 1993; Kosterman & Feshbach, 1989; Worchel & Coutant, 1997). Thus, patriotism primarily involves positive affect toward one's nation. Nationalism, in contrast, has a more cognitive focus. It involves a set of beliefs about the position of one's nation in the world, and in particular, beliefs about the superiority of one's nation compared to others and the importance of promoting the interests of one's own nation above all others (Feshbach, 1990, 1994; Feshbach & Sakano, 1997; Hurwitz & Peffley, 1993; Kosterman & Feshbach, 1989; Worchel & Coutant, 1997). Mummendey et al. (2001) suggest that nationalism is specifically related to intergroup differentiation, the desire to positively differentiate one's own nation from others.

Examination of the scales developed to assess patriotism and nationalism provides additional insight into their different emphasis on affective versus cognitive factors. In a U.S. sample, Kosterman and Feshbach (1989) examined forms of national attachment and found evidence of separate patriotism versus nationalism factors. The Patriotism Scale they developed on the basis of this analysis includes items reflecting pride and collective esteem (see Luhtanen & Crocker, 1992) for their nation. Sample items of the patriotism scale are, "I am proud to be an American," and, "The fact that I am an American is an important part of my identity." In contrast, the Nationalism Scale they developed focuses on exerting and maintaining status, prestige, and the relative welfare of the nation. This scale includes items such as, "In view of America's moral and material superiority, it is only right that we should have the biggest say in deciding United Nations policy," and, "The important thing for the U.S. foreign aid program is to see to it that the U.S. gains a political advantage." A similar distinction between patriotism and nationalism has been found in other countries, such as Japan (Feshbach & Sakano, 1997), and in our Canadian study that we will be describing in more detail in the next section. Of interest, nativists, as assessed in the Australian research described earlier, are especially likely to endorse items that seem to tap into nationalism, such as "Australia should follow its own interests even if that course of action was to lead to conflict with other nations" (Jones, 1999).

Although they are conceptually distinguishable, patriotism and nationalism are not completely unrelated empirically. Correlations between the Kosterman and Feshbach measures range from .28 in their original sample to .41 in our Canadian sample. Nonetheless, the validity of the distinction is evident through examination of their ability to predict other attitudes. For example, although Republicans in the United States score higher in both patriotism and nationalism than do Democrats, the difference in nationalism between Republicans and Democrats is much greater (Kosterman & Feshbach, 1989). In addition, nationalism more strongly predicts prowar attitudes and pronuclear armament attitudes than does patriotism (Feshbach, 1990, 1994; Kosterman & Feshbach, 1989), and more strongly predicts willingness to limit individual civil and political rights (Diaz-Veizades, Widaman, Little, & Gibbs, 1995). Thus, patriotism seems to be a more benign form of national attachment, whereas nationalism more specifically reflects group interest and protection of the national status quo.

Internationalism and Support for a World Government

Identity and attachment may also be defined at a more broad level, at an international level. Two related concepts of relevance to international identity and attachment are internationalism and support for world government. Internationalism involves concern for global welfare and support of mutual assistance among nations (Hurwitz & Peffley, 1993; Kosterman & Feshbach, 1989). Internationalism seems to have an empathic and altruistic nature, and to involve identification with a world community. Thus, although it may involve a political orientation, it also seems to include a belief in and identification with an international community involving all nations. Support for a world government seems to be more cognitive and pragmatic, involving support for a world government or authority rather than national governments (Hurwitz & Peffley, 1993; Kosterman & Feshbach, 1989). Kosterman and Feshbach's (1989) development of patriotism and nationalism measures, as described earlier, also included items intended to assess internationalism and support for a world government, and indeed separate factors were also obtained that correspond to these concepts. Thus, for example, the scale to assess internationalism includes items such as, "We should teach our children to uphold the welfare of all people everywhere even though it may be against the best interests of our own country," and "The position a U.S. citizen takes on an international issue should depend on how much good it does for how many people in the world, regardless of their nation." Sample items on the world government scale include, "All central governments ought to be abolished and replaced by one central world government," and "The U.S. should never give up its military power to a strong world government" (reverse scored).

Perhaps not surprisingly, internationalism and support for a world government tend to be positively related, with an intercorrelation of .29 in the original sample (Kosterman & Feshbach, 1989) and .31 in our Canadian sample. Nonetheless, they do show some discriminant validity in their ability to predict attitudes toward relevant social issues. For example, although both are negatively related to nuclear armament attitudes, the relation for internationalism is somewhat stronger (Kosterman & Feshbach, 1989). In addition, internationalism is highly predictive of the belief that everyone, irrespective of who they are, is entitled to an adequate standard of living (i.e., food, housing, medical care), whereas support for a world government is unrelated to this view (Diaz-Veizades et al., 1995). In the United States, Democrats score higher in both internationalism and support for a world government than do Republicans, and the size of this effect is quite similar for the two measures (Kosterman & Feshbach, 1989).

Given the definitions of nationalism and internationalism and the items used to assess them, one might assume that nationalism and internationalism are opposite ends of a continuum. That is, one might assume that an individual who is high in nationalism—believing in the need to put the welfare of one's own nation above the welfare of others—would necessarily be low in internationalism. The data, however, do not support such a unipolar view. Although nationalism and internationalism are negatively related, the relation is in fact quite weak, with intercorrelations of −.18 in both the original Kosterman and Feshbach (1989) sample and in our Canadian sample. These orientations therefore seem to represent different types of social identities (Brewer, 2000), rather than measures of a single dimension of inclusiveness and exclusiveness. Thus, to understand attitudes toward immigrants and immigration, it would seem to be worth investigating the role of both national and international identity.

PREDICTING ATTITUDES TOWARD IMMIGRANTS AND IMMIGRATION

Several previous studies have examined the role of construal of national identity and national attachment in predicting attitudes toward immigrants and immigration. In his analysis of construal of national identity in Australia, Jones (1997, 1999) included an examination of the relation between definitions of national identity and perceptions of immigrants and their impact on Australia (see also Pakulski & Tranter, 2000). He found that those who held nativist as opposed to civic/cultural perceptions of national identity were especially likely to believe that immigrants have a negative impact on Australian society, including increasing crime rates and taking jobs away from Australian-born individuals. Nativists were also more likely than civic/culturalists to agree that the number of immigrants to Australia should be reduced substantially. Pakulski and Tranter (2000) suggest that the attitudes toward immigrants held by nativists are evidence of protectionism, rather than hatred or xenophobia. Irrespective of whether the basis is ingroup favoritism or outgroup derogation (see Brewer, 1999), it is certainly the case that individuals who define the national ingroup in more exclusionary, nativist terms hold less favorable perceptions of immigrants.

In addition to individual differences in civic/culturalist versus nativist orientations, different subgroups within the same society may systematically differ in their emphases on these factors in their subgroup identities. Maddens,

Billiet, and Beerten (2000; see also Billiet, Maddens, & Beerten, 2003), who examined the role of identity in predicting attitudes toward "foreigners" in Belgium, focused on differences in the nature of identification with the two subnational regions in the country, Wallonia and Flanders. These researchers proposed that Walloons are especially likely to construe Walloon identity in terms of willingness to accept the rules and promote the socioeconomic interests of the region, much like civic/cultural identity, and that the Flemish are especially likely to construe Flemish identity in terms of a relatively static cultural heritage that is determined through descent, similar to nativist identity. In a national survey, they found that among Walloons, increased Walloon identity was associated with more favorable attitudes toward immigrants, whereas among Flemings, increased Flemish identity was associated with less favorable attitudes toward immigrants, including perceptions of economic and cultural threat from immigrants. Thus, as in the Jones (1997, 1999) analysis, individuals who identify strongly with a more exclusionary definition of the ingroup feel more threatened by immigrants.

In terms of the role of national attachment in predicting attitudes toward immigrants and immigration, only one previous study has specifically examined the distinct roles of patriotism versus nationalism. Blank and Schmidt (2003) examined the relations between nationalism versus patriotism and devaluation of foreigners in East and West Germans. Although their assessment of nationalism was quite similar to that of Kosterman and Feshbach (1989), their assessment of patriotism was somewhat different, focusing more on pride in democratic principles and constructive criticism of the nation. Their results revealed that in both East and West Germans, higher nationalism was associated with increased devaluation of foreigners, whereas higher patriotism was associated with decreased devaluation of foreigners.

Although additional studies have not specifically focused on the distinction between patriotism and nationalism, by looking at the items used to assess national attachment, we can loosely classify relevant studies as having assessed predominantly patriotism or nationalism. For example, in an analysis of national survey data in Canada, Berry and Kalin (1995) found a significant positive correlation between "Canadianism" and tolerance of ethnic immigrant groups. The "Canadianism" measure included items such as, "I am proud to be a Canadian." Thus, we would classify such a measure as primarily tapping patriotism. Similarly, in analysing Eurobarometer data collected in 15 Western European countries, Jackson, Brown, Brown, and Marks (2001) found a negative, though nonsignificant, relation between national pride and endorsement of sending immigrants back to their country of origin.

Overall, then, the results of these studies suggest that national attachment primarily assessed in terms of patriotism does not predict increased rejection of immigrants, and if anything, predicts increased acceptance of immigrants. In contrast, national attachment assessed in terms of nationalism is indeed predictive of increased rejection of immigrants.

What relations might we find for internationalism and support for a world government? Once again, although previous studies have not specifically examined the role of these variables in predicting attitudes toward immigrants and immigration, there are some relevant data that bear on this issue. In particular, in examining attitudes toward immigration to the United States in national survey data, Espenshade and Hempstead (1996) found that individuals who believed that the United States has a responsibility to provide assistance to other countries—perhaps a proxy measure of internationalism—had more favorable attitudes toward immigration to the United States. In addition, they found that individuals with a global perspective on economic issues—perhaps more related to support for a world government—also had more favorable attitudes toward immigration to the United States. Thus, internationalism and support for a world government seem to predict more positive attitudes toward immigration.

To explore the role of patriotism, nationalism, internationalism, and support for a world government in immigration attitudes more fully, we conducted a study in which we assessed these variables using the Kosterman and Feshbach (1989) measures described earlier, and examined their relations with attitudes toward immigrants and immigration. Participants were students at a Canadian university who were recruited for a study of Attitudes toward Social Issues. Embedded in a larger survey of social attitudes, we included the measures of patriotism, nationalism, internationalism, and support for a world government, adapted to apply to Canadian respondents. We also assessed attitudes toward immigrants and immigration, using several closed-ended and open-ended measures. Attitudes toward immigration to Canada were assessed on several bipolar measures (e.g., "Do you agree or disagree that immigration to Canada should be encouraged?"), which were averaged to produce a single attitude toward immigration score. Overall attitudes toward immigrants were assessed in a similar manner (e.g., "How positive or negative do you feel toward immigrants?"). In addition, we included open-ended measures to assess three important components of attitudes toward immigrants: stereotypes (beliefs about the characteristics of immigrants), symbolic beliefs (beliefs about the values of immigrants), and emotions (feelings toward immigrants; Esses, Haddock, & Zanna, 1993; Esses & Maio, 2002). Participants were asked to provide lists of the characteristics of immigrants, values of immigrants, and their own feelings toward immigrants. They were then asked to rate the valence of each response provided. For each measure, an average valence score was then determined (see Esses et al., 1993; Esses & Maio, 2002).

Based on the previous literature, we hypothesized that patriotism would be weakly related to attitudes toward immigrants and immigration, and would certainly not predict less favorable attitudes. In contrast, we expected that because nationalism involves a belief in the superiority of one's own nation and desire to protect group interests, nationalism would predict less favorable attitudes toward immigrants, who are not members of the national ingroup, and toward their immigration to one's nation. In addition, based on the previous literature, we hypothesized that internationalism, and perhaps to a lesser extent support for a world government, would predict more favorable attitudes toward immigrants and immigration.

Results supported our hypotheses (see Table 14.2). Patriotism was not significantly related to attitudes toward immigrants or immigration on any of our measures. In contrast, nationalism showed a significant negative relation with overall attitudes toward immigrants, perceived values of immigrants, and emotions toward immigrants. In addition, in regression analyses including both patriotism and nationalism, nationalism significantly accounted for unique variance in predicting overall attitudes toward immigrants and emotions toward immigrants, whereas patriotism had no unique role to play.

Internationalism showed strong effects in the opposite direction. That is, internationalism showed strong positive relations with attitudes toward immigrants and immigration on all of our measures. Support for a world government showed a similar pattern of findings, though the effects were consistently weaker. In regression analyses including both internationalism and support for a world government, internationalism significantly accounted for unique variance in predicting all of the criterion measures, whereas support for a world government had no unique role to play.

Thus, national attachment predicts negative attitudes toward immigrants only when that national attachment takes the form of nationalism. In addition, internationalism has a unique role to play in predicting positive attitudes toward immigrants and immigration.

The results regarding nationalism and patriotism are consistent with the findings of research by Mummendey et al. (2001) on the role of national identification and pride in predicting derogation of foreigners. Mummendey et al.

TABLE 14.2 Relations Between National and International Identity and Attitudes Toward Immigrants and Immigration

Measure	Attitudes toward immigrants	Immigrant stereotypes	Immigrant values	Immigrant emotions	Attitudes toward immigration
Patriotism	.07	−.02	−.11	−.07	.08
Nationalism	−.20*	−.17	−.20*	−.23*	−.08
Internationalism	.55**	.42**	.35**	.38**	.54**
World government	.17	.24*	.15	.21*	.21*

Note: $N = 97$–103. $*p < .05$, $**p < .001$ (two-tailed).

proposed that national identification and pride would only be associated with derogation of foreigners when they are based on intergroup comparisons with other nations. Such comparisons, they suggested, resemble nationalism in eliciting a sense of superiority to other nations, whereas national identification and pride without comparisons with other nations more closely resemble patriotism. In order to test their hypothesis, they used a priming procedure in which participants were asked to make a positive evaluation of their own nation through (a) comparisons with other nations (intergroup comparisons), (b) temporal comparisons with the past (temporal comparisons), or (c) without reference to a particular comparison standard (control). Across four studies conducted in Britain and Germany, Mummendey et al. found support for their hypothesis; overall, national identification and pride significantly predicted derogation of foreigners living in one's country only in the intergroup comparison condition. Linking these findings to nationalism and patriotism, they suggested that nationalism should predict rejection of foreigners, whereas patriotism should not, which is indeed what we obtained in our correlational study.

Thus far, we have examined the nature of national and international identification and have explored their relation to people's inclusive or exclusive attitudes toward immigrants. These relations have been examined correlationally. In the next section of this chapter we examine experimentally the relation between the salience of an inclusive national or international identity and attitudes toward immigrants and immigration. In particular, we investigate whether an emphasis on the inclusiveness of these identities can improve immigration attitudes.

IMPROVING ATTITUDES TOWARD IMMIGRANTS AND IMMIGRATION

The findings discussed in the previous section suggest that national and international identity may play an important role in determining attitudes toward immigrants and immigration. Positive attitudes toward immigrants and immigration are important for promoting social harmony and for avoiding unnecessary conflict over immigration. These favorable relations have obvious benefits for receiving nations. Thus, in this section we consider ways to promote positive attitudes toward immigrants and immigration among members of the receiving society, based on the findings regarding national and international identity discussed in the previous sections. In particular, we describe the research we have conducted using persuasive communications that target national and international identity in an attempt to improve attitudes toward immigrants and immigration.

Our approach builds on research on the Common Ingroup Identity Model (see Gaertner & Dovidio, 2000; Gaertner, Dovidio, Anastasio, Bachman, & Rust,

1993; Gaertner, Dovidio, Nier, Ward, & Banker, 1999), which has demonstrated the benefits of recategorizing ingroup and outgroup members as members of a more inclusive, superordinate group. Gaertner, Dovidio, and their colleagues propose that increasing the salience of a common ingroup identity (for example, by emphasizing membership in shared social categories or interdependence between groups) produces more positive attitudes toward former outgroup members through processes involving pro-ingroup bias. When members of a former outgroup begin to be considered part of the ingroup, the cognitive and motivational processes that contribute to ingroup favoritism become redirected to improve attitudes and foster more positive orientations to these newly defined members of the ingroup (see Gaertner & Dovidio, 2000). Moreover, as Gaertner et al. (1999; see also Chapter 11 in this volume) note, the development of a common ingroup does not require that each group abandon its former identity completely. People possess multiple identities (Brewer, 2000), which can be salient alternatively or simultaneously. It is therefore possible (and sometimes beneficial) for group members to maintain hyphenated, or dual, identities (see also Hornsey & Hogg, 2000).

Manipulation of National Identity

The Common Ingroup Identity approach fits well with the findings we discussed earlier regarding national identity and attachment. That is, as we discussed, previous research has demonstrated that a more inclusive definition of national identity—civic/cultural national identity—is related to more favorable responses to those who are trying to enter the ingroup, immigrants. Thus, promotion of a common national ingroup, including nonimmigrants and immigrants, may foster positive attitudes toward immigrants. In addition, a strong national attachment need not detract from these positive effects if such attachment takes the form of patriotism—positive affect for the national ingroup.

In our first study, we manipulated information about the national ingroup presented in persuasive messages, taking into account the factors that might promote positive attitudes toward immigrants and immigration. In particular, in the context of a study of Attitudes toward Social Issues, participants at a Canadian university were presented with one of four fictitious editorials about immigrants and immigration developed for use in this research: neutral, emphasizing common ethnic roots, emphasizing common national identity, or emphasizing both common ethnic roots and common national identity. Following some filler measures, we then assessed attitudes toward immigrants and immigration using the closed-ended scales described earlier.

In this study, we also assessed individual differences in Social Dominance Orientation (belief in inequality and support for hierarchies in society; Pratto, 1999; Sidanius & Pratto, 1999), because individuals high in social dominance orientation have been found to hold particularly unfavorable attitudes toward immigrants and immigration (Esses, Dovidio, Jackson, & Armstrong, 2001; Esses, Jackson, & Armstrong, 1998). In addition, Social Dominance Orientation has been found to be strongly related to nationalism in American samples (Pratto, Sidanius, Stallworth, & Malle, 1994) and in our Canadian sample described earlier, with less consistent relations with patriotism across these samples. Thus, we were especially interested in determining whether our persuasive messages would be effective in changing the attitudes of high social dominance oriented individuals.

The neutral editorial presented general and benign information about immigrants, such as vague demographic information and transportation used for immigration. For example, it stated that, "Some immigrants to Canada live in urban centers, whereas others take up residence in rural areas," and "Many are between the ages of 12 and 65 at the time of their arrival in Canada, with a relatively even balance of males and females." The remaining three editorials all focused on a common ingroup that includes immigrants and nonimmigrants, though in different ways. At the same time, they all promoted pride in Canada. The editorial emphasizing common ethnic roots was intended to form a connection between participants and immigrants through a common history of immigration. It reminded participants that immigrants of different ethnic backgrounds have a long history in Canada, and that they themselves could likely trace their own ethnic roots (though not the *same* ethnic roots for all people). For example, it stated, "Many ethnic groups in Canada today are descended from people who immigrated to Canada within the past century," and "Canada has a long tradition of immigration, as is evident from the large number of different ethnic groups in this country." In other words, this editorial suggested that most Canadians are "ethnics" of some sort. The editorial emphasizing common national identity similarly was intended to form a connection between immigrants and nonimmigrants, but through a common present and future, rather than past. To do so, it emphasized a united national identity that includes both native-born individuals and immigrants in what it means to be Canadian. For example, it stated, "Whether we immigrated to Canada yesterday or several generations ago, we are all united today in our common Canadian identity," and "Today's immigrants are tomorrow's Canadians." The final editorial included passages from both the common ethnic roots and the common national identity editorials. Thus, the latter three editorials all promoted a civic/cultural conception of national identity, based on nonimmigrants and immigrants being part of the national fabric and having a common allegiance to Canada.

In terms of attitudes toward immigrants, we found that across individuals high and low in social dominance orientation, the three editorials designed to induce a common, inclusive national identity produced more positive attitudes than did the neutral editorial. Because of our particular interest in changing the attitudes of people high in social dominance orientation, we investigated this

TABLE 14.3 Attitudes Toward Immigrants as a Function of Social Dominance Orientation and Manipulation of Perceived Common Ethnic Roots and Common National Identity

		Message		
Social dominance	Neutral	Common ethnic roots	Common national identity	Common roots and identity
Low	1.77_a	2.65_a	2.28_a	2.59_a
High	1.28_a	1.85_{ab}	2.12_b	2.47_b

Note: $N = 160$. Possible range $= -4$ to $+4$. Across rows, means not sharing a common subscript differ at $p < .05$ (Tukey's test).

effect further as a function of Social Dominance Orientation. As shown in Table 14.3, individuals low in social dominance orientation showed a tendency to respond more favorably to immigrants when a common identity was induced, though none of the individual comparisons to the neutral condition were statistically significant. Individuals high in social dominance orientation, however, showed significantly more favorable attitudes toward immigrants, compared to the neutral editorial condition, following the persuasive communications that emphasized a common national identity or both common ethnic roots and a common national identity. Thus, for individuals high in social dominance orientation who tend to hold especially unfavorable attitudes toward immigrants, it seems that promotion of a common civic/cultural national identity that includes immigrants in the national ingroup is effective for improving attitudes toward immigrants.

In contrast to the results for attitudes toward immigrants, no significant effects were found on attitudes toward immigration. Nevertheless, although our manipulations of the salience of an inclusive national identity did not directly produce more positive attitudes toward immigration, over time such attitudes might develop through familiarity and contact with immigrants, which are more likely to occur when favorable attitudes toward immigrants exist (see Gaertner et al., 1999). In addition, whereas our manipulation of national identity focused on the relation of other people to one's nation (i.e., who may be defined as an ingroup member), manipulations that emphasize common, superordinate connections across groups might promote more positive attitudes toward immigration, perhaps even more so than toward immigrants. We investigate this possibility in the next section.

Manipulation of International Identity

In our second study, we focused on internationalism, while also building on the promotion of a common ingroup, in this case, a common international ingroup.

In a similar context to the previous study, participants were presented with one of three editorials and, following some filler measures, were asked to indicate their attitudes toward immigrants and immigration on bipolar scales. Once again we also assessed individual differences in Social Dominance Orientation because of our particular concern with improving the attitudes of high social dominance oriented individuals. In addition, our correlational study described earlier found that Social Dominance Orientation was negatively related to internationalism.

The first editorial, the neutral editorial, once again provided general and benign information about immigrants. The second editorial focused on a common international identity and attempted to promote internationalism. For example, it stated that, "No longer can we consider ourselves to be separate nations. We are, in a very real sense, all part of a single large community, united as citizens of the world," and "The arbitrariness of where we are born will soon no longer determine our lifelong prospects." The final editorial focused on a dual national and international identity. While promoting the same international identity as the second editorial, it also suggested that national and international identities will soon coexist. For example, it stated that, "We will soon identify and operate as citizens of the world, as well as citizens of Canada," and "As we are moving in the direction of a Global Union, our Canadian and international identities will coexist."

In contrast to the previous study, in this study we found no significant effects on attitudes toward immigrants. In terms of attitudes toward immigration, however, we found a significant effect of the editorials for high social-dominance oriented individuals, but not for low social dominance oriented individuals (see Table 14.4). Individuals high in social dominance orientation showed significantly more favorable attitudes toward immigration following the persuasive communications that emphasized a common international identity

TABLE 14.4 Attitudes Toward Immigration as a Function of Social Dominance Orientation and Manipulation of Perceived International Identity

Social dominance	Message		
	Neutral	International identity	National and international identity
Low	1.86$_a$	1.77$_a$	1.35$_a$
High	−.65$_a$	.68$_b$	.53$_b$

Note: $N = 85$. Possible range = −4 to +4. Across rows, means not sharing a common subscript differ at $p < .05$ (Tukey's test).

or a dual national and international identity, compared to the neutral editorial condition. Thus, for individuals high in social dominance orientation who tend to hold especially unfavorable attitudes toward immigration, it seems that promotion of internationalism and an international identity, whether replacing national identity or combined with national identity, is effective for improving attitudes toward immigration.

Summary

Our goal was to determine whether manipulations of national and international identity could be used to promote more favorable attitudes toward immigrants and immigration, particularly among high social dominance oriented individuals. We found that the persuasive communications promoting social inclusiveness in the form of a common national identity that included nonnative born individuals in the national ingroup improved attitudes toward *immigrants*, particularly among high social dominance oriented individuals. In addition, we found that the persuasive communications promoting internationalism and a common international identity improved attitudes toward *immigration*, particularly among high social dominance oriented individuals. In retrospect, it is perhaps not surprising that the common national identity messages were more effective in improving attitudes toward immigrants than attitudes toward immigration because they specifically focused on accepting immigrants as part of the national ingroup. In contrast, the common international identity messages implied that national boundaries are unimportant and thus had their impact on attitudes toward immigration, rather than attitudes toward immigrants. In combination, these two types of messages would likely be effective in promoting both favorable attitudes toward immigrants and immigration.

IMPLICATIONS AND CONCLUSIONS

At a theoretical level, the findings regarding patriotism and nationalism support the basic tenet of Social Identity Theory (Tajfel & Turner, 1979) that the motivation to achieve positive group distinctiveness may lead to derogation of outgroups. In particular, when national attachment takes the form of nationalism—belief in the superiority of one's nation over others—increased attachment is associated with unfavorable attitudes toward immigrants. However, when national attachment involves positive affect toward one's nation, patriotism, without a necessary belief in national superiority, no relation with attitudes toward immigrants is evident. This suggests that positive ingroup identity may result from favorable comparisons with other groups, including outgroup derogation, but also suggests that such comparisons are not necessary in order to evaluate one's own group in a positive light (see also Brewer, 2001).

The research also supports the Common Ingroup Identity Model (see Gaertner & Dovidio, 2000; Gaertner et al., 1993; Gaertner et al., 1999) in finding that more inclusive definitions of national identity—civic/cultural—and manipulations designed to promote inclusion of immigrants in the national ingroup both promote more favorable attitudes toward immigrants. Thus, the salience of a common ingroup identity, emphasizing membership in a shared national category and interdependence between nonimmigrants and immigrants, produces more positive attitudes toward immigrants. As Gaertner et al. (1999) have suggested, however, it is not the case that a common national ingroup requires that immigrants necessarily give up their former ethnic identity in order to be perceived in a positive light. Rather, as our experiment on national identity demonstrated, a dual identity in which ethnic groups maintain their ethnic identity while joining in a common national identity is also of benefit (see Hornsey & Hogg, 2000). The findings regarding internationalism also support the notion that the salience of a shared international category and interdependence between nations may have positive effects on immigration attitudes, and that such effects do not require that national identity be abandoned.

The findings described in this chapter also provide insight into cross-national differences in immigration attitudes and policy, historical trends in immigration attitudes and policy, and strategies for promoting more favorable attitudes.

There are important cross-national differences in how national identity is defined which may help to explain parallel differences in immigration attitudes and policy. For example, countries such as Germany that have favored a relatively strict nativist national identity would be expected to have correspondingly more restrictive immigration policies and generally unfavorable attitudes toward immigrants. In contrast, countries such as Canada that have favored civic/cultural definitions of national identity would be expected to have more open immigration policies and promote favorable attitudes toward immigrants. Overall, such differences do seem to be evident, though a more rigorous examination of this issue is warranted. In these different contexts, patriotism may also have a different role to play, with patriotism in a more nativist national context perhaps leading to rejection of immigrants and patriotism in a more civic/cultural national context potentially having no or positive effects on acceptance of immigrants. Thus, examination of the interaction between national identity and attachment would also be of interest.

Over time, too, there may be considerable variation in national identity and attachment that may, in turn, predict trends in immigration attitudes and policy. As discussed earlier, during times of national crisis and threat there seems to be an increase in nativist sentiment and nationalism. Relatedly, large scale immigration, particularly from new and unfamiliar source countries, can be directly associated with increased concern over national self-definition and nativist sentiments (e.g., Feagin, 1997; Jaret, 1999). In addition, nativist national identity may reinforce perceptions of threat from immigrants (e.g., Jones, 1997, 1999; Maddens et al., 2000; Pakulski & Tranter, 2000), perhaps because nativist identity may be tied to a belief that one's interests are rooted in the group. During times of national crisis and threat, then, one would expect that anti-immigrant attitudes and support for more restrictive immigration policies would be evident, and this does indeed seem to be the case (see Jaret, 1999, for an analysis of anti-immigrant attitudes in the United States in the late 1800s and 1900s). It is important to note, however, that in terms of both crossnational comparisons and analyses of trends over time, it is likely that forms of national identity/attachment and immigration attitudes may be mutually reinforcing. That is, more exclusionary national identity and attachment may both cause and result from unfavorable immigration attitudes.

In addition to contributing to a more complete understanding of immigration attitudes, the research has important implications for promoting more favorable attitudes. First, the findings suggest that instilling national pride in members of a nation need not come at the expense of excluding newcomers. Rather, only when patriotism moves into nationalism and when national identity is defined at a nativist level do such negative consequences seem to occur. This suggests that national programs designed to promote a healthy sense of national identity would do well to focus on national pride and attachment to the national ingroup, without utilizing comparisons with other nations (see also Mummendey et al., 2001). In order to promote favorable attitudes toward immigrants, such programs might also take advantage of the findings suggesting that promotion of a common national identity, including both nonimmigrants and immigrants in the national ingroup, fosters more favorable attitudes toward immigrants, particularly among those who show the strongest tendency to generally derogate immigrants, individuals high in social dominance orientation.

Programs designed to foster acceptance of immigration and immigrants might also focus on promoting an internationalist perspective. By training members of a nation, particularly children, to be concerned about the welfare of all people, regardless of national origins, and to think of themselves as members of an international community, we will not only foster increased tolerance in general, but more specifically, openness to immigration and immigrants. As mentioned previously, this does not need to come at the expense of national attachment and pride. Rather, positive forms of national attachment and an international perspective may coexist, and together move us in the direction of a truly harmonious and open society.

REFERENCES

Bar-Tal, D., & Staub, E. (1997). Introduction: Patriotism: Its scope and meaning. In D. Bar-Tal & E. Staub (Eds.), *Patriotism in the lives of individuals and nations* (pp. 1–19). Chicago: Nelson Hall.

Berry, J. W., & Kalin, R. (1995). Multicultural and ethnic attitudes in Canada: An overview of the 1991 national survey. *Canadian Journal of Behavioural Science, 27*, 301–320.

Billiet, J., Maddens, B., & Beerten, R. (2003). National identity and attitude toward foreigners in a multinational state: A replication. *Political Psychology, 24*, 241–257.

Blank, T., & Schmidt, P. (2003). National identity in Germany: Nationalism or patriotism? An empirical test with representative data. *Political Psychology, 24*, 289–312.

Branscombe, N. R., & Wann, D. L. (1994). Collective self-esteem consequences of outgroup derogation when a valued social identity is on trial. *European Journal of Social Psychology, 24*, 641–657.

Brewer, M. B. (1999). The psychology of prejudice: Ingroup love or outgroup hate? *Journal of Social Issues, 55*, 429–444.

Brewer, M. B. (2000). Reducing prejudice through cross-categorization: Effects of multiple social identities. In S. Oskamp (Ed.), *Reducing prejudice and discrimination* (pp. 165–183). Hillsdale, NJ: Erlbaum.

Brewer, M. B. (2001). Ingroup identification and intergroup conflict: When does ingroup love become outgroup hate? In R. D. Ashmore, L. Jussim, & D. Wilder (Eds.), *Social identity, intergroup conflict, and conflict reduction. Rutgers series on self and social identity, Vol. 3* (pp. 17–41). London, UK: Oxford University Press.

Citrin, J., Reingold, B., & Green, D. P. (1990). American identity and the politics of ethnic change. *Journal of Politics, 52*, 1124–1154.

Condor, S. (2001). Commentary: Nations and nationalisms: particular cases and impossible myths. *British Journal of Social Psychology, 40*, 177–182.

Diaz-Veizades, J., Widaman, K. F., Little, T. D., & Gibbs, K. W. (1995). The measurement and structure of human rights attitudes. *The Journal of Social Psychology, 135*, 313–328.

Doosje, B., & Ellemers, N. (1997). Stereotyping under threat: The role of group identification. In R. Spears, P. J. Oakes, N. Ellemers, & S. A. Haslam (Eds.), *The social psychology of stereotyping and group life* (pp. 257–272). Malden, MA: Blackwell.

Dovidio, J. F., & Esses, V. M. (2001). Immigrants and immigration: Advancing the psychological perspective. In V. M. Esses, J. F. Dovidio, & K. L. Dion (Eds.), *Immigrants and immigration. Journal of Social Issues, 57*, 375–387.

Espenshade, T. J., & Hempstead, K. (1996). Contemporary American attitudes toward U.S. immigration. *International Migration Review, 30*, 535–570.

Esses, V. M., Dovidio, J. F., & Hodson, G. (2002). Public attitudes toward immigration in the United States and Canada in response to the September 11, 2001 "Attack on America." *Analyses of Social Issues and Public Policy, 2*, 69–85.

Esses, V. M., Dovidio, J. F., Jackson, L. M., & Armstrong, T. L. (2001). The immigration dilemma: The role of perceived group competition, ethnic prejudice, and national identity. In V. M. Esses, J. F. Dovidio, & K. L. Dion (Eds.), *Immigrants and immigration. Journal of Social Issues, 57*, 389–412.

Esses, V. M., Haddock, G., & Zanna, M. P. (1993). Values, stereotypes, and emotions as determinants of intergroup attitudes. In D. M. Mackie & D. L. Hamilton (Eds.), *Affect, cognition and stereotyping: Interactive processes in group perception* (pp. 137–166). San Diego: Academic Press.

Esses, V. M., Jackson, L. M., & Armstrong, T. L. (1998). Intergroup competition and attitudes toward immigrants and immigration: An instrumental model of group conflict. *Journal of Social Issues, 54,* 699–724.

Esses, V. M., & Maio, G. R. (2002). Expanding the assessment of attitude components and structure: The benefits of open-ended measures. In W. Stroebe & M. Hewstone (Eds.), *European review of social psychology: 12* (pp. 71–101). Chichester, UK: John Wiley.

Feagin, J. R. (1997). Old poison in new bottles: The deep roots of modern nativism. In J. F. Perea (Ed.), *Immigrants out! The new nativism and the anti-immigrant impulse in the United States.* New York: New York University Press.

Feshbach, S. (1990). Psychology, human violence, and the search for peace: Issues in science and social values. *Journal of Social Issues, 46,* 183–198.

Feshbach, S. (1994). Nationalism, patriotism, and aggression: A clarification of functional differences. In L.R. Huesmann (Ed.), *Aggressive behavior: Current perspectives* (pp. 275–291). New York: Plenum.

Feshbach, S., & Sakano, N. (1997). The structure and correlates of attitudes toward one's nation in samples of United States and Japanese college students: A comparative study. In D. Bar-Tal & E. Staub (Eds.), *Patriotism in the lives of individuals and nations* (pp. 91–107). Chicago: Nelson Hall.

Gagnon A., & Bourhis, R. Y. (1996). Discrimination in the minimal group paradigm: Social identity or self-interest? *Personality and Social Psychology Bulletin, 22,* 1289–1301.

Gaertner, S. L., & Dovidio, J. F. (2000). *Reducing intergroup bias: The Common Ingroup Identity Model.* New York: Psychology Press.

Gaertner, S., Dovidio, J. F., Anastasio, P. A., Bachman, B. A., & Rust, M. C. (1993). The common ingroup identity model: Recategorization and the reduction of intergroup bias. In W. Stroebe & M. Hewstone (Eds.), *European review of social psychology: 4* (pp. 1–26). Chichester, UK: John Wiley.

Gaertner, S., Dovidio, J. F., Nier, J. A., Ward, C. M., & Banker, B. S. (1999). Across cultural divides: The value of a superordinate identity. In D. A. Prentice & D. T. Miller (Eds.), *Cultural divides: Understanding and overcoming group conflict* (pp. 173–212). New York: Russell Sage.

Greenberg, J., Solomon, S., & Pyszczynski, T. (1997). Terror management theory of self-esteem and cultural worldviews: Empirical assessments and cultural refinements. In M. P. Zanna (Ed.), *Advances in experimental social psychology* (Vol. 29, pp. 61–139). Orlando, FL: Academic Press.

Hornsey, M. J., & Hogg, M. A. (2000). Intergroup similarity and subgroup relations: Some implications for assimilation. *Personality and Social Psychology Bulletin, 26,* 948–958.

Hurwitz, J., & Peffley, M. (1999). International attitudes. In J. P. Robinson, P. R. Shaver, & L. S. Wrightsman (Eds.), *Measures of political attitudes* (pp. 533–590). San Diego: Academic Press.

Jackson, J. S., Brown, K. T., Brown, T. N., & Marks, B. (2001). Contemporary immigration policy orientations among dominant-group members in Western Europe. In V. M. Esses, J. F. Dovidio, & K. L. Dion (Eds.), *Immigrants and immigration. Journal of Social Issues, 57,* 431–456.

Jaret, C. (1999). Troubled by newcomers: Anti-immigrant attitudes and action during two eras of mass immigration to the United States. *Journal of American Ethnic History*, 18 (3), 9–39.

Jones, F. L. (1997). Ethnic diversity and national identity. *Australian and New Zealand Journal of Sociology, 33*, 285–305.

Jones, F. L. (1999). *Diversities of National Identity in a Multicultural Society: The Australian Case*. Revision of paper presented at the 14th World Congress of Sociology, Montreal, Canada.

Kosterman, R., & Feshbach, S. (1989). Toward a measure of patriotic and nationalistic attitudes. *Political Psychology, 10*, 257–274.

Luhtanen, R., & Crocker, J. (1992). A collective self-esteem scale: Self-evaluation of one's social identity. *Personality and Social Psychology Bulletin, 18*, 302–318.

Maddens, B., Billiet, J., & Beerten, R. (2000). National identity and the attitude toward foreigners in multi-national states: the case of Belgium. *Journal of Ethnic and Migration Studies, 26*, 45–60.

Mummendey, A., Klink, A., & Brown, R. (2001). Nationalism and patriotism: National identification and out-group rejection. *British Journal of Social Psychology, 40*, 159–171.

Pakulski, J., & Tranter, B. (2000). Civic, national and denizen identity in Australia. *Journal of Sociology, 36*, 205–222.

Perreault, S., & Bourhis R. Y. (1999). Ethnocentrism, social identification, and discrimination. *Personality and Social Psychology Bulletin 25*, 92–103.

Pratto, F. (1999). The puzzle of continuing group inequality: Piecing together psychological, social, and cultural forces in social dominance theory. In M. P. Zanna (Ed.), *Advances in experimental social psychology* (Vol. 31, pp. 191–263). San Diego: Academic Press.

Pratto, F., Sidanius, J., Stallworth, L. M., & Malle, B. F. (1994). Social dominance orientation: A personality variable predicting social and political attitudes. *Journal of Personality and Social Psychology, 67*, 741–763.

Rothgerber, H. (1997). External intergroup threat as an antecedent to perceptions in in-group and out-group homogeneity. *Journal of Personality and Social Psychology, 73*, 1206–1212.

Sidanius, J., & Pratto, F. (1999). *Social dominance: An intergroup theory of social hierarchy and oppression*. New York: Cambridge University Press.

Stephan, W. G., & Stephan, C. W. (2000). An integrated threat theory of prejudice. In S. Oskamp (Ed.), *Claremont symposium on applied social psychology* (pp. 23–46). Hillsdale, NJ: Erlbaum.

Tajfel, H., & Turner, J. C. (1979). An integrative theory of intergroup conflict. In W. G. Austin & S. Worchel (Eds.), *The social psychology of intergroup relations* (pp. 33–48). Monterey, CA: Brooks/Cole.

Turner, J. C., Hogg, M. A., Oakes, P. J., Reicher, S. D., & Wetherell, M. S. (1987). *Rediscovering the social group: A self-categorization theory*. Oxford, UK: Basil Blackwell.

Worchel, S., & Coutant, D. (1997). The tangled web of loyalty: Nationalism, patriotism, and ethnocentrism. In D. Bar-Tal & E. Staub (Eds.), *Patriotism in the lives of individuals and nations* (pp. 190–210). Chicago: Nelson Hall.

Author Index

Abrahams, D., 115
Abrams, D., 16, 67, 93, 97, 99, 102–103, 148, 153, 162, 164–172, 174–179, 181–182, 195–196, 198, 247, 296
Abramson, L., 118
Adair, R.K., 29, 35–36
Adelson, J., 224, 227
Adler, P., 153–154
Adler, P.A., 153–154
Adorno, T.W., 216
Agarie, N., 31
Ainsworth, M.D., 28
Akerstrom, M., 153
Albrecht, S., 116, 123
Allen, I.L., 293, 295
Allen, V., 163
Allen, V.L., 149, 154–155
Alley, T.R., 303
Allison, K.W., 71
Allport, G.W., 70, 72, 247–248, 251, 271–272, 297
Ambady, N., 102
Amorso, D.M., 216, 218, 222
Anastasio, P.A., 246, 248, 253, 255, 327–328, 333
Anderson, N.B., 71
Anderson, S.K., 303
Andrews, D.L., 54
Annandale, N., 203
Aquino, K.F., 18
Archer, D., 65, 236
Armstead, C.A., 119
Armstrong, T.L., 329
Aron, A., 113–115, 194, 275, 278–279, 283
Aron, E.N., 113–115, 278
Aronson, E., 151, 260
Aronson, J., 71, 73, 75
Aronson, V., 115
Arroyo, C.G., 123
Asch, S., 163, 232
Asher, S.R., 33, 35
Asher, T., 69

Ashford, S.J., 142
Ashforth, B.E., 142, 148–150, 156–157
Askari, N.H., 90
Associated Press, 294
Austin, J.T., 282
Axelrod, R., 28

Bachman, B.A., 246, 248, 253, 255–256, 327–328, 333
Banaji, M.R., 68
Bandura, A., 113
Banker, B.S., 253, 256, 328, 330, 333
Banks, M., 220, 295
Barash, D.P., 28
Bargh, J.A., 77
Barker, R.G., 153, 235
Barnes, G., 234
Barnett, W.S., 235
Baron, R., 272
Baron, R.A., 31
Bar-Tal, D., 321
Bartels, J.M., 30, 33
Bat-Chava, Y., 123
Bates, I., 220
Batson, C.D., 275
Batts, D., 269
Baumann, D.J., 33
Baumeister, R.F., 27–30, 32–33, 35–37, 39–40, 47–49, 52–56, 59, 63–64, 70, 76, 90, 92, 115, 120–122, 148
Becker, H.S., 2
Beerten, R., 323–324, 323, 334
Beike, D.R., 194
Bellour, F., 96
Ben Brika, J., 274
Ben-Ari, R., 295
Benson, D., 267
Berkowitz, L., 163
Berreuta-Clement, J.R., 235
Berry, J.W., 250–251, 324
Bettelheim, B., 302
Beyer, J.A., 29

Beyer, J.M., 149, 153–154
Biehl, J.K., 54
Bienvenue, R.M., 294
Biernat, M.T., 168, 295
Bigler, R.S., 310
Billiet, J., 323–324, 334
Billig, M.G., 100
Billings, L.S., 168
Black, D., 213, 228
Blackstone, T., 65
Blader, S.L., 21, 193
Blank, T., 324
Blascovich, J., 22, 166
Blevins, T., 47, 90
Bloom, B.L., 35
Boal, F.W., 269–271, 274, 284
Bobo, L., 20
Bodenhausen, G.V., 168
Bonner B.L., 93–95, 97, 102, 105, 107
Borden, R.J., 198
Bosma, H., 303
Bourassa, L., 150
Bourguignon, D., 96, 173
Bourhis, R.Y., 115, 197, 318
Bowlby, J., 28, 64, 91
Bown, N.J., 93, 99, 162, 168, 174–178, 181, 196
Bowyer Bell, J., 266
Box, S., 224
Boyanowsky, E., 163
Boyd, C., 295
Boyle, K., 269
Braithwaite, J., 232, 234
Branscombe, N.R., 67, 76, 89, 96, 99, 100–101, 107, 116, 119–120, 123, 125, 168, 172, 202, 204, 318
Brazil, D.M., 247
Breakwell, G., 220
Brehm, J., 275
Brewer, M.B., 33, 50, 90, 92, 99–100, 102–104, 107, 120, 122, 162, 164, 193–194, 246, 248, 250, 254, 272, 318, 323, 328, 332
Briar, S., 230
Brickman, P., 80
Brown, D., 220, 224
Brown, K.T., 324
Brown, R.J., 31, 165–166, 168, 234, 251, 254, 271–273, 275, 277, 318, 321, 326–327, 334
Brown, T.N., 324
Brownell, K.D., 71
Buckley, K., 31, 40
Buhrmester, D., 115

Bukowski, W.M., 29, 33
Bundy, R.P., 100
Burger, J.M., 198
Burris, C.T., 95
Burton, F., 267
Burwen, L., 216
Bushman, B.J., 39
Buss, D.M., 28
Butemeyer, J., 247
Buunk, B.P., 127, 251, 256
Bynner, J., 220

Cacho, J., 30, 32
Cadinu, M.R., 165
Cairns, D., 31
Cairns, E., 266–274, 276–277, 280–284
Cameron, L., 170–171
Campbell, D.T., 163, 216
Campbell, W.K., 30, 39
Cannon, W.B., 154
Caporael, L.R., 162
Capozza, D., 96
Carmichael, P., 271, 283
Carroll, J.L., 220, 228
Carter, A.A., 294
Cartwright, D., 70
Carver, C., 114
Carver, M.D., 90
Case, T.I., 57–58
Castano, E., 96, 99, 166, 172–173
Casto, R., 118
Catanese, K.R., 30, 36, 40
Cecil, C.L., 247
Charitides, L., 226
Charlesworth, R., 33
Chavira, V., 123
Chavous, T.M., 123
Cheek, J.M., 28
Chein, I., 294
Cheung, C.K.T., 29, 33, 40, 48, 50, 52, 90, 122
Cheung, S., 120–121
Children's Literature Review Board, 309
Chiriboga, D.A., 125–127
Choi, H.-S., 138
Choi, W., 29, 33, 40, 48, 50, 90, 122
Chokel, J.T., 126
Christian, J.N., 168
Cialdini, R.B., 33, 198
Ciarocco, N.J., 30, 33, 121
Cihangir, S., 193

Cini, M.A., 90, 138
Citrin, J., 317–318
Citron, A.F., 294
Clark, J.P., 218
Clark, R., 71
Clark, V.R., 71
Clement, R.W., 165
Coates, D., 80
Coats, S., 91
Cochrane, S., 182
Codol, J-P., 92
Cohen, L.L., 119
Cohn, E., 80
Coie, J.D., 29, 33
Cole, S.W., 74
Colella, A., 137
Coleman J.M., 93–95, 97, 102, 105, 107
Coleman, H.L.K., 255, 258
Coleman, J., 168, 172
Condor, S., 275, 320
Cooley, C.H., 148
Cooper, M.L., 73–74
Copper, C., 258
Corfield, V.K., 226
Corneille, O., 163
Cornell, J.C., 271, 283
Cornwell, B., 80
Cosmides, L., 115
Coull, A., 172–173
Coutant, D., 317, 321
Cox, M., 118, 122
Cox, R., 118, 122
Cozzarelli, C., 73–74
Craig, J., 270, 276–277
Craighead, W.E., 51
Crandall, C.S., 66, 79
Crocker, J., 64–65, 67–68, 71–72, 75–76, 78, 80, 95, 102, 119, 321
Croker, V., 53, 56
Cropanzano, R., 37
Cross, J., 119
Cruikshank, M., 53, 56
Cuervo, D., 30, 33
Cullen, J.L., 218
Currey, D.P., 57
Czajka, J.A., 37

Dalton, B., 57
Danziger, K., 223
Darby, J., 268–269, 271, 267, 269
Darley, J., 192

Darley, J.M., 226
Davis, A., 64
Davis, J., 163
Davis, M.H., 275
Dawson, K., 275
Day, E.A., 247
Dazzi, C., 96
de Nicholas, M.E., 198
Deci, E.L., 113, 118
Degoey, P., 76
DeLongis, A., 35
Demetriou, A., 226
Demoulin, S., 65, 162, 167
Dennis, J., 215–217
Desch, L.W., 303
Desforges, D.M., 273
Devine, P.G., 166, 168, 272
Dhavale, D., 122
Diaz-Loving, R., 272
Diaz-Veizades, J., 322–323
Diener, E., 71
Diener, M., 71
Dion, K.K., 74–75
Dion, K.L., 123
Dishion, T., 230
Dittes, J.E., 52, 116, 125
Dodge, K.A., 33
Doherty, P., 269
Doosjc, B., 16, 101, 107, 202, 318
Dougill, M., 93, 99, 175–177
Dovidio, J.F., 246–248, 251–259, 318–319, 327–330, 333
Downey, G., 64
Downey, K.T., 71
Downs, D.L., 28, 55, 90
Duck, J.M., 179
Dunn, S., 269–270, 274, 282–283
Duran, A., 272
Durkheim, E., 2, 35
Durkin, D., 214
Dutton, D.G., 115
Dweck C.S., 118

Easton, D., 215–217
Ebaugh, H.R.F., 142, 157
Eccles, J.S., 123
Eisenberg, N., 220, 228
Eisminger, S., 293
Ellemers, N., 16, 72, 101, 107, 115, 164, 202, 318
Elliot, K., 120–121

Emler, N., 194, 217–218, 220–229, 231–233
Enge, R.S., 151
Enright, R.D., 276
Ensari, N., 273
Epstein, A.S., 235
Erdley, C.A., 33
Ericson, E.E., 293, 310
Erikson, E.H., 70
Espenshade, T.J., 325
Esses, V.M., 275, 318–319, 325, 329
Etcoff, N.L., 296
Eurich-Fulcer, R., 272
Exline, J.J., 33
Ezrakhovich, A., 120–121

Fahey, J.L., 74
Faludi, S., 152
Farina, A., 64, 67, 72, 74
Farren, S., 269
Farrington, D.P., 220, 222, 236
Faulkner, S.J., 52
Fay, M.T., 268
Feagin, J.R., 310, 319, 333
Feather, N.T., 198, 202
Feeney, B., 268
Feldman, D.C., 151
Fenigstein, A., 52
Fenn, C.B., 127
Ferguson, D.L., 276
Ferguson, M.J., 119
Feshbach, S., 106, 317–318, 320–325,
Festinger, L., 163, 192
Fielding, K.S., 179, 192, 202–203
Finkel, E.J., 247
Fischer, G.W., 296, 309
Fischer, K., 75
Fiske, S.T., 164, 246, 248, 273, 296
Fitzgerald, L.F., 75
Flament, C., 100
Flesch, R., 304–305
Foels, R., 307
Folkman, S., 35
Ford, C.E., 198
Forsyth, D.R., 166
Foster-Fishman, P.G., 193
Frable, D.E., 65, 76–77
Fraley, B., 114
Francis, L.J., 268
Franke, R., 73
Frazier, S., 247
Freedman, S., 276

Freeman, S., 198
Frenkel-Brunswik, E., 216
Freud, S., 33, 35
Fried, M., 296
Friedman, M.A., 71
Fromkin, H.L., 92
Fry, P.S., 226
Fukuyama, F., 29
Fulk, J., 37
Fuquay, J., 294
Furth, H.G., 217

Gaertner, L., 79
Gaertner, S.L., 246–248, 251–257, 259, 319, 327–328, 330, 333
Gagnon, A., 318
Gallagher, A.M., 269–271, 282
Gallgher, T., 268
Garbarino, J., 29
Gardner, W., 50
Gardner, W.L., 33, 90, 102, 122
Garfinkel, H., 149, 154
Garst, E., 275
Gassin, E.A., 276
Gaunt, R., 65, 162, 167
Gecas, V., 113
Geller, D.M., 51, 118, 120–121
Gerard, H.B., 151
Gergen, K.J., 64
Gerton, J., 255, 258
Gest, S.D., 33
Gibbons, J., 119
Gibbs, K.W., 322–323
Gibson, H.B., 218
Gilbert, D.T., 197, 200
Giller, H., 223
Glaser, B.G., 149
Glazer, J.A., 33
Goffman, E., 2, 64–65, 69, 72, 74
Gold, L.J., 226
Gooden, M.P., 254
Goodstein, L., 51, 118, 120–121
Goodwin, J.S., 35
Gorden, C., 119
Gottman, J.M., 51
Gould, S.J., 303
Govan, C.L., 53, 56–58
Graen, G.B., 197
Graetz, K., 79
Graham-Bermann, S.A., 33
Gramzow, R.H., 73–74

Granic, I., 230
Grauerholz, E., 302, 309
Graumann, C.F., 294, 297
Green, B., 224
Green, D.P., 317–318
Greenberg, E., 215, 218, 220
Greenberg, J., 68, 70, 114, 294–295, 317
Greenland, K., 272
Greenlee, A., 303
Greenwald, A.G., 58
Griffiths, C.T., 234
Groenewoud, J.T., 273
Gross, S., 167
Gross, T.E., 303
Gruter, M., 51

Haber, J., 117
Hadden, T., 269
Haddock, G., 275, 325
Hagendoorn, L., 274
Hains, S.C., 163, 179, 247
Hall, N.E., 218
Hamberger, J., 274–276
Hamilton, A., 269
Hamilton, D.L., 19, 163
Hamilton, W.D., 28
Hamlet, M.A., 198
Hansell, S., 222
Harano, R.M., 29
Harbison, J., 268
Harding, J., 294
Hargreaves, D.H., 222
Haritos-Fatouros, M., 150
Harrington, D.M., 29
Harris, D.B., 303
Harris, J., 269
Harris, R., 274
Hart, D., 247
Hartup, W.W., 33
Harvey, J., 125
Harvey, R.D., 76, 119, 123
Harwood, J., 272
Haslam, S.A., 93, 96–97, 164, 175–176, 179–180, 278
Hastings, R., 117
Hastorf, A.H., 64, 72, 74
Hatfield, E., 115
Haupt, A.L., 126
Hautaluoma, J.E., 151
Hayes, B.C., 269, 284
Hazen, B.S., 293

Heaven, P., 220
Hempstead, K., 325
Henry, S., 278
Henson, M., 93, 99, 174–178, 181, 196
Herek, G.M., 66, 71
Hess, R.D., 214–216
Hetherington, E.M., 118, 122
Hewstone, M., 161, 195, 234, 250–251, 254, 256, 261, 266, 269–277, 279–281, 283–284
Higgins, E.T., 22, 113
Hilton, J.L., 226
Hinsz, V.B., 193
Hirschfeld, L.A., 295
Hirschi, T., 222
Hodges, J.A., 198
Hodson, G., 318
Hoey, S., 76–77
Hogan, R., 28, 33
Hogg, M.A., 16, 67, 76, 92, 97, 99, 102, 148, 153, 163–168, 179, 182, 192–193, 195–199, 203, 246–247, 318, 328, 333
Holgate, S., 47, 90
Holland, J., 266
Hollander, E.P., 153, 179
Holtz, R., 167
Homish, L., 229
Hong, G., 57
Hopkins, N., 194–195, 197, 234
Hornsey, M.J., 192–193, 328, 333
Houlette, M., 252
Howard, J.M., 247
Howard, R., 163
Howe, K., 303
Howlett, K., 231
Hoyle, R.H., 57
Hu, L.T., 250
Huddy, L., 296
Hughes, J., 269, 271, 283
Hunt, W.C., 35
Hunter, J., 231
Huo, Y.J., 255
Hurwitz, J., 321–322
Hutchison, P., 162, 168, 172–173
Hyers, L.L., 119

Iannaccone, L.R., 154
Insko, C.A., 52, 57, 247
Islam, M.R., 256, 272
Ivanov, P., 293
Iverson, A., 115
Izmirlieva, V., 293

Jackson, J., 274
Jackson, J.M., 125
Jackson, J.S., 324
Jackson, L.M., 95, 329
Jacobs, A., 150
Jaggi V., 231
Jahoda, G., 68
James, W., 48–49
Jamieson, L., 220
Janda, L., 37
Janis, I.L., 163, 182
Jaret, C., 317–319, 333–334
Jencks, C., 222–223
Jenkins, R., 267
Jerrems, A., 120–121
Jetten, J., 19, 67, 76, 98, 101, 107, 193
Joesten, J., 293
Johnson, B., 247
Johnson, C., 258, 294–296, 298, 300
Johnson, D.W., 260, 303
Johnson, J.D., 257
Johnson, K.M., 257
Johnson, R.T., 260
Jolles, J., 303
Jones, E.E., 64, 72, 74, 101
Jones, F.L., 319–321, 323–324, 334
Jones, J.M., 260
Jones, W.H., 28, 90
Jöreskog, K.J., 277
Jost, J.T., 68
Judd, C.M., 103–104, 163, 296

Kafati, G., 251, 254, 257, 259
Kahneman, D., 167
Kaiser, C.R., 66, 73, 78, 123
Kaldegg, G., 304
Kalin, R., 324
Kameda, M., 31
Kameda, T., 193
Kang, M., 275
Kanter, R.M., 150, 295
Karuza, J.Jr., 80
Katovich, M.A., 151
Keane, M.C., 271, 274, 284
Kedem, P., 295
Kelley, H.H., 116, 125
Kelly, D.H., 222
Kelters, S., 268
Kemeny, M.E., 74
Kendrick, D.T., 33
Kenny, D.A., 115, 272

Kerr, A., 120–121
Key, C.R., 35
Keys, C.B., 193
Khleif, B.B., 295, 297
Kibler, J.L., 166
Kidder, L., 80
Kiecolt, K.J., 274
Kieffer, S.C., 303
Kimball, W.H., 51
Kirkland, S.L., 294–295
Kirkpatrick, L.A., 31
Klandermans, B., 20
Klein, G., 303
Klink, A., 318, 321, 326–327, 334
Knox, C., 269, 283
Ko, T., 120
Kohen, J.A., 117, 125
Kohlberg, L., 224
Kosterman, R., 317–318, 320–325
Kowalski, R.M., 29, 39, 47–48, 54, 90
Kozar, R., 247
Krueger, J., 165
Kruglanski, A.W., 166
Kuethe, J.L., 302
Kulik, J.A., 31
Kulla, C., 296
Kunda, Z., 165
Kurz, E., 303
Kurzban, R., 5, 66–67, 69, 162

Ladd, G.W., 33
LaFromboise, T., 255, 258
Lam, A., 53, 56
Lanieck, D.L., 273
Larson, J.R.Jr., 193
Lassegard, M.-A., 198
Laub, J.H., 29, 232
Lawler, K.A., 119
Lazarus, R.S., 35
Leader, T., 307
Leary, M.R., 5, 27–29, 31–32, 39–40, 47–49, 52, 54–55, 63–64, 66–67, 69, 70, 72–73, 76, 90, 92, 107, 115, 118, 120–121, 126, 148, 162
Leekam, S.R., 171
Leemans, V., 173
Leggett, E.L., 118
Leith, K.P., 36
Lemaine, G., 274
Lemert, E.M., 2
Lemonick, M.D., 54

Leonard, L., 152
Leventhal, G.S., 225
Levin, S., 106, 272
Levine, J.M., 90, 137–138, 141, 143, 148, 152, 154–157, 163, 192
Levine, M., 231
Levinson, D.J., 216
Levy, K., 220
Levy-Weiner, N., 295
Lewicki, R.J., 150
Lewis, A., 163
Lewis, C.A., 266
Lewis, M., 151–152
Leyens, J-P., 65, 96, 162, 166–168, 172, 195
Lichter, J.H., 303
Lickona, T., 216
Liebkind, K., 278
Liebman, R.C., 195
Lin, M., 246, 248
Lind, A.E., 255
Lind, E.A., 226
Lindsey, S., 55–56
Linville, P., 296, 309
Lipsey, M., 234, 236
Liska, A.E., 222
Little, T.D., 322–323
Livingstone, D.N., 271, 274, 284
Lodewijkx, H.F.M., 151
Loeber, R., 229
Lois, J., 153
Lord, C.G., 273
Louis, M.R., 142, 150
Luhtanen, R., 95, 102, 321
Lynch, J.J., 36
Lynham, D., 223

MacCallum, R.C., 282
MacDonald, D., 30, 40
Machleit, U., 275
Mackie, D.M., 22, 296
MacMullen, J., 294
Macrae, C.N., 19, 168
Maddens, B., 323–324, 334
Magnusson, J., 79
Maio, G.R., 325
Major, B., 64–65, 67–68, 70–80, 119
Malle, B.F., 329
Malone, P.S., 197, 200
Mann, J.A., 248, 252
Manstead, A.S.R., 76, 98
Maras, P., 273

Marcus, D.K., 90
Marks, B., 324
Markus, H., 64, 72, 74
Marques, J.M., 93, 99, 103, 153, 162, 165, 167–172, 174–178, 181, 195–196, 198
Martin, R., 195, 197–198
Martinez-Taboada, C., 165, 169, 196
Martins, L.L., 253
Marushiakova, E., 296
Maslow, A.H., 113
Mason, I., 179
Mason, J.A., 273
Masser, B., 166, 273
Massey, C.R., 222
Masters, R.D., 51
Mathews, A., 275
Mathewson, G.C., 151
Matoka, K., 247
Mawby, R., 228
McAlister, A.L., 278
McAllister, I., 269, 284
McAuliffe, B.J., 193
McBride, R.S., 29
McCall, G.J., 116
McClelland, D.C., 302
McClenahan, C., 269–270, 274
McCoy, S.K., 70–71, 77–79
McCreary, A., 268
McElligot, S., 79
McGarry, J., 266
McGarty, C., 96–97, 164, 166, 175–176, 179–180, 278
McGhee, D.E., 58
McIlraith, S.A., 57
McKee, I., 202
McKenna, K.Y.A., 77
McKittrick, D., 268
McLaughlin-Volpe, T., 113–114, 117, 275, 278–279, 283
McLernon, A., 276–277
McLernon, F., 266, 284
McNamara, C.C., 33
Mead, G.H., 148
Meertens, R.W., 274
Melichar, J., 127
Menard, S., 223
Mendes, W.B., 22
Mendoza-Denton, R., 64
Menninger, K., 35
Mercer, G.W., 267
Merton, R.K., 2

Milardo, R.M., 116
Milgram, S., 232
Milkie, M.A., 302, 309
Miller, C.T., 66, 71–74, 123
Miller, D.T., 64, 72, 74, 167
Miller, J.A., 309
Miller, N., 167, 248, 272–273
Milliken, F.J., 253
Mills, J., 151
Minto, B., 96
Mitchell, J.K., 268
Mitchell, T.M., 151
Mize, J., 33
Moffitt, T., 223
Monson, D.L., 303
Monteith, M.J., 166, 168
Montoya, M.R., 247
Morand, D.A., 142
Moreland, R.L., 28, 89–90, 137–138, 141, 143, 148, 152, 154–157, 192
Morgan, V., 269–270, 274, 283
Morrissey, M., 268
Morse, B.J., 223
Moscovici, S., 162, 195, 217–218, 226
Moskowitz, G.B., 247
Moxon-Browne, E., 270
Mueller, P.M., 73
Mugny, G., 162, 195
Mulder, M., 197
Mullen, B., 163, 165, 250, 258, 294–296, 298, 300, 305, 307, 309
Mullin, B-A., 102
Mummendey, A., 106, 167, 258, 318, 321, 326–327, 334
Munford, M.B., 123
Murphy, J., 91
Murphy, D., 267
Murray, C., 218
Murray, C.R., 270
Murray, D., 269, 271
Murrell, A.J., 248, 252
Murtagh, B., 269
Myers, A.M., 74–75
Myklebust, H.R., 304

Nasby, W., 115
Nash, H., 303
Nathan, L.E., 274
Nekuee, S., 274
Nelsen, E.A., 220, 228
Nelson, G., 114

Nemeth, C., 193, 195
Neter, E., 113
Neuberg, S.L., 69, 164, 246, 248
Newcomb, A.F., 29, 33
Nezlek, J.B., 47, 90
Ng, S.H., 197
Ngai, M.M., 298, 300
Nichols, D.R., 294, 296
Nicholson, N., 142
Niedenthal, P.M., 194
Nielsen, W.A., 294
Niemann, Y.F., 253–254
Niens, U., 269–271, 274, 276, 283–284
Nier, J.A., 253, 256, 328, 330, 333
Noel, J.G., 96, 101, 107, 116, 120, 168, 172
Noor, M., 284
Norman, C.C., 113–114, 278
Northern Ireland Council for Educational Development (NICED), 283
Northern Ireland Life and Times Survey, 270
Nuss, C.K., 30, 37
Nuwer, H., 152

Oakes, P.J., 92–93, 96–97, 99, 164, 175–176, 179–180, 198, 246, 318
O'Brien, M., 295
Ogbu, J.U., 75
Ohana, J., 217–218, 226, 228
Ohbuchi, K., 31
O'Leary, B., 266
Oleson, K.C., 165
Olson, L.M., 276
O'Neal, E.C., 31
O'Neil, R., 224
Onorato, R., 175–176
Opotow, S., 66–67
Oppes, T., 193
Osgood, D.W., 294–295, 299–301, 304–305, 307
Otten, S., 247
Owens, P., 193

Pàez, D., 21, 153, 162, 165, 167–169, 172, 195–196
Pakulski, J., 320, 323, 334
Paladino, M-P., 162, 166–167, 172–173
Paladino, P.M., 65
Palmonari, A., 220, 228
Palmore, E.B., 294–295
Pankiw, B., 294
Paolini, S., 272, 279
Paris, M., 114

Park, B., 103–104, 247, 296
Parkes, C.M., 118
Parkhurst, J.T., 33
Parsons, C., 231
Patnoe, S., 260
Pattee, L., 29
Patterson, G.R., 236
Peck, R.L., 29
Pedersen, A., 58
Peffley, M., 321–322
Pemberton, M.B., 57
Pennebaker, J.W., 21, 37, 73–74
Pepitone, A., 118, 121
Peplau, L.A., 90
Perlman, D., 90
Perner, J., 171
Perreault S., 318
Perry, D.G., 33
Perry, L.C., 33
Perry, R.P., 79
Pescosolido, B.A., 302, 309
Petee, T.A., 29
Peterson, A.M., 294
Peterson, C., 294–295, 299–301, 304–305, 307
Petrocik, J.R., 106
Pettigrew, T.F., 247–248, 250, 261, 271–276, 278, 282
Phillips, S., 29, 39, 48, 54
Phinney, J.S., 123, 276
Piaget, J., 214, 216
Pickett, C.L., 33, 50, 90, 92–95, 97, 99, 100, 102–105, 107, 120, 122
Piers, G., 35
Pietrzak, J., 64
Piliavin, I., 230
Pinkley, R.L., 57
Pinter, B., 247
Pittinsky, T.L., 102
Pittman, T.S., 101
Pizzuto, C., 307
Plant, E.A., 166, 168, 272
Platow, M.J., 179–180
Platt, L., 76–77
Pomare, M., 252
Poole, M., 268–269, 271, 275
Poole, M.A., 270
Poresky, R.H., 302
Portes, A., 20
Postmes, T., 54, 168, 193
Pratto, F., 68, 106, 328–329
Predmore, S.J., 49, 122

Prentice, D.A., 167
Price, J., 79
Prins, K.S., 251, 256
Purdie, V.J., 64
Putnam, R.D., 20, 29
Pyszczynski, T.A., 68, 70, 114, 294–295, 317

Quinn, D.M., 80
Quinton, W.J., 70–71, 78–79

Rabinowitz, V.C., 80
Rahn, W., 275
Ramirez, A., 273
Ramsey, S.L., 273
Rands, M., 116
Randsley de Moura, G., 179, 181 162, 168, 182
Ratcliff, C.D., 273
Reed, A., 18
Reed, M.D., 222
Reese, W.A.II., 151
Rehak, P.J., 51
Reicher, S.D., 54, 92, 97, 99, 164, 168, 193–195, 197–198, 220–221, 223, 225–229, 230–233, 246, 318
Reingold, B., 317–318
Reiss, A.J., 222
Renshaw, P.D., 33
Reuters, 294
Reynolds, K.J., 179–180
Rhodes, A.L., 222
Rice, D.R., 295–296, 298, 300, 305, 307
Richards, B.C., 37
Richards, C., 73–74
Richardson, D.R., 31, 52
Richman, A., 29
Ridge, M.L., 304–305, 308
Rigby, K., 218
Rimé, B., 21
Ring, K., 67
Rittwager, F.J., 151
Roback, A.A., 293, 295, 297, 310
Robalo, E.M., 168
Robinson, G., 266, 271
Robrts, K., 220
Roccas, S., 194
Rocha, S.A., 168
Rodgers, J.S., 19
Rodin, M., 79
Rodriguez-Perez, A., 65, 162, 167
Rodriguez-Torres, R., 65, 162, 167
Ropp, S.A., 275, 278–279, 283

Rose, R., 267, 270
Rosenberg, M., 71, 148
Ross, L., 197, 200
Rothbart, M., 165, 247
Rothgerber, H., 247, 317
Rottman, L., 115
Rouse, T.P., 149
Routh, D., 234
Rowley, S.J., 123
Rozell, D., 294–296, 298, 300
Rubchinsky, K., 275
Rubin, M., 161, 273
Rubini, M., 220, 228
Ruble, D.N., 142, 149
Ruderman, A.J., 296
Ruffman, T., 171
Rump, E., 218
Rusbult, C.E., 127
Ruscher, J., 273
Rust, M.C., 246, 248, 253, 255, 327–328, 333
Rutland, A., 170–171
Rutter, M., 223
Ryan, C.S., 138, 148, 154, 296
Ryan, R.M., 113, 118

Sachdev, I., 115, 197
Sager, K., 275
Sakano, N., 321
Salovey, P., 296
Saltzstein, H.D., 125
Sameroff, A., 123
Samet, J.M., 35
Sampson, R.J., 29, 232
Sanchez, F., 79
Sanford, R.N., 216
Sani, F., 193, 195
Sarbin, T.R., 154–155
Scarberry, N.C., 273
Schachter, S., 163, 192
Schaller, M., 295
Scheier, M., 114
Schein, E.H., 142
Scher, S.J., 35
Scherbaum, C., 65
Schmader, T., 71, 75, 78–79
Schmidt, P., 324
Schmitt, M.T., 67, 76, 89, 99–100, 107, 119, 123, 120, 125, 204
Schneider, B., 137
Schofield, J.W., 272
Schofield, P., 218

Schonert-Reichl, K.A., 33
Schooler, T.Y., 55–56
Schopler, J., 57, 247
Schreindorfer, L.S., 66
Schwartz, J.K.L., 58
Schwartz, N., 303
Schwartz, W., 149
Schweinhhart, L.J., 235
Sciacchitano, A.M., 73
Scott, R.A., 64, 72, 74
Scott, W.A., 294–295, 299–301, 304–305, 307
Sedikides, C., 79
Seidman, E., 142, 149
Seligman, M., 118
Sellers, R.M., 123
Serôdio, R.G., 103, 168–169, 196, 198
Seron, E., 96, 99, 173
Shah, J., 22
Shapiro, M.J., 298
Shaver, P., 115
Shaw, M.E., 163, 192
Sherif, C.W., 170
Sherif, M., 20, 163, 170, 192
Sherman, J.W., 166, 168
Sherman, L., 234
Sherman, S.J., 19, 163
Shih, M., 102
Sidanius, J., 68, 106, 272, 328–329
Sigelman, L., 198
Silver, M., 51, 118, 120–121
Silvia, P.J., 204
Simmel, G., 2
Simmons, R.G., 71
Simon, B., 296
Sinclair, S., 106
Singer, M., 35
Skinner, E.A., 118
Slee, P., 218
Slim, R., 57
Sloan, L.R., 198
Smart, L., 74
Smith, A., 271, 283–284
Smith, C., 165
Smith, D.L., 150, 152
Smith, D.M., 69
Smith, E.E., 294
Smith, E.R., 22, 91, 114, 278, 296
Smith, H., 76
Smith, H.H., 255
Smith, H.J., 255
Smith, L., 29, 39, 48, 54

Smith, M.A., 123
Smyth, M., 268–269
Snider, K., 253–254
Snoek, J.D., 49, 52, 116, 120–122, 124
Snow, J.H., 303
Snyder, C.R., 92, 198
Solomon, S., 68, 70, 114, 317
Sommer, K.L., 33, 48–49, 56, 120, 122
Somner, K.L., 121
Sörbom, D., 277
Soriano, F.I., 273
Sorrentino, R.M., 113
Spanier, G., 118
Spears, R., 16, 54, 67, 76, 98, 101, 107, 164, 168, 193, 202
Sprecher, S., 118, 127
Srull, T.K., 37
St. James, A., 222, 224, 232
Stacey, B.G., 215
Stallworth, L.M., 329
Stasser, G., 193
Staub, E., 321
Staw, B.M., 193
Steele, C.M., 64–65, 67–68, 71, 73, 75, 119
Stein, S., 74–75
Stephan, C.W., 272, 275–276, 318
Stephan, W.G., 318
Stephen, T., 126
Sternberg, W.C., 51, 118, 120–121
Stewart, D.D., 193
Stott, C., 230
Stouthamer-Loeber, M., 223, 229
Strang, H., 234
Strauss, A.L., 149
Strausser, K.S., 126
Stringer, M., 231
Stryker, S., 148
Stucke, T.S., 29–30, 48, 52, 54, 56, 121
Subkoviak, M.J., 276
Sutton, J.R., 195
Sutton, R.I., 150
Svensson, A., 193
Swan, S., 75
Swart, L.A., 166
Swim, J.K., 119
Syroit, J.E.M.M., 151

Taft, R., 296
Tajfel, H., 16, 67, 72, 76, 100, 148, 164, 198, 246–248, 254, 318, 332
Takaki, R., 298, 300

Takeuchi, D.T., 29, 35–36
Tambor, E.S., 28, 55, 90
Tarry, H., 223
Tate, J.D., 276
Taylor, D.M., 231
Taylor, M.S., 142
Taylor, S.E., 74, 113, 296
Taylor, S.L., 31
Teasdale, J., 118
Terdal, S.K., 28, 55, 90
Tesser, A., 67, 101
Testa, M., 73, 78
Thabes, V., 126
Thompson, F., 218
Thompson, H.L., 52
Thompson, L.L., 152
Thorne, A., 198
Thornton, C., 268
Thurner, M., 125–127
Tice, D.M., 29–30, 47–48, 52, 54, 56, 64, 90, 121
Tillman, M.H., 304
Tindale, R.S., 193
Tisserand, D.J., 303
Tooby, J., 115
Torney, J.V., 214–216
Tranter, B., 320, 323, 334
Traupmann, J., 115
Tremblay, R.E., 214
Trew, K., 267–268, 270–271, 274, 283
Trice, H.M., 142, 149, 153–154
Tropp, L.R., 114, 194, 248, 272, 276
Trout, D.L., 35
Tuchman, G., 309
Tudor, M., 114
Turner, J.C., 16, 67, 72, 76, 92–93, 96–97, 99, 148, 164–165, 175–176, 179–180, 182, 198, 246–249, 254, 278, 318, 332
Twenge, J.M., 29–30, 32–33, 36–37, 39–40, 48, 52–54, 56, 59, 71, 121
Tyler, T., 76, 225–226
Tyler, T.R., 21, 193, 226, 255
Tynan, D., 53, 56

Uhl-Bien, M., 197

Vaes, J., 65, 162, 167
Valencia, A., 31
Validzic, A., 247, 254
Van Ausdale, D., 310
van Avermaet, E., 162

Van Boxtel, M.P.J., 303
van de Vliert, E., 149
Van Gennep, A., 142
van Knippenberg, D., 180, 196–197
van Laar, C., 272
Van Leeuwen, M.D., 273
Van Maanen, J., 142
van Oudenhoven, J.P., 251, 256, 273
Van Rijswijk, W., 72
Vaughan, D., 119
Vaught, C., 150, 152
Vescio, T.K., 168, 295
Viki, G.T., 168
Virtanen, S., 296
Visscher, B.R., 74
Vivian, J., 273, 275, 277
Voci, A., 272–274, 276–277, 279–281, 284
Voelkl, K., 78
Volkmer, R., 202
von Hippel, W., 254

Wachtler, J., 193
Wade, G., 254, 275
Wagner, U., 274–275
Wahl, O., 63, 67, 73
Waldo, G.P., 218
Walker, I., 58
Walker, M.R., 198
Wallace, J., 37
Walsh, A., 29
Walster, E., 115
Walster, G.W., 115
Wann, D.L., 96, 101, 107, 116, 120, 168, 172, 198, 202, 318
Wanous, J.P., 137
Warburton, W., 31, 59
Ward, C., 256
Ward, C.M., 328, 330, 333
Ware, E.E., 216, 218, 222
Watson, R.P. 231
Waugh, C.E., 31
Wayment, H.A., 113
Weber, M., 219
Webster, D.M., 166
Webster, G.D., 31
Weeden, K., 198
Wegner, D.M., 74
Wei, E., 229
Weigart, A.J., 117
Weikart, D.P., 235

Weil, S., 296
Weiner, B., 79
Weiss, R.J., 33
Wenninger, E.P., 218
Wentzel, K.R., 33
Wenzel, M., 106, 167, 258
West, D.J., 220, 222, 236
West, S.C., 273
Wetherell, M.S., 92, 97, 99, 101, 164, 182, 198, 246, 318
Wheeler, L., 125
White, R.W., 113, 268
White, S.W., 35
Whyte, J., 266–271,
Wiatrowski, M.D., 222
Wicker, A.W., 192
Widaman, K.F., 322–323
Widdicombe, S., 149
Wieselquist, J., 57
Wilder, D.A., 247–248, 272–273
Wildschut, T., 247
Williams, D.R., 29, 35–36, 71
Williams, J.A., 275
Williams, K.D., 29, 31, 33, 35–36, 40, 47–51, 53–58, 63, 70, 90, 120–122, 125, 155, 191
Willis, H., 161, 273
Willis, P., 223
Wills, T.A., 67
Wilpizeski, C., 118, 121
Wilson D.L., 222
Wilson, M., 52
Wilson, R., 268
Wilson, T.D., 55–56
Wilson, T.M., 198
Wimmer, H., 171
Winerip, M., 150
Wingert, M.L., 137
Winkel, R., 40
Winslow, D., 152
Wintermantel, M., 294
Witte, E., 163
Wittenbaum, G.M., 193
Wong, C.A., 123
Wooffitt, R., 149
Worchel, S., 247, 317, 321
Wotman, S.R., 115
Wright, S.C., 114, 194, 275, 278–279, 283
Wu, C., 276
Wuthnow, R., 195

Wyer, N.A., 166
Wyer, R.S., 37

Yang, P.Q., 300
Yohannes, J., 295
Yoshikawa, H., 235
Yzerbyt, V.Y., 96, 99, 163, 166, 168, 172–173, 195

Zadro, L., 47, 50, 57, 122
Zanna, M.P., 226, 275, 325
Zick, A., 274
Zigler, E., 123
Ziller, R.C., 149, 156
Zobel, M., 296
Zubek, J.M., 73–74
Zuckerman, M., 303

Subject Index

Abortion/pregnancy, 73–74
Adolescents
   Delinquency, 218–221
African-Americans, 68, 75, 78, 309
Aggression, 129
   Need to belong, 28–32
Antisocial behavior, 29, 48
   Ostracism, 51–54
Attachment theory
   Marginal group membership, 91–92
Authority, attitudes and perceptions of (*see* delinquency)

"Black sheep effect", 162, 168–169

Children, 33, 59, 170–172, 214–218, 302–305
   School shootings, 28–29, 39–40, 48, 54, 128–129
Cognitive development
   Delinquency, 224–225
Cognitive dissonance, 150–151
Cognitive representations
   Ethnic groups, 293–310
Common ingroup identity model (CIIM), 246–261
   Commitment, 253–254
   Contact hypothesis, 247–248, 253
   Dual identity, 254–259
   Ethnic groups, 327–328, 333
   Explanation of, 249–251
   Intergroup bias, 246–249, 251–253
   Minority groups, 250–251, 253–254, 255–256, 258–259
   Social categorization, 246–247
   Status, 257
Conflict
   Northern Ireland, 265–269
Conformity, 51
Contact hypothesis, 271–283
   Common ingroup identity model, 247–248, 253
   Northern Ireland, 271–283

Control, 54–55
   Group socialization model, 148
   Self-expansion model, 118

Delinquency, 211–237
   Adolescents, 218–221
   Children, 214–218
   Cognitive development, 224–225
   Education, 221–224
   Exclusion, 231–236
   Intergroup relations, 229–231
   Procedural fairness/legitimacy, 225–227
   Uncertain protection, 227–229
Developmental processes, 169–172
Deviance, 65,
   Marginal group membership, 93, 98, 99
Deviant group members, 161–182
   "Black sheep effect", 162, 168–169, 195–196
   Developmental processes, 169–172
   Entitativity, 163
   Leadership, 178–182
   Norms, 165–168, 169, 173–178, 179–182
   Social identity theory/self-categorization theory, 164–165, 179
   Social self-regulation model, 167–168
   Stereotype maintenance, 172–173
   Subjective group dynamics model, 165–182, 196
Divorce, 123, 125, 126–127

Education
   Delinquency, 221–224
   Intergroup contact, 280–282, 283
   Segregation, 270–271
Emotion, 64
   Need to belong, 40
   Self-expansion model, 118, 119
Entitativity
   Deviant group members, 163
Ethnic groups, 106–107, 293–310, 317–334
   Attitudes towards, 323–332

SUBJECT INDEX

Ethnic groups – continued
  Cognitive representations (ethnophaulisms), 293–310
  Common ingroup identity model, 327–328, 333
  Direct exclusion, 296–302, 305–310
  Indirect exclusion, 302–310
  International identity and, 320, 322–327, 330–332
  National identity and, 319–322, 324–330
  Social dominance orientation, 328–334
  Social identity theory (SIT), 318, 332
Ethnophaulisms (see ethnic groups: cognitive representations)
Evolutionary theory, 28, 51, 70

Gender stereotypes, 175
Group composition (see group socialization model)
Group socialization model, 137–156
  Boundary control, 137–138
  Control, 148
  Need to belong, 148
  Role transitions, 139–156
  Status, 149, 153

HIV, 74
Homosexuality, 66, 73, 74, 75

Identification
  Stigma, 66, 67, 69, 76, 77, 78
Identity salience, 101–103, 106
Immigrants/immigration (see ethnic groups)
Implicit attitudes, 55–58
Ingroup overexclusion effect, 96
Intelligence
  Need to belong, 37–38
Intergroup bias
  Common ingroup identity model, 246–249, 251–253
Intergroup contact
  Northern Ireland, 274–283
Intergroup relations
  Delinquency, 229–231
Internet, 77

Leader-member exchange (LMX) theory, 197–198
Leaders/leadership, 56–57
  Deviant group members, 178–182
  Marginalization, 196–198

Legitimacy
  Delinquency, 225–227
  Stigma, 66–67, 79–80

Marginal group membership, 89–108
  Attachment theory, 91–92
  Deviance, 93, 98, 99
  Identity salience, 101–103, 106
  Ingroup-outgroup perceptions, 90, 103–105
  Intergroup boundaries, 96–101
  Optimal distinctiveness theory, 92, 104, 194
  Self-categorization theory, 93, 96, 97, 98–99
  Self-esteem, 102
  Self-expansion model, 120
  Self-stereotyping, 93–96
  Social identity theory, 100–101
  Stereotypes, 102
Marginalization, 191–204
  Leadership, 196–198
  Motivational processes, 198–204
  Self-enhancement, 200
  Social identity theory, 196–199
  Types, 192–198
  Uncertainty reduction hypothesis, 195–196, 199
Meaningful existence, 54–55
Mental health, 35, 71
Mental illness, 67, 73
Minority groups
  Common ingroup identity model, 250–251, 253–254, 255–256, 258–259
Mood
  Need to belong, 40
  Self-expansion model, 118

Narcissism (or individual differences)
  Need to belong, 38–40
Need to belong, 28–40, 50, 51, 54–55, 90
  Aggression, 28–32
  Group socialization model, 148
  Intelligence, 37–38
  Mood, 37, 40
  Narcissism (or individual differences), 38–40
  Prosocial behavior, 32–35,
  Self-defeating behavior, 35–37
  Self-esteem, 39–40
Norms
  Deviant group membership, 165–168, 169, 173–178, 179–182
Northern Ireland, 265–285
  Contact hypothesis, 271–283

SUBJECT INDEX

Conflict, 265–269
Intergroup contact, 274–283
Policy implications, 283–284
Segregation, 269–271

Obesity, 67, 75
Ostracism, 29, 47–60
Antisocial behavior, 51–54
Prosocial behavior, 49–51
Self-expansion model, 121, 122, 125

Power (*see* status), 50
Prejudice, 70–71, 119, 123
Procedural fairness (*see* legitimacy)
Prosocial behavior, 49–51
Need to belong, 32–35
Ostracism, 49–51
Psychoanalytic theory, 33

Racism (*see* prejudice), 119
Relationships, 29, 64, 75
Self-expansion model, 114–130

Segregation
Education, 270–271
Northern Ireland, 269–271
Self-categorization theory (SCT – *see* social identity theory)
Self-defeating behavior
Need to belong, 35–37
Self-efficacy
Self-expansion model, 117, 122
Self-enhancement
Marginalization, 200
Self-esteem, 28, 64, 50, 51, 54–55
Marginal group membership, 102
Need to belong, 39–40
Self-expansion model, 116, 118, 123, 126
Stigma, 67, 71
Self-expansion model, 113–130
Control, 118
Emotion, 118, 119
Group membership, 114–130
Marginal group membership, 120
Mood, 118

Ostracism, 121, 122, 125
Relationships, 114–130
Self-efficacy, 117, 122
Self-esteem, 116, 118, 123, 126
Status, 115–116
September, 11 67, 317
Sexism (*see* prejudice), 119
Social categorization
Common ingroup identity model, 246–247
Social comparison, 67
Social dominance orientation (SDO)
Ethnic groups, 328–334
Social identity theory (SIT), 249, 254
Deviant group members, 164–165, 179
Ethnic groups, 318, 332
Leadership, 196–199
Social self-regulation model
Deviant group members, 167–168
Sociometer theory, 28, 55, 126
Status, 32, 65–66
Common ingroup identity model, 257
Group socialization model, 149, 153
Self-expansion model, 115–116
Stereotype maintenance
Deviant group members, 172–173
Stigma, 64–80
Identification and, 66, 67, 69, 76, 77, 78
Legitimacy, 66–67, 79–80
Self-esteem, 67, 71
Status and, 65
Stress and coping, 72–80
Stress and coping
Stigma, 72–80
Subjective group dynamics (SGD) model
Deviant group members, 165–182
Suicide, 35
System justification theory, 68–69

Terror management theory, 67–68

Uncertainty reduction hypothesis, 195–196, 199

Women, 75, 78